THE AGATE BASIN SITE

This is a volume in the series
STUDIES IN ARCHAEOLOGY
Under the consulting editorship of Stuart Struever,
Northwestern University

A complete list of titles in this series appears at the end of this volume.

THE AGATE BASIN SITE

A Record of the Paleoindian Occupation of the Northwestern High Plains

george c. frison

Department of Anthropology
University of Wyoming
Laramie, Wyoming

dennis j. stanford

Department of Anthropology
National Museum of Natural History
Smithsonian Institution
Washington, D.C.

ACADEMIC PRESS

A Subsidiary of Harcourt Brace Jovanovich, Publishers
New York   London
Paris   San Diego   San Francisco   São Paulo   Sydney   Tokyo   Toronto

ACADEMIC PRESS, INC.
111 Fifth Avenue, New York, New York 10003

United Kingdom Edition published by
ACADEMIC PRESS, INC. (LONDON) LTD.
24/28 Oval Road, London NW1 7DX

Library of Congress Cataloging in Publication Data
Frison, George C.
    The Agate Basin site.

    (Studies in archaeology)
    Includes index.
    1. Agate Basin Site (Wyo.) 2. Paleo-Indians—Great
Plains. 3. Great Plains—Antiquities. I. Stanford,
Dennis J. II. Title. III. Series.
E78.W95F73   978.7'15   82-6637
ISBN 0-12-268570-9   AACR2

PRINTED IN THE UNITED STATES OF AMERICA
82 83 84 85   9 8 7 6 5 4 3 2 1

TO ROBERT E. FRISON AND WILLIAM SPENCER

who discovered the Agate Basin site
and recognized its value.

CONTENTS

one
INTRODUCTION

george c. frison

two
ARCHAEOLOGY

Contents

three
LITHIC TECHNOLOGY

four
FAUNAL STUDIES

Contents

five
PALEOECOLOGICAL STUDIES

six
SUMMARY AND CONCLUSIONS

george c. frison
dennis j. stanford

CONTRIBUTORS

Numbers in parentheses indicate the pages on which the authors' contributions begin.

john albanese *(309), Smithsonian Institution affiliate, Casper, Wyoming 82601*

jane m. beiswenger *(349), Department of Botany, University of Wyoming, Laramie, Wyoming 82071*

bruce a. bradley *(181, 209), Complete Archeological Service Associates, Cortez, Colorado 81321*

carolyn craig *(157), Department of Anthropology, University of Wyoming, Laramie, Wyoming 82071*

emmett evanoff *(357), Department of Geological Sciences, University of Colorado, Boulder, Colorado 80309*

george c. frison *(1, 27, 37, 76, 135, 143, 157, 173, 178, 209, 240, 261, 361), Department of Anthropology, University of Wyoming, Laramie, Wyoming 82071*

rhoda owen lewis *(353), Metcalf-Zier Associates, Boulder, Colorado 80301*

clayton marlow *(344), Department of Range Management, Montana State University, Bozeman, Montana 59717*

richard g. reider *(331), Department of Geography, University of Wyoming, Laramie, Wyoming 82071*

dennis j. stanford *(76, 361), Department of Anthropology, National Museum of Natural History, Smithsonian Institution, Washington, D.C. 20560*

danny n. walker *(270, 274), State Archeologist Office, Wyoming Recreation Commission, Laramie, Wyoming 82070*

george m. zeimens *(213), State Archeologist Office, Wyoming Recreation Commission, Laramie, Wyoming 82070*

PREFACE

The Agate Basin site is only one of many Paleoindian sties that have been investigated, but for which analysis and publication of results are lacking. It is the type site of the Agate Basin cultural complex and its data therefore should be made available to students of the Paleoindian. This book accordingly attempts to bring together all the known data from the Agate Basin site locality.

The authors have attempted to evaluate the Agate Basin site from the perspectives of a number of separate disciplinary approaches, with guiding principles being that paleoecological reconstructions are possible and that they can be used as a medium within which to observe human behavior. Because Paleoindian sites of the size and complexity of Agate Basin are rare, and because adequate protection seems assured, as much as possible of the site has been left intact for future investigators.

The book is primarily directed to professional archaeologists interested in Paleoindian studies. The avocational archaeologist with similar interests should also find it of use. Those interested in topics that include reconstruction of paleolandforms, stream transport, soils, and taphonomy should also find something of at least passing interest.

Illustrations are liberally provided, both to make the reader familiar with the site and the general area, and as a means for referring to complete cultural assemblages. It is felt that this type of presentation allows the reader to apply to the data whatever interpretive device or model he or she sees fit, and also facilitates comparison with data from other archaeological sites.

The book consists of six chapters. Chapter 1 introduces the reader first to the general area of the High Plains and then to the particular area of the Agate Basin site. The site has been known since the late 1930s. It actually consists of several sites, which are integrated by a common drainage system. These sites have witnessed a number of investigations, ranging in character from legitimate to entirely predatory, in the years following their discovery. Chapter 1 also presents a history of these investigations and the collections known to have been taken from the site.

Chapter 2 deals specifically with the archaeological aspects of the Agate Basin site locality, which has produced Clovis, Folsom, Agate Basin, and Hell Gap components. These are presented in eight sections with topical titles beginning with the cultural stratigraphy and continuing with the evidence from the various cultural components. Bone and antler technology, raw stone flaking materials, and radiocarbon dating are also treated separately.

Chapter 3 is a technological study. The first section deals with observations on lithic technology. It is followed by a short section on fluting of Folsom projectile points.

Chapter 4 is a taphonomic treatment of the faunal remains. The first section describes bison butchering and is followed by a section on the dynamics of the bison population based mainly on dental observations. Bison taxonomy and procurement are considered in the two sections that follow and a short section is devoted to butchering of nonbison materials. Finally, the complete faunal list recovered and reconstruction of the paleoecology based on small animals recovered are presented.

Chapter 5 includes studies of a number of paleoecological components, including geology, soils, vegetation, pollen, phytoliths, and gastropods. The geological data were indispensable to the final interpretations of the site. The soil, vegetation, and gastropod data also aided in paleoecological studies; the pollen and phytolith studies, however, were inconclusive.

Chapter 6 is an attempt to abstract the preceding chapters into a statement describing Paleoindian lifeways based on the relatively disparate avenues of research involved in six years of fieldwork and laboratory analysis. This chapter also attempts to place the Agate Basin site locality within the framework of other, related, Paleoindian studies. These interpretations, it should be emphasized, are largely hypothetical and will be subject to constant revision as Paleoindian studies continue and methodologies improve.

ACKNOWLEDGMENTS

Testing, excavation, and analysis of the Agate Basin site and materials, during the period 1971–1980 was supported by the University of Wyoming, The Smithsonian Institution, the Wyoming Recreation Commission, the Wyoming Archeological Foundation, and the National Science Foundation (Grant No. BNS 7905852). The 1961 excavations were supported by a grant from the National Geographic Society.

The authors thank a number of persons, including William Bass, for making available the results of the 1961 field excavation; Robert Frison, Jr., for donating the Robert Frison, Sr., collection of Agate Basin Materials for study; George Agogino for his help with the Brewster site materials; C. Vance Haynes for his field notes taken at the Agate Basin site after the 1961 excavations; and H. Marie Wormington for her continual encouragement and the benefit of the unequaled breadth and depth of her knowledge of Paleoindian studies. James Duguid and Louis Steege donated their collections from the Brewster and Agate Basin sites to the Smithsonian Institution.

The senior author is deeply indebted to the Smithsonian Institution and particularly the Department of Anthropology for their support, which led to the granting of one of the first three board of regents fellowships and thus allowed a full year of research on the Agate Basin materials. Discussions with colleagues, in particular, Waldo Wedel, the late Clifford Evans, William Fitzhugh, T. Dale Stewart, and Gary Haynes, were of inestimable value to the completion of the project. Robert Stuckenrath gave special care to radiocarbon samples. Victor Krantz produced the excellent photographs of artifacts. Marcia Bakry illustrated the artifacts and bison dentitions, which are without question the finest in existence. George R. Lewis and Ellen Paige drafted the numerous excellent site maps. The laboratory staff of the Department of Anthropology at the Smithsonian Institution were particularly helpful during the year of residence, which was deeply appreciated. A special note of thanks is expressed to Gretchen Ellsworth of the Grants and Fellowships Department at the Smithsonian Institution along with many others of the staff there, whose efforts allowed the stay at the Smithsonian to be a full year of research. Clayton Ray and Robert Purdy identified faunal remains from the Agate Basin site.

Reading and suggestions for revisions on the Agate Basin local fauna section were done by Holmes Semken. The same was done for the gastropod section by John Hanley, Kenneth Carpenter, and Alberta Settle.

The senior author is especially indebted to Mr. and Mrs. Thomas Beebe and Jesse and Kathy Schultz for the hospitality extended at their ranch during the years of fieldwork at the Agate Basin. Thanks are due also to Wayne Peterson and Robert Sheaman for the use of their private lands during this same period. Stan Renner, another nearby rancher, helped many times with the loan of tools and equipment. Josephine Spencer made the collection of the late William Spencer available for study. Adrian Hannus provided a helicopter and Jesse Schultz provided an airplane for taking aerial photographs.

The sources of raw material figured strongly in the Agate Basin site analysis. Many of these sources are on private land and many landowners, including Leonard Degering, Artie Joss, Rebel Coffee, and George Lynch were particularly cooperative in allowing access. Robert Alex and part of his staff offered their services for a day to visit quarry sources in South Dakota and provided samples from a number of others.

In other areas, "Bison Pete" Gardner provided innumerable samples of bison for biological study and allowed us the benefit of his superior knowledge of bison behavior. It was a privilege to share his many and varied experiences with bison both dead and alive. The Wyoming Game and Fish Department is also acknowledged for providing biological specimens that aided in faunal analysis of the Agate Basin materials.

June Frison, the senior author's spouse, typed numerous drafts of the manuscript during the period of residence at the Smithsonian Institution and, in addition, was cook, purchasing agent, and general camp manager for six years of field excavations at the Agate Basin site. Terri Craigie was largely responsible for typing and organizing the final draft of the manuscript. Laura Mai and Mary David also helped in typing the manuscript.

Laboratory workers over a period of years included Richard Blatchley, Dan Eakin, Karen Bridger, Caren Collins, and Carol Frison Grace. Field crew supervisors over the years include William Bass for the Smithsonian expedition in 1961, George Zeimens, Charles Reher, Bruce Bradley, and Danny Walker. Field crew members, in alphabetical order, included Evelyn Albanese, Dale Austin, Jean Bedord, Walter Birkby, Richard Blatchley, Manton Botsford, Cindy Bradley, Karen Bridger, Carolyn Buff, Susan Bupp, Caren Collins, Carolyn Craig, Dave Darlington, Zach Deiss, Bob Dunnell, Dan Eakin, Dave Eckles, Jodee Eckles, Julie Francis, Gene Galloway, Charles Gossard, Travis Gray, John Greer, Jeff Hauff, Dan Hayes, Ross Hilman, Jack Hofman, Pat Mansfield Hofman, Paul Hokenstad, Harold Howells, John Jameson, Junko Kawaguchi, Marcel Kornfeld, Larry Lahren, Mary Lou Larson, Thomas K. Larson, Sherry Landry, Merry Lang, Roy Larrick, Bill Latady, Rich Laurent, Rhoda Lewis, Julie

Longenecker, Gordon Marlatt, Dave McGuire, Donna McGuire, Judy Michaelsen, Mark E. Miller, Pete Milne, Ann Mitchell, John Mitchell, Steven Moore, Frances Mundt, Linda Nicholas, Bob Peterson, Grove Ohelan, Joe Pinner, Judy Pinner, Dave Reiss, Mary Ann Robeson, Richard Robrock, Paula Rosa, Paul Sanders, Lee Carol Scutt, John Seeger, Susan Schock, Gail Slutszky, F. E. "Kim" Smiley, Robert Swaim, Paula Ingram Tibesar, William Tibesar, Larry Todd, Sandra Myers Todd, Pat Treat, Larry Welty, and Sandy Zeimens.

Due to the length of time and the number of individuals involved in the Agate Basin project, some deserving of credit have inevitably been overlooked. To those, our sincere apologies and appreciation.

one
INTRODUCTION
george c. frison

The Agate Basin site is one of a number of Paleoindian sites on the Northwestern High Plains. These sites, found in late Pleistocene and early Holocene geologic deposits, are providing us with an ever increasing data base for the Clovis, Folsom, Agate Basin, and Hell Gap cultural complexes (Figure 1.1). Sites associated with the procurement of large herbivores are best known, largely because of their high archaeological visibility. At the Agate Basin site, for example, a large communal bison kill took place in an arroyo; its existence was revealed by bison bone and projectile points found eroding from the arroyo bank.

Site exposure is primarily the result of geologic conditions. High topographic relief, moderate amounts of yearly precipitation, and large seasonal extremes of temperature, common on the High Plains, provide situations that encourage erosion and deposition. The distribution of precipitation events and small increases or decreases in amounts can result in dramatic changes in vegetative cover over short periods of time. The disastrous effects of the 1930s dust bowl days on crop production and the animal carrying capacity of the High Plains provide a prime example (J. E. Weaver 1968). Changes in vegetation and in the water table, in turn, strongly affect the processes of erosion. Where these conditions prevail, the probability that archaeological sites will be exposed is high, but so is the probability of subsequent site destruction.

The shortgrass High Plains, although inhospitable in many ways, were and still are attractive to large herbivores. Even though the grasses are relatively short and sparse, they are high in protein and are available in some form all year. However, they are sensitive to changes in moisture, and animals depending on them would have to adjust their populations accordingly. A series of good grass years could witness significant increases in the populations of such animals as

FIGURE 1.1   Clovis, Folsom, Agate Basin, and Hell Gap sites in Wyoming and adjacent areas: 1: Anzick; Clovis (Lahren and Bonnichsen 1974). 2: Hanson; Folsom (Frison and Bradley 1980). 3: Colby; Clovis (Frison 1976, 1978b). 4: Sister's Hill; Hell Gap (Agogino and Galloway 1965). 5: Carter/Kerr-McGee; Clovis, Folsom, Agate Basin, Hell Gap (Frison 1977). 6: Morgan; Folsom (Frison 1978b). 7: Mud Springs; Folsom (Frison 1978b). 8: Casper; Hell Gap (Frison 1974). 9: Johnson; Folsom (Galloway and Agogino 1961). 10: Lindenmeier; Folsom (Wilmsen and Roberts 1978). 11: Dent; Clovis (Figgins 1933). 12: Frazier; Agate Basin (Wormington, personal communication, 1976). 13: Jones–Miller; Hell Gap (Stanford 1978). 14: Hell Gap; Goshen, Folsom, Midland, Agate Basin, Hell Gap (Irwin-Williams *et al.* 1973). 15: Agate Basin; Clovis, Folsom, Agate Basin, Hell Gap. 16: Dutton; Clovis (Stanford 1979).

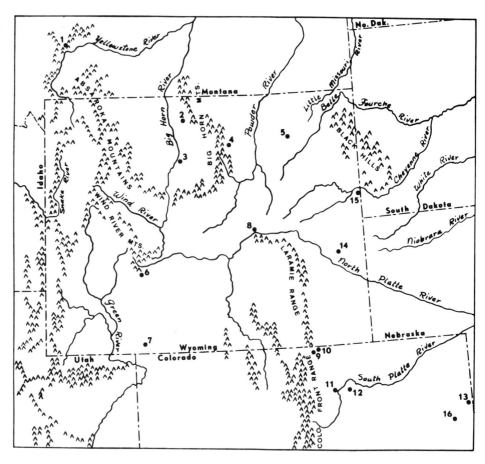

the bison, where females reproduce at 3 years of age. A combination of poor grass and hard winters, on the other hand, would quickly reduce animal numbers.

Small, nomadic human groups were able to survive on the shortgrass Plains in late Pleistocene–early Holocene times by systematically exploiting plant and animal resources, including the large herbivores. These groups possessed the knowledge and the technology necessary to trap and kill animals. They were familiar enough with animal behavior to take advantage of the natural topography in their procurement efforts, but they were also able to modify natural conditions to achieve the same ends. Even so, they were not able to perfect procurement techniques to the extent that the bison were threatened. The predator–prey relationships between man and other large herbivores, such as the horse and the camel, are not yet well understood. There is no question that the two species mentioned were present on the Plains in Paleoindian times, but the reasons for their disappearance are not yet known. The effect of human predation on animal populations is one of the major issues in Paleoindian studies today (see P. S. Martin 1967; P. S. Martin and H. E. Wright 1967). This study of the Agate Basin site deals mainly with bison procurement and utilization, however. It is the authors' belief, based on this and a number of other bison kills, that the site represents patterned human behavior rather than fortuitous encounters with animals in a favorable location.

The Agate Basin site epitomizes the Paleoindian bison kill preserved by aggradation in an arroyo shortly after deposition and exposed later by degradation. Its future would have been determined primarily by geologic processes had it not been observed after exposure. Further erosion might have destroyed the entire site, or a reversal of the process to a period of filling of the present arroyo might have once more sealed the remainder of the site for some time. One part of the site, in Area 3, was exposed and resealed in this manner, as the site profiles demonstrate.

The evidence from the Agate Basin site and several other bison kill sites (see, e.g., Frison 1974; Frison *et al.* 1976; Stanford 1974; Wheat 1972) indicates that much of the cultural activity of Paleoindian hunters engaged in communal large-animal kills occurred along and in streams and dry arroyos. The potential for destruction of these sites through geologic activity is high; in fact, the ones that are preserved, such as Agate Basin, are in reality accidents of preservation. Our methodology does not yet allow us to reliably predict how many Paleoindian sites have been destroyed, are exposed but not yet located, or are still sealed in undisturbed geologic deposits.

Since High Plains Paleoindian sites are contained in geologic contexts, archaeologists must use the heuristic potential of the full range of earth sciences in their investigations. Unfortunately, the interests of the Paleoindian archaeologist seldom coincide with the mainstream of studies in other disciplines. We cannot, for example, offer the botanist substantial parts of plants for identification and our use of the results may not be for taxonomic purposes. Faunal remains may have passed through cultural events that create unfamiliar situations for the paleontologist. The response of an animal population to predation by Paleoindian hunters selecting nursery herds is an alien situation for the wildlife biologist who is interested in the present-day response to the present-day hunting of male animals. Also, the late Pleistocene and early Holocene deposits in which the sites are found are not highly regarded by geologists. The deposits contain little in the way of resources with economic value and encompass a period of time too short to have witnessed what are generally regarded as great geologic changes. Consequently, their study is not in the mainstream of geologic interest, and anthropological archaeologists, who without exception lack adequate training in geology, find it difficult to obtain the kind of geologic expertise they need.

The archaeologist as a result must be innovative but extremely careful in interpreting the results obtained by using the methodology of an unfamiliar discipline. It is appropriate and fair to mention also that anthropologists observe the same phenomenon when persons in other disciplines attempt to use the methodology of anthropology in their interpretations. In the final analysis, however, the interpretation of archaeology is accomplished through the broader methodology of anthropology. The archaeologist must be able to interpret the results of other disciplinary efforts correctly or the input to anthropology will be in error. The development of better methods is essential.

As a direct result of natural forces, Paleoindian sites on the High Plains are severely limited in number. The investigation of one such site destroys a part of a very small and very valuable data base. The Agate Basin site has now witnessed nearly four decades of such destruction, most of it for the purpose of learning about Paleoindian archaeology but entirely too much for the selfish purpose of individual ownership of artifacts. It is somewhat comforting to know that a significant portion of the site remains intact and in a situation that offers maximum protection. This constitutes a very important resource and one that deserves every effort at preservation so that future Paleoindian archaeologists will be assured of an adequate data base as the methodology of investigation is improved.

THE SITE LOCALITY   The north and south forks of Moss Agate Creek and their tributaries meander through a rough, deeply dissected area extending into the low hills south of the Cheyenne River along the Wyoming–South Dakota boundary, close to the southern end of the Black Hills. Moss Agate Arroyo is a short tributary of Moss Agate Creek, and it in turn has a number of smaller tributary arroyos. It begins as a shallow, flat-bottomed arroyo, becoming wider and deeper as it approaches its confluence with Moss Agate Creek (Figure 1.2). The bottom of the arroyo is matted with tall grasses and the channel meanders within the confines of the banks, which are low and gently sloping toward the head of the arroyo but become higher and more abrupt downstream. The original Agate Basin site consisted of two exposures of Agate Basin cultural levels toward the upper end of Moss Agate Arroyo (Figures 1.3 and 1.4). Elevation at the site datum at Area 2 is 1189 m (3900 feet) above sea level.

Site Areas.   The Agate Basin site locality is in sections 10, 15, and 16, T 39 N, R 60 W, Niobrara County, Wyoming, and sections 7 and 18, R 1 E, T 8 S, in Fall River County, South Dakota (Figure 1.5). Within this area are 11 known Paleoindian site exposures (Figure 1.4). Some of these are in situ; others are redeposited. In section 15 Area 1, is the original discovery location and the site of the first systematic excavations, carried out in 1942 by the Smithsonian Institution. An in situ Agate Basin component was present. Area 1 was excavated by the Smithsonian again in 1961, and the University of Wyoming in 1975. Area 2 is split by the line between sections 15 and 16 and was discovered at about the same time as Area 1. It was badly disturbed before the 1961 Smithsonian excavations. In situ Agate Basin and Folsom components were present. The University of Wyoming tested Area 2 in 1972 and carried out annual field excavations from 1975 to 1980. Area 3, about 100 m west of Area 2 in section 16, was found in the late 1950s. A small excavation was conducted in 1959 by the University of Wyoming; this excavation became known as the Brewster site. Area 3 contains in situ Hell Gap and Folsom components, and Agate Basin components were mentioned in the original Brewster site report (Agogino and Frankforter 1960). The University of Wyoming continued excavations at Area 3 in 1977, 1979, and 1980. Area 4 is a small exposure a few meters west of Area 3. Tests were made there by the University of Wyoming in 1977 and 1980, but the material appears to be redeposited. The same is true of Area 5, which is several hundred meters west of Area 4. Tests of Area 5 in 1977 and 1979 by the University of Wyoming revealed small amounts of redeposited cultural materials. Area 6 is several hundred meters east of Area 1 in section 15 and to date has produced only redeposited materials. The Smithsonian Institu-

FIGURE 1.2 **Aerial views of the Agate Basin site looking northwest. Arrow in each indicates Areas 1 and 2.**

tion excavated this area in 1961, and the University of Wyoming excavated in 1975 and 1976, both with negative results. All six exposures discussed so far are located along what in Paleoindian times was the same arroyo.

Area 7 is on a present tributary arroyo about 150 m south of Area 6 and is manifest by three thin levels of apparently redeposited material, all containing charcoal, flakes, and bone. This was apparently some distance from the old arroyo in Paleoindian times and may have been associated with one of its tributaries. Area 8, the Schultz site, is several hundred meters southeast of Area 7, and it was also along the old arroyo in Paleoindian times. This site contains an in situ Agate Basin component, but has only been minimally tested. Area 9, in

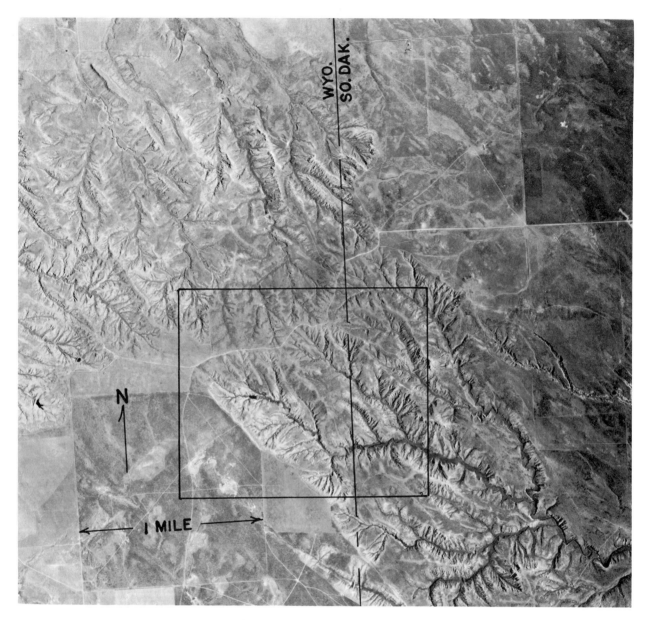

FIGURE 1.3 **Aerial view of the Agate Basin site area.**

another tributary of Moss Agate Arroyo, is the location of an in situ Clovis component. This has been named the Sheaman site, after the present landowner, Robert Sheaman of Gillette, Wyoming, and was excavated by the University of Wyoming in 1977, 1978, and 1979. The site is about 100 m from the Wyoming–South Dakota line in section 10. Areas 10 and 11 are exposures in arroyo banks in sections 7 and 18 in South Dakota. Both areas appear to consist only of redeposited cultural materials, but they have not been investigated thoroughly.

Physical Environment. In both Moss Agate Arroyo and Moss Agate Creek water flows only during spring runoff and heavy rains, although seepage

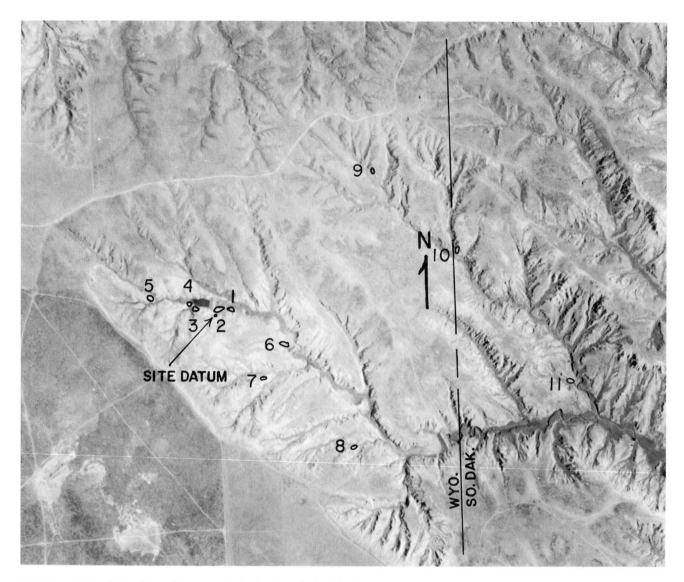

FIGURE 1.4   Enlarged view of part of Figure 1.3 showing locations of Paleoindian site exposures.

areas and stagnant ponds are common during spring and early summer. There is a flowing spring directly across the arroyo from Area 2, and another a few meters from the Sheaman site. The volume of water in both springs is low, and during extremely dry years they may cease flowing by late summer. Both springs draw water from deep snowbanks on the leeward side of the divide between Moss Agate Arroyo and the Cheyenne River.

Headward erosion of the Moss Agate Arroyo system has resulted in the rough, deeply dissected topography in the immediate vicinity of the Agate Basin site and over the low divide to the north separating Moss Agate Creek from the Cheyenne River (Figure 1.2). Past these rough areas or "breaks" are rolling hills, gentle slopes, and a more mature topography. Prominent also are horizontal sandstone and shale formations interbedded with softer materials, creating perpendicular bluffs and steep talus slopes in the more eroded areas. Particularly

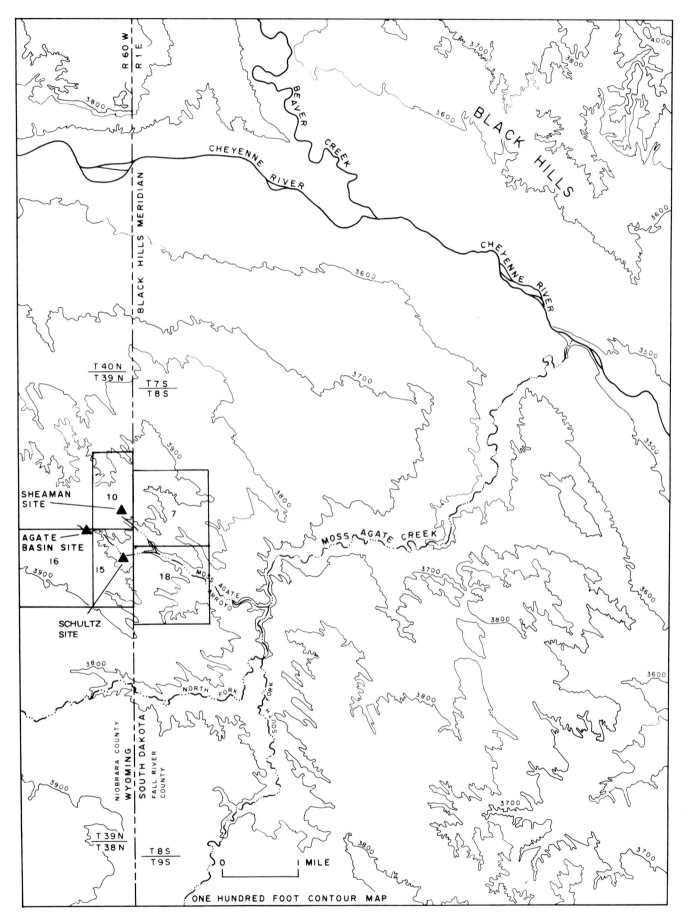

FIGURE 1.5 Agate Basin site location and topographic map.

noticeable is a long, narrow, flat-topped mesa known as the Twentyone Divide rising abruptly 60 m above the surrounding country about 10 km north of the Agate Basin site.

About 6 km north of the Agate Basin site is the Cheyenne River. This stream and its several branches begin about 100 km west of the Agate Basin site in the bandlands country of east-central Wyoming. Its headwaters do not reach the high elevations and no large, permanent springs are in the area. Consequently the flow of the Cheyenne River fluctuates greatly; the river may be nearly dry one day and bank full the next depending on runoff conditions. The stream has a low gradient and a wide floodplain.

The Black Hills extend about 100 miles from southeast to northwest across the Wyoming–South Dakota line, with about three-fifths in the latter state. They constitute a prominent uplift, reaching to 2207 m (7242 feet). They are rough and timber covered, but numerous wide, open, grass-covered corridors make travel through them not difficult. Several live streams flow east out of the Black Hills, but there are none to the west in the southern part. Water for humans and livestock has always been a problem historically in the Agate Basin area. The Cheyenne River flows southeast around the southern tip of the Black Hills and then bears northeast toward the Missouri River. The Agate Basin site is about 15 km from the southwestern edge of the Black Hills.

Climate.   Yearly precipitation in the Agate Basin area averages 12–14 inches, which is sufficient for a continuous grass cover. Sagebrush also dominates the vegetation cover in well-drained areas; greasewood dominates in low, flat, saline areas along floodplains. Cottonwoods, brush thickets, and patches of tall, coarse ryegrass mark the Cheyenne River floodplain. Arroyo bottoms are covered with thick stands of grass, which attract all grazing animals. Ponderosa pine covers most of the Black Hills, but patches of quaking aspen are seen. Canyon bottoms within the Black Hills are lined with brush thickets.

Seasonal changes in this part of the High Plains are of considerable magnitude and often abrupt. Winter temperatures regularly drop below −30°F. Prevailing winds are out of the northwest and create even lower chill factors. The constant wind moves the snow, filling depressions and creating deep drifts on the leeward side of ridges. However, this keeps the windward sides of ridges bare, an important factor in the survival of the large, grazing animals. Winter chinook winds are not uncommon, but they can be a mixed blessing, since they often melt only part of the snow; a quick temperature reversal can create a solid ice sheet that seals the grass away from the animals. In late March the winter snows begin to melt, but spring blizzards are common well into May and are often deadly to all living things.

In normal years, the moisture and warmer weather that come in late April and early May combine to produce new grass, so that by June the entire countryside resembles a green carpet. Feed is abundant, and grazing animals rapidly gain weight and lose their rough winter coats. The young are born and grow rapidly. It is without doubt the most favorable time of the year for animals. Usually by the first part of July, however, the grass is forced into maturity by hot winds and dry weather. By August the country is brown and the fat hardens on the animals, which helps prepare them for winter survival.

Snow and frost are to be expected any time after the first of September, although some of the best weather of the year comes during this month. By October, the snow begins to lie longer in the higher elevations and on north-facing slopes. By late November, winter is once more to be expected at any time, bringing below-zero temperatures and drifting snow.

There is a great deal of climatic variation from year to year on the High Plains. One winter may be mild or "open," whereas the next may be exactly the opposite. If spring rains do not materialize, the result is a shortage of summer feed. Open winters are enjoyed by humans and animals alike but the lack of winter moisture can have adverse affects on the growth of spring grasses. A dry spring and summer may not be too serious if an open winter follows. But if a hard winter follows, populations of grazing animals can be decimated. This has been demonstrated many times in the historic record and undoubtedly applied throughout prehistory also.

For all of the unfavorable comment on High Plains winters, they can be survived with relatively few problems even with a prehistoric technology. The human subsistence strategy has always been to prepare for and expect a bad winter regardless of past conditions. This is strongly suggested by the evidence recovered in the Agate Basin site investigations and in all High Plains archaeological sites.

The Paleoindian use of the Agate Basin site locality apparently spanned a time of significant climatic change, the late Pleistocene to the early Holocene. Temperatures, precipitation, growing seasons, and other climatic factors were undergoing great changes from around 12,000 to 10,000 years ago if the present body of data on climatology is correct (see, e.g., Bryson 1974). It would be a mistake to assume that present conditions at the Agate Basin locality can be used to describe those at the beginning of known human occupation there.

Some of these environmental changes are suggested by the small fauna recovered at the site (see Walker, this volume, Chapter 4, Section 6). That the landforms were quite different, at least with regard to the arroyo system in the immediate site locality, is demonstrated by the reconstructions of earlier landforms based on present remnants (see Albanese, this volume, Chapter 5, Section 1). Both pollen and phytolith studies were inconclusive, because the necessary elements were either lacking or poorly preserved (see Beiswenger and Lewis, this volume, Chapter 5, Sections 4 and 5). However, the charred remains of quaking aspen (*Populus tremuloides*) in the Hell Gap component suggest that there were stands of this species at the site around 10,000 years ago. In fact, a small stand of aspen was discovered in 1980 only 14 km east of the Agate Basin site (see Marlow, this volume, Chapter 5, Section 3).

If, as the geologic evidence indicates, Moss Agate Arroyo had a wide, flat bottom, steep, high banks, and fewer tributaries in late Pleistocene and early Holocene times, its past and present appearance contrasted sharply. If the vegetation consisted of less sagebrush, more brush, trees, and taller grasses, this also would have altered its appearance. That significant changes of this nature were occurring during late Pleistocene–early Holocene times is strongly suggested by the aggrading of the old arroyo as shown by site profiles, and by the loss of some fauna and the appearance of others as shown by the faunal remains.

More than six decades have passed since the historic discovery of the Agate Basin site. The exact date is not known, but it is believed that the site was discovered around 1916 by William Spencer, a livestock owner and operator living in the southern Black Hills near Edgemont, South Dakota. Many explanations—some pure conjecture, some based on the collection and analysis of data—have been presented to account for this phenomenon of bison bones eroding out of a stratum near the top of an arroyo bank along with projectile points of exceptionally fine workmanship. Excavations at the site have similarly ranged from artifact collection to serious undertakings whose purpose was understanding and explanation.

Spencer probably first noticed the site during a visit to the spring directly across the arroyo from the site. This spring was one of a very few sources of potable water in the area, and many homesteaders living nearby visited it regularly in the early part of the present century. Others besides Spencer must have noticed the bones, since they were quite visible and would have aroused anyone's curiosity.

Spencer collected several broken projectile points that had eroded out of the bone level and were exposed on the steep talus slope below. He recovered at least one more while removing bones protruding from the bank. He died in 1977, and whether he performed any serious digging into the site deposits is not known. From all reports, however, it is not believed that he did anything more than superficially probe the edge of the bone deposits.

R. E. Frison, an uncle of the senior author, was the regional game warden for this area of Wyoming during the early 1940s and had long been a collector of artifacts. He was also a longtime acquaintance of one of the discoverers of the Lindenmeier Folsom site, Roy Coffin of Fort Collins, Colorado. As a result, he developed an interest in Paleoindian studies and soon became knowledgeable enough to recognize a number of Paleoindian projectile point types.

In the spring of 1941, a chance meeting occurred between R. E. Frison and William Spencer at an informal gathering of persons interested in local historical phenomena. The gathering took place in a picnic area in a cottonwood grove on the wide floodplain along the Cheyenne River, a few kilometers north of the Agate Basin site. Spencer happened to have with him several broken projectile points from the Agate Basin site, which he showed to the group. Frison recognized these pieces as being unique and very likely quite old. It was the spring of 1942 before the two managed to visit the site together, and a small amount of probing into the bone bed yielded three broken projectile points. Frison sent one of these and some bison teeth from the site to Frank H. H. Roberts, archaeologist at the Smithsonian Institution. This resulted in test excavations in July 1942. The actual excavating was done by Frank H. H. Roberts, his brother, H. B. Roberts, and R. E. Frison, and occurred in what is here designated Area 1.

There are several extant photographs of the 1942 excavations. One of these (Figure 1.6) was taken at the beginning of the excavation. It is difficult to tell for certain, but it is believed that this represents the cleanup stage from earlier digging. If so, the amount of previous site disturbance was minimal. The excavation later in the season (Figure 1.7) reveals a large bone bed with bone well preserved compared to that found in subsequent excavations in Area 2. There

FIGURE 1.6   Beginning of excavations at Agate Basin, 1942, in Area 1. Note that there is no visible evidence of digging at Area 2.

FIGURE 1.7   Excavations in Area 1, 1942. Note the highly visible bone bed and the large pile of bison bone on the arroyo bank.

FIGURE 1.8 **Photograph taken in 1980 at the exact location shown in Figure 1.7.**

was no visible disturbance in Area 2 at this time (Figure 1.6). Little if any change can be detected in the general area between 1942 and 1980 (Figure 1.8), except for the removal of material for a dam to form a stock-watering pond during the 1960s, and the similar removal of material in the excavation of Area 2.

A brief note on the site was published by Roberts (1943). The work in 1942 was severely limited by World War II. Under normal circumstances a full-scale excavation would almost certainly have been initiated within the next few years. R. E. Frison did make some later visits to the site between 1942 and 1946, and he collected several more artifacts. Both he and Roberts were aware of similar materials eroding out of the arroyo bank now designated Area 2, and Frison collected the base of one Agate Basin projectile point from there between 1942 and 1945.

Further mention of the Agate Basin site and pictures of some of the projectile points did not appear in the literature until several years later (Roberts 1951). At that time there was insufficient evidence to assign either a reliable or absolute relative date to the Agate Basin cultural complex. However, a few years later (Wheeler 1954) the Agate Basin projectile point was described as a type on the basis of materials recovered at the Agate Basin site in 1942.

Roberts had also found Hell Gap projectile points at Agate Basin but at the time these were not recognized as either a point type or a cultural complex. The provenience of these specimens is lacking, so they may not have been recovered in situ. The Folsom components that would have clarified the stratigraphic relationships between the Folsom and Agate Basin cultural complexes still lay undisturbed in other parts of the site.

The technological excellence expressed in the Agate Basin projectile points at the site proved irresistible, and consequently the site suffered continual depredation. Roberts' work was confined to the eastern end of the site (Area 1, Figure 1.4) although as has been mentioned he was well aware of another exposure of bone and artifacts (Area 2, Figure 1.4). Collectors dug to some extent in both site areas before Roberts was able to return to the site in 1961.

One of the persons who visited the Agate Basin site in the late 1950s was James Duguid, a geology student at the University of Wyoming, who noticed bones, charcoal, and artifacts eroding out of an arroyo bank about 85 m west of Area 2. Probing into the bone level, Duguid recovered two Folsom projectile points. This discovery led to a small excavation by the University of Wyoming in 1959, under the direction of George Agogino with W. D. Frankforter as paleontologist and C. V. Haynes as consulting geologist. This was the excavation that came to be known as the Brewster site (Agogino and Frankforter 1960), after an Iowa man who appeared and offered to do volunteer work there. The Folsom component was confirmed and found to underlie what were then believed to be Agate Basin components. The Brewster site was considered to be separate from the Agate Basin site, although today there is no question that it is part of the same site. This was also Roberts' opinion (1961a: 132); he was aware of the exposure of the cultural level that later became known as the Brewster site (now Area 3; see Figure 1.4).

The first major excavation at the Agate Basin site was conducted in 1961 by William M. Bass of the University of Kansas and Frank H. H. Roberts of the Smithsonian Institution. Funds were supplied by the National Geographic Society (Grant No. 329). At the beginning of the investigations, it was noted that extensive damage had been done by collectors to the Agate Basin components in Areas 1 and 2 (Figure 1.9). However, the major excavations during 1961 were in Area 2 (Figure 1.10). The remainder of Area 1 was excavated, but the artifact collectors had left little. Unfortunately, much of the effort in 1961 was expended in cleaning up the site so that proper excavation could proceed.

In addition, several areas along the south bank of the arroyo were tested in 1961; a small area adjacent to the Brewster site excavation was later proven to contain part of a Hell Gap component (Figure 1.10). Area 6, about 200 m downstream from the Areas 1 and 2, was also tested. Two short reports were published on these investigations (Bass 1970; Roberts 1961b); Roberts (1961a) also published a slightly expanded statement that presented Agate Basin as a cultural complex.

The 1961 excavation trenches were not filled and unfortunately provided ideal guide markers for the projectile point collectors. Consequently much of the site, especially in Area 2 and to a lesser extent in Areas 1 and 3, was lost to the collectors throughout the 1960s. James Duguid, who, subsequent to locating the Brewster site, had also discovered the Hell Gap site about 110 km south of the Agate Basin site, dug and collected materials from Agate Basin between 1961 and 1967, as did Louis Steege of Cheyenne, Wyoming, a member of the Wyoming Archaeological Society. All the material they collected at the Agate Basin site has been given to the Smithsonian Institution and is of some value, but exact provenience is lacking, bones were not mapped or saved, and the exact areas excavated were not carefully recorded.

Several hundred meters downstream from Area 1 is a livestock pond built in

FIGURE 1.9 **The Agate basin site as it appeared at the beginning of the 1961 Smithsonian field season (top); extensive digging into the Agate Basin component in Area 2 (bottom).**

the 1950s. The dam was constructed from dirt scooped out of the arroyo bottom and from the south arroyo bank. This excavation exposed several dark strata containing redeposited charcoal and bone. Out of the deepest of these levels, Duguid recovered a toothed bone flesher thought to be of Folsom age (see Chapter 2, Section 6). It is now believed that this artifact was redeposited from upstream, since excavations in this site area in 1975 and 1976 revealed scattered bone fragments, small flakes, and charcoal but nothing that appeared to be in situ. Duguid also discovered and dug into the Paleoindian exposure known as the Sheaman site (Area 9), which is of Clovis age.

Shortly after the 1961 excavations by Roberts and Bass, another livestock reservoir was constructed in Moss Agate Arroyo at the Agate Basin site, this time at Area 2 (see Figure 1.2, bottom). Although the fill material was taken from both the bottom and the south bank of the arroyo, site components were not seriously disturbed by these excavations. However, some disturbance did result from the preparation of the base for the dam, and the water in the pond

FIGURE 1.10 Excavations in Areas 1 and 2 in 1961 (top), and tests in Area 3 (bottom). B indicates the Brewster site excavations in 1959. [*Photo by William Bass*]

has backed up to the Brewster site area, causing considerable cutting into the south arroyo bank. This has been greatly accelerated by the increased use of the area around the pond by livestock. Fortunately most of the archaeological components are deeply buried well away from the edge of the stock pond, and their chances of destruction are minimal.

In 1972 the senior author was conducting archaeological work about 100 km to the north in the Wyoming Black Hills when he decided to test the Agate Basin site in order to acertain if any of the site remained. A 5 × 10 foot test of the Agate Basin component in Area 2 revealed that artifact hunters were still finding undisturbed deposits with considerable amounts of bone. It also indicated a strong possibility that more remained. A visit to the site in August 1975 revealed extensive looting, and consequently a crew from the University of Wyoming and the Wyoming State Archeologist's Office spent over 2 weeks investigating the site. A large segment of an undisturbed bone bed was exposed in Area 2, but excavations showed that very little remained intact in Area 1. A large bone sample and a number of projectile points and tools were recovered, but all were in disturbed deposits resulting from earlier digging. An intensive geologic study of the entire locality was begun at this time.

In 1976, excavations were conducted at Agate Basin in late May and early June, a period of nearly 3 weeks, this time with additional monetary aid from the Smithsonian Institution through the efforts of the junior author. Most work centered in Area 2, although one test was made in Area 6. As already mentioned, this bone level had been exposed earlier by reservoir construction and was tested by Bass and Roberts in 1961, but with almost totally negative results. Some cultural material—a few small flakes of quartzite and chert recovered on a water-screen—was found in association with the bone but nothing recovered was diagnostic; this is now believed to be entirely redeposited material. Several deep backhoe trenches were dug in the vicinity of Area 6 in 1976 to provide profiles for continued geologic study.

Another 2 weeks were spent at Agate Basin in 1977. Test and profile trenches were dug by backhoe in the Brewster site area to determine if any in situ cultural deposits remained. The stratigraphy was found to conform quite closely to that described by Agogino and Frankforter (1960), but no diagnostic artifacts were recovered. However, in what was later confirmed to be a Folsom level, one male and one female bison skull were recovered along with several long bones. All were badly distorted by pressure from overlying deposits, in some places 4 m thick, so only a few reliable skull measurements were possible. This proved later to be a Folsom level and was, in addition, almost certainly a remnant of the Brewster site Folsom level described by Agogino and Frankforter (1960). A level above the Folsom level contained bone, flakes, and fragments of two Hell Gap points. One of these later proved to be a basal fragment of Hell Gap type, since the remainder had been recovered in a different part of the same bone level by Bass and Roberts in 1961 during their tests in Area 3. It seems almost certain that one cultural level that Agogino and Frankforter regarded as an Agate Basin component was in reality Hell Gap, but their interpretation was a reasonable one in view of the absence of diagnostic projectile points. No cultural materials were recovered in what was apparently an extension of Agogino and Frankforter's Agate Basin component. Another small section of the Agate Basin level in Area 2 was also dug during the 1977 field season.

A visit to the Agate Basin site area in 1973 had revealed a buried component exposed in an arroyo bank about 1 km northeast of the actual Agate Basin site (the Sheaman site, Area 9; see Figure 1.4). It had been dug into earlier, and bone fragments and quartzite and chert flakes were present in the backdirt, but no diagnostic materials were seen. It was later confirmed that this had first been tested by Duguid at about the same time as his discovery of the Brewster site. A small test made in 1977 by the senior author revealed a well-defined cultural level heavily impregnated with red ocher; bone fragments and flakes were found, but there was nothing of diagnostic value. However, the condition of the bone and the red ocher suggested a Paleoindian age. The site is close to the head of an arroyo that drains into Moss Agate Arroyo, the same arroyo that contains the Agate Basin site.

In 1978, tests below the main Agate Basin level in Area 2 revealed another cultural level. Three weeks of fieldwork proved this to be an in situ Folsom component that produced a large assemblage of stone tools, debris from projectile point manufacture, and faunal materials. No cultural material was found below the Folsom level, although several bones and charcoal in lower levels hinted strongly at the possibility of earlier components.

The excavation at the Sheaman site was expanded in 1978 and resulted in the recovery of a large number of core and biface reduction flakes. A cylindrical ivory object, tapered on one end and pointed on the opposite end, was recovered. It is almost identical to bone objects recovered in Clovis sites (see, e.g., Lahren and Bonnichsen 1974), strongly suggesting that the Sheaman site was a remnant of a Clovis occupation.

Also surveyed in 1978 was a section of Moss Agate Arroyo downstream from the Agate Basin site. The survey revealed the Schultz site, where another Agate Basin component was eroding out of the arroyo bank (Area 8, Figure 1.4). A small test confirmed the presence of bison bone, Agate Basin points, tools, and debitage. No attempt was made to excavate further in this area but future problems may warrant an investigation. Also noted at this time was a small

FIGURE 1.11 Archaic period fire pit exposed at the surface along Moss Agate Arroyo.

exposure of bone and flakes close to the surface along a short tributary of Moss Agate Arroyo (Area 7, Figure 1.4). As at the Sheaman site, the appearance of the bone suggested a Paleoindian age. The area had been tested earlier by unknown person or persons, and a 1979 test revealed three levels contained within a vertical distance of less than 30 cm. The bone fragments, charcoal, and flakes found in these levels appear to be redeposited. A charcoal date of nearly 10,000 B.P. confirms their Paleoindian age.

Eight weeks were spent at the Agate Basin site in the summer of 1979. Efforts were directed toward geologic and soils studies and also toward the Folsom component in Area 2. At the Brewster site (Area 3), 4 m of overburden were removed, revealing a small in situ Hell Gap component and an overlying unidentified component. Still lower stratigraphically was a Folsom component. As in Area 2, there are still lower levels containing charcoal, bone, flakes, and at

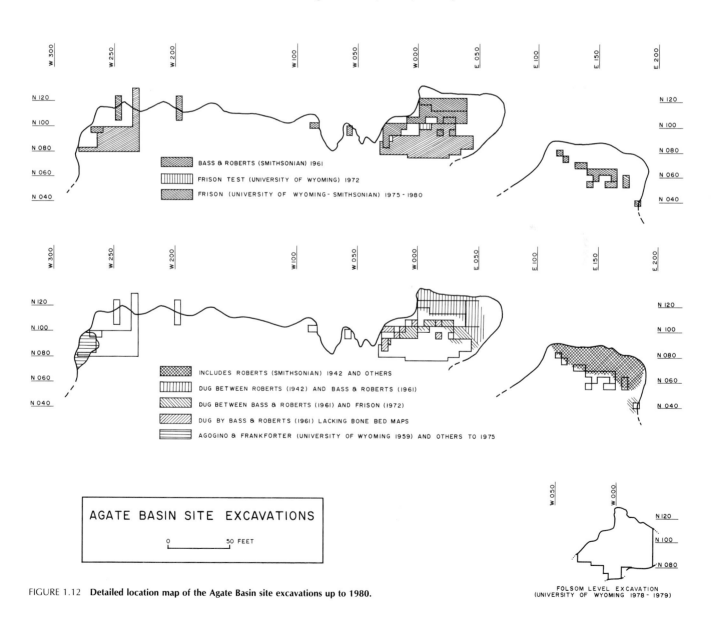

FIGURE 1.12   Detailed location map of the Agate Basin site excavations up to 1980.

least three tools. Cultural affiliations are as yet unknown, but a camel bone was recovered in these lower levels and two radiocarbon dates on charcoal of around 11,500 B.P. indicate an age equivalent to Clovis.

A week's work at the Sheaman site in the fall of 1979 resulted in the recovery of a Clovis projectile point, several tools, and debitage further indicating that this is a true Clovis component. Another week late in the fall of 1979 was spent doing geologic mapping of the locality as far downstream as the confluence of Moss Agate Arroyo and the arroyo in which the Sheaman site is located.

In 1980, two trenches were dug in Area 3 in order to resolve the stratigraphy in the old arroyo deposits. This resulted in a better definition of the stratigraphy in the old arroyo as well as the Hell Gap and Folsom components located the year before. Three Hell Gap components and two Folsom components, all in situ, are now known to be present in Area 3. The redeposited cultural levels below the Folsom levels are still unresolved.

One day was spent investigating a number of in situ Archaic period fire pits along Moss Agate Arroyo (Figure 1.11) in order to obtain radiocarbon dates that might aid in obtaining minimum dates for the existence of the present-day Moss Agate Arroyo. No further excavations are planned for the Agate Basin locality at this time.

This record of activity (Figure 1.12) at the Agate Basin site covers about 65 years. Geologic studies indicate that a large part of the Agate Basin site still lies intact under a thick cover of alluvial and colluvial material in preserved parts of the old arroyo. Some of this will undoubtedly contain in situ site components, although most will be redeposited. Undoubtedly much remains to be learned about the site both geologically and archaeologically.

ARTIFACT COLLECTIONS

Conclusions on the Agate Basin site as it is presently known are based on the examination of the field notes of the investigators and the materials they collected. It is the shared opinion of the authors, and of archaeologists in general, that the interpretation of another person's archaeological field notes and collected materials is not an ideal situation. The second investigator can never view the context from which the site assemblage was taken or interpret the results in the same way and consequently as well as the original investigator. In this particular situation, however, both authors have been able to establish a close familiarity with the site and the collections. In fact, the senior author over a period of 8 years has excavated more of the site, and has recovered more site data than all other site investigators combined. As a result, the authors do claim adequate site familiarity to perform the final analysis. Even so, it is freely admitted that we will never be able to view the Agate Basin site as it was viewed by Frank H. H. Roberts, the first professional archaeologist to investigate a part of the site (Area 1) that was apparently quite different from the ones excavated later.

As noted in an earlier section, the Agate Basin site investigations have covered nearly four decades, and several individuals, both amateurs and professionals, have been deeply involved. As a result, the site data were collected by persons with different levels of expertise, and different perspectives. Therefore it is necessary for us to give a detailed account of the collections that comprise the data base for the Agate Basin site, and to provide some knowledge of the individuals involved, so that those reading this book may better evaluate the validity of the data and how this may have affected the final interpretations.

Unfortunately, the recovery data on the Roberts collection are not good. The original field notes for the 1942 investigation have not appeared, and only the unprovenienced artifacts remain. In addition, none of the persons involved in the 1942 excavations is living, and verbal accounts can no longer be recovered.

The Roberts Collection

The material collected in 1942 by Roberts consists of 60 consecutively numbered artifacts. Forty-eight of these numbers comprise 46 projectile points, since three numbered specimens fit together to make up the proximal end of one point. In addition, three projectile points are not numbered. One of these is almost certainly the point found by C. V. Haynes shortly after the Bass and Roberts excavations in 1961 and subsequently sent to Roberts. Haynes had visited the Agate Basin site to examine and take notes on the geology, and, while there, he found the projectile point in the wall of an old excavation (Haynes, personal communication). The second specimen was apparently thought by someone to be part of the base of another point, and the two pieces were even glued together at one time. However, both are distal ends of projectile points and are of noticeably different grades of materials; neither the breaks nor the flake scars match. We do know that the specimen was one found by Roberts, since it is pictured in both his 1951 and 1961 articles. The third specimen is a midsection of an Agate Basin projectile point for which there are no known provenience data.

Five of the 60 numbered specimens are biface fragments. One of these fragments appears to be a midsection of an Agate Basin projectile point made into a tool that morphologically and functionally is a combination of an end scraper and a graver. Another biface is in two pieces, one part found by Roberts in 1942 and the other found by the University of Wyoming in 1975. Two other bifaces were probably also broken knives, and the last biface is actually a chopper. Five items are flake tools, and there are two bone fragments that were probably thought to have been tools. Their past use is questionable; they can only be regarded as broken bison bone. Deterioration often produces conditions suggestive of wear on edges of broken bone.

There is a considerable amount of evidence that most of the Roberts collection was recovered from Area 1. Roberts (1951:127) indicated that this was the location of the 1942 excavations and this was also said to be the case by R. E. Frison during his numerous discussions with the senior author. However, both Roberts and R. E. Frison were also aware of the bone exposed in the arroyo bank in Area 2.

About half of the projectile points from the Roberts collection were made of what is believed to be Knife River flint. The senior author also recovered several projectile points from Area 1, and all demonstrate heavy patination, as do the projectile points from the Roberts collection that were made of Knife River flint.

In contrast, projectile points of the same material from Area 2 do not demonstrate this high degree of patination. The same is true of the R. E. Frison collection; those specimens from Area 1 are heavily patinated, whereas one specimen known to be from Area 2 is not. Apparently something in the soil chemistry of the two areas affected the Knife River flint differently. The patination process is so advanced on some of the Knife River flint specimens that the functional utility of the points would now be seriously affected.

The R. E. Frison Collection

R. E. Frison was able to work at the Agate Basin site periodically with Frank H. H. Roberts and the latter's brother, H. B. Roberts, in the summer of 1942. During this period and on several other visits to the site, he acquired at least 14 and probably 15 projectile points from the Agate Basin site, mostly from Area 1. The 14 remaining specimens have been donated to the University of Wyoming by Robert Frison, Jr. One of the specimens is the distal end of an Agate Basin projectile point; the proximal end was recovered in Area 1 by the senior author. The distal end of another specimen came from Area 1 and another piece was found in the William Spencer collection.

Any discussion of the Roberts and R. E. Frison collections must include mention of Roberts' (1951, 1961a) publications on the site. According to the later account (1961a), 32 projectile points were recovered in situ in the 1942 excavations. In the same publication (p. 131), Plate 3 illustrates 58 separate pieces described as those points collected during the 1942 test excavations (see also Wormington 1957:142). Of the specimens illustrated (Figure 1.13), numbers 2, 4, 5, 10, 11, 13, 23, 37, and 56 were part of the R. E. Frison collection but 37 and 56 have since disappeared (see also Figure 1.14). All the remaining specimens in Plate 3 (Roberts 1961a) are accounted for in the Roberts collection. This means that at least 15 of the specimens in Figure 1.13 were not found in situ but we do not know which ones these are.

Roberts also noted (1961a:126) that, besides the 32 points found in situ, he studied 38 points from various local collections. Whether or not this group of 38 specimens includes the 9 in Figure 1.13 from the R. E. Frison collection plus the 15 in Figure 1.13 not found in situ in 1942 is not known. It is not unlikely, however, that Roberts was able to acquire or at least borrow for study some specimens from other local collections and used them in the illustration in Figure 1.13. If this was the case, the 15 specimens unaccounted for could be part of the 38 specimens from other collections. At least some of the 38 specimens must have been part of the William Spencer collection, discussed next. It should be mentioned that the photograph in Roberts' 1951 article (p. 19) is the same as that in the 1961 article (1961a) except that both sides were cropped.

The Spencer Collection

During his years as a stockman, William Spencer gathered a number of artifacts, and at least 13 of these were collected at the Agate Basin site. Some were surface finds in the immediate site area, others were found on the talus slopes between the bone level and the arroyo bottom, and the remainder were found in very superficial attempts at digging into the bone bed in Areas 1 and 2. Closer provenience of these specimens is not known. Several specimens known to have been in the collection are now missing.

One of the Spencer collection artifacts is a midsection of an Agate Basin point that matches the distal end of one recovered by R. E. Frison in Area 1. Although the basal part of the specimen is still missing, it demonstrates perhaps as well as any specimen the excellence in flint technology attained by the Agate Basin cultural complex (see Chapter 2, Figure 2.59).

The Duguid Collection

James Duguid has been credited with the discovery of the Brewster site (Agogino and Frankforter 1960) and in addition collected extensively at the Agate Basin site. The Duguid collection includes the two Folsom points from the Brewster site. Another Folsom point in the Duguid collection was found on the backdirt pile in Area 2 sometime after the Smithsonian (Bass and Roberts) excavations in 1961, but whether or not this was backdirt from these excavations or from someone digging for artifacts is not known.

A serrated bone flesher was recovered by Duguid in Area 6. This specimen was almost certainly redeposited, but site geology indicates that the unit from which it was recovered is probably also of Folsom age. Two artifacts were recovered by Duguid from the Sheaman (Clovis) site about .8 km northeast of the main site area. The remainder of the Duguid collection consists of tools and projectile points from various parts of the site. Two Hell Gap points were surface finds from the vicinity of Area 2, and several Agate Basin points and tools were excavated from Areas 1 and 2. Several other stone tools from the Duguid collection lacked sufficient provenience data to allow them to be used in the analysis.

The Bass–Roberts Collection

Material in the Bass–Roberts collection was gathered during the Smithsonian Institution excavations in the summer of 1961. Most of those specimens regarded as artifacts were numbered from 1 through 65, and 20 are projectile points from Areas 1, 2, and 3. At least 30 more specimens are stone tools but the identification of 4 items as bone tools is highly questionable. The remaining specimens in this series of numbers consist of surface finds and miscellaneous items.

Several hundred other items in the collection include stone, bone, charcoal samples, shell, and miscellaneous items, as well as some artifact material. These items were given a different set of numbers, from 501 through 746. This entire collection is well documented with adequate provenience data and field notes.

The Wheeler–Shippee Collection

The Wheeler–Shippee collection consists of 13 miscellaneous stone items and 6 animal bones gathered as surface finds in 1951. Its usefulness in the final site analysis is very low because of a lack of provenience data.

The Mallory Collection

The Mallory collection also consists of surface finds—28 stone items and 18 animal bones—collected in 1967 by Oscar Mallory. As with the Wheeler–Shippee collection, its usefulness in site interpretations is minimal.

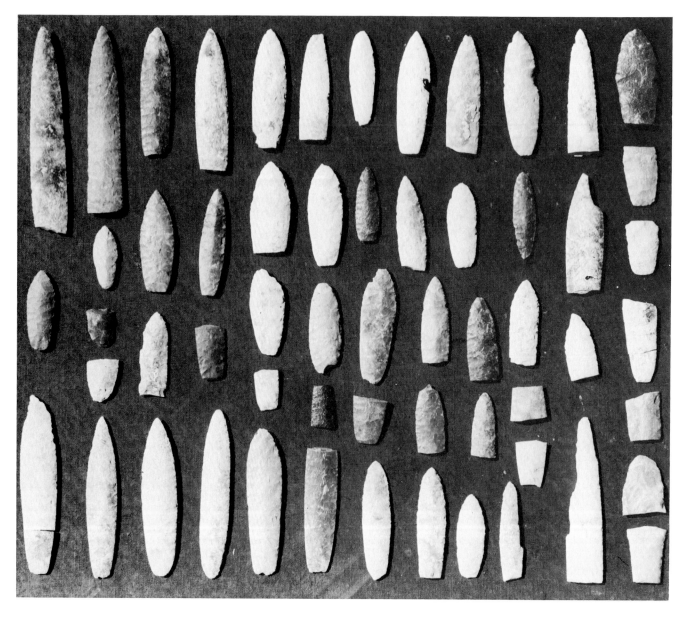

FIGURE 1.13 **Projectile points illustrated by Roberts (1951, 1961a).**

The University of Wyoming Collection

By far the largest of the collections, the University of Wyoming collection consists of materials gathered by the senior author from 1972 through 1980. Over 1100 cataloged artifacts and more than 3000 identified bones are included, along with over 25,000 associated items of debitage and unidentified bone. This collection and the associated multidisciplinary studies provide the major body of interpretative data for the final site interpretations.

The Steege Collection

In the collection of Louis Steege are a number of items, of which only five are of diagnostic value and need to be mentioned. One is a projectile point of

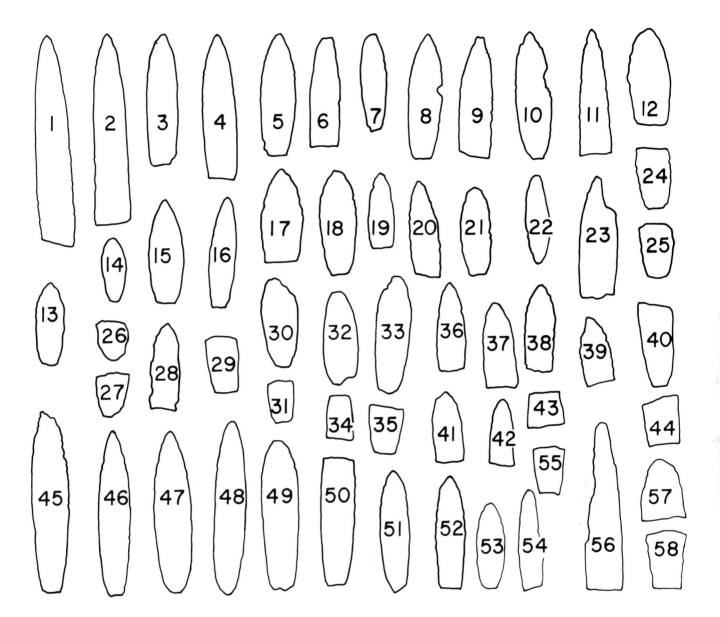

FIGURE 1.14 **Key to projectile points in Figure 1.13.**

Knife River flint recovered from the main Agate Basin level in Area 2. Another is the Agate Basin projectile point that came from the Brewster site (see Agogino and Frankforter 1960:103); the remaining three specimens came from the surface in the vicinity of Areas 1 and 2. As with the Duguid collection, many other items lacked sufficient provenience data to be usable in the final analysis.

The Tubbs family have lived near the Agate Basin site for a number of years. One member collected a large side scraper from the Agate Basin bone bed prior to the University of Wyoming–Smithsonian excavations in 1975. The artifact (Figure 2.62a) was donated to the University of Wyoming in 1975.

The Tubbs Collection

Together these collections comprise the tangible body of evidence from the Agate Basin site. The following chapters deal with the description, analysis, and interpretation of the materials contained in these collections and the contexts from which they were recovered.

two
ARCHAEOLOGY

1. STRATIGRAPHY

george c. frison

The stratigraphic relationships between cultural levels at the Agate Basin site are demonstrated by vertical profiles taken at several site locations. There are three main areas of site excavations. At the first, designated as Area 1, initial investigations began in the summer of 1942. Area 2 was the focus of excavation in 1961. Area 3, generally referred to as the Brewster site, was first excavated in 1959, but extensive excavations occurred there in 1977, 1979, and 1980; a small test excavation was made in 1961. The cultural components and their stratigraphic relationships are different in all three areas, although they were deposited in the bottom of the same arroyo. The basic horizontal unit of excavation was a 5-foot square. This unit was used by the Smithsonian in 1961 and was carried through all subsequent excavations to prevent confusion. The exception is the Sheaman site, a Clovis component, which was some distance from the three main site areas and was excavated in metric units.

Data for the 1942 excavation of Area 1 are lacking, and most of the site was destroyed before the first major excavations occurred, in 1961. Bass and Roberts' 1961 field notes indicate that a few small areas of the bone bed were intact at that time. According to Roberts (1961a:126) the bone bed was at a depth of 4 feet at the termination of the 1942 work. Unfortunately, we do not know the exact location of this observation. Photographs of the excavation (Figure 2.1; see Roberts 1951, 1961a) demonstrate a bone bed continuing on

SITE AREA 1

FIGURE 2.1 **Excavations and exposed
bone bed in Area 1, 1942.**

into the sloping south bank of the present arroyo. The entire bone bed had been
destroyed by the time the University of Wyoming–Smithsonian excavations
began in 1975.

In 1961, Bass and Roberts made an east–west profile of a partially excavated 5-foot-square unit (Figure 2.2) that shows the Agate Basin bone bed just
slightly over 3 feet below ground surface. This is probably a short distance south

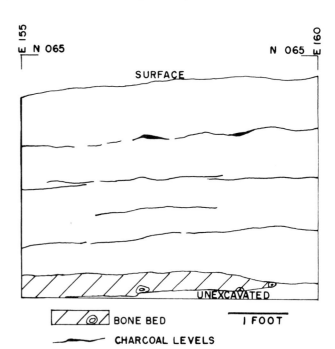

FIGURE 2.2 **East–west profile in
Area 1.** [*Redrawn from Bass and
Roberts 1961.*]

and east of the site of the 1942 photograph, and the slope of the ground surface brings it closer to the bone bed. Roberts (1961a:128) noted also that the "stratum was relatively level as it continued into the bank," so that the depth of the bone bed was determined by ground surface topography. It appears that the bone bed in Area 1 was deposited on the floodplain on the south side of the old arroyo channel, and both terminated where the old arroyo bank sloped rapidly upward. The 1975 University of Wyoming–Smithsonian excavations in Area 1 (see Figure 1.12) revealed the south bank of the old arroyo, but the entire bone bed to the north of this had been removed. Tests below the Agate Basin level revealed no deeper cultural levels, so little more can be said about the stratigraphy of Area 1.

Better data are available for Area 2. A north–south profile (Figure 2.3) and an east–west profile (Figure 2.4) demonstrate the relationship between cultural strata. A thick, redeposited, dark level underlying the Folsom level in Area 2 contains charcoal and bone fragments but no stone flakes or artifacts. The Folsom level directly above is essentially in situ and in some places there is a thin, barely perceptible lighter-colored sterile level between the two levels. **SITE AREA 2**

There is good separation between the Folsom level and the overlying Agate Basin bone bed level, which is also in situ. However, some of the Folsom cultural materials were suspended in the matrix above the actual floor. This probably resulted from the scouring of parts of the Folsom level by runoff water heavily laden with silt and other debris. Some of the Agate Basin materials were below the bone bed in the upper part of the sterile level. Much of this displacement undoubtedly resulted from rodent activity. There is also a strong suggestion that large animals trampled the bone bed when it was wet, forcing some materials into the matrix below.

Above the Agate Basin level and separated by a sterile level of varying thickness was another dark level containing redeposited charcoal, flakes, broken bone, and artifacts. Two projectile point bases (Figure 2.54u, x) found in this level are probably Hell Gap, an assumption based on the manufacturing technology. A very small charcoal sample from the level is dated at 10,200 ± 2000 years B.P. (RL-738); because of the large plus–minus figure, this date may not be too informative.

Both Folsom and Agate Basin cultural strata are relatively level in north-south profile to the north end of the excavations, but to the south both levels slope rapidly into the old arroyo channel (Figure 2.3). Both strata slope gently downstream as shown in east–west profile (Figure 2.4). This is demonstrated also in a topographic map of the Folsom level (Figure 2.5); the Agate Basin level follows a similar configuration.

There were some changes in Area 2 between 1961 and 1979. A comparison of Bass and Roberts' 1961 field excavation map and the Folsom level excavation maps of 1979 and 1980 reveals a marked change in the configuration of the south bank of the modern arroyo. This change probably resulted from ground disturbance caused by the construction of a dam across the present arroyo to form a stock-watering reservoir in 1962.

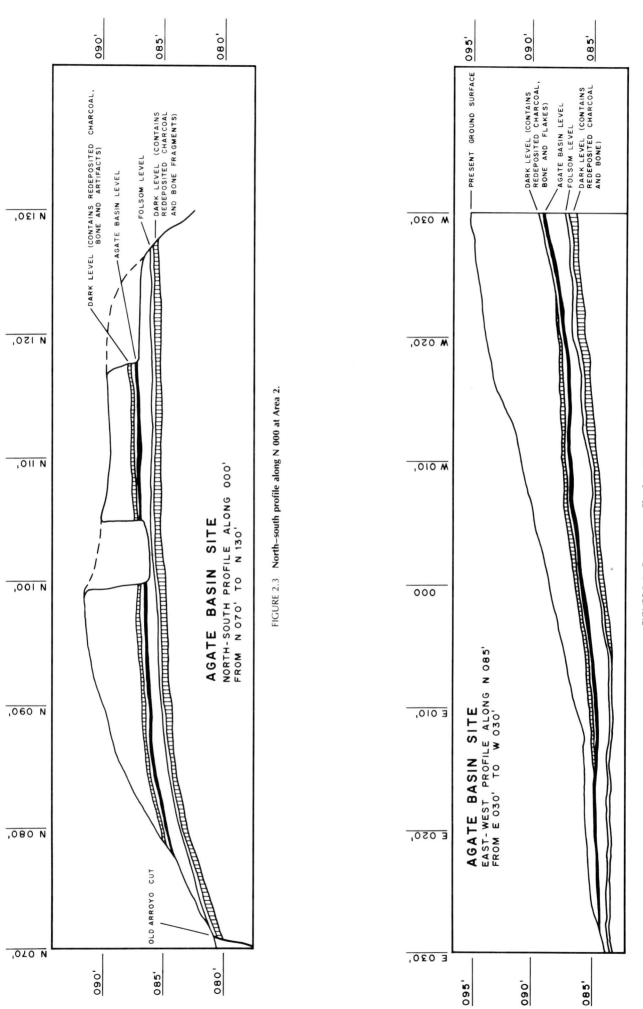

FIGURE 2.3 North–south profile along N 000 at Area 2.

FIGURE 2.4 East–west profile along W 085 at Area 2.

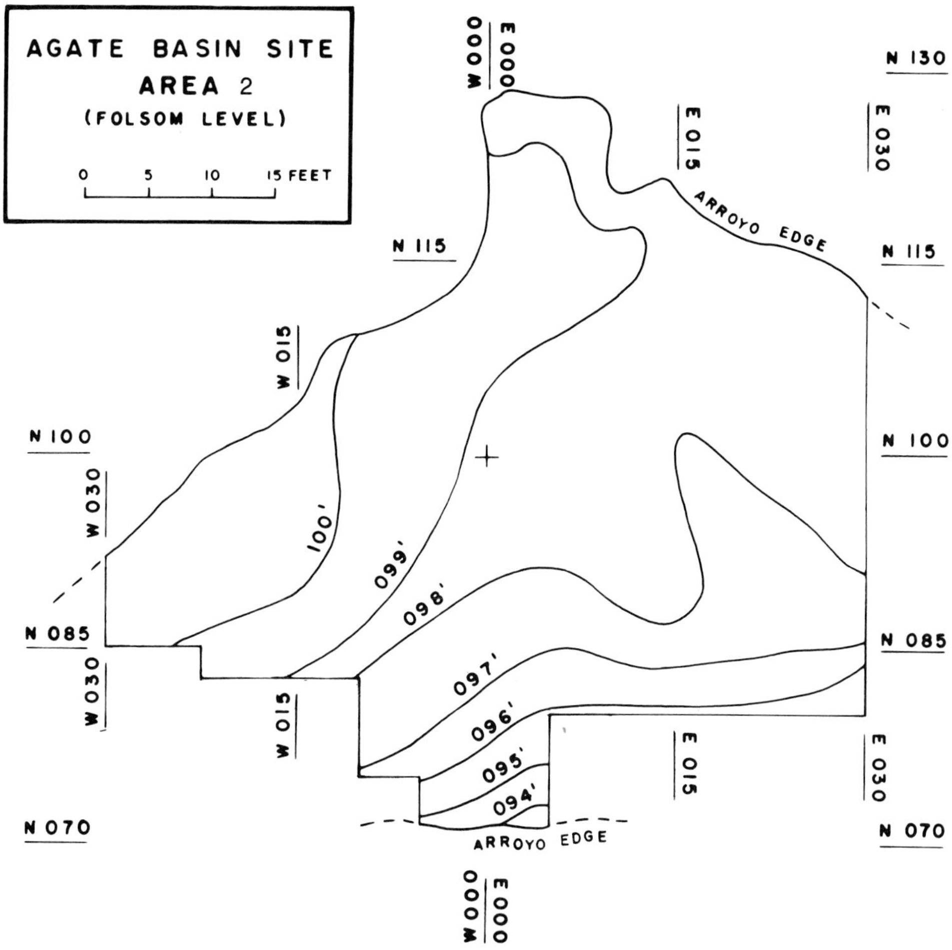

AGATE BASIN SITE
AREA 2
(FOLSOM LEVEL)

0   5   10   15 FEET

FIGURE 2.5 **Topographic map of the Folsom level in Area 2.**

Apparently, the Bass and Roberts excavations in 1961 did not penetrate below the Agate Basin levels, except for one 5 × 5 foot unit (W 025–030, N 085–090). This unit was excavated through both the Agate Basin and Folsom levels, and an Agate Basin type projectile point was recovered in the Agate Basin level. Bones were recovered and mapped in the Folsom level but not in the Agate Basin level, since only a few scattered fragments were recorded there. The recorded profile of this unit (Figure 2.6) was of special importance in integrating the Bass and Roberts field data with those of the University of Wyoming–Smithsonian excavations, but the excavators in 1961 were unaware that they had found a Folsom level. This is not surprising since there was very little in the way of diagnostic material in this part of the site and the Folsom level itself was indistinct except for a few bones directly above the underlying, dark, redeposited level.

SITE AREA 3

The University of Wyoming–Smithsonian team excavated in Area 3 during 1977, 1979, and 1980. Profiles demonstrate both redeposited and in situ cultural levels. The oldest known level containing cultural materials is relatively thick

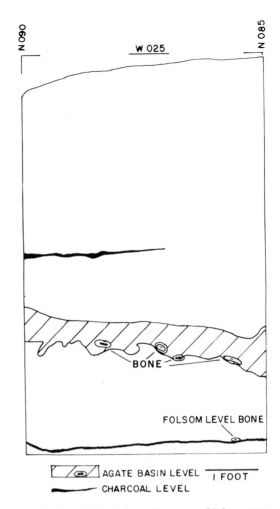

N 090

W 025

N 085

BONE

FOLSOM LEVEL BONE

AGATE BASIN LEVEL   1 FOOT
CHARCOAL LEVEL

FIGURE 2.6   **North–south profile along W 025.** *[Redrawn from Bass and Roberts 1961.]*

and dark. Small amounts of bone, along with two simple stone tools (Figure 2.79j, k), comprise the presently known cultural materials. This level is believed to correlate with a similar stratum underlying the Folsom level in Area 2.

Two thin in situ Folsom levels occur above the thick, dark level and above this are at least three in situ Hell Gap levels (Figure 2.7). To the south and west, the Hell Gap levels merge into a single level. These cultural levels are all on the south side of the old arroyo (Figures 2.8–2.11); no cultural levels were encountered on the north side (Figures 2.8–2.11), although the present arroyo has cut quite deeply into the old arroyo deposits on that side.

An arroyo cut postdating the deposition of the Hell Gap components destroyed an unknown amount of the Hell Gap bone bed (Figure 2.9), but was not deep enough to affect the Folsom and older components. Excavations in 1980 (Figures 2.9–2.12) were specifically for the purpose of clarifying site stratigraphy. However, the excavations were not extended far enough south to allow a complete profile of the old arroyo. All profile locations are shown (Figure 2.13) in relationship to the different site areas. The profile maps indicate a high probability of extensive cultural deposits remaining between Area 2 and Area 3.

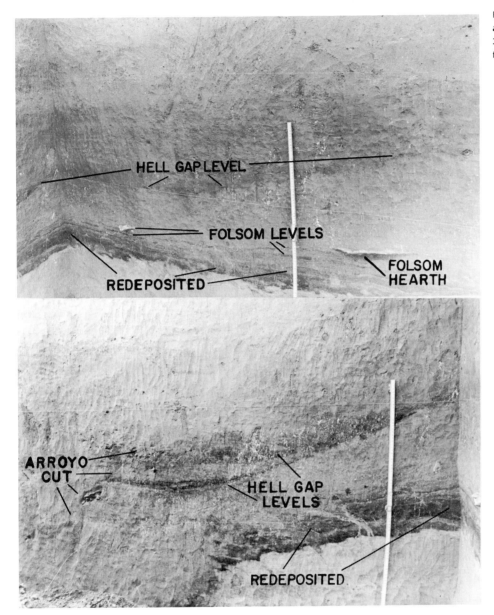

FIGURE 2.7   **View of the east–west (top) and north–south (bottom) profiles in Area 3 taken in 1980 (see Figures 2.9 and 2.10 for detail).**

They are deeply buried, and since the present arroyo shows no tendency to move in their direction, their protection seems certain. In addition, between Areas 3 and 6 (Figure 1.4) the old arroyo deposits are intact and the presence of in situ cultural components here is almost a certainty.

Moderate rodent activity throughout most of the site deposits accounts for some of the minor amounts of displacement of cultural materials. Stream cutting, filling, and transport within the arroyo bottom might also have been partly responsible. Some parts of older cultural components might have been exposed during the times of later components. Whatever the explanation, minor mixing of components did occur.

Fire pits dating to the Late Plains Archaic period were found along both sides of the present Moss Agate Arroyo for its entire known length (Figure 1.11).

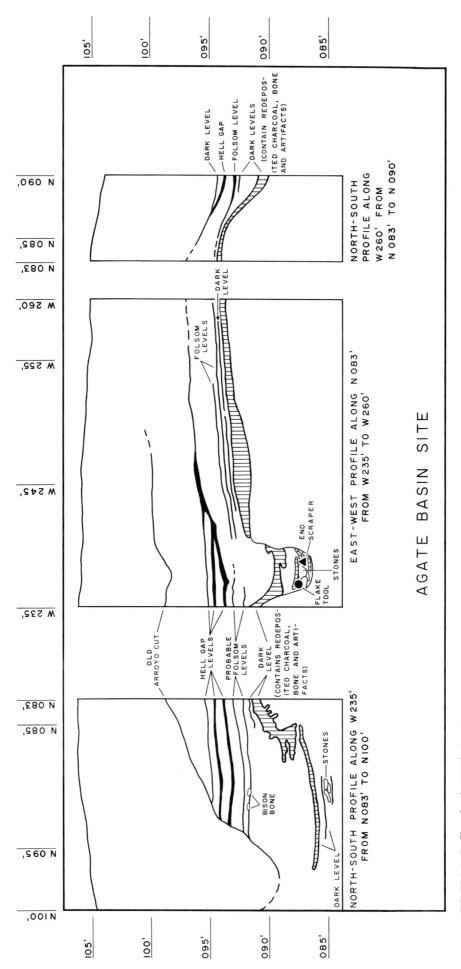

FIGURE 2.8 **Profiles taken in 1978 in Area 3.**

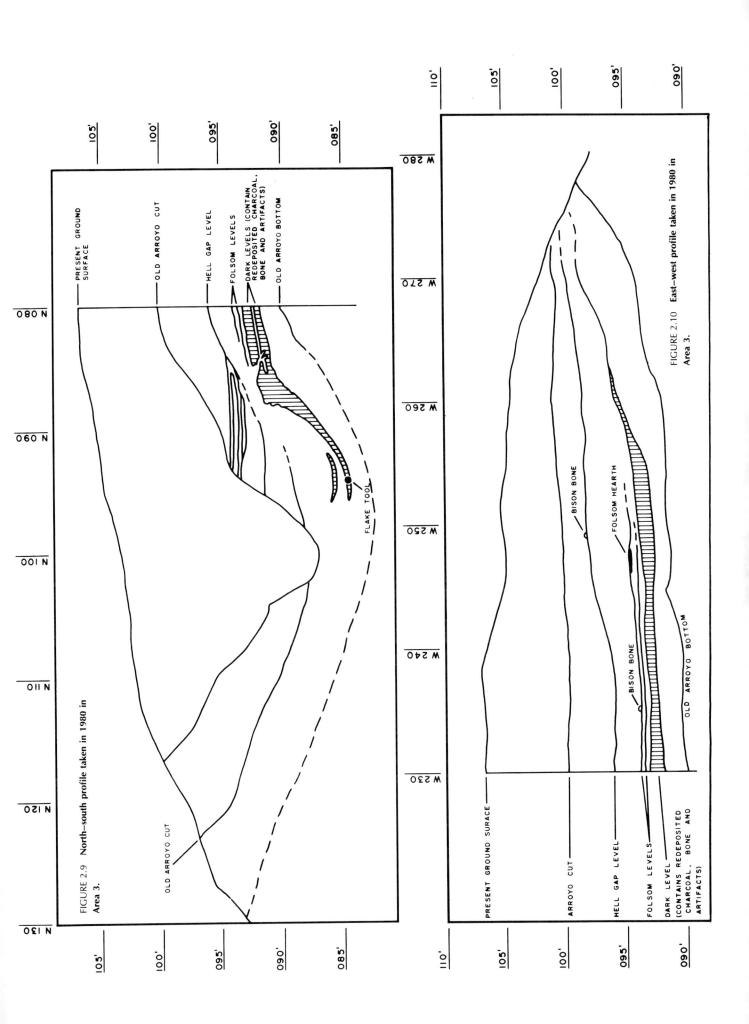

FIGURE 2.9 North–south profile taken in 1980 in Area 3.

PRESENT GROUND SURFACE

OLD ARROYO CUT

HELL GAP LEVEL

FOLSOM LEVELS

DARK LEVELS (CONTAIN REDEPOSITED CHARCOAL, BONE AND ARTIFACTS)

OLD ARROYO BOTTOM

OLD ARROYO CUT

FLAKE TOOL

FIGURE 2.10 East–west profile taken in 1980 in Area 3.

PRESENT GROUND SURACE

ARROYO CUT

HELL GAP LEVEL

FOLSOM LEVELS

DARK LEVEL (CONTAINS REDEPOSITED CHARCOAL, BONE AND ARTIFACTS)

BISON BONE

FOLSOM HEARTH

BISON BONE

OLD ARROYO BOTTOM

FIGURE 2.11 **View of north–south profile taken in 1980 across the old arroyo in Area 3, demonstrating arroyo cutting into Paleoindian deposits (see Figure 2.9 for detail).**

FIGURE 2.12 **Aerial view of walls for profiles in Figures 2.9 and 2.10, June 1980. Undisturbed deposits are still present in the old arroyo between Areas 2 and 3.**

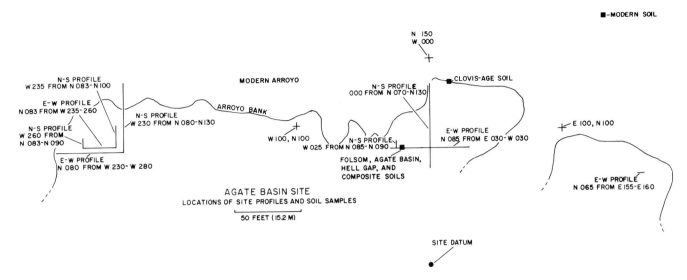

FIGURE 2.13   **Locations of profiles and soil samples taken at the Agate Basin site.**

Diagnostic artifacts of the same age are also found regularly on the surface. Less common surface finds (Figure 2.79 m, n) are projectile points of the Early Plains Archaic or Altithermal period (about 8000–5000 years ago); however, no dated evidence or in situ deposits of this period have yet been found in the Agate Basin site locality. The arroyo cut that removed part of the Hell Gap bone bed in Area 3 (Figures 2.9 and 2.11) may have been of Altithermal age, but this remains unproven.

Part of what appears to be an Early Plains Archaic projectile point was found several years ago eroding out of a stratum about 50 m downstream from Area 1 and on the same side of the present arroyo. Several flakes and bone fragments were in the same stratum but its geologic relationship to the Paleoindian levels is not known. The presence of diagnostic artifacts is strongly indicative that Early Plains Archaic groups were present; future site work may eventually resolve this question.

2.   FOLSOM COMPONENTS
george c. frison

In situ Folsom occupation levels appeared in Agate Basin site Areas 2 and 3. In Area 2, the Folsom component was separated stratigraphically from an overlying Agate Basin level. In Area 3, two in situ Folsom components were present, overlain by three Hell Gap components. The lower Folsom component in Area 3 is almost certainly an extension of the one excavated by Agogino and Frankforter (1960) at the Brewster site. No Folsom cultural component could be found below the Agate Basin level in Area 1, although several deep tests were made there.

The Folsom components in Areas 2 and 3 are separated horizontally by about 80 m, but there is almost unequivocal evidence of a close association between the two areas. Part of a channel flake (Figure 2.26u) recovered in Area 3 had been removed from a projectile point preform (Figure 2.26s) that was recovered in Area 2. Part of the channel flake (Figure 2.26t) removed from the opposite side of the preform was recovered in Area 2, close to the preform. In addition, part of a retouched flake tool (Figure 2.22b) was found in 1961 by Bass and Roberts on a point-hunter's backdirt pile in Area 3, and another fragment of the same tool was recovered in situ in the Folsom level in Area 2 during the 1978 excavations. It is assumed that Paleoindian levels between Areas 1 and 2 are still present, covered by several meters of overburden.

The Folsom occupation level in Area 2 slopes to the south, away from the present arroyo and toward the channel of the arroyo present during that period of Paleoindian times (Figure 2.5). The occupation level itself rests on the floodplain of the old arroyo, which apparently did become flooded during periods of heavy runoff. The location would have been safe from flooding throughout most winters, although in historic times a sudden thaw in late January or February has produced enough unseasonal runoff to overflow the main channels of similar arroyos. Such an event would almost certainly have proven disruptive to human activity in the arroyo bottom, particularly if frozen meat was being stored, which is believed to be the case.

In the direction of the old arroyo, the Folsom occupation level in Area 2 appears as a darkened stratum, but the stratum is lost in the opposite direction. A thick, dark stratum containing redeposited charcoal and occasional bone fragments is directly below the Folsom level. The actual limits of the depression containing the largest hearth in the northern section of the Folsom level were difficult to determine, because it was intruded into the underlying dark level, which closely resembled the hearth contents in this part of the site. A suggestion of more than one level is present in part of the Folsom component; this may indicate more than a single component, or it may simply be the result of rapid buildup of material toward the lower parts of the site caused by human activity over short periods of time. More than one component may be indicated by the different raw flaking materials found in the higher (northern) part of the site and in the lower (southern) part. There is some evidence to support the presence of a former structure in the higher part; the somewhat weaker evidence for a structure in the lower part is probably due to different kinds of geologic activity. If these two structures were actually present, the change in raw materials could indicate two separate occupations. On the other hand, it could be argued that the site represents a communal kill effort that brought together different band segments. Obviously this is all speculation that could be continued indefinitely with no conclusive results.

Another unique feature that allowed the Folsom cultural levels in Areas 2 and 3 to be readily defined was the presence of red ocher throughout. The same phenomenon appeared in the Clovis level at the Sheaman site (discussed later in this chapter), and throughout the Folsom levels at the Hanson site (Frison and Bradley 1980). The red ocher appeared as a stain that contrasted sharply with the surrounding matrix; numerous small lumps up to 5 cm in diameter were also seen. The reddish stain tended in many instances to collect at the lower surfaces of both stone and bone materials in the Folsom level, but not in levels above or below. The presence of this material seems unquestionably cultural but whether it was used as a coloring agent or in religious or some other context or both is not known. Various color grades of ocher occur locally.

The Folsom levels are in situ in Areas 2 and 3, but there is some evidence of redeposited Folsom materials immediately above the level in Area 2. A few bone fragments, flakes, and artifacts were distributed as much as 1–5 cm above the actual habitation level; these items probably were moved short distances by the scouring action of runoff water and were subsequently redeposited. The problems that arise in interpreting cultural components laid down in active arroyo bottoms are very different from those encountered in interpreting site components laid down on the terraces of the same arroyos. There is every reason to assume that other site activities were carried on away from the arroyo bottom at the Agate Basin site, but these locations have been lost through degradation, leaving only the evidence lying in the old arroyo bottom. The need for more and better geologic expertise becomes immediately apparent, because whether or not the site in question is on an arroyo bottom, a terrace, or other geomorphic feature is crucial to the accuracy of the final interpretations.

The most visible feature in the Area 2 Folsom component was a scattered bone bed containing remains of several bison, pronghorn, canids, and rabbits (Figures 2.14 and 2.15). A single fragment was identified as part of a mandible of *Platygonus compressus*. Butchering, population, seasonality, and taxonomic studies of the faunal remains are treated in following chapters. The bison remains dominate the faunal assemblage and are believed to represent a winter kill.

The distribution of certain features in the Folsom level argues strongly for the former presence of one and possibly two structures. The higher (north) area of the site (see Figure 2.5) is less disturbed than the lower (south) side, and the distribution of flakes and tools, combined with a barely perceptible change in the color and texture of the cultural deposits in both areas, suggests a floor. A well-defined hearth about 30 cm in diameter was contained in a shallow basin 8 cm in maximum depth. A concentration of tools (Figure 2.16) and flakes (Figure 2.17) was present toward the north part of the postulated structure and the absence of these to the south of this area may indicate special activity areas. Bone is also relatively absent in this area (Figure 2.14).

A bison rib was pushed or driven into the ground below the original surface at least 10 cm (Figure 2.18) and probably more since the end below the old floor level was badly deteriorated. Although any interpretation is highly speculative, the rib could have served as a peg to anchor some sort of a hide cover that was stretched over a conical or dome-shaped structure. Another rib was treated similarly in the south part of the site in the other area suspected of being the location of a structure. There are several apparently nonartifact stones of various sizes in both areas; these may have been used in conjunction with pegs to

FEATURES IN SITE AREA 2

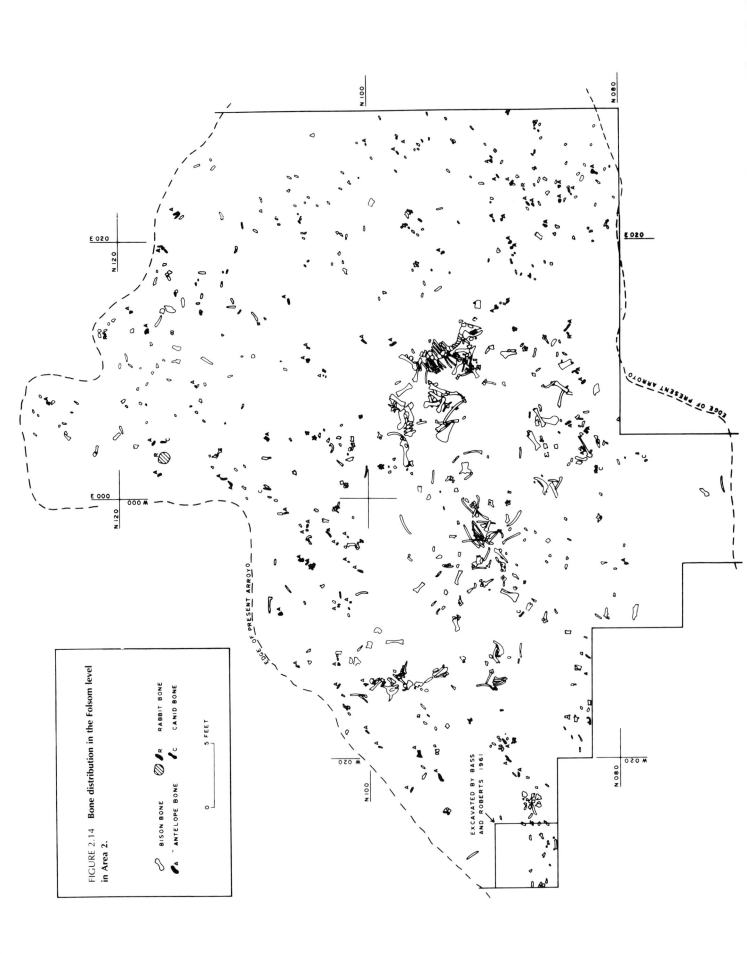

FIGURE 2.14 Bone distribution in the Folsom level in Area 2.

BISON BONE

ANTELOPE BONE

RABBIT BONE

CANID BONE

0   5 FEET

EDGE OF PRESENT ARROYO

EDGE OF PRESENT ARROYO

EXCAVATED BY BASS AND ROBERTS 1961

FIGURE 2.15   **Part of the bison bone bed (top) and a bison calf skull (bottom) from the Folsom level in Area 2.**

hold down a hide cover. However, there is no discernible pattern suggesting an outline form, such as the familiar circular tipi ring structures of the Archaic and Late Prehistoric periods.

Inside the postulated structure at the northern part of Area 2 were two flake concentrations. The larger contained 4680 flakes; the smaller, 770 (Figure 2.17). Within the larger were several artifacts, including tools, projectile point preforms, channel flakes, and bone-needle fragments; the smaller flake area contained no tools. Both piles demonstrated several relatively large flakes (over 2.5 cm in maximum diameter) but most were small, recoverable on a 1.70 mm (.0661 inch) mesh water-screen but not on a screen of the standard quarter-inch

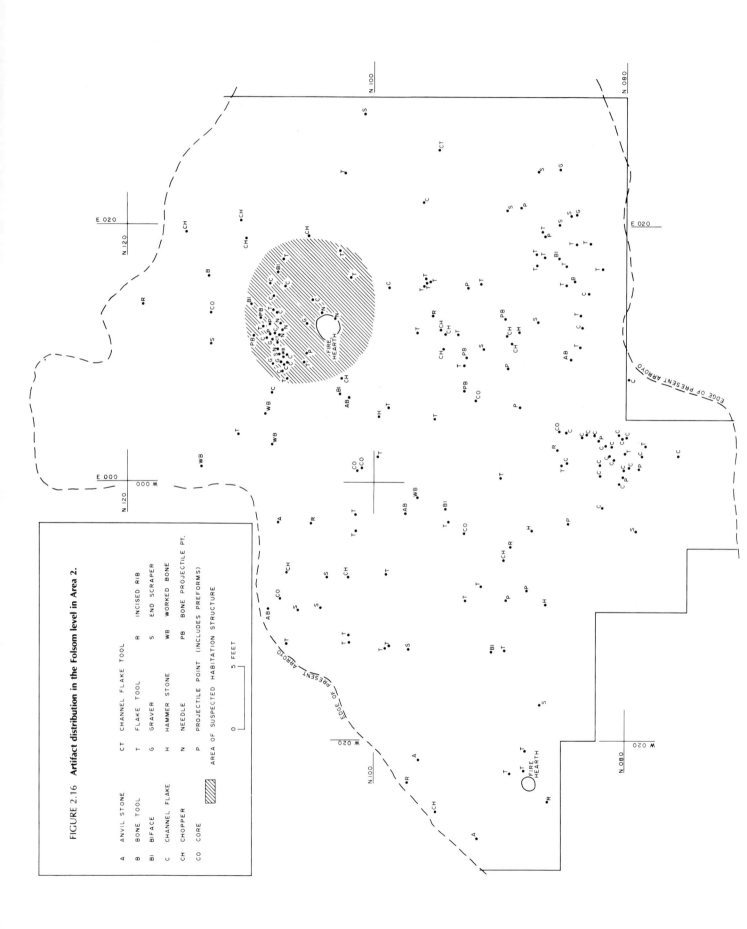

FIGURE 2.16 **Artifact distribution in the Folsom level in Area 2.**

A   ANVIL STONE   CT   CHANNEL FLAKE TOOL
B   BONE TOOL   T   FLAKE TOOL   R   INCISED RIB
BI   BIFACE   G   GRAVER   S   END SCRAPER
C   CHANNEL FLAKE   H   HAMMER STONE   WB   WORKED BONE
CH   CHOPPER   N   NEEDLE   PB   BONE PROJECTILE PT.
CO   CORE   P   PROJECTILE POINT (INCLUDES PREFORMS)

     AREA OF SUSPECTED HABITATION STRUCTURE

0   5 FEET

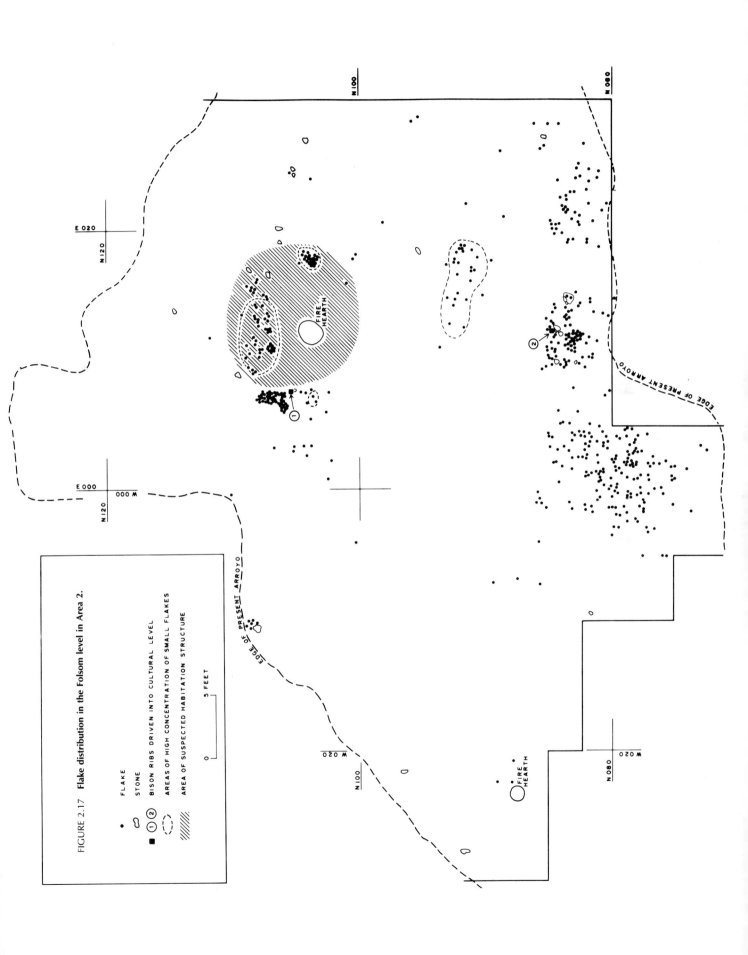

FIGURE 2.17 Flake distribution in the Folsom level in Area 2.

FLAKE

STONE

① ② BISON RIBS DRIVEN INTO CULTURAL LEVEL

AREAS OF HIGH CONCENTRATION OF SMALL FLAKES

AREA OF SUSPECTED HABITATION STRUCTURE

0   5 FEET

FIRE HEARTH

FIRE HEARTH

EDGE OF PRESENT ARROYO

EDGE OF PRESENT ARROYO

FIGURE 2.18 **Bison rib in the Folsom level in Area 2.**

mesh. Outside of the postulated structure area were two more concentrations of the same kind of relatively large biface reduction flakes, but none of the smaller ones.

The south area of the Folsom component also contained a large number of flakes, but more disturbance could be detected here. Burning by either cultural or natural causes, or both, destroyed much of the lithic material, especially the small flakes. Many calcined bone fragments testify also to the former presence of extreme heat. As a result of the extent and intensity of the fire, no definite prepared hearths could be detected. A small surface hearth was present in the extreme western part of the area, but evidence of cultural activity there was meager compared to that in the eastern part.

Although there was good separation of Folsom and Agate Basin cultural levels in Area 2, there were a few instances of mixing of cultural materials, part of which is attributed to moderate amounts of rodent activity. Bass and Roberts in 1961 recovered part of a flake tool (Figure 2.23b) in the Agate Basin level, and the remainder of the tool was found in situ in the Folsom level in 1979. There is no doubt that this tool was originally from the Folsom level, since several either manufacture or sharpening flakes that match flake scars on the tool were recovered in one of the flake concentrations. Bass and Roberts also recovered three broken channel flakes, one of which fits onto another section recovered in the Folsom level in 1980. However, the Folsom component was essentially intact. The only part disturbed by recent activity was the area between Bass and Roberts' work in 1961 and that of Frison in 1975; here artifact hunters had penetrated the Folsom level. This damage was minimal, however, and in an area of low concentration of cultural materials.

The Folsom flaked stone technology and typology are treated elsewhere, as are raw material types and sources. This discussion deals mostly with descriptive and functional aspects of the assemblage. Several categories of tools were recovered and, as at the Hanson site (Frison and Bradley 1980), composite use of tools was the rule rather than the exception. A single flake tool, for example, may have a scraping edge, a cutting edge, a notch, and a sharp corner, each probably used in a different task. Scraping edges were generated in many ways—for example, by flaking at the desired angle, or utilization of sharp edges at various angles formed by accidental or deliberate breaks, or using hinge fractures. A thin edge may also have acquired a steep retouch through scraping use. Breakage and reuse were common; a tool often changed form and function through its lifetime of use. All of these factors must enter into any discussion of tool function, manufacture, and use in the Folsom assemblage.

End Scrapers.   A wide range of morphological characteristics are seen in Folsom end scrapers. They were made from percussion flakes, and in nearly all cases the working edge is opposite the bulb of percussion and varies in outline form from slightly convex (Figure 2.19b) to strongly convex (Figure 2.19f). Careful flake selection negated the need to modify the flakes other than to produce a working edge or edges, so the dorsal surfaces are unworked. Working edges are usually at right angles to the long axis of the flake (Figure 2.19f), although exceptions occur (Figure 2.19d, k). Sharp, well-defined corners are common on working edges (Figure 2.19c) and may be accentuated by spurs at one end (Figure 2.19e, k) or at both ends (Figures 2.19b, 2.20b, and 2.21w, x) of working edges. Notches were sometimes placed just below one corner of the working edge (Figure 2.19d, i). In two cases (Figure 2.19a, j), one corner of the working edge was missing, perhaps deliberately removed. There is evidence of scraping use on the sharp edges formed by the break and the ventral flake faces, as well as the flaked working edge.

The lateral edges of end scrapers often demonstrate deliberate preparation and use of working edges so that some of these (Figures 2.19b, i; 2.20b) could also be classified as side scrapers. On one of these specimens (Figure 2.19i) the right edge was modified by a steep retouch to form what could almost be described as a graver with a blunt point. The lateral edges of another specimen (Figure 2.19k) were unmodified except for a fine, denticulate edge retouch. The left side, which had a relatively low edge angle (31°), was used in cutting; the right edge angle was steeper (37°), apparently for use as a side scraper. This specimen has a blunt graver point on the right edge similar to that shown in Figure 2.19i, and it also demonstrates use-wear similar to that of Figure 2.19i. In addition, a deliberately formed notch present on the left edge demonstrates use-wear; this notch weakened the artifact so that it broke transversely from the bottom of the notch to the opposite side. No subsequent evidence of use can be detected on either piece in the vicinity of the break. On two others (Figures 2.19f, j), the lateral edges were not modified by any retouch but they demonstrate edge damage that is not believed to represent deliberate edge dulling for hafting purposes. A V-shaped notch is present on the left lateral edge of another

Tools Made of Flakes and Blades

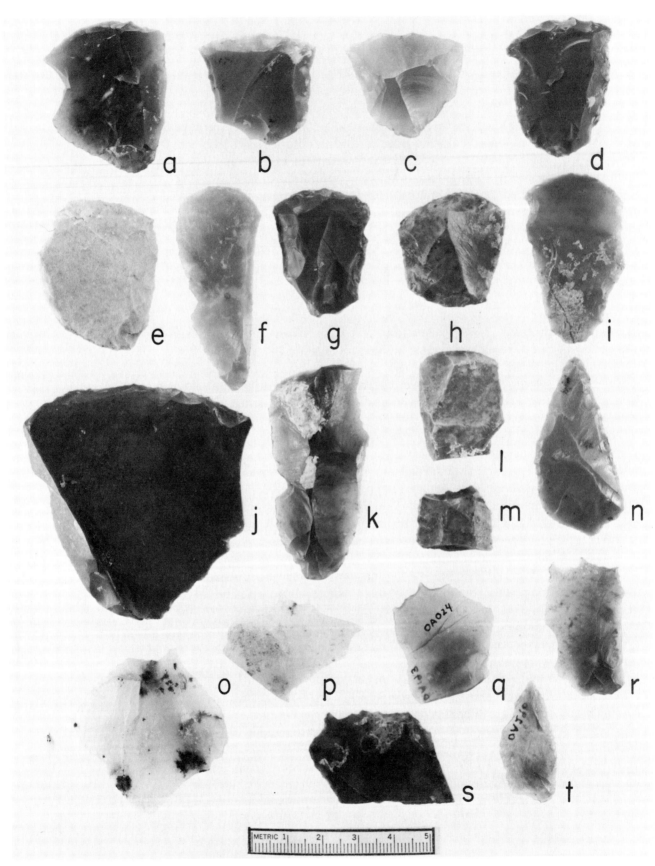

FIGURE 2.19 **End scrapers (a–l) and gravers (m–t) from the Folsom level in Area 2.**

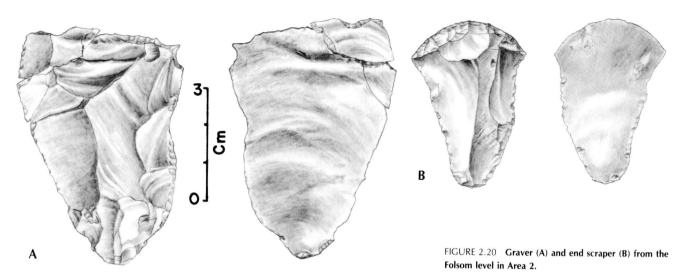

FIGURE 2.20 **Graver (A) and end scraper (B) from the Folsom level in Area 2.**

specimen (Figure 2.19f); the remainder of this edge demonstrates cutting use, and the opposite lateral edge demonstrates scraping use.

The size range of end scrapers is large, as is the degree of convexity of working edges. Angles on working edges range from about 54° to about 75°. One specimen (Figure 2.19b) was apparently either modified slightly or sharpened at the site, since three flakes from one of the small flake concentrations match flake scars on the working edge. Wear on working edges varies greatly and is manifest only in the form of a polish on edge projections on some specimens. On one specimen (Figure 2.19a) the wear can be seen in the form of striations over the working edge and at right angles to it. On others, the working edges demonstrate a light to heavy step-fracturing, which should reflect harder use.

A unique end scraper (Figure 2.21a) is one on which the working edge was formed only by the application of notches of varying sizes, making an irregular denticulate edge at an angle to the longitudinal flake axis. The lateral edges of this specimen also demonstrate heavy use-wear but were not deliberately denticulated. From the interpretations of use on all of the end scrapers, it would be erroneous to regard this category of tools as being restricted to what are normally considered as end-scraper tasks; in fact, most are multipurpose tools.

Side Scrapers.   It is also difficult to assign side scrapers to discrete categories because of the composite nature of their use. They were made on percussion flakes and blades modified only to form the desired working edge. On one quartzite specimen (Figure 2.22a), the entire edge of the flake except for the immediate area of the striking platform, which is still intact, was modified to form working edges. This tool could also have been classified as an end scraper, although three side-scraping edges were also present. It was broken, and both pieces demonstrate use subsequent to breakage. Angles of working edges vary from the end-scraper section directly opposite the bulb of percussion, which is about 79°, to the side-scraper working edges, which range from 53 to 65°.

A chert side scraper (Figure 2.23b) also demonstrates a high incidence of composite tool use. A long, slightly convex, scraping edge is present on one side,

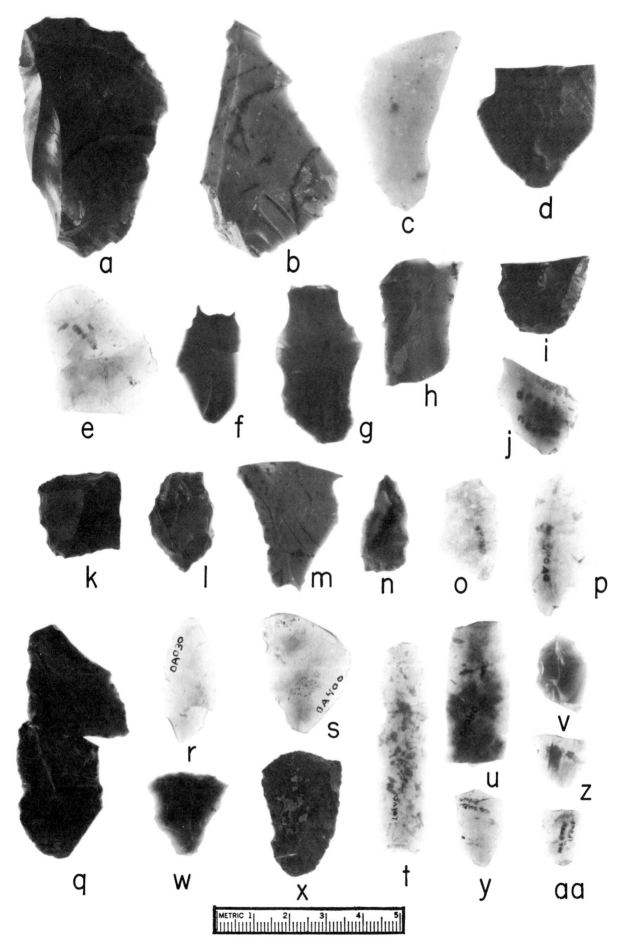

FIGURE 2.21   Flake tools (b–s, v), end scrapers (a, w, x), and channel-flake tools (t, u, y–aa) from the Folsom level in Area 2.

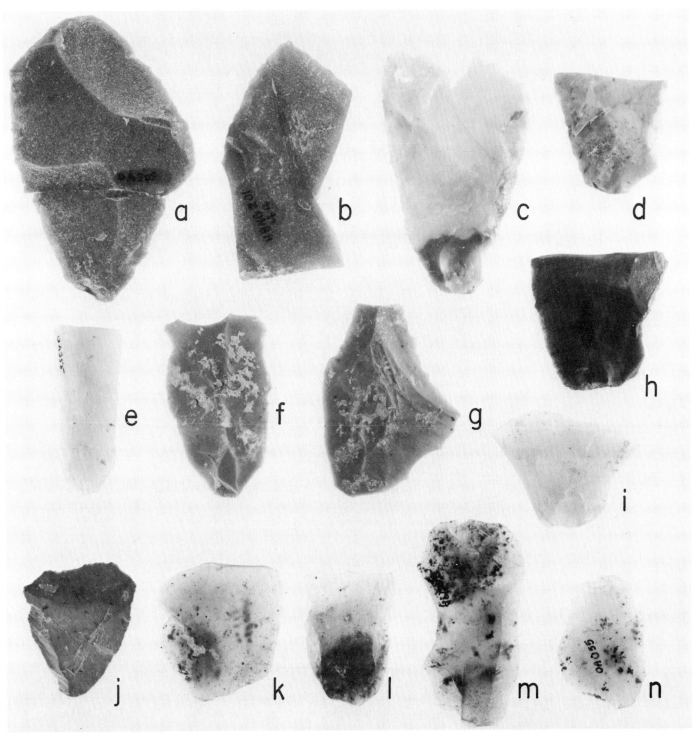

FIGURE 2.22 **Flake tools (a–d, f–n) and blade tool (e) from the Folsom level in Area 2. Part of b was recovered in Area 3.**

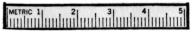

a dull graver point is present on one end with a sharp graver point adjacent, and three shallow notches appear on the other edge. As already mentioned in a previous section, either sharpening or manufacture flakes for this tool were recovered in a pile of flakes in the Folsom level. The angle of the main working edge is about 68°. The scraper was broken, with no evidence of use subsequent to breakage. A relatively thin (6.3 mm) chert flake (Figure 2.23a) demonstrates a prepared, nearly straight scraping edge (edge angle 48°) and an unprepared but heavily used cutting edge (edge angle 24°) on the opposite side. The distal end of the blade terminates in a hinge fracture, so that the ventral surface meets the dorsal surface at an angle of about 60°. This forms a slightly concave scraping edge 20 mm long, which demonstrates scraping use in the form of wear striations. The working edge is situated, probably fortuitously, so that scraping was performed toward the direction of the dorsal surface. Nearly identical use of a hinge fracture is present on a thicker (10.3 mm) flake (Figure 2.23f) with a wider (31 mm) working edge (edge angle 68°); there is evidence of heavier use that resulted in a light step-fracturing. A straight, prepared side-scraper edge (edge angle 63°) is also present adjacent to the hinge fracture and on the opposite side is a shallow notch (Figures 2.22h and 2.24). Hinge-fracture tools are discussed in detail in the Hanson site report (Frison and Bradley 1980:90–93) and also later on in this section on flake tools.

One chert blade (Figure 2.23e) demonstrates two long, nearly straight, scraping edges (edge angles about 50°), one prepared and one demonstrating only use-wear. The two edges converge toward the striking platform and the distal corners are pointed and dulled from use; the edge of the concavity between the two distal corners is dulled from heavy use. Other side scrapers are less complex, with two opposed working edges (Figure 2.23h) or single working edges (Figures 2.23g and 2.22c).

A unique side scraper (Figure 2.19n) made on a chert flake has two straight scraping edges (edge angles about 48°) that converge to a blunted point and actually form a relatively sharp-pointed end scraper or graver. A convexity continuous with one working edge is finely serrated and is functionally a cutting edge (edge angle 20°), with light use-wear on the points between the serrations. This tool demonstrates a rapid change in use from the scraping edge to the immediately adjacent cutting edge.

One quartzite side scraper (Figure 2.22b) is incomplete, but a steep pressure retouch is present on the entire edge of what remains. The tool was broken, probably deliberately, by a radial break in the same manner as was determined on a similar flake tool at the Hanson site (see Frison and Bradley 1980:98). Of the two pieces recovered, one came from Area 2 and the other from Area 3, a distance of nearly 100 m. It is highly probable that this tool was deliberately broken in order to make several tools in the manner described in the discussion of the Hanson site tool assemblage.

A variation of the side-scraper category is that consisting of relatively small, thin flakes with a delicate, steep retouch on all or nearly all of the dorsal edges (Figure 2.21o, r) excluding the striking platform. These are probably best described as raclettes (see Bordes 1972:84, Figure 5).

Cutting Tools.   A common and efficient method of preparing cutting tools was to serrate the working edge. Variation is seen in the size and spacing of the

FIGURE 2.23   Flake tools (a–c, f–k) and blade tools (d, e) from the Folsom level in Area 2. Part of b was recovered in the Agate Basin level.

FIGURE 2.24 **Flake tool from the Folsom level in Area 2.**

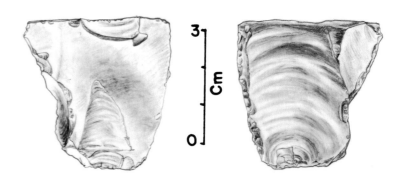

nicks that produce the serrated edges. Angles of working edges of cutting tools are realtively low in comparison to edge angles of scrapers, and in the Folsom tools they vary from about 18° to about 40°. Some cutting edges on side-scraper tools have already been described.

One chert blade (Figure 2.23d) has one edge serrated and dulled from use; the opposite edge is also dulled, probably as a backing. The distal end terminates in a hinge fracture that executes nearly a 180° turn. The rounded end that resulted is polished from an undetermined use. Two relatively large chert flakes (Figure 2.23i, k) and a quartzite flake (Figure 2.23j) demonstrate similar cutting-edge preparation and use-wear. Smaller flakes with edge angles as low as about 15° (Figure 2.22g, i, k, n) and finely serrated edges were probably cutting tools, as were similar flakes (Figure 2.22f, l, m) that were not serrated but demonstrate cutting use. One blade (Figure 2.22e), triangular in transverse cross-section, has working-edge angles of 24° and 50°. Both edges are unmodified, but demonstrate dulling from cutting use.

The finely serrated cutting edge is found also on very thin flakes (2–3 mm) having extremely low edge angles (about 10°). Edges this thin are easily damaged. Two flakes (Figure 2.21e, h) demonstrate concave, convex, and straight working edges with use-wear in the form of a light polish. Short segments of finely serrated cutting edges are present also along both sides of a flake adjacent to a graver point (Figure 2.21v).

Gravers.   Gravers were made on thin percussion flakes and demonstrate a wide range of variation in size, shape, number, and placement of points. Composite use is well demonstrated in this tool category also. The graver points were formed in most cases by flaking two adjacent concavities on the edge of a flake. The manner in which the two concavities meet determines the outline form, and point thickness is determined by the thickness of the flake. Some of these gravers are extremely delicate tools with narrow stems and thin, sharp points (Figures 2.19t and 2.21n); others are very much the opposite (Figure 2.19o). However, all were made of excellent quality chert. Two adjacent points on the same tool may be of similar morphology (Figure 2.21f) or slightly different (Figure 2.19q), which could and probably does reflect different tasks. On both these specimens the flakes were broken and the parts matched. The pieces of the flakes opposite the points were found in large flake concentrations, suggesting deliberate breakage and subsequent abandonment. In fact, on one (Figure 2.21f) a definite impact point is present on the flake face, which further supports the idea of deliberate breakage. This could be an indication that the tools were hafted, since in their present form they would function better as graving tools when hafted. However, they would probably function better not hafted if the broken pieces were joined.

Three separate graver points are present on a thin (2.77 mm) flake tool (Figure 2.19r), each one slightly different in morphology. In addition, one straight edge of the flake adjacent to the striking platform is dulled from cutting or sawing use. Three adjacent points (Figure 2.19m) are also seen on a thicker (4.2 mm) flake, but these points are of different morphology and probably different function than those of Figure 2.19r. Two specimens made on relatively thin (1.7 mm and 2.1 mm) flakes (Figures 2.19t and 2.21n) have single graver points directly opposite the striking platform. On the former, the slightly convex edge extending from the graver point to the striking platform demonstrates a finely serrated retouch on the dorsal side, forming a steep scraping edge (edge angle about 65°). On another graver the point is at one corner, and four shallow notches are present, two along each lateral edge of the flake (Figure 2.21g).

One graver in particular merits a careful description (Figure 2.20a). It was made on a wide, thin (4 mm) flake of exceptionally fine chert. The graver point was placed at one corner, and most of the remainder of the edge of the flake demonstrates light but extensive cutting use (edge angles about 18–22°). Either a flaw in the material or heavy use resulted in the breakage of the corner of the flake opposite the graver point, and subsequent to this, the distal end of the flake adjacent to the graver point was prepared and used in scraping (edge angle 55°). The broken pieces were recovered in close proximity to the tool itself.

Graver points were formed by flaking on the dorsal side of the flake. On one exception (Figure 2.19s) alternate flaking is seen, which should reflect a difference in function, probably boring in contrast to grooving. Some of the end-scraper spurs (Figure 2.19k) might be better described as graver points, but their use as gravers is conjectural.

Other variations in manufacture are present. One other graver point is different, having been made by flaking a deep concavity adjacent to a transverse break (Figure 2.21m), which may reflect a special use. What appears to be a fortuitously formed graver point on the end of a thin flake (2.0 mm) demonstrates use, and a lateral edge of the same specimen was used as a delicate cutting tool after the working edge was finely serrated (Figure 2.21p).

Channel-Flake Tools.   One hundred and twenty channel-flake fragments and a single complete specimen were recovered in the Folsom components at the Agate Basin site. Out of these only two (Figure 2.21t, u) demonstrate unequivocal evidence of tool use; three others may have been lightly used (Figure 2.21y, z, aa). Both of the former are midsections of channel flakes. All of the nearly straight edge of one (Figure 2.21t) is dulled through use, probably as a cutting tool. The other (Figure 2.21u) has two alternate corners reduced by fine pressure flaking to form a backing, and the other alternate corners demonstrate evidence of light use as cutting tools. The three others are striking-platform ends of channel flakes, and one or both corners at the transverse breaks appear dulled probably from undetermined use.

Hinge Flake Tools. In the Hanson site tool assemblages were a number of flakes terminating with hinge fractures that were used for various tasks. When the hinge fracture met the dorsal flake surface at a right angle (or less), the resulting edge was often used as a scraper. When the fracture hinged all the way, the hinge sometimes demonstrated a polish as if it had been used to finish a hide or perform a similar task (see Frison and Bradley 1980:90–92). Four of these hinge-fracture tools have already been described (Figures 2.23a, d, f; 2.24). Another flake tool (Figure 2.21s) has a complete (180°) hinge fracture on the distal end and a use-polish over the entire hinge. The corners of the tool at the edges of the hinge demonstrate scraping use. This tool is nearly identical to a Hanson site tool (Frison and Bradley 1980:Figure 58d). It was suggested in the same report (p. 91) that the hinge may have served as a kind of shoe to pass over some material (e.g., wood or hide), and the notches at the side may have scored or scratched the material. Another flake (Figure 2.21b) terminates in a narrow hinge fracture that demonstrates a polish. The lateral edges of the same tool demonstrate light use, probably as a cutting tool. Polish such as demonstrated on these hinge fractures can be produced by rubbing against something like a suspended hide to loosen the fibers.

Bend Break Tools. Another category of flake tools is identical to a group found at the Hanson site. This category consists of percussion flakes that were broken transversely to provide a sharp corner or corners. In some cases one or both lateral edges of the snapped flake were modified in side-scraper fashion, so these tools may be identified as broken side scrapers. However, it was common practice to place a notch on the edge in a direction proximal to the break, probably to accentuate the sharp corner or corners of the tool. Two examples of this are present in the Agate Basin assemblage (Figures 2.21j and 2.22d). On two others (Figures 2.21d, i) there is clear evidence of impact where the flakes were deliberately snapped. Also, although the point formed at the juncture of the break and the lateral edge was clearly used, no notch was present on the lateral edge adjacent to the point. These are referred to as *bend break tools* (Frison and Bradley 1980:91–95). There is a strong indication that the angle of breakage was controlled to provide the desired point shape. Another flake broken in the same manner (Figure 2.21q) demonstrates heavy damage from scraping at the sharper corner formed by the break and one lateral edge. The remainder or distal end of the flake was recovered, and it also demonstrates heavy edge damage from some scraping task. Both pieces were used intensively subsequent to breakage.

Notches. Notches of various sizes and shapes were an integral part of the Folsom tool assemblage and were apparently in regular use in conjunction with other working-edge types, as has been indicated in the preceding discussion. One additional flake (Figure 2.21c) has no use or modification other than a carefully prepared, shallow notch at one corner.

Wedges. The breakage of a number of tool fragments suggests damage greater than and different in kind from that accomplished by normal use of either hand-held or hafted tools. Two specimens strongly suggest wedging of material by pounding. One (Figure 2.21,l) has one sharpened end, and another end battered presumably by pounding. The tool is thick enough (9 mm) and shaped in the proper manner to withstand strong abuse. Another specimen (Figure 2.21k) is of similar thickness and has a wider point and larger platform for the poll of the hammerstone to strike. By actual experiment, either style of wedge can withstand the abuse necessary to split, for example, the metatarsal of a bison.

Bifaces

Biface tools are poorly represented in the Agate Basin Folsom assemblage. One (Figure 2.25b) is similar to a knife type from the Hanson site (Frison and Bradley 1980:Figure 21). Both working edges are alternately beveled (edge angles about 40°) and there is evidence of use subsequent to breakage on one end. Two pieces of bifaces (Figure 2.25c, d) were subjected to extremely damaging use that strongly suggests the pounding resulting from use as a wedge. A convexity on one specimen (Figure 2.25c) was deliberately shaped by percussion; the opposite surface is flat and shows evidence of heavy and repeated pounding. These may be part of a larger category of wedges, since battering is present on relatively broad platforms opposite relatively blunt edges (edge angles 40–65°). This also could have occurred subsequent to breakage, and the specimens may only represent parts of some former tool type or types. One exhausted core (Figure 2.25g) is regarded as a biface and appears to have been modified into a small chopper-like tool. Included as a biface is a cutting tool (edge angle 40°) made from a piece of plate chalcedony 1 cm thick (Figure 2.25e).

Two other bifaces appear to have been broken in manufacture. One is of quartzite and represents a high degree of skill in flaking a relatively poor quality material (Figure 2.25a). Extremely thin (5.5 mm), this biface broke from a perverse fracture in what was probably the final flaking sequence and was discarded; there is no evidence of use. Both ends are also missing. The two remaining biface specimens (Figure 2.25f, h) also broke early in the manufacture sequence and demonstrate no observable evidence of use.

The remaining bifaces from the Folsom level in Area 2 appear to be related only to projectile point manufacture technology. There are some possible exceptions, however. One fluted biface may have been modified into a small knife-like tool (Figure 2.26a). A preform was destroyed on the second flute with an *outre passe* type of break. The sides and distal end were then modified by a denticulate retouch (Figure 2.26f). Three specimens may have been completed projectile points and may also have been used. Two (Figure 2.26c, h) were fluted; the third (Figure 2.26g) has the apperance of being fluted but is actually a thin flake that was modified by shaping to the desired outline form. One Folsom projectile point base from the James Duguid collection (Figure 2.41b) was a surface find from Area 3. This was a completed specimen and may have been broken from use. Folsom projectile point manufacture is discussed in Chapter 3.

Other Stone Tools

Choppers.   Twelve specimens from the Folsom component in Area 2 are classified as choppers. As a group they vary considerably. Most reflect the simplest of manufacture technology with only the minimum of modification of

FIGURE 2.25A,B **Bifaces from the Folsom level in Area 2.**

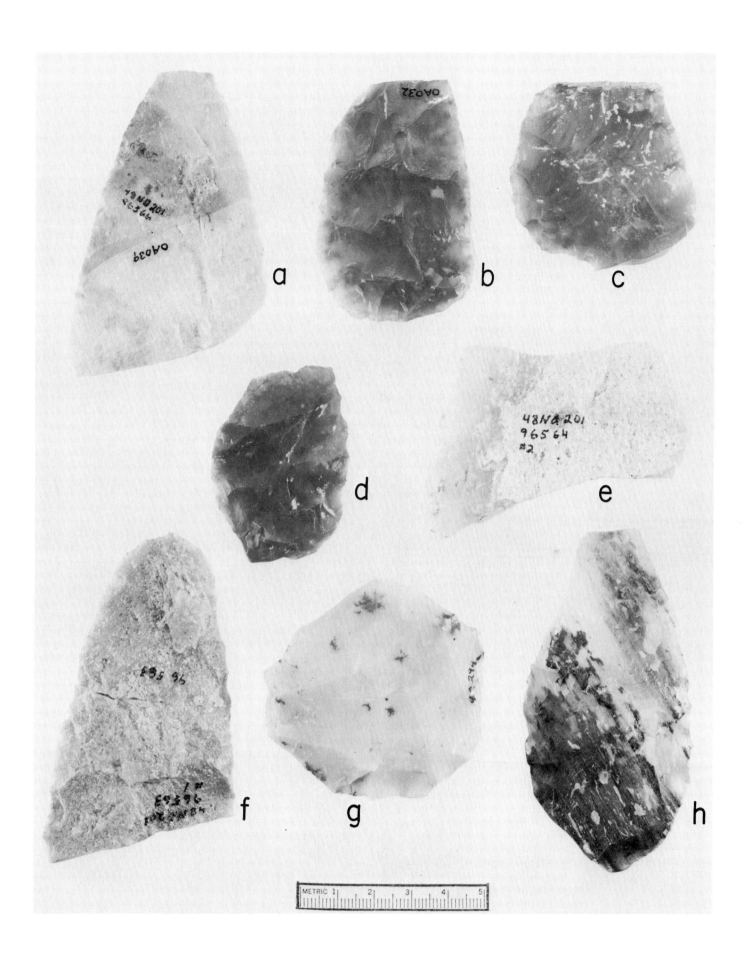

FIGURE 2.26A,B Bifaces and channel flakes related to projectile point manufacture from the Folsom level.

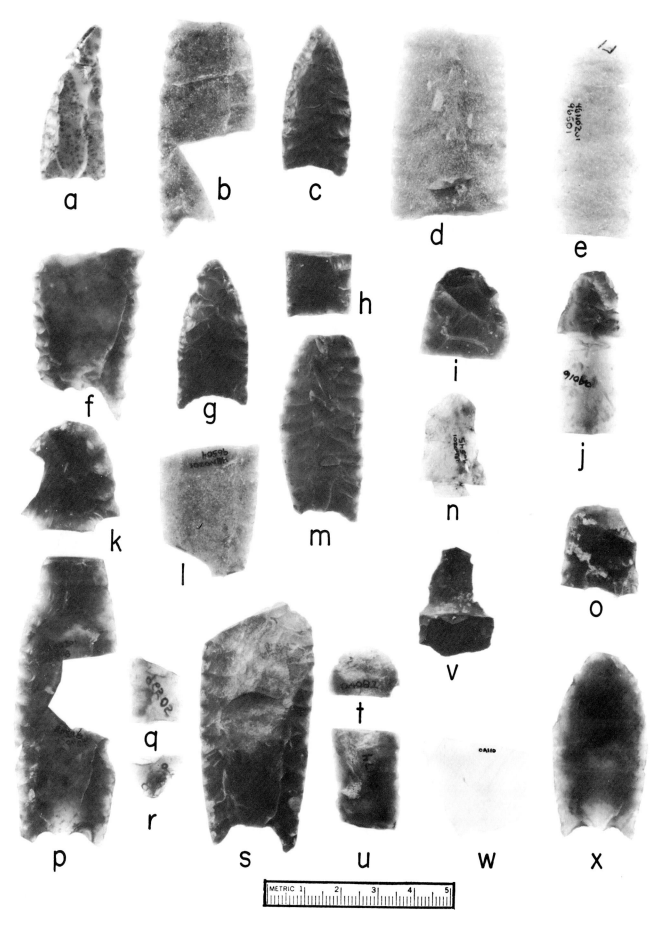

a   b   c   d   e

f   g   h   i   j

k   l   m   n   o

p   q   r   s   t   u   v   w   x

METRIC 1   2   3   4   5

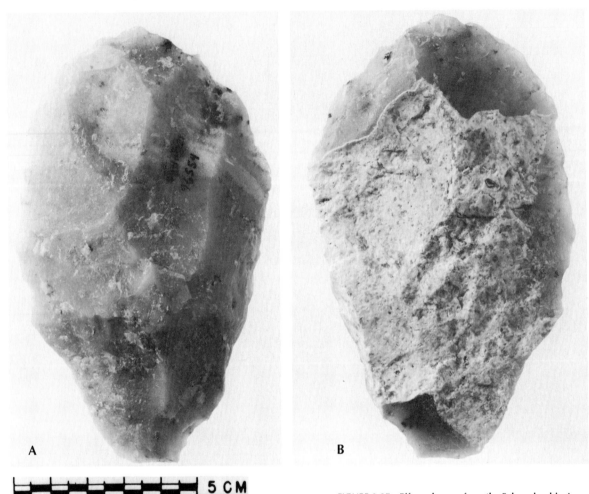

FIGURE 2.27 Biface chopper from the Folsom level in Area 2.

angular, coarse-grained quartzite and granite cobbles found locally. Only one that could be classified as a biface (Figure 2.27) demonstrates a somewhat higher level of sophistication and care in preparation. It has a rounded chopping edge (edge angle 63°) on one end and a narrow wedge-like chopping edge (edge angle 54°) opposite. It was recovered in direct context with several disarticulated and butchered skeletal parts of a bison calf, suggesting its possible function.

Quartzite and granite specimens demonstrate only the most minimal preparation of working edges. Most working edges are relatively wide (Figures 2.28 and 2.29), but some are narrow (Figure 2.30) or pointed (Figure 2.31), and edge angles vary from 55 to 65°. Two of the granite specimens (Figures 2.28a and 2.29) have a few flakes removed to establish a working edge, but the general appearance of working-edge damage suggests that these specimens have been used for breaking or crushing rather than for chopping. One quartzite chopper (Figure 2.28b) demonstrates working-edge preparation by removal of several flakes bilaterally along one edge of a flattened cobble (33.7 mm thick) to form a steep (70°) angle. This specimen was recovered directly under the rib cage of the partially articulated female bison (Figure 2.15). The two other quartzite chop-

a

b

FIGURE 2.28 **Granite (a) and quartzite (b) choppers from the Folsom level in Area 2.**

FIGURE 2.29 Granite chopper from the Folsom level in Area 2.

FIGURE 2.30 Quartzite chopper from
the Folsom level in Area 2.

FIGURE 2.31 **Pointed quartzite chopper from the Folsom level in Area 2.**

METRIC 1 2 3 4 5 6 7 8 9 10 11 12 13 14

FIGURE 2.32 **Heavy chopper or anvil stone from the Folsom level in Area 2.**

pers (Figures 2.30 and 2.31) are slabs that were broken from larger pieces partially along natural cleavage planes; slight further modification by percussion formed the working edges.

These tools probably saw varied uses. They may have been used directly against flesh and bone in the butchering process. They may also have been used in pairs, one as an anvil stone held under a bone or cartilage to be crushed or severed by the other used as a chopper. They may have been used in conjunction with an anvil stone that was stationary on the ground. A larger chopper may have been held in one hand while the bones were held and smashed against it with the other hand.

Anvil Stones. One quartzite specimen (Figure 2.32) is thicker (9.4 cm) and much heavier than any of the other choppers, and may have been an anvil stone. One end was modified by removal of a few large percussion flakes to form a wide, blunt edge. It could have been used as a heavy hammerstone to crush large animal bone, or it could have been placed with the working edge up, to be used as an anvil for breaking bones, perhaps in conjunction with a hammerstone. Many functions other than bone breakage could be proposed. We know that this specimen was shaped at the location, since the percussion flakes removed were recovered in the same immediate area.

Hammerstones. One hammerstone was made from a flattened sandstone cobble 37 mm thick (Figure 2.33). Around most of its perimeter is evidence of heavy pounding in the form of step-fracturing. One flake was replaced in its

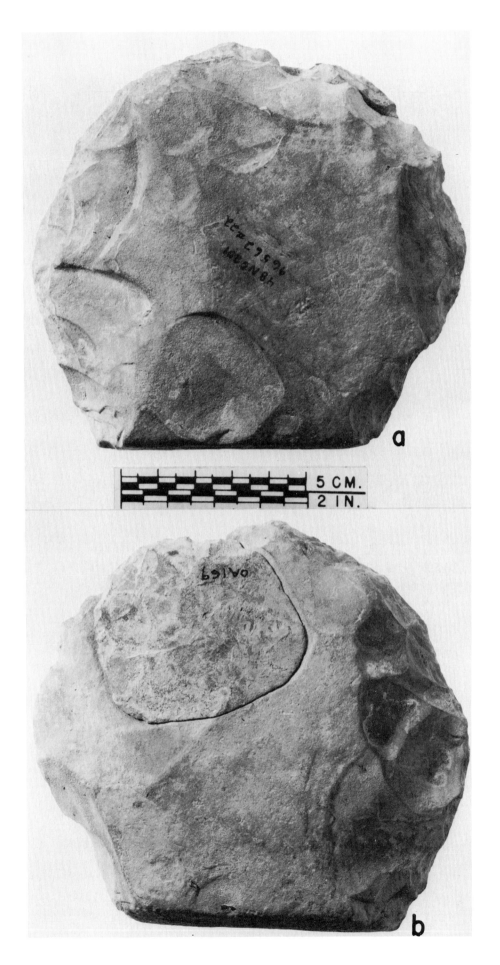

FIGURE 2.33 **Sandstone hammerstone from the Folsom level in Area 2.**

A

B

FIGURE 2.34 Sandstone abrader from the Folsom level in Area 2.

flake scar (Figure 2.33b). It is believed that this flake was removed from use rather than from deliberate percussion flaking. The rough, irregular edge of the tool was further reduced by battering, but the force was not sufficient to produce additional step-fracturing.

The remaining part of the edge of the same tool is an elongated platform 75 mm long and 30 mm wide. It is ground to a smooth surface that is slightly higher (2 mm) in the center, producing a keeled effect parallel to its long axis. A few use flakes have produced step fractures along the edges of this smoothed working surface; in addition, a light pecking is present over much of this same smoothed surface. One side of the specimen demonstrates a light abrading use.

Its use is highly speculative. A similar but smaller object was found at the Hanson site (Frison and Bradley 1980:102), and another object in the Sheaman site Clovis component bears some resemblance (discussed later in this chapter), but both of these lack the ground platform on the edge. A suggestion is that it was used in many ways, such as in breaking large bones, abrading hides, and as a light hammerstone in percussion flaking or wedge driving. The sandstone itself is an unusually fine grade and unlike any presently known to be available from the immediate site area.

Abrading Stones. An angular block of sandstone (Figure 2.34) varying from 31 to 55 mm in thickness demonstrates extensive abrading use. The edges are rounded, and dim grooves in a number of directions are present on both sides. In addition, part of one side (Figure 2.34b) shows deep pecking marks of unexplained origin but suggestive of a deliberate pecking. Most of the surface of

FIGURE 2.35 **Sandstone abrader from the Folsom level in Area 2.**

FIGURE 2.36 **Abrading stone from the Folsom level in Area 2.**

the specimen is coated with red ocher. Another abrader (Figure 2.35) is of a similar grade of sandstone, angular in shape, and characterized by abrading marks and grooves over the entire surface. It was in two pieces found close together, and no apparent use was made of the tool subsequent to breakage. One side (Figure 2.35, left) has a long, diagonal depression, as if it had been used to smooth a rounded surface. A fragment of still another abrader is of a much finer-grained sandstone, and the grinding has a heavy coating of red ocher, which may indicate the original function of the tool. Sandstone of the quality and texture of both of these tools is available in quantity within a kilometer of the site.

The soils in parts of the Agate Basin site cause decomposition of some sandstone, and several pieces were reduced to uncemented concentrations of sand grains. Since this material is alien to the immediate site area and was therefore probably brought to the site, these pieces are probably also the remains of abrading tools.

FIGURE 2.37   **Polishing stone from the Folsom level in Area 2.**

In addition to these sandstone tools, there are two other specimens of different materials. One is a triangular piece of stone 22 mm thick. One side is flat; the opposite side is covered with calcite crystals (Figure 2.36). The points of the highest crystals are worn, as if the stone had been used as an abrading tool. Calcite crystal is relatively soft and would abrade without damaging material such as wood or hide. In fact, use of a similar piece to soften a piece of buffalo hide produced excellent results. It is also possible that this piece was collected merely for its unusual appearance. The second specimen is a flat slab of a soft, white, unidentified stone 20 mm thick, used as some sort of polishing tool (Figure 2.37). One side is convex and demonstrates a polish as if it were held in one hand and rubbed over a soft surface such as a partially tanned hide. It may have been a hide-finishing tool.

Red Ocher Grinding Slab.   A flat slab of dolomite (Figure 2.38) averaging 35 mm in thickness and triangular in outline has a small, worn depression about 2.5 mm deep and 56 mm in diameter toward the narrow end. Much of the relatively rough remaining area of the surface was coated with a layer of red ocher up to 1 mm thick. The bottom surface of the stone was also heavily stained. This was almost certainly a grinding slab for pulverizing red ocher.

FIGURE 2.38   **Red ocher grinding slab from the Folsom level in Area 2.**

Cores   There is limited evidence of core reduction in the Folsom assemblage, and five used and/or exhausted cores were recovered. Only one (Figure 2.25g) was slightly modified, perhaps for use as a small chopping tool. The others were apparently discarded after either successful or unsuccessful attempts at core reduction. Four of these are of chert found near the site area; the other is silicified wood that may or may not be local. The cores demonstrate the same reduction strategy as those from the Agate Basin component. Since the local material is difficult to flake successfully, no highly patterned core reduction sequences were accomplished. Core reduction strategies are discussed in Chapter 3.

Flakes   A total of 18,755 flakes were recovered from the Folsom level in Area 2. The largest number of flakes come from concentrations of small flakes (see Figure 2.17) of a size recoverable only on fine mesh water-screens. By weight, however, the largest share consists of larger core and biface reduction flakes. Some core and biface reduction was performed at the site, but most was probably done elsewhere. Selected flakes were then brought to the area to be used as tools. Projectile point manufacture was a major activity at the Agate Basin Folsom level, which helps to account for the large number of small flakes present. The various aspects of stone flaking technology are treated in Chapter 3.

FIGURE 2.39 **Bison skull from the lower Folsom level in Area 3.**

Two superimposed in situ Folsom levels were found in Area 3. As has been indicated, the lower may be an extension of the Folsom level earlier described in the Brewster site report (Agogino and Frankforter 1960). A small bison bone pile was recovered along with scattered bison bone throughout most of the level. One bison skull was nearly complete (Figure 2.39) but was badly distorted from the pressure of the overburden.

The only artifacts recovered in this level were associated with a shallow hearth several meters away (Figure 2.40). The hearth was well defined and was confined with in a shallow basin about 6 cm deep. Very little charcoal remained, apparently the result of nearly complete combustion of materials. Several calcined small bone fragments were recovered in and near the hearth. Three of these were parts of larger objects that may have been decorative (Figure 2.114c, d, e). Another bone fragment is cylindrical, 11.5 mm long and 5.0 mm in diameter; it may have been a section of an awl or bone projectile point.

Stone artifacts include a preform that was apparently broken in an unsuccessful fluting attempt; one corner of its base was subsequently modified to form a graver tool (Figure 2.41d). None of the remainder of the tool demonstrates evidence of use. Another tool (Figure 2.41i) is a thin (.19 mm) biface reduction flake with the graver point placed opposite the striking platform. Edges and projections of the same tool demonstrate light use. Two end scrapers were recovered; one (Figure 2.41g) has definite projections or spurs at each end of the

FOLSOM LEVELS IN SITE AREA 3

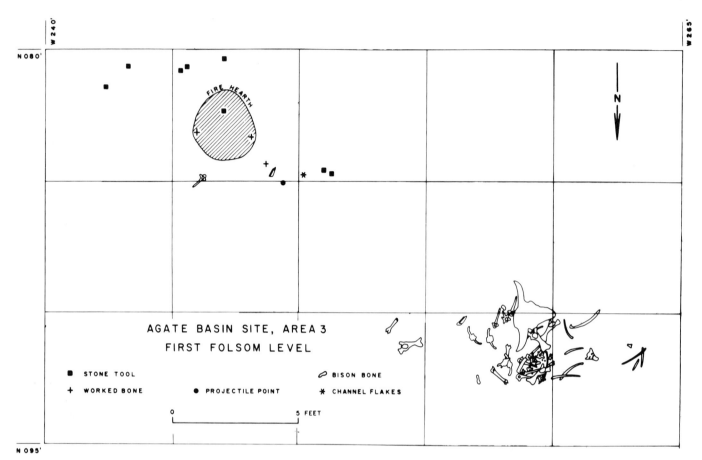

FIGURE 2.40   **Map of the lower Folsom level in Area 3.**

working edge (edge angle 60°); these are somewhat reduced as a result of relatively damaging use. The breakage of the proximal end suggests that it might have resulted from use, which might indicate that the tool was hafted for better leverage and control while it was being used. Another end scraper (working-edge angle 76°) has a spur at one corner of the working edge, a graver point at the other end, and another, less prominent graver point about midway between the first point and the base (Figure 2.41j). The end-scraper working edge on this specimen demonstrates reduction in the form of step-fracturing, suggesting relatively hard use.

Another tool was made of a relatively thick (5.7 mm) chert flake and is somewhat different. Two straight scraping edges (edge angles about 50°) converge to form a sharp graver point. Between one scraping edge and the base of the flake is a notch with a working-edge angle of about 62° (Figure 2.41f). Part of a channel flake (Figure 2.26u) recovered in this level fits on a preform (Figure 2.26s) found in the Folsom level in Area 2. At least three other burned stone fragments are parts of unidentifiable flaked stone objects.

Two Folsom projectile points, one nearly complete (Figure 2.41a) and the other a basal fragment (Figure 2.41c), were recovered in the Brewster site excavations (Agogino and Frankforter 1960). They are part of the Duguid collection and are shown here because they were not illustrated in the original report.

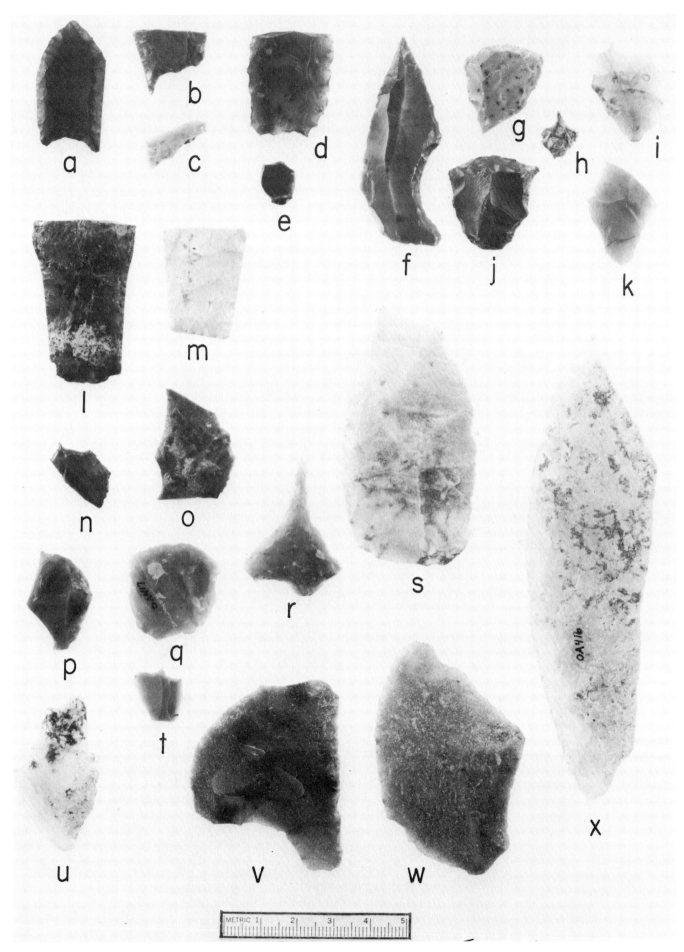

FIGURE 2.41 **Artifacts from the Folsom (a–k) and Hell Gap (l–x) levels in Area 3.**

FIGURE 2.42   **Hearths in the lower (a) and upper (b) Folsom levels in Area 3 (see Figure 2.10).**

The second Folsom level is directly above the lower one. Its areal extent is not known at this time. A shallow hearth similar to the one in the lower level (13.1 cm deep) was present (see Figure 2.42). Bison bones are scattered throughout the level and one lumbar sequence was articulated (Figure 2.43). Some of the bones were relatively well preserved and demonstrate marks that probably reflect butchering (see the section on treatment of postcranial elements). A humerus and part of a canid maxillary were also recovered. A channel flake (Figure 2.41e) and a small flake tool (Figure 2.41k) found in the hearth deposits had been burned, as had a small graver made on a thin (1.6 mm) flake (Figure 2.41h) just outside the hearth. Two other burned and fire-fractured stones also appear to be tool fragments. One may be part of an end scraper; the other is too badly fragmented to be identified.

Calcined bone fragments were present in the hearth; one is a small fragment of a needle midsection (see Table 2.1, Section 6). A fragment of a bison rib from just outside the hearth demonstrates part of a transverse cut similar to that on specimens recovered in the Folsom component in Area 2.

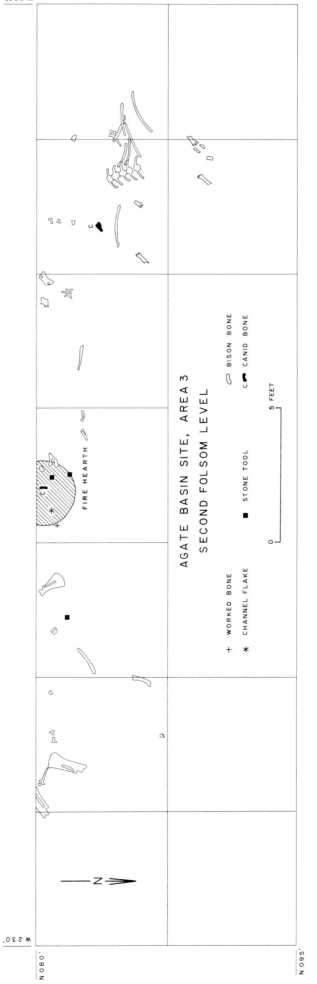

FIGURE 2.43 Map of the upper Folsom level in Area 3.

Flakes   Other than the tools, no large core or biface reduction flakes were found in either of the Folsom levels in Area 3. However, water-screening of the cultural levels produced 880 small flakes in the area in and around the hearth in the upper level, and 325 small flakes in the same area in the lower level. Most of these are pressure and percussion flakes but several are larger fragments resulting from intense heat.

3.   AGATE BASIN COMPONENTS
george c. frison and dennis stanford

There was one in situ Agate Basin component in Areas 1 and 2. Both areas contained bison bones in varying concentrations and degrees of disarticulation and breakage. Unfortunately, very little is known of Area 1. According to Agogino and Frankforter (1960), there was an Agate Basin component or components in Area 3, but none. were found in the areas excavated by Bass and Roberts in 1961 or by the University of Wyoming–Smithsonian team in 1977, 1979, and 1980. A detailed bone bed map of Area 2 was constructed using the data from the Bass and Roberts Excavations in 1961 and the University of Wyoming excavations from 1975 through 1979 (Figure 2.44). The map excludes parts of the bone bed damaged by artifact hunters but enough remains to allow meaningful interpretations. It is also somewhat schematic in nature to allow better clarity. This bone bed directly overlies the Folsom bone bed and is separated from it by a sterile level (Figures 2.45 and 2.46). The relationships between Agate Basin and Folsom levels in Area 2 were stratigraphically well demonstrated at the close of the 1979 field season (Figure 2.47). Since the interpretations of the Agate Basin component center around the bone bed, several assumptions should be stated.

First, there is no doubt of the in situ nature of the bone bed in the Agate Basin component, although it was covered by material brought directly by water transport. The bone bed itself by its very nature was undoubtedly instrumental in trapping and holding the overlying material. In such a situation, some contamination of the component is inevitable since cultural activities must have occurred both up and down the arroyo bottom as well as in the immediate area of the bone bed, and some cultural material would have been moved and redeposited by stream transport.

Second, there did appear to be at least one and possibly two relatively heavily concentrated areas of bone toward the bottom center of the map. In one concentration there were several articulated units. Away from these two areas, the bones are scattered and disarticulated, and they demonstrate a higher incidence of breakage.

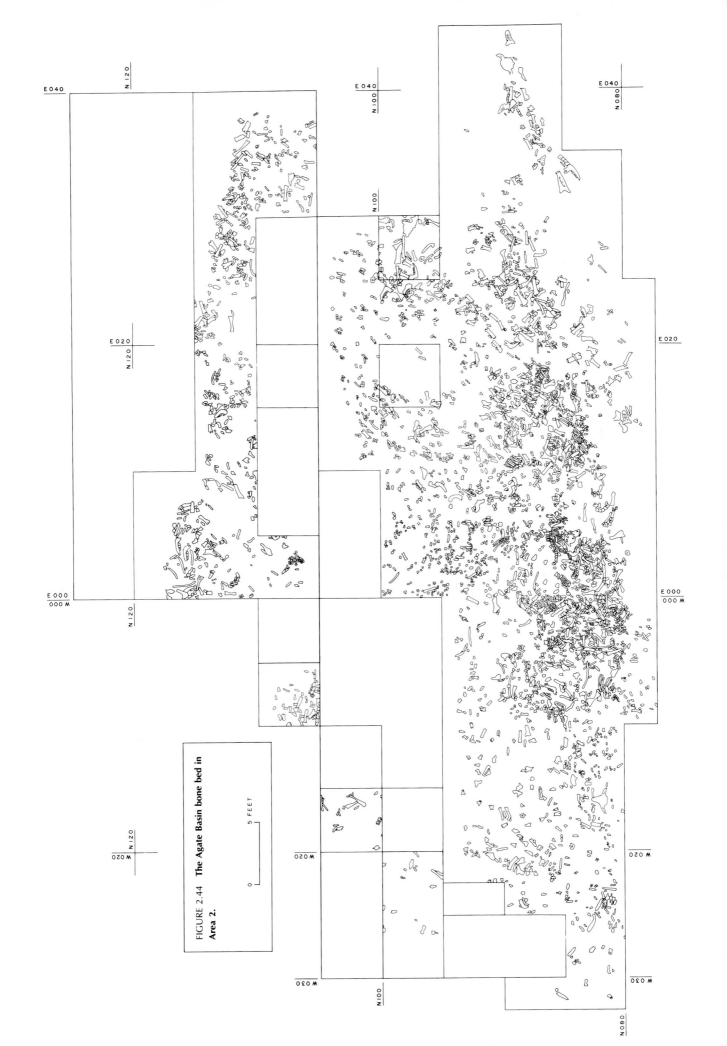

FIGURE 2.44 The Agate Basin bone bed in Area 2.

5 FEET

FIGURE 2.45 Excavations in the Agate Basin bone bed in Area 2 in 1976.

FIGURE 2.46 Excavations exposing part of the Folsom bone bed (bottom) directly under the Agate Basin bone bed (top) in Area 2 in 1978. Arrow points to the same post in each photo.

FIGURE 2.47   **The Agate Basin level (a) and the Folsom level (f) in 1979.**

Third, within the confines of the bone bed was an assemblage of weaponry, tools, and flakes that, along with the bones, are herein used to explain the cultural activities that occurred there.

Fourth, animal population studies (see Chapter 4) indicate a cold weather period of site occupation and animal-procurement events. It is assumed that the animal-procurement events were communal, and designed to provide more food than could be immediately consumed. Short-term preservation and storage of surplus meat is thought to have been through freezing. The bone bed in the Agate Basin component is interpreted as representing the partial remains of one and possibly two piles of partially dismembered and subsequently frozen bison carcasses from which parts were extracted as needed and processed for consumption on a relatively flat area immediately adjacent to the meat piles.

Fifth, we can observe only the excavated bone bed area because geologic activity since its deposition has removed the remainder of the site context. We can only guess the amount and kind of concomitant cultural activity that took place in the remainder of the arroyo and the site vicinity. Geomorphic reconstructions of past landforms based on small remnants are general and therefore limited in the amount of interpretation they can provide for the archaeologist.

The bone bed described is the main feature of the Agate Basin component. Its raison d'être reflects the main purpose of the archaeological investigations of the site. It follows that the investigator is inevitably channeled into describing the artifact assemblage within functional categories related to the reasons for the presence of the bone bed.

STONE ARTIFACT
ASSEMBLAGE

Projectile Points

The Agate Basin site projectile points are the type site specimens, and illustrations of some have been published. Roberts (1951) illustrated 36 broken and complete specimens at about three-quarters scale. A decade later he (Roberts 1961a: Plate 3) illustrated 58 specimens at about one-third scale. As was mentioned in Chapter 1, the 1961 illustration was actually the complete version of the photograph published in 1951; both sides had been cropped in the 1951 publication. The same photograph was also published by Wormington (1957), and has been reproduced here for reference purposes (Figure 1.13). It illustrates most of the Roberts Smithsonian Institution collection as well as nine specimens from the R. E. Frison collection.

In the same article Roberts (1961a) illustrated three of the specimens at near actual size. The third specimen in this illustration (Roberts 1961a:Plate 4) is actually Nos. 9 and 55 of another illustration (Roberts 1961a:Plate 3). The base on this third specimen was described as concave, which is erroneous since the base shape resulted from either a manufacture or—more likely—a usage break. In addition, Nos. 26 and 57 are tools and Nos. 12 and 58 are Hell Gap projectile points.

A total of 169 broken and complete Agate Basin projectile points are in the known collections from Areas 1 and 2 and from the surface near the site area (see Figures 2.48–2.59). Many more were taken by collectors but those presently known are believed to represent by far the larger proportion of the actual total. This is based on an estimation of the amount of the site area excavated by the Smithsonian Institution and the University of Wyoming versus that known to have been destroyed by artifact hunters. Technological aspects of Agate Basin projectile point manufacture are treated in Chapter 3 and the following considers only their general characteristics and ranges of variation.

Of the 169 projectile points, 72 are made of what is probably Knife River flint, 59 are of other chert, 37 are of quartzite, and 1 is of porcellanite. Evidence of use is present in the form of impact breaks, most of which were probably produced as they were driven into buffalo with throwing sticks and possibly thrusting spears. The nature of the breakage on some could probably be used to argue for velocities higher than those normally obtained with a thrusting spear (see e.g., Figures 2.49g, 2.53b, n; 2.57f; and 2.59c, d). Many kinds of impact damage can be identified, ranging from only a loss of the sharp point to crushing and various kinds of flake removal on the distal end (see, e.g., Figures 2.48c, e, m; 2.49o; 2.52k; 2.53l; 2.55g; 2.56a, b; and 2.59c, d). Removal of long, thin flakes along blade edges was common also (Figures 2.49e, 2.51d, and 2.53b, n). Snap breaks occurred at almost any point between base and tip, but the areas closer to both ends were particularly vulnerable to this type of breakage.

Much of the variation in the projectile points resulted from the reshaping of broken pieces. Resharpening the tip was common, and the amount of reshaping needed was determined by the distance from the tip that the break occurred. This reworking of projectile points can usually be observed from abrupt changes in the original flaking pattern, outline form, and longitudinal and transverse cross-section. Reshaping seldom was done with the expertise demonstrated on the first completion. In fact, reshaping was usually carelessly executed with an apparent disregard for the excellence of the technology expressed originally (see, e.g., Figure 2.55c, g). On other specimens it is less easy to detect (Figures 2.51i and 2.55a) but still quite obvious.

Broken bases were reshaped also. The original projectile point configuration usually included a rounded base (Figures 2.48a, 2.49j, 2.51g, 2.53o, and 2.56j). When a break was close to the base, usually only a grinding of the resulting sharp corners was needed (Figures 2.48i, 2.51m, and 2.55j). Another method was to drive short, burin-like spalls off one or both corners before grinding (Figures 2.51e, 2.52c, 2.55d, and 2.56a). The result was often a straight base (Figures 2.52b and 2.55d), and breaks at an angle often destroyed the symmetry of the point (Figure 2.53m).

The quality of the original workmanship varies, but the flaking is usually well executed, with flake scars at right angles to the longitudinal axis of the projectile point. Departure from this pattern is rare and can be seen minimally on two specimens (Figures 2.51, l; 2.58k) where there is a noticeable trend to a diagonal flake removal. The former specimen is unique in that the distal end was reshaped by an alternate bevel. Flake scars usually cover both faces and leave no evidence of original dorsal or ventral flake surfaces, with few exceptions (Figures 2.49k and 2.52b). However, in some cases the flaking pattern of an earlier reduction sequence can be detected where the last flaking sequence failed to reach the center.

Transverse cross-sections are usually smoothly lenticular, a fine retouch having been applied to the blade edges to ensure smooth margins. In only two cases can a definite center ridge be observed (Figures 2.50p and 2.51j), and the former demonstrates the sharp center ridge on one side only. Longitudinal cross-sections were carefully controlled also, and taper evenly to both the tip and the base. Grinding of the blade edges usually extended from just around the basal corners up to or nearly to the point of greatest width. On specimens with narrow, rounded bases (Figures 2.48a, 2.49f, and 2.52h), the grinding may be continuous around the base, but it is invariably lighter on the basal extremity than on the edges. However, in most cases the bases are not ground.

Another noticeable feature of the Agate Basin projectile points is the lack of a twist longitudinally, a feature common to the Hell Gap projectile points from the Casper site. Consequently, blade edges, almost without exception, are straight from base to tip. A suggestion of a stem and shoulders reminiscent of those on Hell Gap projectile points appears on a few specimens (Figures 2.50g; 2.52g, h; 2.53e; and 2.54b), and it is not difficult to conceptualize the change in projectile point style from Agate Basin to Hell Gap. It is difficult, however, to understand the change in terms of function. Agate Basin points are structurally sound, haft well, penetrate easily, and are extremely lethal when used with either a throwing stick or a thrusting spear on large animals such as bison. This assumed superiority was apparently not enough to deter the change to the broad, relatively blunt-pointed Hell Gap projectile point, which may have had superior functional attributes that we are not yet aware of. Several true Hell Gap projectile points were recovered in the excavations and as surface finds prior to the University of Wyoming–Smithsonian excavations beginning in 1975 (Figures 2.50e, m; 2.54a; 2.56m, t; and 2.57o, p). These are discussed in a later section.

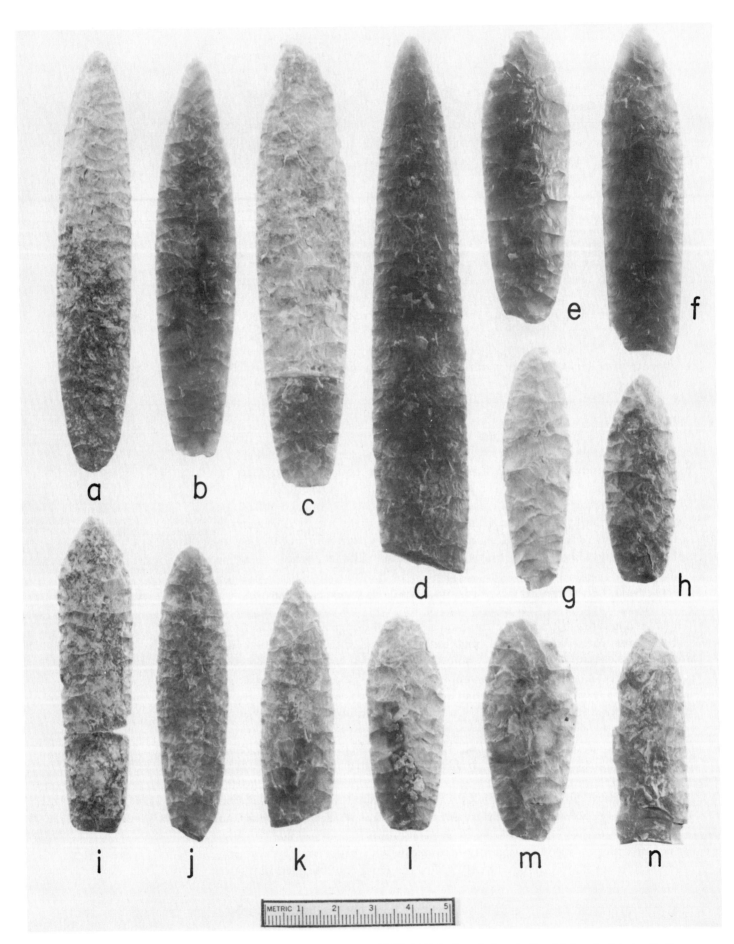

FIGURE 2.48A,B Agate Basin projectile points from the Roberts collection.

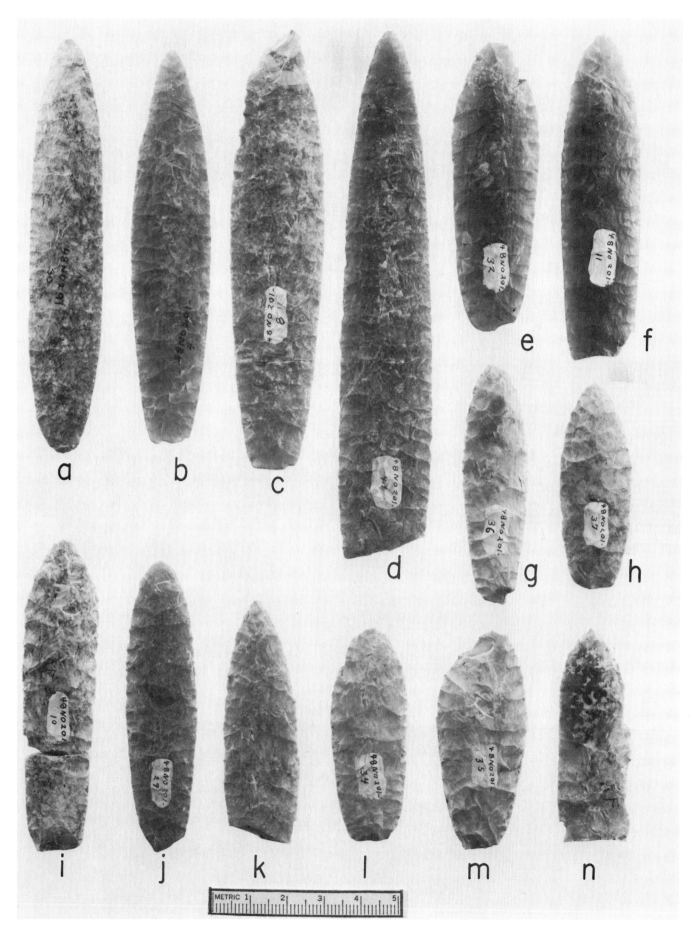

a   b   c   d   e   f

g   h

i   j   k   l   m   n

METRIC 1   2   3   4   5

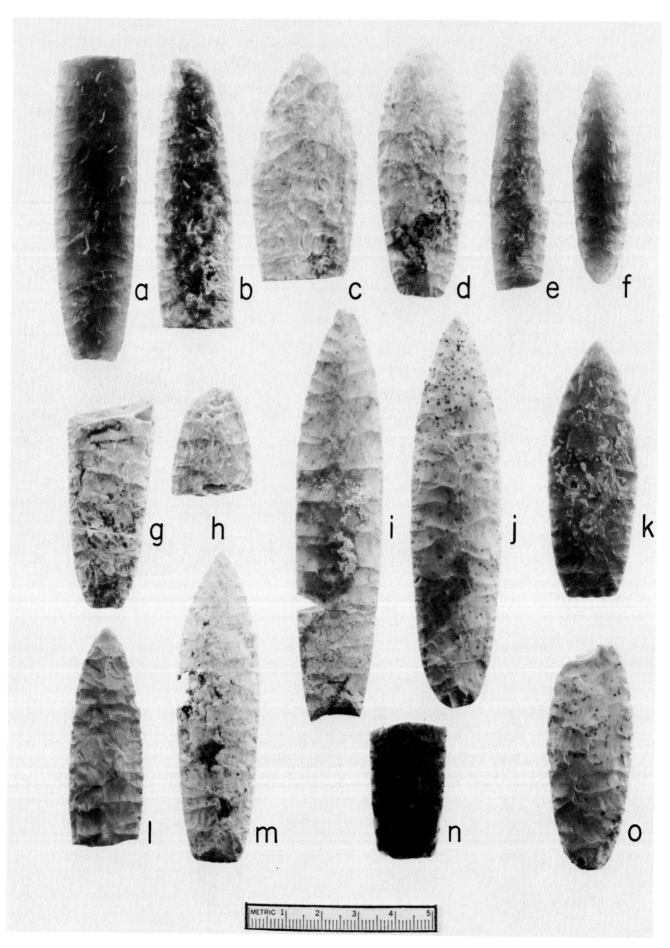

FIGURE 2.49A,B Agate Basin projectile points from the Roberts collection.

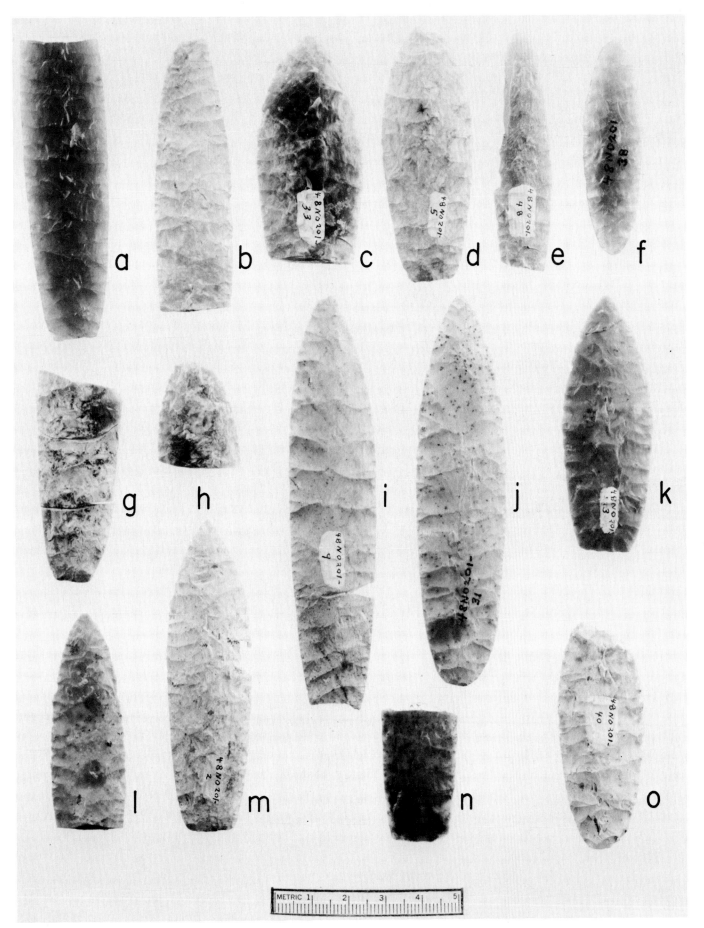

FIGURE 2.50A,B **Agate Basin projectile points (a–d, f–l, m–r, t) and Hell Gap projectile points (e, m, s) from the Roberts collection.**

FIGURE 2.51A,B Agate Basin projectile points from the R. E. Frison collection.

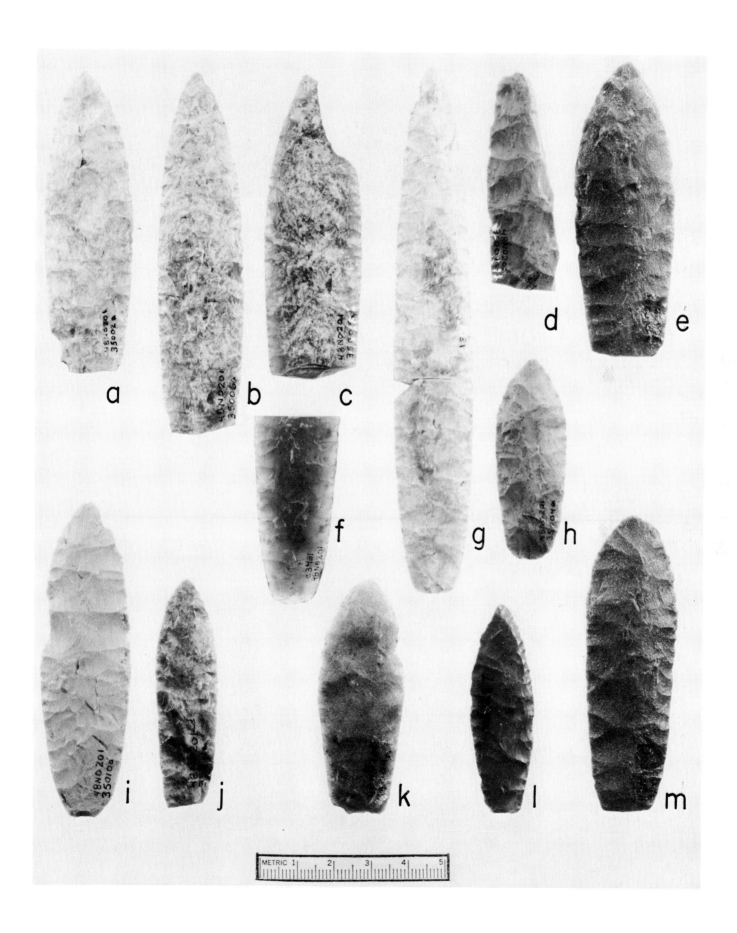

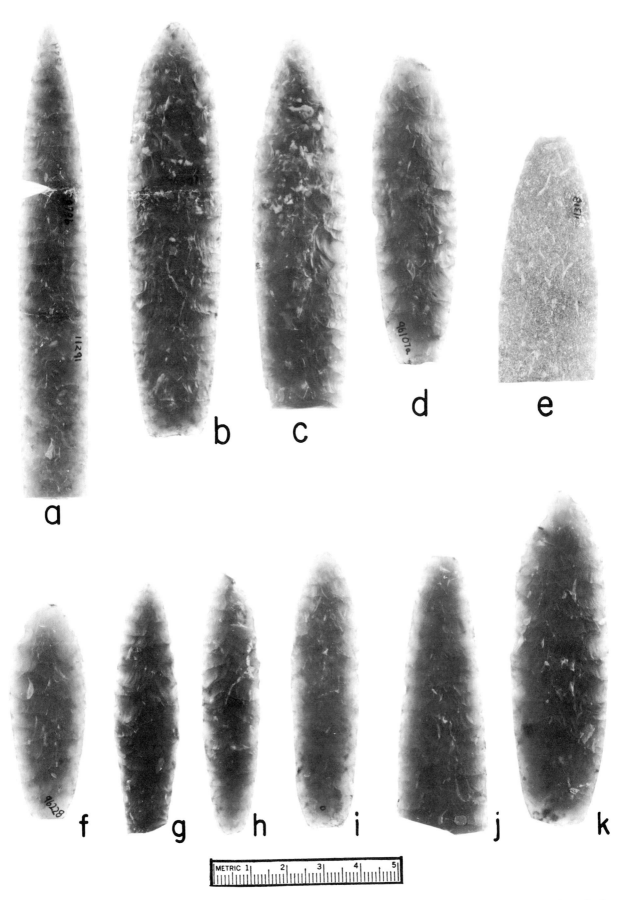

FIGURE 2.52A,B Agate Basin projectile points from the University of Wyoming collection.

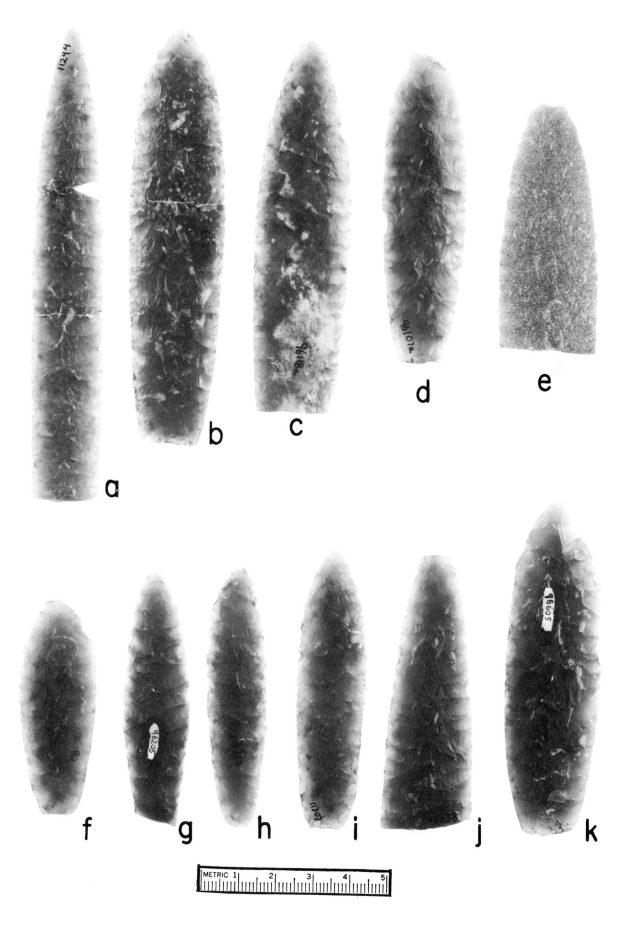

a

b

c

d

e

f

g

h

i

j

k

METRIC 1 2 3 4 5

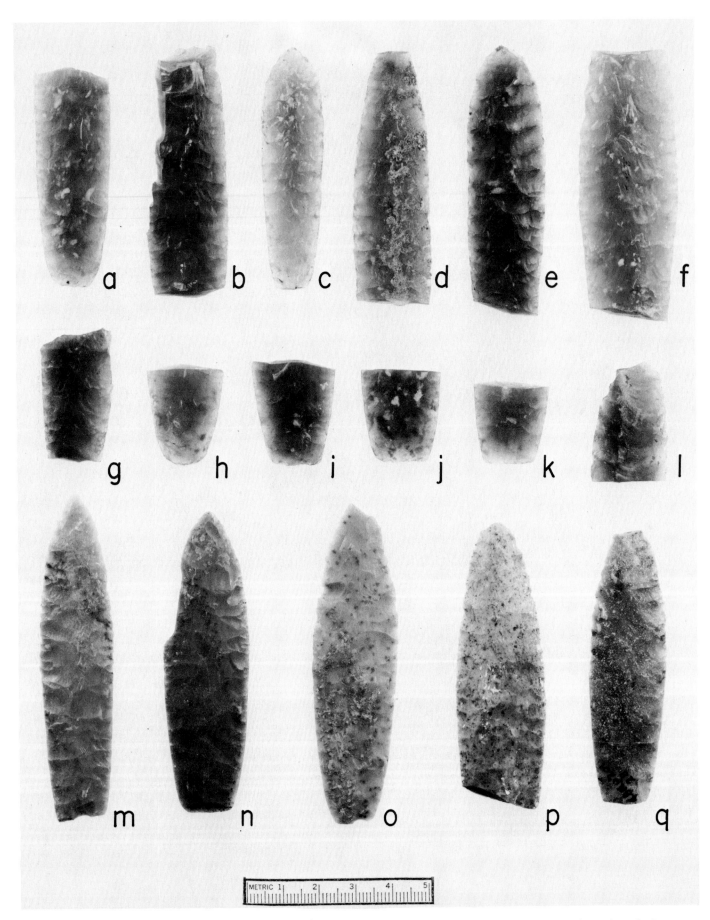

FIGURE 2.53A,B Agate Basin projectile points from the University of Wyoming collection.

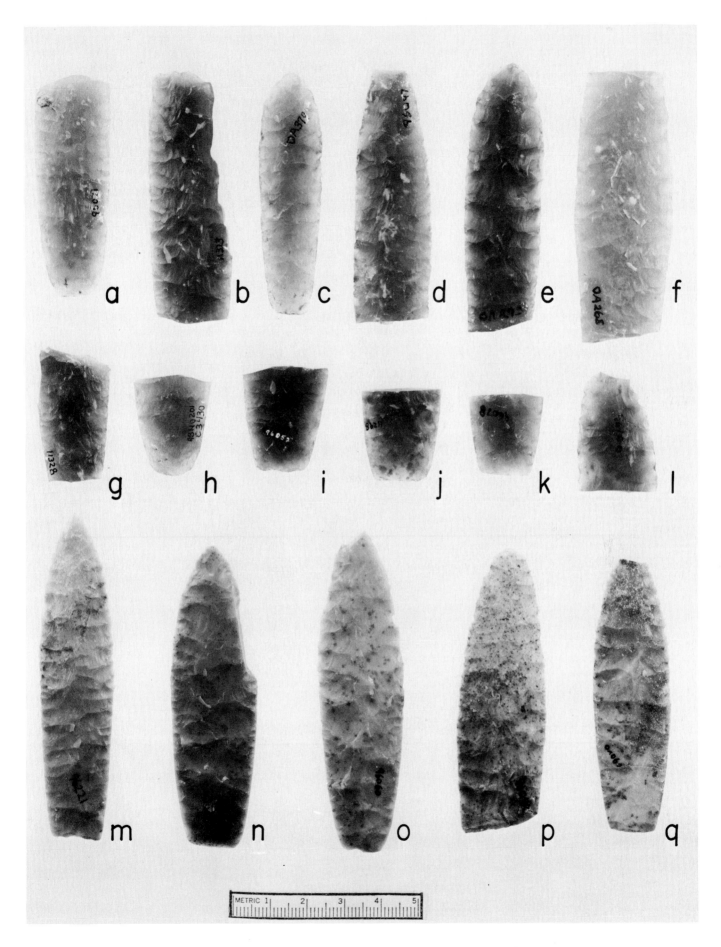

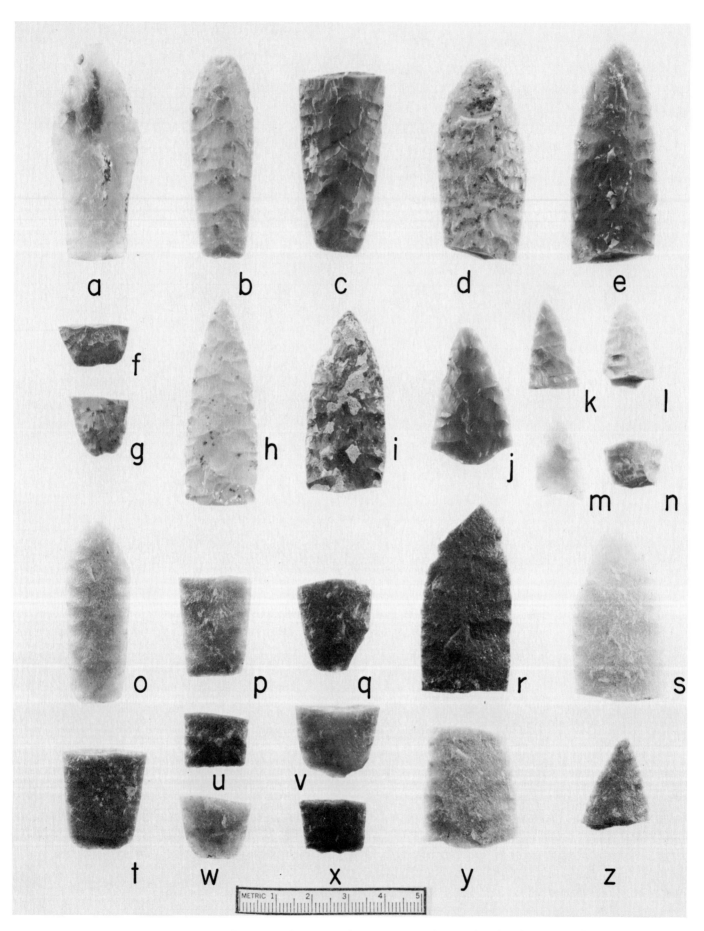

FIGURE 2.54A,B **Hell Gap projectile point (a) and Agate Basin projectile points (b–z) from the University of Wyoming collection.**

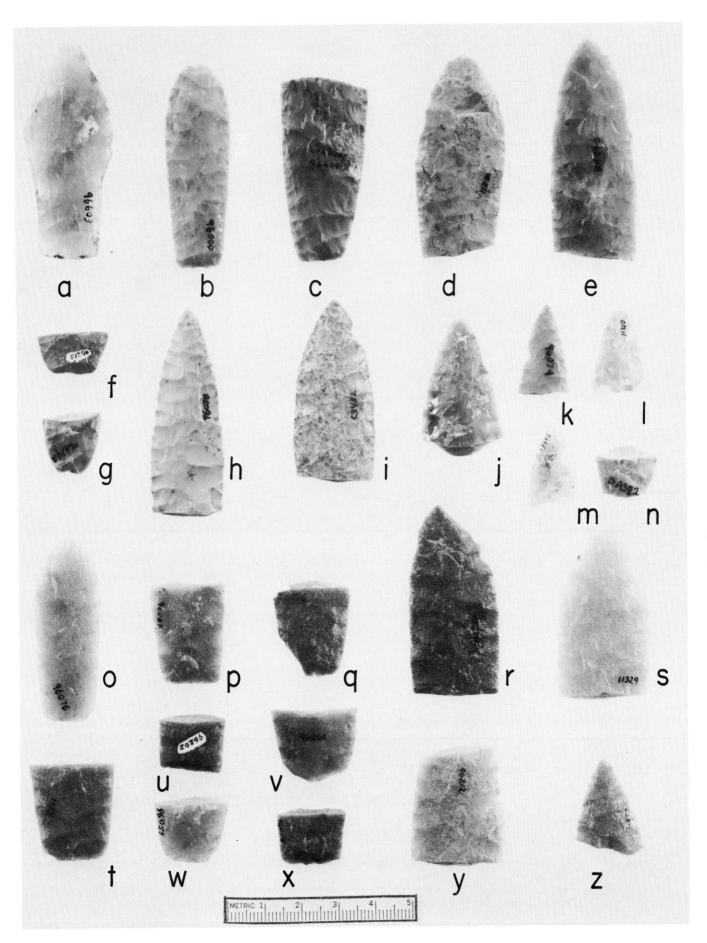

a   b   c   d   e

f

g   h   i   j   k   l

m   n

o   p   q   r   s

t   u   v   w   x   y   z

METRIC 1   2   3   4   5

FIGURE 2.55A,B Agate Basin projectile points from the University of Wyoming collection (a–i, o) and the Steege collection (j–n).

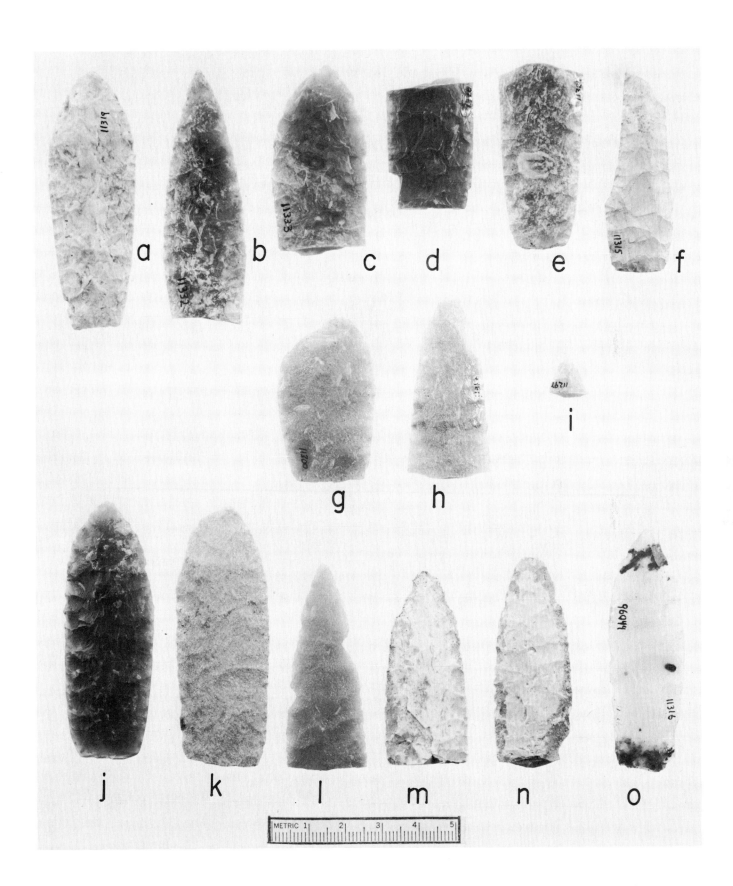

a b c d e f

g h i

j k l m n o

METRIC 1 2 3 4 5

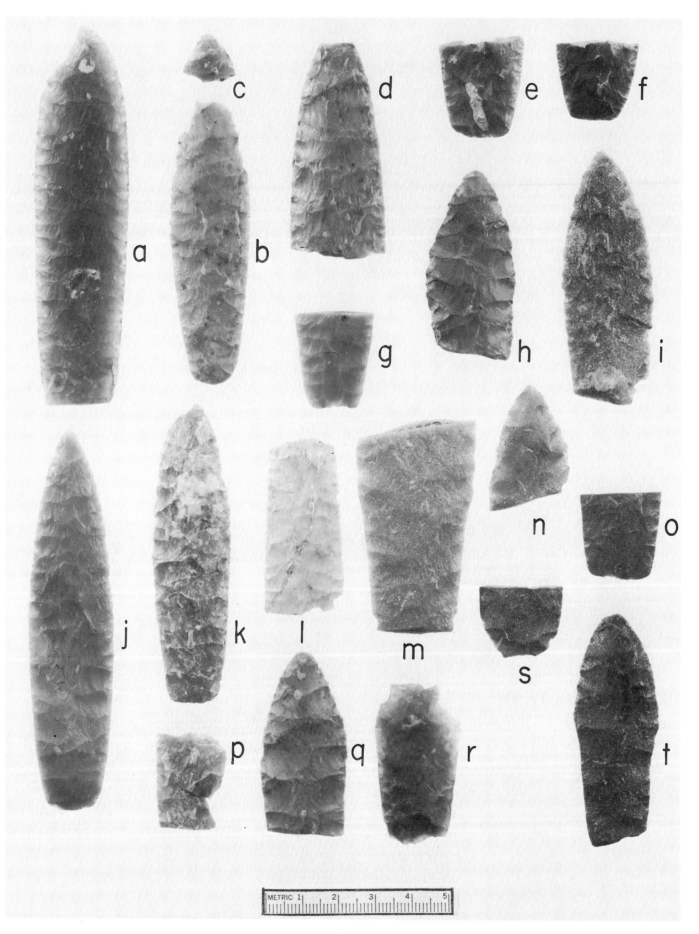

FIGURE 2.56A,B Agate Basin projectile points (a–l, n–q,s), and Hell Gap projectile points (r, m, t) from the Bass and Roberts 1961 collection.

a b c d e f g h i j k l m n o p q r s t

METRIC 1 2 3 4 5

[99]

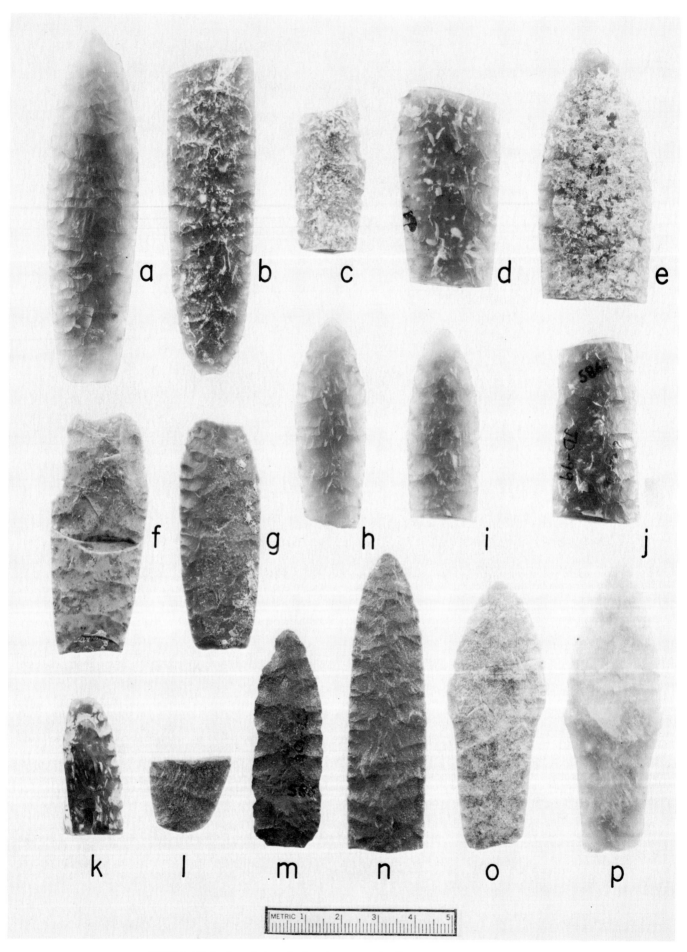

FIGURE 2.57A,B Agate Basin projectile points (a–n) and Hell Gap projectile points (o–p) from the James Duguid collection.

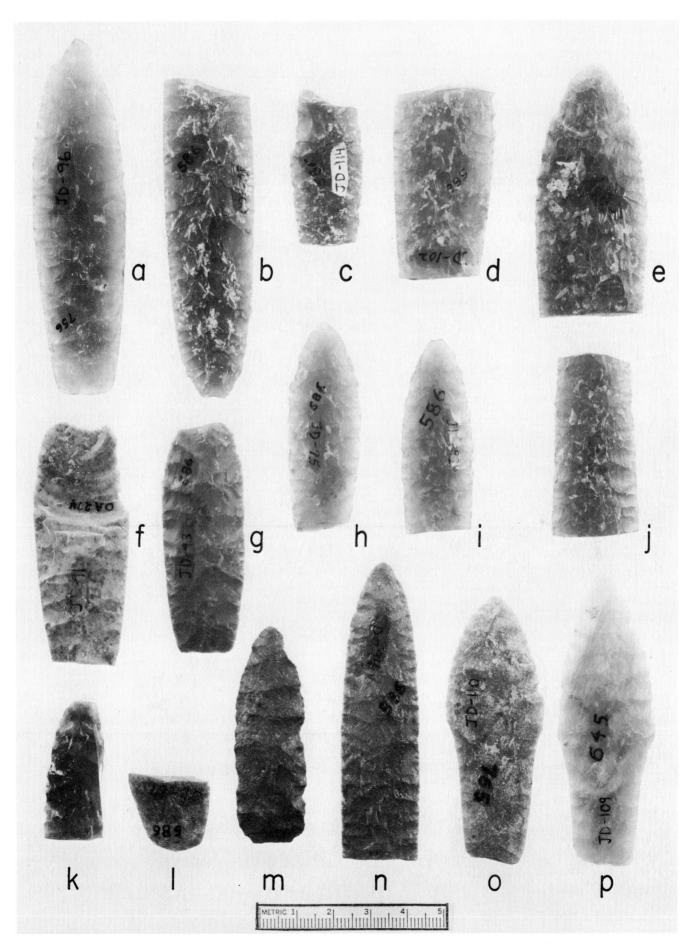

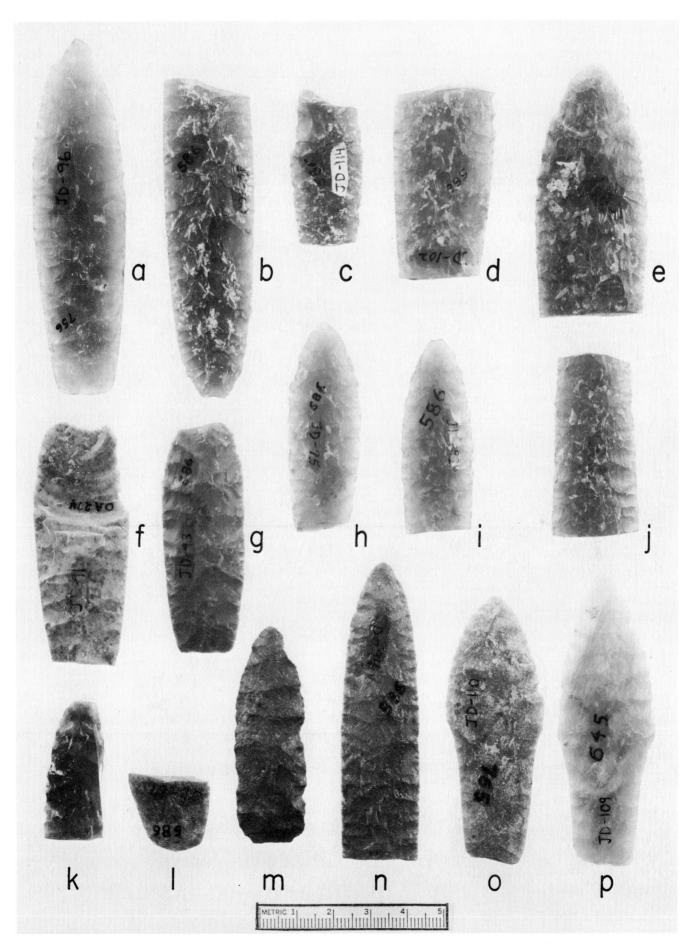

a b c d e

f g h i j

k l m n o p

METRIC 1 2 3 4 5

[101]

FIGURE 2.58A,B **Agate Basin projectile points (a–e, g–l) and a Folsom preform (f) from the William Spencer collection.**

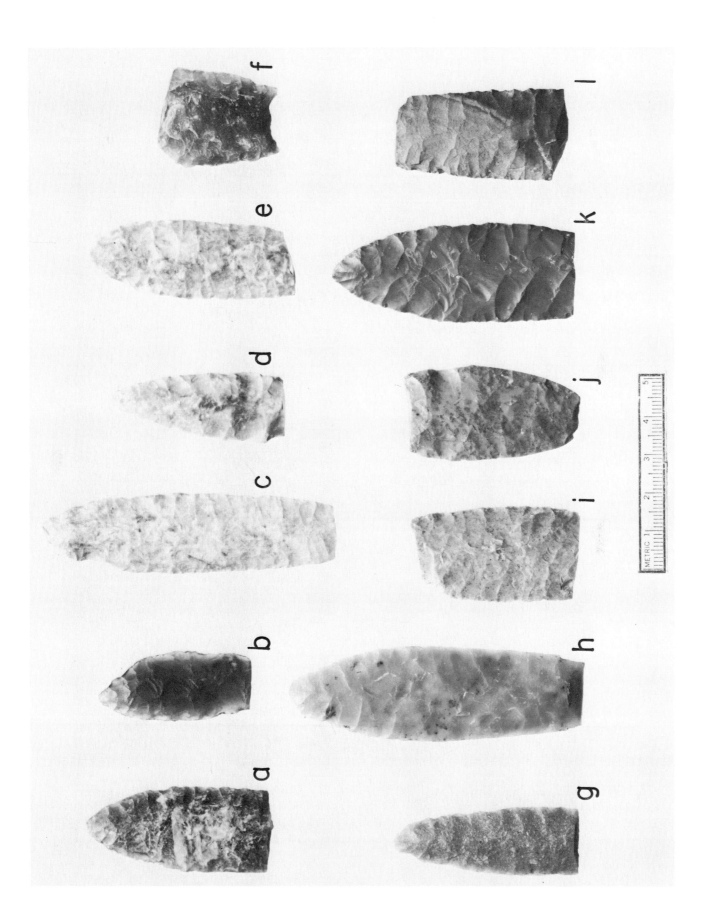

FIGURE 2.59 Agate Basin projectile point distal end from the R. E. Frison collection and midsection from the William Spencer collection (a, b), and a nearly complete specimen recovered during the 1976–1981 excavations (c, d).

The excellence of Agate Basin manufacture technology is well demonstrated by two of the specimens, although neither may be typical of the majority of Agate Basin projectile points. One (Figure 2.59a, b) was made of an especially fine chert very likely obtained from the Hartville uplift, an extensive source of high-quality cherts that begins about 80 km (50 miles) southwest of Agate Basin. The specimen is incomplete but was probably reused as a projectile point in its present form. The extreme tip was broken and reshaped slightly; one corner of the base was burinated either deliberately or accidentally, and both corners were then reduced slightly by grinding. One blade edge has several nicks that are nearly identical to those produced in experiments by contact with a bison rib during penetration. The specimen snapped transversely as the result of a small crystal pocket present in the material and edge grinding extended just distal to the break. If the symmetry applied to other Agate Basin projectile points can be applied to this specimen, which is likely, this artifact was originally at least another 3 or 4 cm longer. The distal end was recovered during excavations in Area 1 in 1942, and the midsection was found in the Spencer collection in 1980.

The other specimen (Figure 2.59c, d) is of Knife River flint, and it also is incomplete. Part of the distal end is missing, which indicates a heavy impact, probably with a bison rib or—more likely—a long bone. One impact flake recovered extends for some distance proximally on one face of the projectile point and hinged out abruptly. The remaining impact flakes for the distal end were not recovered.

Another break occurred just proximal to the beginning of the edge grinding. This break also demonstrates the results of heavy impact. A contact area between the two pieces is present in the center, but small wedge-shaped pieces were broken out on both sides and were not recovered. There is a strong suggestion that a twist was applied along with the back pressure upon impact, and also that the break occurred just distal to the end of the hafting element.

Still another break is present closer to the base. This one is more of a snap or bend break but still it demonstrates the results of back pressure. It undoubtedly occurred in that part of the point that was covered by the hafting element, and there is no evidence here of twisting. A flake was removed, giving the point the appearance of a concave base. The different breaks are shown in both face and edge views (Figure 2.60a, b) and the part of the point believed to have been covered with the hafting element is also suggested (Figure 2.60c).

Similar results have been observed in the actual spearing of domestic cattle and bison with a thrusting spear and a notched wooden foreshaft to hold the projectile point. Experimental specimens were bound in wooden foreshafts with sinew alone and also with sinew and pitch. When a direct hit against bone occurred, the bases of the points were driven with great force against the base of the notches. When the force exceeded the breaking point of a projectile point that was properly seated and bound in the foreshaft, breaks similar to that shown in Figure 2.60 were common. In the case of the projectile point Figure 2.59c and d, the point base was driven both downward and sideways against the base of the wooden notch, and flakes were dislodged that angled upward toward the opposite face of the point (Figure 2.60c). In cases where the projectile point bindings failed because of improper application, the bases of the points were

FIGURE 2.60 **Suggested impact breakage on the specimen shown in Figure 2.59 c and d.**

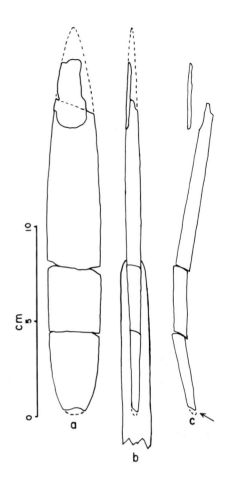

driven backward, splitting the foreshaft. The point usually broke in these situations also.

A further suggestion based on observations of projectile points damaged in the experimental spearing of large animals is that the point in Figure 2.59c and d probably struck a long bone such as a humerus (a regular occurrence when one aims for the rib cage) rather than a rib. Moreover, the anterior sides of *Bison* ribs are more rounded than those of *Bos* and a projectile point tends to slide around the rib and penetrate the rib cage of the former more so than the latter, where the tendency is for the point to penetrate the bone.

As we saw for the specimen in Figure 2.59a and b, it is possible to estimate the original length of a projectile point using a type concept expressed on other Agate Basin points unaltered from their original finished condition. For the point shown in Figure 2.59c and d, using Bradley's indices (see Chapter 3, Table 3.9, points OA176, OA458, 96094, 96094a), the total length was 205 mm, give or take a millimeter or so; blade length was 120 mm, and stem length was 85 mm. The following ratios were calculated: maximum length/maximum width = 7.19; blade length/maximum width = 4.21; blade length/stem length = 1.41. These measurements and ratios may be slightly erroneous but not significantly so.

The breakage demonstrated by the projectile point shown in Figure 2.59c and d is not unique to the Agate Basin projectile point assemblage. Another specimen in particular (Figure 2.49i) demonstrates an almost identical pattern of basal damage. This specimen was recovered by Roberts, who described it as a point with a concave base (Roberts 1951:131), but the change from a rounded base and the break distal to the base almost certainly resulted from heavy impact.

Although a number of the Agate Basin projectile points evidence an excellence in manufacture that transcends functional needs in terms of lethal effects on large animals such as the late Pleistocene *Bison,* there seems to have been no hesitation to use such specimens. We do not know at this time whether or not there were projectile points or other flaked stone items reserved for ritualistic contexts and not associated with the actual spearing of animals. Miniature projectile points in the Jones–Miller site of Hell Gap age may have been ritualistic objects used by a shaman, as the junior author has suggested (Stanford 1978:96–97), but nothing of this nature is known to have been found at the Agate Basin site. However, a miniature projectile point recovered at the Muddy Creek site (Frison 1978b:Figure 5.40d) in a context associated with communal bison procurement appears somewhat anomolous and may have been part of a shaman's equipment. The ethnographic literature is rich in instances of supernatural activity associated with communal bison procurement (see, e.g., Chittenden and Richardson 1905:1028–1029; Fletcher and La Flesche 1906:281; Gilmore 1924:209; Grinnell 1961:12–14; Mandelbaum 1940:190–191), and there seems no reason that it would not have been part of the cultural content of Paleoindian lifeways as well.

A brief description of Agate Basin projectile points as a type was published by Wheeler (1954). At that time Wheeler believed that they resembled projectile points from the Ray Long site 22 km east of the Agate Basin site, at the Angostura Reservoir in Fall River County, South Dakota. However, further observations caused Wheeler to reclassify the Ray Long points as Angostura. Wheeler may have been influenced to some degree by the erroneous identification of the bison from the Agate Basin site as a modern form.

Flake and Blade Tools

The stone tool assemblage recovered from the Agate Basin component in Area 2 includes a limited number of functional tool types that, in general, appear to have been designed for use in preparing bison carcasses for human consumption as well as other products of nonfood use. The tools are relatively simple in manufacture and design. Most were apparently made elsewhere and brought to the site, although some tool manufacture occurred there.

The most common tool category consists of large percussion flakes with various kinds of modifications on the edges of the dorsal surfaces. A deliberate percussion flake removal technique to produce tools is evidenced by a number of specimens. A percussion flake was first removed in such a manner as to produce a relatively flat surface on the core. This flat surface later became the dorsal side of the flake intended for a tool, and further core reduction was deliberately planned to achieve this end. The ideal and actual result in many cases was a flake of relatively even thickness that required no further modification other than edge preparation to form a completed tool. Flake thickness varies from about 6 to 17 mm, and a single flake may vary considerably in thickness from one part of the flake to another.

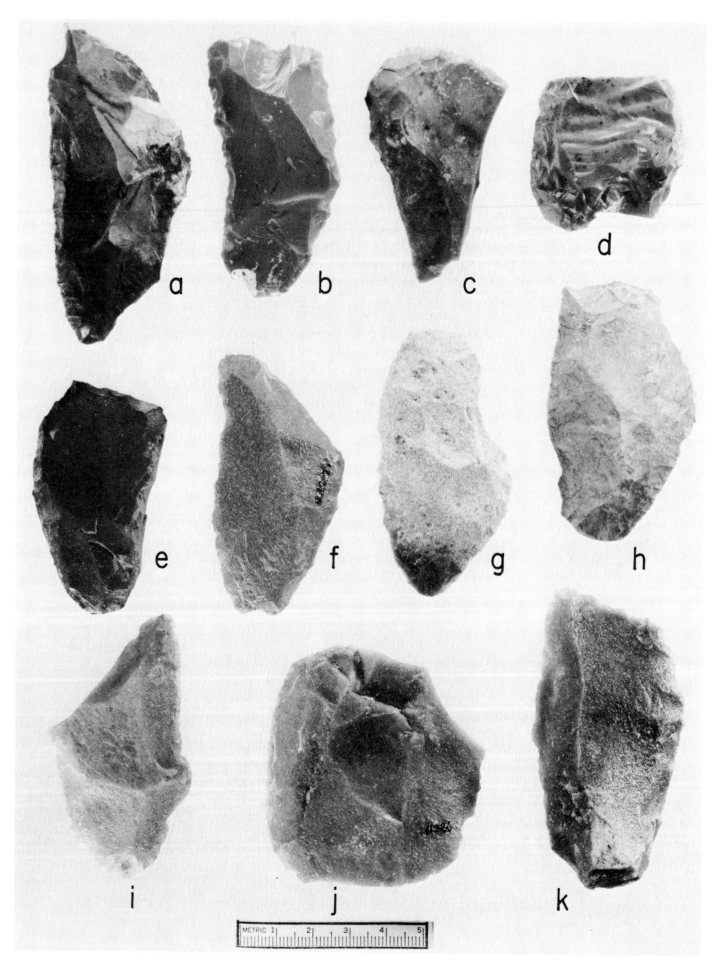

a b c d

e f g h

i j k

METRIC 1 2 3 4 5

FIGURE 2.61 Flake tools from the Agate Basin level in Area 2.

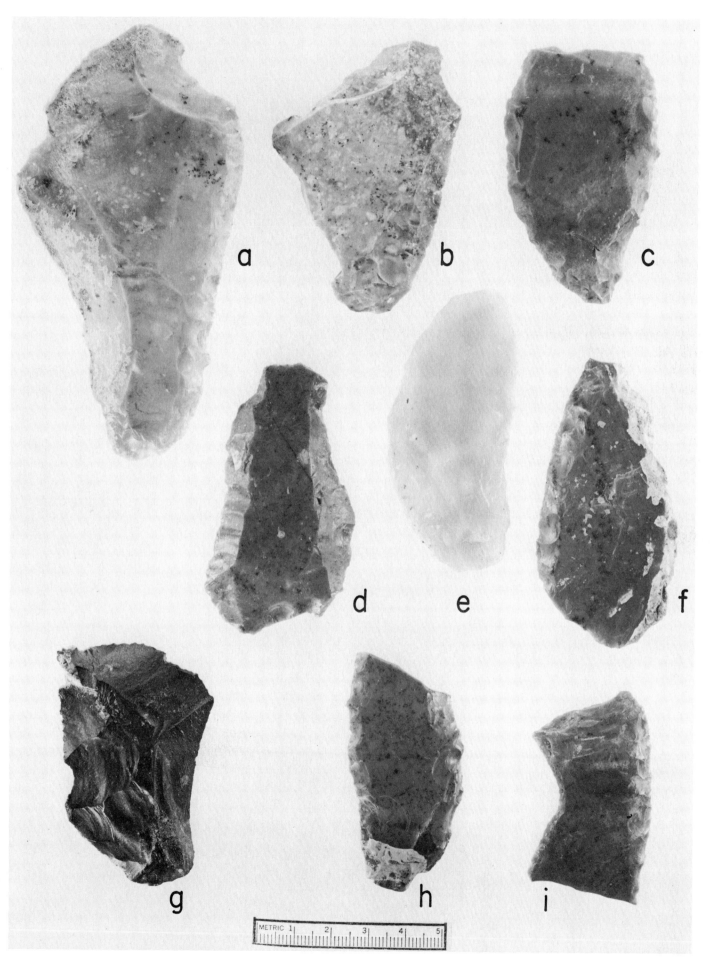

FIGURE 2.62   Flake tools from the Agate Basin level in Area 2. One (a) is from the Tubbs family collection.

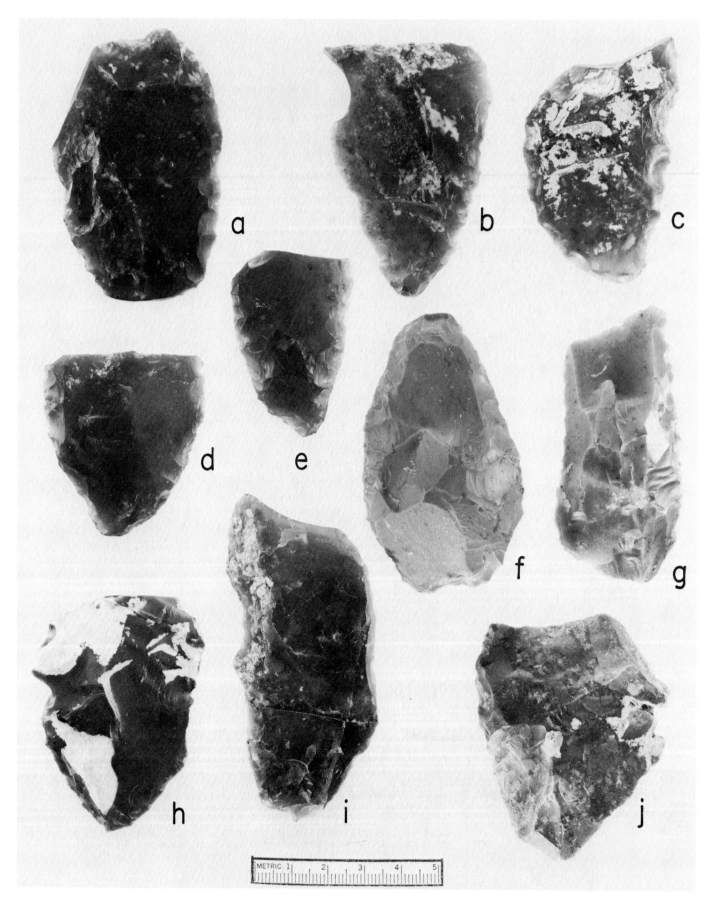

FIGURE 2.63 **Flake tools from the Agate Basin level in Area 2.**

FIGURE 2.64 **Large end scraper from the Roberts collection (a) and flake and blade tools (b–n) from the Agate Basin levels in Areas 1 and 2.**

The configuration of the working edges varies considerably. They may be nearly straight (Figure 2.61a), concave (Figure 2.65a), or convex (Figure 2.61g), along with varying degrees of the last two conditions. A tool may have only a single working edge (Figure 2.62f) or as many as three (Figure 2.61f). In some cases, the entire perimeter of the flake may have been used (Figure 2.63f). Working edges in nearly all cases were prepared by deliberate percussion flaking (Figure 2.61a, j) or a tool may rarely demonstrate heavy use of an edge without any modification (Figure 2.62d). It is common for one edge to demonstrate deliberate preparation and another edge of the same tool to demonstrate only edge modification through use (Figure 2.62a). One deliberate method of edge preparation was to nick the edges of the flake at regular intervals, which resulted in a denticulate effect (Figure 2.62g).

In general, working-edge angles of these tools vary considerably and suggest combinations of both cutting and scraping use. A single working-edge angle (Figure 2.61f) may vary from about 35° to about 55°, which is believed to be strongly indicative of use in normal butchering work with large animals, where a continual interplay of cutting and scraping with this sort of tool works best in skinning and muscle stripping. Another feature of at least three of these tools is to continue the working edge around a corner of the tool to form what is best described as an end scraper connected to a side scraper edge or edges (Figures 2.63f and 2.65b). This kind of working edge is extremely functional in skinning and muscle stripping large animals. One specimen that is unique in the assemblage is a percussion flake (Figure 2.64b) made of coarse-grained quartzite with a cutting edge (edge angle 39°) formed by pressure flaking. The working edge is extremely dulled, to the extent that it has an abraded appearance and is no longer functional as a cutting tool. This tool was from the 1942 Smithsonian collections. Its exact provenience is not known, but it is believed to have been found in Area 1.

One unusual side scraper was made on a chert blade (11.3 mm thick) with the striking-platform end broken. The break probably occurred before the tool was made, since the prepared working edges do not extend to the break. The working edges are steep (65–80°) and dulled from use. The edges formed by both proximal and distal snap breaks are also worn from use. This may have been an Agate Basin projectile point preform blank before it was broken. The material is identical to that of the large projectile point (Figure 2.65c), and before it was made into a tool it could easily have been made into a typical Agate Basin projectile point. This specimen provided some insight into the ability of Agate Basin knappers to produce blades.

Ends or corners of tools that are either accidentally or purposely snapped to form edges at or near a right angle to the ventral flake surface also demonstrate scraping use (Figure 2.61c). Sharp graver points were formed on edges (Figure 2.61e), corners (Figure 2.65b), and ends (Figure 2.61a) of tools. Although their purpose is highly speculative, such modifications of tools are very useful in tasks like removing the tendons from legs of large animals.

A number of tools were made on smaller flakes, and in general represent a category of tools more delicate and specialized than the heavy butchering tools just described, although some appear to be smaller versions of the same tool types. One (Figure 2.66h) is a wide, thin (4.5 mm) flake with steep scraping

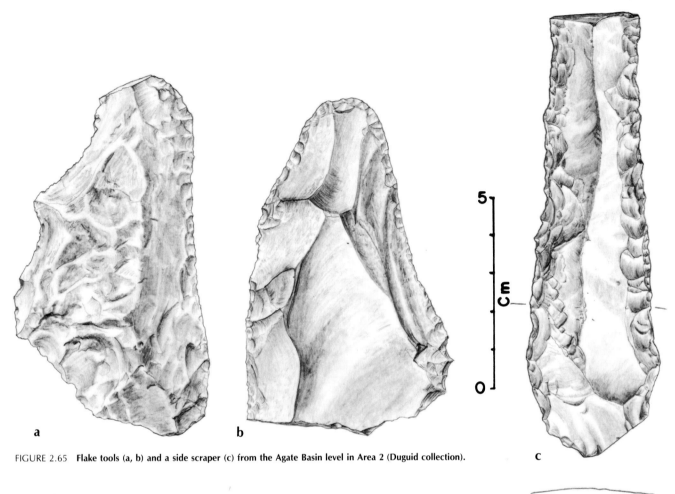

FIGURE 2.65   **Flake tools (a, b) and a side scraper (c) from the Agate Basin level in Area 2 (Duguid collection).**

edges on both sides. One corner has two adjacent graver-like points and the other corner has a rounded projection, demonstrating heavy use, probably as a cutting tool. Another flake tool (Figure 2.66d) has a straight and a concave scraping edge, as well as a single graver point on a corner. In addition, the distal end demonstrates a heavy use retouch from scraping use. Still another flake tool (Figure 2.66e) has two steep scraping edges that terminate in a sharp graver point. Two flakes demonstrate heavy working-edge use but no deliberate edge preparation. One of these (Figure 2.66b) has a graver point on one end and two notches along one edge. The other (Figure 2.66g) has a similarly placed graver point and a small rounded projection adjacent that resembles a small end scraper. Adjacent to this is a notch; another shallow notch appears farther around the edge. All of these working-edge features demonstrate relatively heavy use.

Gravers.   More typical graver tools include one (Figures 2.66f and 2.67b) made on a thin (2 mm) flake. The delicate graver point is adjacent to a pressure-flaked scraping edge. Three graver points are positioned around the end of another flake (Figure 2.66a), and edges of the flake are unmodified. One is a low-angle (25°) cutting edge; the edge opposite is a high-angle (52°) scraping edge. Both demonstrate heavy use. A sharp graver point was formed fortuitously

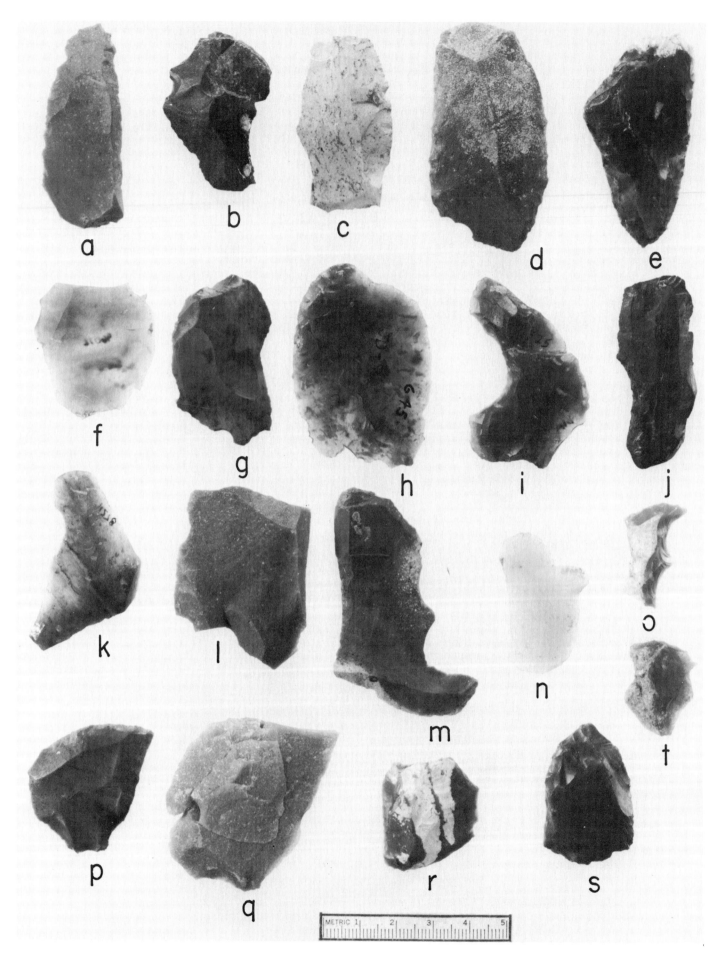

FIGURE 2.66 **Flake tools from the Agate Basin level in Area 2.**

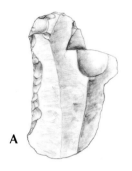
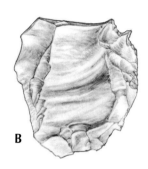
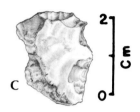

FIGURE 2.67   **Flake tool (A), graver (B), and composite tool from the Agate Basin level in Area 2.**

at the corner of another flake (Figure 2.66c) and it demonstrates unmistakable evidence of use. Adjacent to the graver point is a convex, pressure-flaked cutting edge (edge angle 32°) interrupted with a notch along one side of the flake. Another tool is probably more of a convergent scraper than a graver (Figure 2.66p). In this case a steep convex scraping edge (edge angle 65°) meets a straight cutting edge (edge angle 38°) to form a sharp point that demonstrates graver use. The scraping edge is dulled from use, as is the cutting edge. A shallow notch is present at the other end of the cutting edge adjacent to the striking platform.

One tool in the graver category appears to have been designed and used for a special purpose (Figure 2.68). The graver point was formed on the end of a

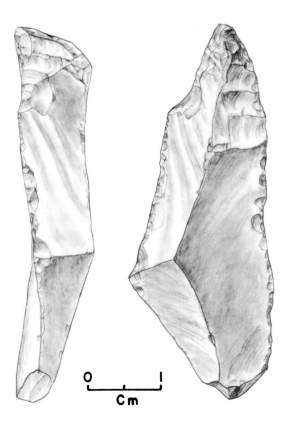

FIGURE 2.68   **Composite graver and cutting tool from the Agate Basin level in Area 2.**

thick flake and is slightly asymmetrical. The point is extremely thick, and buttressed, as if a narrow sharp point was needed for unusually heavy use.

Notches. Notched tools are common. They occur in a wide variety of sizes and shapes, although notched working edges usually appear in conjunction with other working-edge types to form composite tools. Many notches might be regarded as an extension of the range of concave working edges. Working-edge angles are relatively steep (65–75°) and are placed in various locations with regard to flake morphology but usually along the lateral edges.

Several notched tools have been described earlier, but a number of others deserve mention. On one tool (Figure 2.66k) a notch was deliberately pressure flaked into a less concave scraping edge on a flake. A small notch was similarly formed in the convex cutting edge of another flake (Figure 2.66l). The edge angle of this notch is 68°, whereas the cutting-edge angle is 40°. A large notch (edge angle 67°) occupies most of one side of a flake (Figure 2.66i) and a small area of the side opposite the notch was used as a side scraper (edge angle 53°). A relatively long and shallow notch on the side of a blade terminates at one end with a well-worn graver point (Figure 2.66g). The remainder of the edge of the flake demonstrates use as a cutting tool.

The working edges of one tool indicate several functions. One edge has a concave, pressure-flaked scraping edge (edge angle 50°). Opposite this edge are two notches formed by the accidental or deliberate removal of two arc-shaped pieces of the flake (Figure 2.66m). Both the notches and the point formed between them demonstrate heavy use; part of the remainder of the edge of the flake is abraded from use, partially obliterating an earlier use retouch. Two adjacent notches on a much larger flake tool (Figure 2.63i) form a blunt, well-worn point, and the working edges of the notches are worn in a manner similar to that of Figure 2.66m. On still another specimen, two adjacent notches were present accidentally, forming a dull point between them that was well worn. A long, slightly concave scraping edge is opposite (Figure 2.65a). Part of the remaining edge is unmodified but demonstrates heavy use.

One puzzling tool is made on a thick (8 mm) cortex flake. Two adjacent notches with steep (62°) edge angles are present on one side, and a scraping edge (78° edge angle) is on the distal end (Figure 2.66o). One notch and one end of the scraper edge form a sharp graver point. All edges and the two points demonstrate heavy use. Part of a similar specimen (Figures 2.66t and 2.67c) was also recovered, suggesting that this may be a specialized tool type.

Miscellaneous. Selected biface reduction flakes account for at least four flake tools. The largest (Figure 2.66h) has already been described; another (Figure 2.64j), which is typical of the remaining two, demonstrates a light use retouch along one edge. Core reduction flakes and blades account for at least nine more tools. One of these (Figure 2.66c) has been described as a combination cutting tool and graver. Five tools are blades from core reduction (Figures 2.64c, g; 2.69d–g) on which one or both edges demonstrate a use retouch. Core reduction flakes were used also as tools with no modification to form working edges (Figure 2.69h, i). One core reduction flake has a carefully pressure-flaked

FIGURE 2.69 Hammerstones (a–c), cores (d–e), and flake tools (f–i) from the Agate Basin level in Area 2.

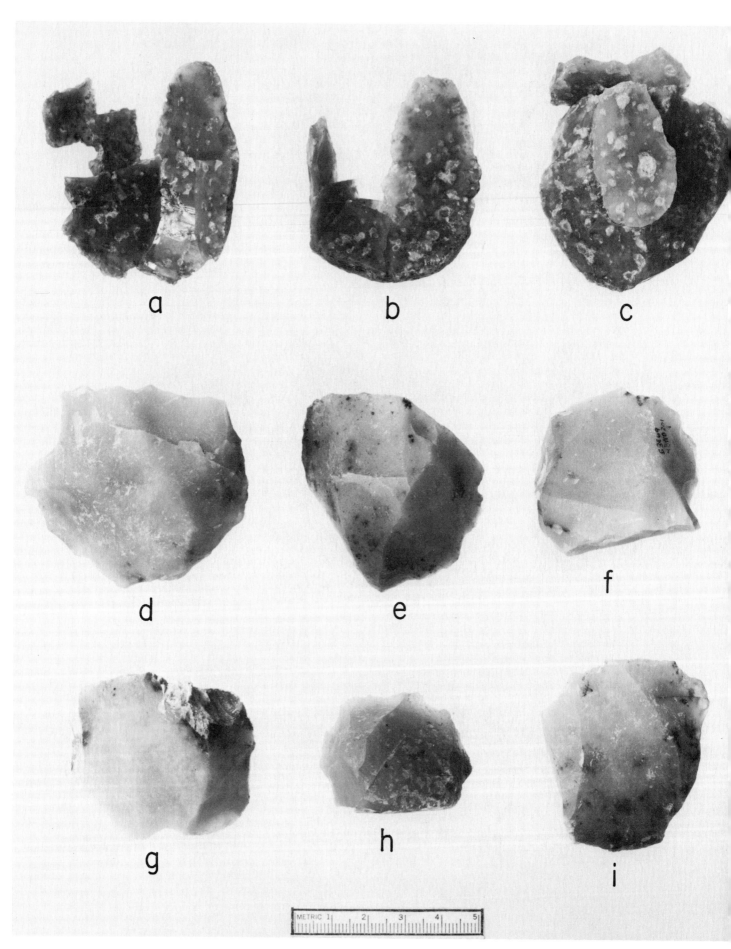

FIGURE 2.70A,B Core reduction flakes (a–c) and cores (d–i) from the Agate Basin level in Area 2.

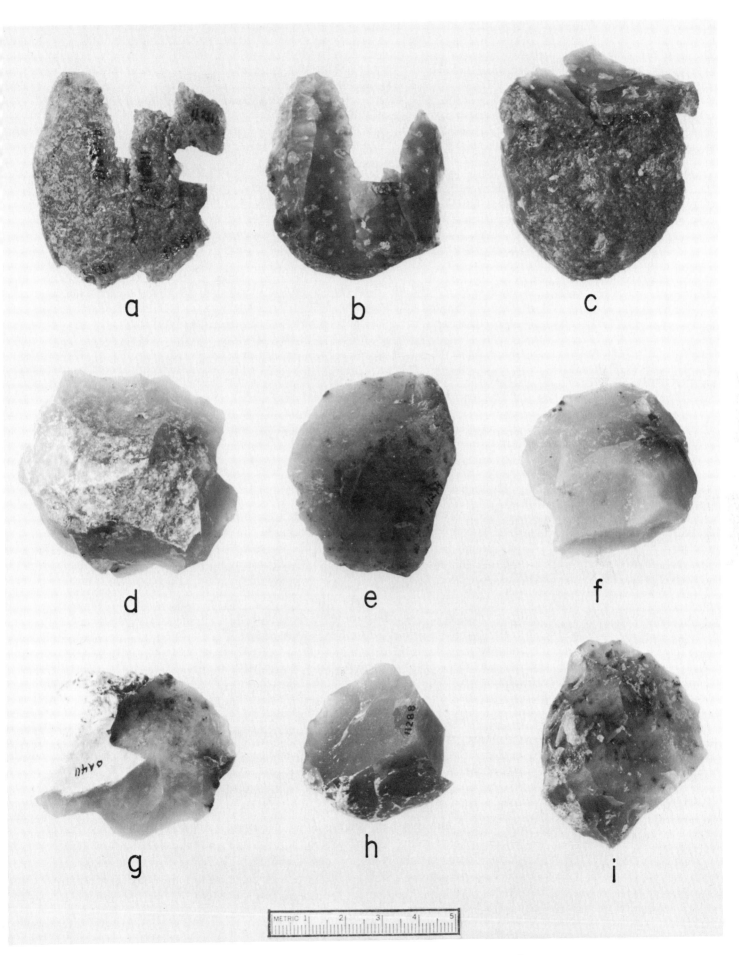

a

b

c

d

e

f

g

h

i

METRIC 1 2 3 4 5

concave edge with a low (34°) edge angle; it was apparently used as a cutting tool (Figures 2.66n and 2.67a).

Several flakes from the reduction sequence of a nodule of local chert were recovered and reassembled. After removal of the cortex (Figure 2.70a) several blades and flakes were removed. At least one blade (Figure 2.70b) and a flake (Figure 2.70c) demonstrate use as cutting tools. The distal ends of several other flakes and/or blades were broken off and discarded, and the missing parts were probably also used as tools.

Five tools are from the Roberts Smithsonian collection and were probably recovered from Area 1. One (Figure 2.64d) is a broken side scraper with steep (68° and 50°) working-edge angles. Another (Figure 2.64b) is a tool with a low-angle (34°) convex working edge. It would be regarded as a cutting tool except that the working edge is worn smooth. The third specimen (Figure 2.64i) has a convex cutting edge (26° edge angle) on one side and a steeper, concave working edge (53° edge angle) opposite. The fourth specimen (Figure 2.64h) is a fragment of a larger tool with a steep pressure retouch along one edge. The last specimen is a blade and has a use retouch along a small portion of one edge (Figure 2.64c). Since certain provenience data are lacking, these artifacts can always be questioned. Most were probably found during excavation, but some were recovered from backdirt of earlier digging. The blade tool (Figure 2.64c) demonstrates patination identical to that on surface finds in the area, and this tool at least may be a surface find.

End Scrapers.   End scrapers were usually made on percussion flakes with the working edge opposite the bulb of percussion. The exceptions (Figure 2.71o, p, r) were made by placing working edges on broken flakes with no discernible patterning in mind. Blades and flakes resulting from core reduction of chert nodules common in the site area provided material for nearly half (nine) of the end scrapers (Figure 2.71a–h, q). Working edges are convex to nearly straight and may or may not be at right angles to the longitudinal axis of the flake. Single spurs (Figure 2.71g) or double spurs (Figure 2.71d) may be present at the corners of the working edge. The working edge of one specimen is accentuated sharply by flaking into the edges of the tool on both sides directly below the corners of the working edge (Figure 2.71m). One unique specimen (Figure 2.71f) has two directly opposed working edges. Another specimen has a slightly asymmetrical working edge and a graver point at one corner of the basal end (Figure 2.71n). One other specimen has a small, sharp graver point on one side, adjacent to one end of the working edge (Figure 2.71a). One specimen (Figure 2.71q) is a wide, core reduction flake with a narrow scraping edge placed at the extreme distal end of the flake directly opposite the striking platform.

Wear on working edges is light to moderate and takes the form of a polish or abrasion at one extreme and step-fracturing at the other extreme. The working edge of one specimen (Figure 2.71i) is dulled, and wear striations at right angles to the working edge are visible. On this specimen the wear has advanced to the extent that the working edge is continuously and evenly smoothed. On other specimens (e.g., Figure 2.71c) the wear has polished the projecting points on the working edge. On the specimen shown in Figure 2.71m the wear was extremely heavy, and the working edge had been largely reshaped by the re-

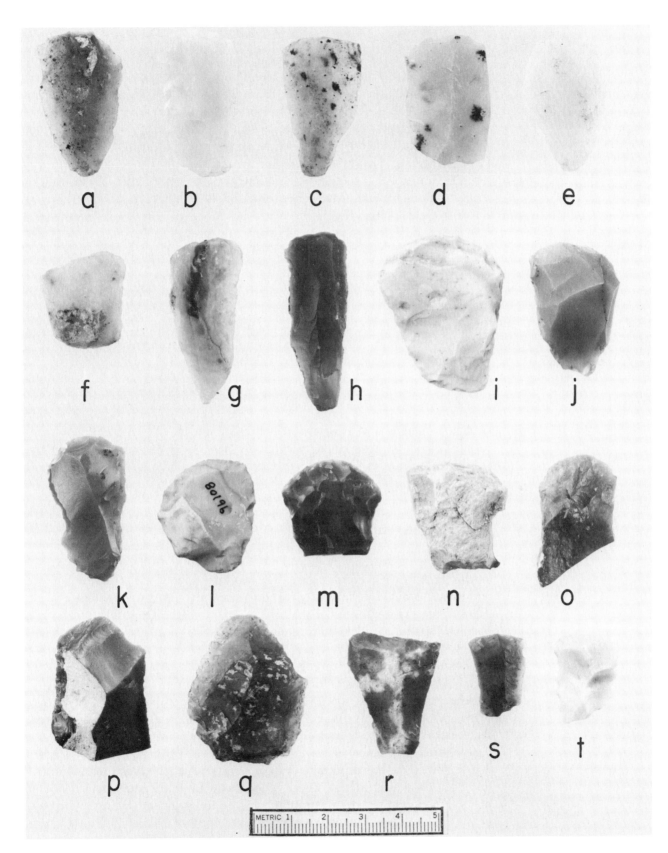

FIGURE 2.71 **End scrapers from the Agate Basin level in Area 2.**

moval of small step-fractures. Working-edge angles vary from one very low value of 55–60° (Figure 2.71p) to around 75–85° for most of the remaining specimens. Low edge angles are found on working edges of end scrapers made from broken flakes, rather than on those made in the more stylized manner where working edges are opposite the bulbs of percussion on selected core reduction flakes. We do not at this time know the significance of this difference in edge angle.

One unusual end scraper was collected by Roberts, presumably in 1942 in Area 1, although exact provenience is lacking. It is a typical end scraper (Figure 2.64a) but much larger than any other in any of the site collections. It is made of a coarse-grained, local quartzite and the working edge angle is 62°. Only a very light dulling of the projections along the working edge can be detected.

Wedges. Several badly fragmented pieces of large percussion flakes with evidence of deliberate edge preparation may be stone wedges that were used for tasks such as bone splitting. Two specimens were reconstructed from debitage recovered in the bone bed level. Both (Figure 2.66q, r) were broken by heavy impact and both have deliberately prepared edges (54° and 48° edge angles) opposite the areas of heavy impact. Both specimens were also structurally able (9.1 mm and 9.9 mm in thickness) to withstand sustained, intensive use. Another specimen (Figure 2.66s) demonstrates deliberate preparation of a wide wedge at one end and a somewhat battered platform end opposite. One hammerstone from the bone bed demonstrates use on one end that is identical to that produced by splitting large animal bones experimentally with wedges.

Bifaces   Biface tools constitute a significant part of the Agate Basin tool assemblage. A smaller number appear to have been discarded in the process of manufacture. One specimen (Figure 2.72a) is complete, bipointed in outline form and plano-convex in transverse cross-section. The working edge is the most convex side and it was formed by flaking toward one face only. The working-edge angle is 40° and the side opposite the working edge was deliberately dulled to form a backing. It is an excellent cutting tool.

Another specimen (Figure 2.72b) is similar, but the transverse cross-section is lenticular and the working edge was formed by a bilateral flaking. The working edge is similar in outline form to that of the first tool and the opposite edge is also backed. One other specimen (Figure 2.72f) is apparently a smaller version of the first two. It was made by a bilateral flaking on a long, thin (5–6 mm) flake. Both edges are sharp with no evidence of backing.

Whether two other bifaces in the University of Wyoming collection (Figure 2.73a, c) were tools is uncertain. Both demonstrate slightly more preparation of one edge compared to the other, which could be interpreted as evidence of deliberate working-edge preparation. One biface fragment (Figure 2.73d) appears to have been broken in manufacture; another (Figure 2.73b) was discarded in an early stage of manufacture. One specimen (Figure 2.72e) is considered a biface tool. The working-edge angle is 38°, and the tool was apparently made by percussion shaping applied to a piece of a broken biface.

Four specimens in the Roberts collection should also be mentioned in the biface category although their exact provenience is not known. One (Figure 2.73j) is probably a midsection of an Agate Basin projectile point that was reworked into a double-ended scraper. One working edge is straight with a sharp graver point at one corner. The other working edge is rounded but slightly asymmetrical in outline form. Both edges demonstrate use-wear in the form of a polish. Another biface may have been a small knife. It resembles a projectile point in outline form (Figure 2.73k) but the base was not completed and the biface could not be hafted as a projectile point in its present condition. The third specimen (Figure 2.73f) is a thick (21 mm) exhausted core with the edges percussion flaked to form a chopper-like tool. The last specimen is the end of a cutting tool (Figure 2.73i) that was backed on one side and a sharp cutting edge (edge angle 38°) was formed opposite. These tools were probably recovered from Area 1.

Four broken bifaces were recovered in the Bass and Roberts excavations in 1961. One (Figure 2.73e) was from Area 1; the other three (Figure 2.73g, h, l) were found in Area 2 and are broken tools. Included also in the biface category are two cutting tools of plate chalcedony. The largest (Figure 2.72c) is 8.5 mm thick and demonstrates a bilateral percussion retouch to form a working-edge angle of 30°. The other specimen (Figure 2.72d) is smaller and thinner (7.0 mm) and has a greater working-edge angle (42°). Both may have been parts of larger tools although both also demonstrate evidence of use in their present form.

Choppers.   One smoothed quartzite cobble 42 mm thick (Figure 2.74, bottom) was shaped into a chopper with a pointed end; another cobble 39 mm thick was shaped into a chopper with a wide point (Figure 2.74, top). The wide proximal end of each of these tools fits comfortably into the palm of the hand and both suggest carefully selected raw materials and prepared working edges. Working-edge angles are 76° and 50° respectively and modification was by percussion flaking.

Five other, larger choppers are also of quartzite but of a grade definitely inferior to that of the first two specimens. Angular blocks of coarse-grained quartzite occur locally and these choppers were crudely shaped from selected blocks of this material. There was little care in edge preparation other than to form sharp working edges (Figure 2.75) that vary in outline form from sharp to wide points. Percussion flakes of this material were present in the bone level, suggesting either manufacture or reshaping of these tools or both in the bone bed at the site. The material is difficult to flake with separation commonly occurring along natural cleavage planes. These choppers are identical in material and similar in manufacture technology and size to choppers from the Folsom level in Area 2.

Hammerstones.   Three small hammerstones (Figure 2.69a–c) were recovered. All are selected river cobbles and could account for the kind of stone flaking activity present. A larger specimen (Figure 2.76) is a quartzite cobble with evidence of battering on both the wide and pointed ends. It could have been used in percussion work to shape the larger choppers and/or drive wedges, as has been mentioned.

METRIC 1 2 3 4 5

FIGURE 2.72A,B Bifaces from the Agate Basin level in Area 2.

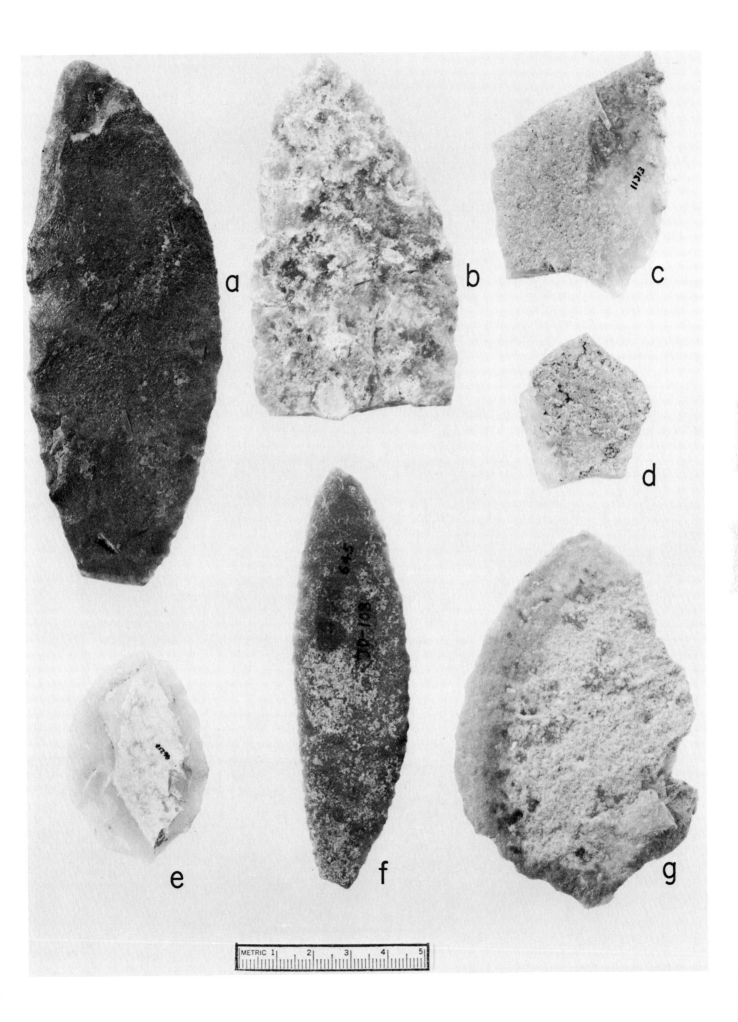

FIGURE 2.73A,B **Bifaces from the Agate Basin levels in Areas 1 and 2.**

a   b   c   d

e

f   g   h

i   j   k   l

METRIC 1   2   3   4   5

FIGURE 2.74   Choppers from the Agate Basin level in Area 2.

Cores   Core technology is treated fully in Chapter 3 and there is only minimal secondary use suggested of used cores as tools. Of over 25 exhausted cores, only 2 specimens (Figure 2.70e, i) demonstrate small areas of battering and step-fracturing on a point or end that may have resulted from deliberate modification and use as small choppers. All cores are of chert obtained in the immediate site vicinity.

FIGURE 2.75 Chopper from the Agate Basin level in Area 2.

FIGURE 2.76   **Hammerstone from the Agate Basin level in Area 2.**

Flakes   The Agate Basin component in Area 1 produced over 4000 flakes. Most of these (by number) were recovered by water-screening of the cultural deposits. Most are quartzite. A smaller percentage are chert and a very few are porcellanite. The great bulk of flakes (by weight) resulted from core and biface reduction; tool-sharpening flakes are relatively rare. In fact, fewer than 10 flakes can be satisfactorily identified as sharpening flakes of the distinctive Knife River flint or similar material, although 7 (22%) of the 32 large tools in the Agate Basin component bone bed are of this material.

Five flakes represent a sharpening effort on one tool from Area 2 made of a distinctive yellow chert (Figure 2.63f) but only a small area of the total working edge of the tool was involved. Other attempts to match sharpening flakes to working edges of tools were not successful. Although large areas of the Agate Basin level were lost the data sample is still large enough to suggest that most tool and projectile point manufacture occurred elsewhere, and that the nature of tool use at Area 2 required a minimum amount of sharpening of tool edges.

Four flakes resulting from projectile point impact were recovered in the Agate Basin assemblages. Projectile point impact on substances such as bone is manifest in several distinctive ways. In most cases, readily identifiable flake types result. Although some impact flakes resemble and can be misidentified as Folsom channel flakes, they are usually distinctive enough to be properly identified. A distinctive feature in this kind of impact-flake removal is a channel similar to that on a Folsom point, beginning at the tip and extending toward the base of the projectile point. An excellent example is present in the Agate Basin projectile point assemblage (Figure 2.53l). One impact flake resembling a Folsom channel flake was matched to the projectile point from which it was removed (Figure 2.59c, d).

Another form of impact flake is a long sliver removed from the blade edge of a projectile point, as can be seen in Figure 2.53n. Two such flakes were recovered in the water-screening in the Agate Basin bone bed matrix. Impact can also result in the shattering of the tip or areas near the tip of the projectile point into fragments so minute that they are seldom recovered. Other results of projectile point impact in bison kills have been described in the context of a Hell Gap bison kill (see Frison 1974:96–98).

Projectile Point Tools

Although approximately 169 known Agate Bison projectile points in all stages of completeness were recovered by excavation and in the immediate vicinity of Areas 1 and 2, there is no evidence to suggest any systematic use or reuse of projectile points as tools. Reshaping of projectile points was a regular occurrence, but this seems to have been mostly for the purpose of reusing them as projectile points, not as tools. Possible exceptions include one specimen recovered by Roberts (Figure 2.73j). However, too little of the original artifact remains to determine whether or not it was originally a projectile point, and its provenience is lacking. Two broken pieces recovered by Bass and Roberts (Figure 2.56h, n) may have been projectile points reused as tools, but they may also have been originally intended as biface tools.

It can be argued that to disdain use of projectile points as tools subsequent to their use as projectile points is not rational behavior, since a complete or broken part of a projectile point may be substituted for a limited number of functional tool types without any modification. However, if Agate Basin projectile points were reused as tools, no attempt was made to alter the morphology of the projectile points or fragments thereof into what would be considered more usable tool shapes. Also, the projectile points recovered in the bone bed do not demonstrate use on the edges comparable to that on the tools.

Experimentation with stone projectile points has revealed much with regard to the damage a stone point undergoes in the process of killing large animals. We know, for example, that impact can remove burin-like spalls from the blade edges of a projectile point upon contact with a rib. In an earlier publication (Frison 1978b:161, 167) it was argued that the presence of five superimposed burin spalls along one blade edge of an Agate Basin projectile point (Figure 2.53b) was difficult to regard as the result of impact, and that it probably resulted from a deliberate burination of the edge to produce either a burin or burin spalls to be used as tools. The truth in this situation is still far from clear.

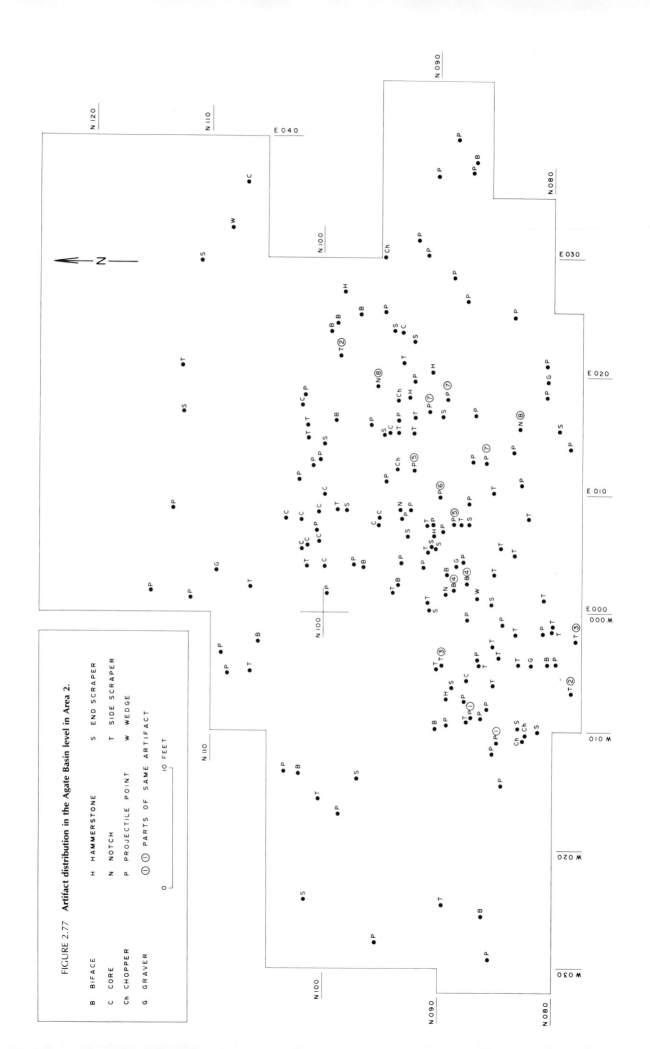

FIGURE 2.77 **Artifact distribution in the Agate Basin level in Area 2.**

B BIFACE   H HAMMERSTONE   S END SCRAPER

C CORE   N NOTCH   T SIDE SCRAPER

Ch CHOPPER   P PROJECTILE POINT W WEDGE

G GRAVER   ① ① PARTS OF SAME ARTIFACT

0   10 FEET

Further experimentation with impact at velocities generated by a throwing stick has produced a wide range of results, so that, based on better evidence, the damage to this particular specimen may have very possibly resulted from impact.

Provenience Summary

Proveniences of projectile points and tools are known for the artifact materials recovered in the Bass and Roberts and University of Wyoming–Smithsonian excavations (Figure 2.77). The proveniences of 11 projectile points and 2 tools are also known from Area 1 (Figure 2.78). The 3 projectile points in Area 1 from outside the Bass and Roberts and University of Wyoming–Smithsonian excavations were found in a small part of the site in which point collectors missed the bottom of the bone bed. The tools from Area 1 include a side scraper (Figure 2.64k) and a biface fragment (Figure 2.73e). Projectile points include 6 from the 1961 Bass and Roberts excavations (Figure 2.56f, j–l, p, q) and 5 from the University of Wyoming–Smithsonian excavations in 1975 (Figure 2.55c, e, g–i). Too few bones were left in place in Area 1 to justify a bone bed map.

THE SCHULTZ SITE ARTIFACTS

The Schultz site is an exposure of an Agate Basin component about 650 m down Moss Agate Arroyo from Area 2 and about 100 m from the mouth of a small tributary arroyo that empties into it (Figure 1.4, Area 8). It was originally either in or along the old arroyo, which was then located some distance west of the present one. The Schultz site was exposed by cutting of the present tributary

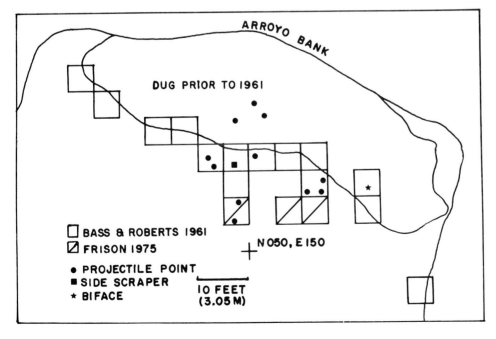

FIGURE 2.78 **Artifact distribution in the Agate Basin level in Area 1.**

FIGURE 2.79 Schultz site artifacts (a–i), artifacts from below the Folsom level in Area 3 (j, k), a Folsom projectile point preform from the Folsom level in Area 2 (l), and two notched projectile points from the surface in the Agate Basin locality (m, n).

arroyo through the deposits in the old arroyo. Only a small test excavation was made here and the results indicated the possibility of an extensive in situ Agate Basin component. However, most of the cultural material recovered was not in situ but was exposed by recent widening of the present arroyo.

Two projectile points were found, one (Figure 2.79a) a midsection, and the other (Figure 2.79b) a base. Shape and manufacture technology are unmistakably Agate Basin. The former was made of a distinctive light-brown chert of unknown origin and the latter was made of a light-tan, fine-grained quartzite that probably was derived from the Morrison (Upper Jurassic) formation. Exposures of this material are numerous and widespread, allowing little possibility of determining an actual quarry source.

Three tools—a small light chopper (Figure 2.79e), a large end scraper (Figure 2.79h), and a part of a biface tool (Figure 2.79d)—are of the same light-brown chert as the projectile point midsection. The chopper was made from a piece of plate chert and is 7.5 mm thick; the rounded point was formed by percussion flaking from both sides. The end scraper was made on a large, broken percussion flake and the working edge is worn from use. It is slightly thicker (8.5 mm) than the chopper and the dorsal flake surface is flat, suggesting that it was struck from another piece of plate chert. The biface fragment (Figure 2.79d) may have been one broken in manufacture, but one end demonstrated heavy use that could have occurred either before or after it was broken. It was made on a piece of plate chert 7 mm thick. Two percussion flakes of this same material (Figure 2.79g, i) demonstrate use-wear on part of their edges.

In addition to these, an end scraper (Figure 2.79c) and a large retouched flake tool (Figure 2.79f) were recovered. Both were made from the local, light-colored, translucent chert. These two specimens are heavily patinated. A bison scapula, a thoracic vertebra, and several long-bone and rib fragments were the only other cultural material recovered in the test. The tan-colored chert to date is alien to other site components in the locality and may be an indication of an Agate Basin occupation separate from that in Areas 1 and 2.

4.   HELL GAP COMPONENTS
george c. frison

Hell Gap components were present above the Folsom components in Area 3. A small in situ bison bone bed was discovered in the first Hell Gap level (Figure 2.80). The presence of other bones deeper in the old arroyo deposits in this area may have resulted largely from cutting into this Hell Gap bone level by later erosional events (see Figure 2.9). The original extent of this bone level is not known, but the edge of it was found by Bass and Roberts in their 1961 excavations. It may also have been reached by the Brewster site excavations in

FIGURE 2.80 **Part of the Hell Gap bone bed in the first Hell Gap level in Area 3.**

1959. This is strongly suggested by the base of a Hell Gap projectile point (Figure 2.56r) found in the wall of the Brewster site by Bass and Roberts in 1961 at what should have been about the right depth. Excavations by the University of Wyoming–Smithsonian team in 1977, 1979, and 1980 required the removal of large amounts of overburden in order to expose more of the bone bed.

The stratigraphy of the site is interesting (Figure 2.8) in that what appears to be a single Hell Gap component divides into two and probably three components farther down the old arroyo from the bone bed. There is, however, no indication of what the separation between the levels represents in passage of time. The accumulation of interim deposits could conceivably represent a very short passage of time, even as little as a few days.

THE MAIN HELL GAP LEVEL

The main Hell Gap level consists of the bone bed, which terminates abruptly close to a hearth (Figure 2.81). The bone and artifact inventory in the bone bed area differs significantly from that in the vicinity of the hearth. This

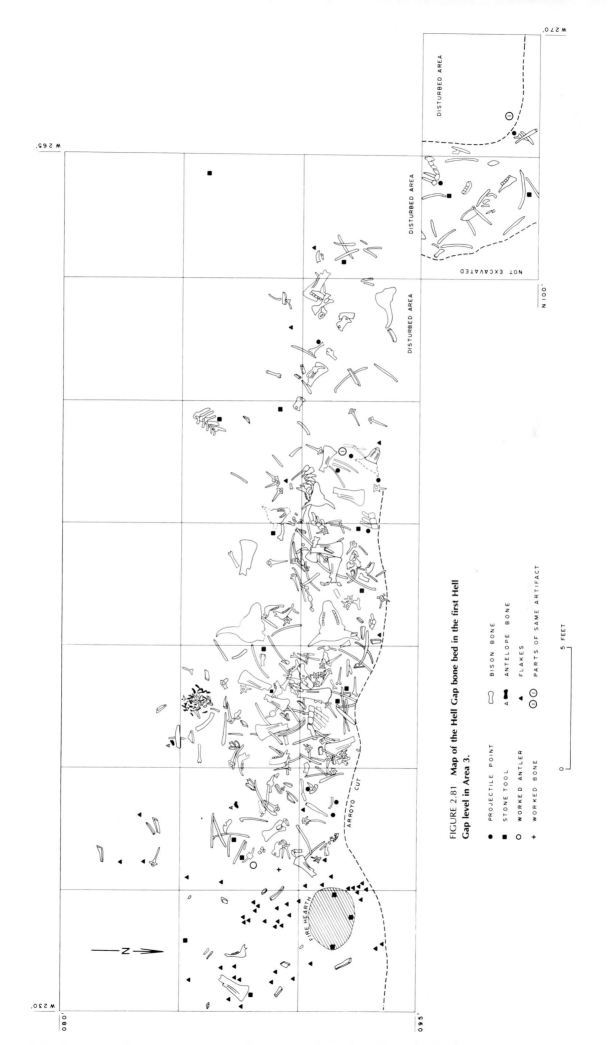

FIGURE 2.81 Map of the Hell Gap bone bed in the first Hell Gap level in Area 3.

PROJECTILE POINT
STONE TOOL
WORKED ANTLER
WORKED BONE

BISON BONE
ANTELOPE BONE
FLAKES
PARTS OF SAME ARTIFACT

0   5 FEET

DISTURBED AREA

NOT EXCAVATED

DISTURBED AREA

DISTURBED AREA

ARROYO CUT

FIRE HEARTH

N

W 265'

W 270'

W 230'

N 100'

080'

095'

FIGURE 2.82   **Sandstone abrader from the first Hell Gap level in Area 3.**

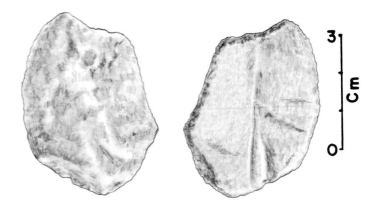

feature is contained within a shallow, oval shaped basin about 7 cm in maximum depth. Combustion within the hearth was nearly complete with only white ash and no charcoal remaining. Several calcined bone fragments and fire-fractured stone tools and flakes were included in the contents of the hearth. One of the tools is a wide quartzite scraper (Figure 2.41v) with both straight (edge angle 55°) and convex (edge angle 55–76°) working edges. It was damaged by heat; two other chipped stone tools were damaged beyond identification as to tool type. At least five biface reduction flakes may have been made into tools but were damaged by heat to the extent that unequivocal evidence for this was lost.

At the edge of the hearth was a sandstone abrader (Figure 2.82). The abraded side is flattened and marked with several grooves at different angles. It may have been an edge-grinding tool used in conjunction with stone flaking. In fact, the quantity and kind of flakes in the area around the hearth indicate both pressure-flaking and percussion-flaking activities. The only other functionally identifiable chipped stone tool from the vicinity of the hearth was a small graver (Figure 2.41t) with an extremely sharp, delicate point. Bone and antler artifacts and manufacture technology are discussed in another section.

The remainder of the Hell Gap artifact assemblage in this level is associated with the bison bone bed. There are seven Hell Gap projectile points (Figures 2.83a–f; 2.56t) with tapered stems and pronounced shoulders. Edge grinding is present on the lateral edges to the beginning of the shoulder. Bases are slightly convex (Figure 2.83f) to rounded (Figure 2.83d), and in the latter case the base is ground. The base of one (Figure 2.56t) was broken at an angle but both corners were ground to remove the sharp corner. The distal end also appears to have been reshaped, and the point was probably reused. This specimen is in two pieces. The distal part was recovered by Bass and Roberts in 1961 and the base was recovered by the University of Wyoming–Smithsonian team in 1977.

The distal end of another specimen (Figure 2.83c) demonstrates reworking, but two others (Figure 2.83a, b) do not. On another specimen recovered by Roberts and Bass (Figure 2.56m) both corners of the broken base were removed by short burin-like spalls and the corners were then ground to remove sharp points. This is identical to a method used in rejuvenating the base of Agate Basin projectile points for reuse.

Two specimens (Figure 2.83d, e) appear to have been heavily impacted, and

FIGURE 2.83   **Hell Gap projectile points (a–f) and flake tools (g–i, k–o) from the first Hell Gap level in Area 3, and a flake tool (j) found nearby.**

both suggest reuse as tools. Sharp edges on both specimens are dulled, suggesting they may have been used as tools while hafted.

The Hell Gap projectile points closely resemble specimens from the Casper site (Frison 1974), which was also a Hell Gap bison kill. The Hell Gap components at both Casper and Agate Basin did not provide good evidence for projectile point manufacture. However, the manufacture technology proposed by Bradley (1974) is probably valid for both Hell Gap components.

At least two Hell Gap projectile points are in the Roberts Smithsonian collection (Figure 2.50e, m) and another (Figure 2.50s) is probably a midsection, but provenience data are lacking. One Hell Gap projectile point (Figure 2.54a) was recovered in the University of Wyoming excavations in the Agate Basin level in Area 2; Hell Gap points also occurred as surface finds in the vicinity of Areas 1 and 2 (Figures 2.57o, p).

The remainder of the artifacts from the Hell Gap bone bed are flake tools of the kind commonly used in butchering and processing large animals. A quartzite side scraper (Figure 2.83g) has one straight and two convex working edges (edge angles 60°, 52°, and 45°). Another specimen (Figure 2.83i) has one straight and one concave edge (edge angles 68° and 60°). Still another (Figure 2.83l) has a concave and a convex working edge (edge angles 60°). A different type of tool (Figure 2.83h) has a short, prepared scraping edge (edge angle 62°) opposite the bulb of percussion. The remainder of the flake edge exclusive of the bulb of percussion is unmodified but demonstrates use as a cutting tool (edge angle 24–28°). Six other fragments are probably parts of similar tools. Another side scraper (Figure 2.83j) was a surface find in the modern arroyo adjacent to the Hell Gap exposure. Although similar in morphology to the others, it provenience is questionable.

The items remaining are flake cutting tools with low working-edge angles (25–30°). Two of chert (Figure 2.83m, n) and one of quartzite (Figure 2.83k) have no edge preparation and demonstrate only use-wear. The last one (Figure 2.83o) was made of porcellanite and has a working edge prepared by a careful pressure flaking that is dulled from use.

Flakes

A total of 1068 flakes were recovered in the upper Hell Gap level. Most were relatively small and were recovered on water-screens. Thirty-four of these from the bone bed area may be tool-sharpening flakes, and these represent only a sample of water-screened deposits from the Hell Gap bone bed area because of equipment failure that prematurely terminated water screening. One of the tools in particular (Figure 2.83i) has the appearance of one that was resharpened repeatedly and was about ready to be discarded. This strongly suggests more tool sharpening than in the Agate Basin level in Area 2 and may have resulted from somewhat different site activities in the two situations.

THE SECOND HELL GAP LEVEL

As illustrated by the profiles in Figure 2.8 and 2.9, the Hell Gap levels appear to merge into a single level at the bone bed in the upstream direction. A second lower productive Hell Gap level appears at the east edge of the excavated area and probably continues downstream. A hearth in a shallow basin (8 cm deep) is present in this level and it is similar to the one in the level above. Tools, projectile points, flakes, and bison bone fragments are present in and around the hearth area (Figure 2.84).

Assembly of several fire-fractured pieces produced the proximal end of an unmistakable Hell Gap projectile point (Figure 2.41, l) made of chert, and the base of a quartzite specimen (Figure 2.41m) was burned but not fragmented. Edge grinding is present to the shoulder of the first specimen and on the edges of the second, which broke just below the shoulder. The base of the first specimen is rounded, whereas the base of the second is straight; no basal grinding is present on either.

One quartzite side scraper (Figure 2.41s) with a convex working edge (edge angle 52°) demonstrates intensive scraping wear in the form of use-flake detachment on the distal end. The edge opposite the scraping edge was backed by grinding. A quartzite percussion-flake tool (Figure 2.41w) has a carefully prepared, flaked, convex cutting edge (edge angle 34°). The opposite edges of this tool are also backed by grinding or cutting use or both. A piece of plate chalcedony 5.6 mm thick has a bilateral percussion retouch along one edge to form a cutting tool (edge angle 35–40°). Sharp projections on the opposite edge have been reduced by grinding (Figures 2.41x and 2.85a).

Smaller tools include a sharp graver point on a relatively thick (4.3 mm) flake. Two other less prominent graver points are spaced around the edge of the same tool (Figure 2.41n). A composite tool found in two pieces (Figure 2.41u and 2.85b) was made on a relatively thick (9 mm) percussion flake. Sharp graver points were placed opposite the bulb of percussion and also on the lateral edge. Between these two are two dull projections that demonstrate heavy use, the remaining naturally steep edges (48° and 50°) on both sides of the bulb of percussion demonstrate intensive scraping use in the form of a combination of small step-fractures and abrading. A long, narrow graver point on a relatively thick (5 mm) flake has a notch opposite the graver point (Figure 2.41r).

Another tool has a graver point placed adjacent to a scraping edge (edge angle 72°) and could be classified as an end scraper with a graver point at one corner of the working edge. Scraping use produced a fine but extensive step-fracturing of the working edge (Figure 2.41p). Another end scarper (edge angle 84°) has a definite spur at one corner of the working edge accentuated by a shallow notch (Figure 2.41q). The specimen was broken and both pieces were recovered. The nature of the breakage strongly suggests that the specimen was hafted in order to increase leverage and improve control during use.

Several core and biface reduction flakes were found around the hearth; many of these were fire fractured. Only one (Figure 2.41o) is unquestionably a tool. It is a relatively thin (2.7 mm) flake with a carefully pressure-flaked concavity or notch (working-edge angle 64°) on one side.

None of the bison bone fragments in the second Hell Gap level demonstrate any evidence of modification, but a modified antler tine was recovered and is described in a later section.

In addition to the larger flakes in the second Hell Gap level (Figure 2.84), there were 1650 small flakes recovered by water-screening. These resulted from

Flakes

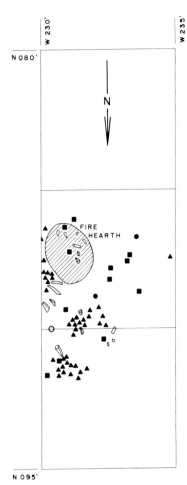

FIGURE 2.84 **Map of the second Hell Gap level in Area 3.**

● PROJECTILE POINT
■ STONE TOOL
▱ BISON BONE
○ WORKED ANTLER
▲ FLAKES

0   5 FEET

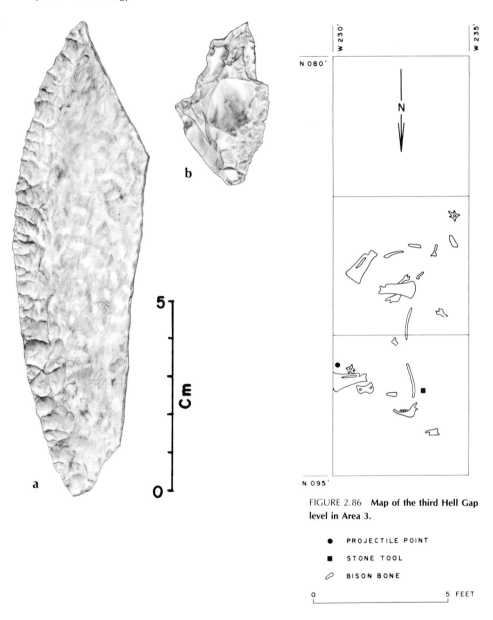

FIGURE 2.85   **Plate chalcedony knife (a) and a flake tool (b) from the second Hell Gap level in Area 3.**

FIGURE 2.86   **Map of the third Hell Gap level in Area 3.**

● PROJECTILE POINT

■ STONE TOOL

⬭ BISON BONE

0   5 FEET

both pressure and percussion work. They are about equally divided between quartzite and chert. No cores or bifaces broken in manufacture were present in either the first or second Hell Gap levels, but parts of both levels remain intact.

THE THIRD HELL GAP LEVEL

Below the second Hell Gap level is another level containing only bison bone and 11 mm of the base of what appears to be a Hell Gap projectile point (Figure 2.86). A piece of a flat quartzite river cobble 7 mm thick, 84 mm wide, and 132 mm long bears no convincing evidence of modification or use but was certainly brought in by human activity and is therefore regarded as a tool. The bison bone consists of both complete bones and fragments but no articulated units. Some also appear to have been broken during butchering and processing activities.

5. THE SHEAMAN SITE: A CLOVIS COMPONENT

george c. frison

The Sheaman site is near the divide between Moss Agate Creek and the Cheyenne River (Figure 1.4, Area 9). A few meters directly east of the site exposure in a small connecting arroyo is a small spring that flows nearly all year, and it may have been instrumental in determining the site location. The Clovis cultural component was exposed through lateral erosion of the arroyo to the east of the spring and only a part remained of what may have originally been a large site. A significant part was lost through digging by artifact hunters (see Figure 2.87a) prior to 1977.

The Clovis cultural materials lay in the bottom of what was at that time a small swale or arroyo with a flat bottom and gently sloping sides. It may have resembled the present arroyo in which the entire bottom is grass covered, and it is too near its headwaters to collect enough water to create a channel through the bottom, as happens a short distance downstream. Several alternating light and dark strata appear in profile (Figure 2.88), but these are apparently paleosols and not of cultural origin.

FIGURE 2.87   **Map of the Sheaman site and excavations (a), and feature and artifact distributions (b).**

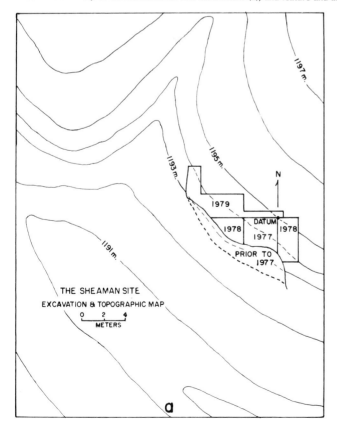
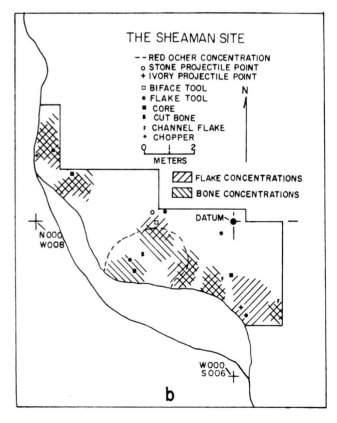

FIGURE 2.88 **Looking north (a, b) and east (c) at the Sheaman site excavations.**

Particularly noticeable in the Clovis cultural component is an oval-shaped area of soil stained with red ocher about 2.5 × 3 m, and from 5 to 8 cm thick (see Figure 2.87b). Most of the red ocher could be seen as a stain or dispersed small particles, although several lumps were recovered. The largest of these lumps is about 5.0 cm in diameter and 1.6 cm thick. The other lumps are much smaller. Two broken bison bones, a distal humerus (Figure 2.89a) and a proximal tibia (Figure 2.89b), were recovered in this area of the site, and both the outside surfaces and the interior cavities were coated with a thick layer of ocher-

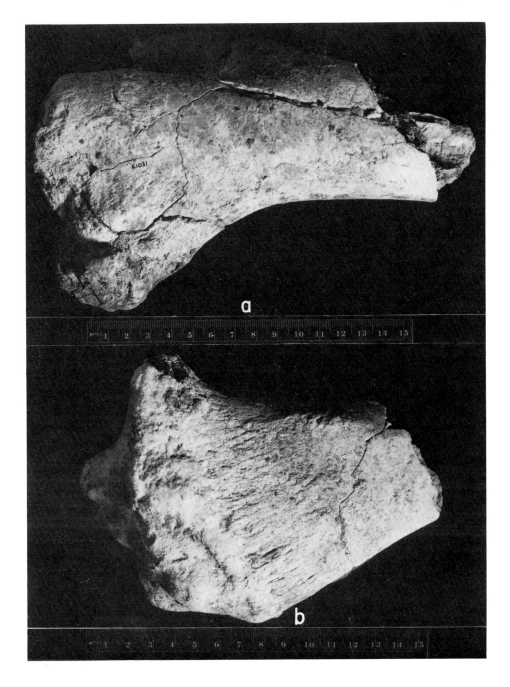

FIGURE 2.89   **Bison humerus (a) and tibia (b) heavily coated with red ocher from the Sheaman site.**

impregnated soil. There is a strong suggestion that the two bones had originally been coated with red ocher, both inside and out, and that some of this ocher had subsequently transferred to the surrounding soil after the bones were covered with alluvium.

Several other bison bone fragments were in the red ocher area and these also were stained with red ocher. Outside this area were several light concentrations of fragmented bison bone. Identifiable among these were a badly burned and decomposed occipital region of a skull, a distal part of an ilium, several rib and thoracic vertebra fragments, a nearly complete dorsal spine of a thoracic vertebra, part of a mandible of a newborn calf, and several individual teeth. Most of the bone outside the red ocher area was coated with a layer of caliche up to 5 mm thick.

No hearths were present in the Clovis level but some charcoal was recovered from immediately above it. This charcoal resulted from an event or events postdating the Clovis occupation. Evidence to support this is seen in the debitage. Flakes in the Clovis level demonstrate a wide range of heat-treating, fracturing, and color alteration. Most of the debitage resulted from biface reduction. Flakes near the top of the Clovis cultural level were fire fractured; these farther down in the level demonstrate different degrees of color alteration, and those still farther down were unaltered. The heat from the fire appears to have been remarkably intense and its effects penetrated a good share of the Clovis cultural level.

The present hypothesis is that the source of the charcoal was a fire in the old

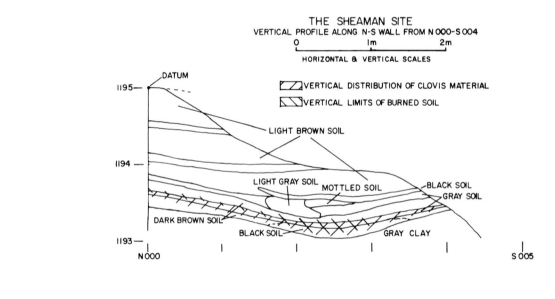

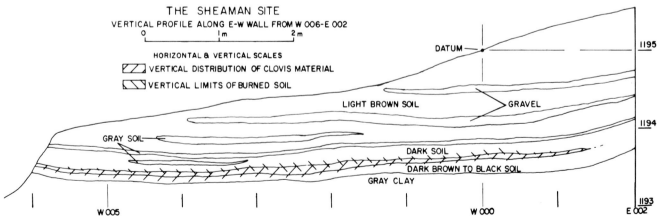

FIGURE 2.90   North–south and east–west profiles at the Sheaman site.

arroyo bottom of sufficient intensity to fracture flakes at or near the surface and alter the color of flakes in relation to their distance from the heat (see Figure 2.90). The time of this fire is suggested by two radiocarbon dates of slightly over 10,000 years B.P. (see Table 2.2 in Section 8, this chapter: RL-1000, RL-1241) or what should be approximately 1000 years later than the Clovis occupation. The fire in question was more than a simple grass fire since considerable heat over a period of time is required to bring the soil to the proper temperature for the successful heat altering of chert, which did occur in this case. Perhaps the arroyo bottom had a thick cover of brush and/or trees at that time. One piece of charcoal from the fire level can be identified to *Populus* sp., which could be quaking aspen (*Populus tremuloides*).

North–south (Figure 2.90a) and east–west (Figure 2.90b) profiles strongly indicate a shallow swale trending from northwest to southeast, and continuing into the wall at E 002m. There is no noticeable channel present in the old swale bottom, which is much like the present-day condition. However, as has been mentioned, a noticeable channel does develop in the modern arroyo a short distance downstream from the site location. There is apparently enough vegetation this close to the head of the arroyo to prevent channel formation until a point farther downstream where increased runoff water is able to penetrate the heavy grass cover.

The Clovis component in the area west of the north–south line through the site datum appears to be in situ, as demonstrated by the flake, bone, and red ocher concentrations. East of this line, however, the cultural materials and their surrounding sediments begin to acquire an aspect of having been moved by stream action. Some of these stream-transported cultural materials remain unexcavated in the bank to the east and south of the excavated area (see Figure 2.87). All indications are that the old arroyo or swale meanders back into the course of the present arroyo a few meters downstream from the south limits of the excavations and disappears.

ARTIFACTS

Two artifacts were recovered by James Duguid from the Sheaman site. One is a chert biface broken during manufacture, which was modified with a bilateral percussion retouch along one edge to form a cutting edge (Figure 2.91a). The biface demonstrates an unquestionable excellence in biface reduction technology. It was apparently broken during manufacture as a result of a flaw in the material. The bilateral retouch was applied subsequent to this manufacture breakage, indicating that it is a complete artifact in its present form and not one broken after it was made. The other specimen is probably a projectile point preform (Figure 2.91b) manufactured from a distinctive banded quartzite. Several flakes of material similar to the latter were recovered in situ in the Clovis component, strongly indicating that the specimen did originate in the Clovis component. However, no flakes resulting from manufacture of this particular biface were recovered. Duguid is confident of the provenience of both of these artifacts from within the Clovis component and since there is only a single component present, he is probably correct.

FIGURE 2.91A,B Bifaces (a, b), projectile point (c), flake tools (d, f), and three conjoined flakes (e) from the Sheaman site.

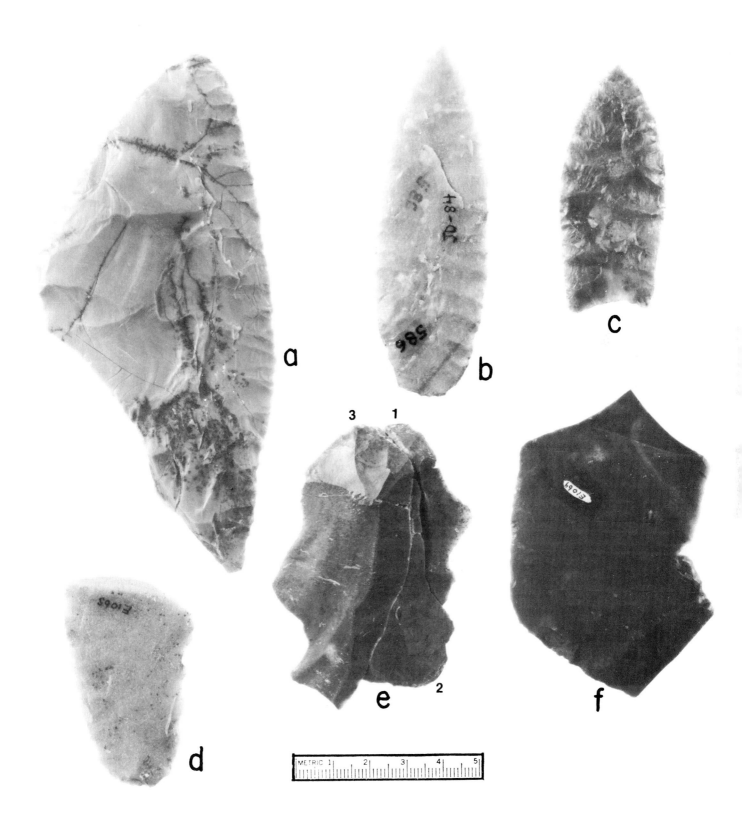

a

b

c

3 1

d

e 2

METRIC 1 2 3 4 5

f

METRIC 1 2 3 4 5

FIGURE 2.92 Biface reduction flake tools from the Sheaman site.

Five large biface reduction flakes (Figure 2.92a, b, d–f) that demonstrate evidence of tool use without further preparation of working edges were recovered from the spoil dirt at the Sheaman site. A similar flake (Figure 2.92c) was recovered in situ in the Clovis level. All of the first group were made of chert, although the latter is of quartzite. Two of the first group (Figure 2.92a, b) are of material identical to several flakes recovered in situ, and all probably resulted from reduction of the same two bifaces. There seems to be little reason to doubt that the five large biface flake tools came from the Clovis level.

Several other stone tools were recovered in the 1977–1979 excavations. One chert tool (Figure 2.91f) is a composite side scraper and double burin. The working edge (edge angle 47°) is straight and demonstrates intense use in the form of a number of small step-fractures. The working edge curves sharply on one end to form what could be considered an end-scraper edge adjacent to the side-scraper edge. End-scraper use is suggested also by the wear pattern.

Both ends of the tool are pointed. The points were formed by burin-like spalls in conjunction with snap breaks. Both sharp ends were used in a direction at right angles to the faces of the flake in a graver-like manner rather than as true burins.

A broken quartzite side scraper has a slightly convex working edge (edge angle 56°). The working edge on the ventral side of the flake was adjusted slightly by a careful percussion retouch (Figure 2.91d). The edge opposite the working edge is backed and there is no evidence of use subsequent to breakage. One chert percussion flake demonstrates a light percussion retouch on both sides adjacent to the striking platform (Figure 2.93a). The left side is a side scraper (edge angle 53°) and the right side is a cutting edge (edge angle 39°); both demonstrate intensive use. The wide, straight edge opposite the striking platform was modified by an intensive scraping use retouch (edge angle 72°).

Another chert side scraper (Figure 2.93b) is broken and badly damaged by heat (edge angle 52°). Heat damage to another chert side scraper (Figure 2.93c) was so extreme that only a fragment of a working edge remains. Another chert percussion flake was snapped transversely in two places (Figure 2.93f) and the right edge demonstrates a steep scraping edge (edge angle 57°). The opposite edge is a sharp cutting edge (edge angle 22°). Both working edges demonstrate intensive use but no use is evident on the transverse break. One large percussion flake (Figure 2.93d) and a much smaller one (Figure 2.93g), both of chert, demonstrate cutting use on one edge (working edges 37° and 35° respectively).

Two chert percussion flakes (Figure 2.93e, h) demonstrate deliberate preparation of convex projections that demonstrate end-scraper use (edge angles 56° and 68° respectively). The larger (Figure 2.93e) has a small area of the flake edge (directly opposite the scraper edge) that demonstrates light cutting use (edge angle 28°).

At least five other flakes demonstrate some suggestion of use by wear patterns that are only visible microscopically. Most of the Sheaman site debitage resulted from biface reduction, and two of the five specimens are broken flakes with barely perceptible use on the edges. In these two instances, the striking-platform ends of two adjacent overlapping flakes (Figure 2.91e, flakes 1 and 3) were found in a debitage pile. The distal ends demonstrating light cutting use were found some distance away. This is strongly indicative that there was care-

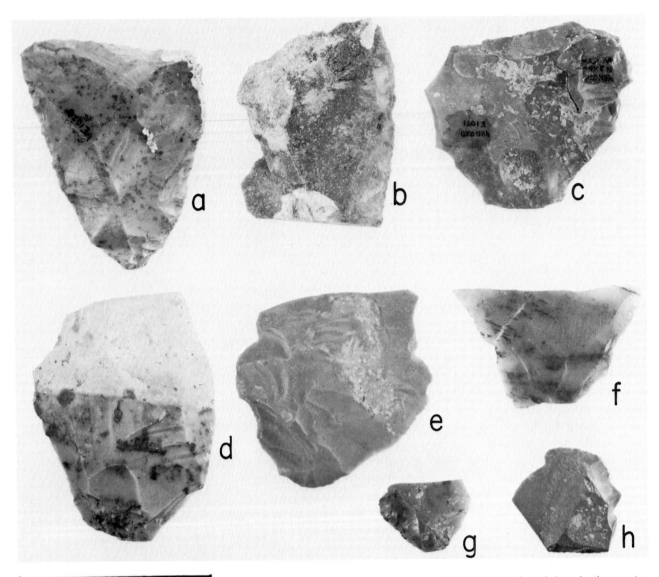

METRIC 1 2 3 4 5

FIGURE 2.93   **Flake tools from the Sheaman site.**

ful selection of the biface reduction flakes for future use as tools. A discussion of Clovis biface reduction strategies and a clearer figure of the conjoined flakes is presented in Chapter 3 (see Figure 3.13c, d).

Clovis Projectile Points   One chert projectile point 67.4 mm long and 29.3 mm wide demonstrates a slightly atypical Clovis manufacture technology in that the flutes have been obliterated to some extent by flaking subsequent to their removal. There is, however, no question that flutes are present. On one side the flute is 22.2 mm in length and is partially obscured by a parallel basal thinning flake 13.9 mm in length. On the opposite side, 20.4 mm of the flute is present. Flakes from the side to remove the step fractures at the end of the flutes are present. One corner of the base of the point is about 1.6 mm shorter than the other, giving the

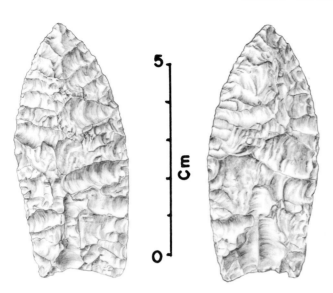

FIGURE 2.94 **Clovis point from the Sheaman site.**

specimen a slightly asymmetrical appearance. The lateral edges are ground for distances of 37.2 mm and 36.1 mm respectively (Figures 2.91c and 2.94).

There is a strong indication that this projectile point was reworked slightly along one side toward the base to correct a flaw of some sort, either a manufacture break or one through use. A definite reworking is observable unilaterally for a distance of 36 mm from the base of the short side. A reconstruction of the point with an addition to match the unmodified side results in a typical Clovis point. The correction of the flaw may have rendered the specimen undesirable to the extent that it was discarded.

Four flakes are unique in their morphology and are believed to be channel flakes. The basis for this determination is an unusual amount of platform preparation in relation to other flakes and/or their flake scar characteristics. One in particular (Figure 2.95) demonstrates grinding on the striking platform and flake scars that meet at right angles to the long axis of the flake. All four specimens are broken close to the striking platform, and a more positive identification would be possible if they were complete. Differences in overall projectile point manufacture technology between Folsom and Clovis make these far less distinctive than Folsom channel flakes, and consequently more difficult to identify.

Channel Flakes

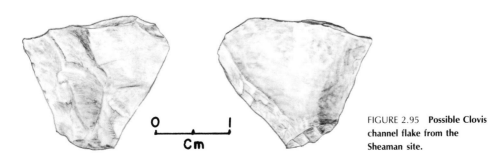

FIGURE 2.95 **Possible Clovis channel flake from the Sheaman site.**

Debitage   Flakes from the Sheaman site total 2792. All are chert, except 109, which are quartzite. Flaking-material sources are discussed later in this chapter but the raw materials at the Sheaman site are of exceptionally high quality for flaking purposes. These flakes appear to represent varying amounts of the reduction sequences of not more than 10 bifaces, and the partial cortex removal from one core. This determination was made on the basis of the color and texture of the raw materials and the context of the various flake concentrations. There were rather discrete boundaries of most the flake concentrations that, according to color and texture, had to derive from the same piece of material. As already mentioned, many flakes were altered in texture and color by heat. Once this was realized, however, it presented little problem since each separate piece of chert material contained dendrites with distinctive patterns that were not altered by the heat.

Further support for the argument that the debitage piles represent biface reduction is demonstrated by reassembly of flakes. In one instance, nearly one entire side and part of the other was reassembled, indicating that a biface no longer present had been produced (Figure 2.96). However, its size and shape strongly suggest that it was a projectile point preform. Its completion must have

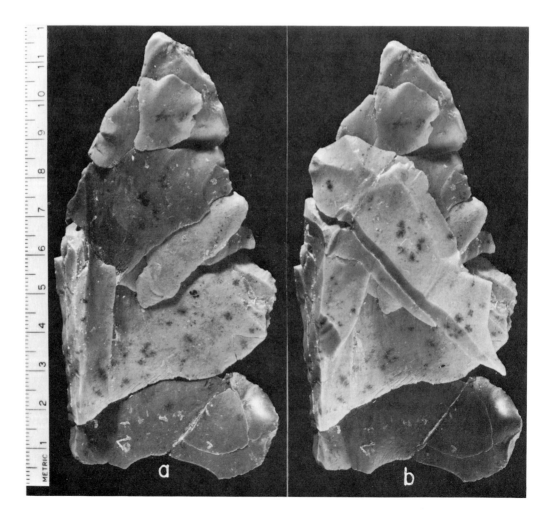

FIGURE 2.96 **Reassembled biface reduction flakes from the Sheaman site.**

5 CM
2 IN

FIGURE 2.97   **Core with several flakes reassembled from the Sheaman site.**

occurred elsewhere, since no flakes beyond the stage of completion represented here were recovered. Several other smaller flake reconstructions were also made, further supporting the argument for biface reduction as the main focus of lithic activity at the Sheaman site (Figures 3.13 and 3.14).

Cores

A core (Figure 2.97) bears evidence of considerable effort but little positive results in producing usable flakes. In fact, many of the cortex removal flakes could be reassembled and the core was discarded long before it was exhausted. This material, the agate found along Moss Agate Arroyo, was difficult to flake, and only a small portion of that available could be flaked with any degree of success. Clovis stone flaking technology as seen at the Sheaman site is discussed in Chapter 3.

Hammerstones

A split quartzite river cobble 39 mm thick (Figure 2.98) was shaped around its entire perimeter by a rough percussion flaking. Superimposed over this on the edges is a light pecking. The cobble resembles a tool from the Folsom level

FIGURE 2.98 **Split quartzite cobble tool from the Sheaman site.**

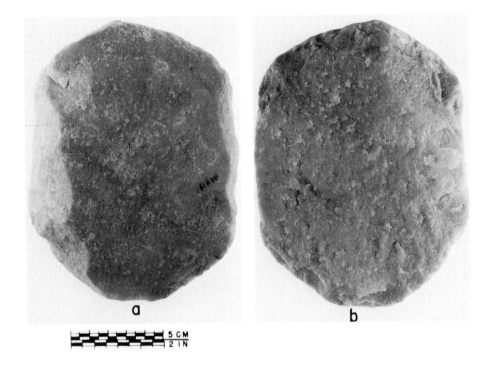

(Figure 2.33) and still another from the Hanson site (Frison and Bradley 1980:Figure 66). It may be a flaking hammer.

Ivory and Bone Artifacts

A carved and polished ivory object 203.4 mm in length was recovered from the Clovis component. It is oval in cross section (13.6 × 12 mm) and tapers gradually toward the distal end, which is broken (Figure 2.99). At its most distally complete part, the cross section is 12.15 × 10.0 mm. The proximal end is terminated with an angular bevel that is 74.7 mm long and perfectly straight, it extends from one side to the opposite across the widest part. When the object was first recovered, its surface demonstrated a high polish, and part of the tapered surface at the proximal end was covered with a pattern of double cross-hatching similar to those from the Anzick site (Lahren and Bonnichsen 1974). The polish has since deteriorated to a dull luster, and most of the marks disappeared shortly after recovery. The remains of some marks that were slightly deeper than others can still be detected, however.

Whether or not the distal end continued to a point is not known but this is certainly suggested. The true function of this and similar objects recovered in Clovis sites remains an open question; they are postulated as having been both foreshafts and actual projectile points. No evidence of ivory artifact manufacture was found at the Sheaman site.

One pronghorn (*Antilocapra americana*) metatarsal was cut in two a short distance from the proximal end. The cut was accomplished with two directly opposing V-shaped notches that reach nearly to the cancellous bone on both sides, and then separation was completed by breaking the remainder of the bone (Figure 2.109i).

The Sheaman site evidence suggests a remnant of a small campsite in the bottom and slopes of a small swale. It does not appear to have been a favorable wet-weather location and may represent activities peripheral to a larger site area. A partial mandible from a *Bison* calf suggests a spring or summer occupation (see Chapter 4, Section 2).

6.   BONE, ANTLER, AND IVORY ARTIFACTS AND MANUFACTURE TECHNOLOGY

george c. frison and carolyn craig

Any discussion of bone, antler, or ivory tool manufacture technology requires a consideration of some very basic concepts. All three of these materials are different in their composition and structure. In order to manufacture tools or perform the necessary breakage for butchering and processing purposes, the butcher or artisan must know how these materials respond to various forces and tools. Bone technology is a subject every bit as complex as stone technology (see, e.g., Bonnichsen 1979), but only a few principles need be mentioned here.

Green or fresh bone behaves differently than dry or cured bone when hit by a hammerstone or chopper with enough force to cause fracturing. Green bone separates with a spiral break. Prehistoric butchers were familiar with the individual bones and knew where to smash a bone to initiate fractures that would serve their purpose—perhaps to expose the interior bone cavities for marrow extraction or to produce tools. Examples can be produced experimentally and can be demonstrated by examples from the site components.

A heavy hammerstone blow to the diaphysis of a bison humerus resting on a solid support results in a depressed fracture with spiral breaks radiating in several directions. The same results can be observed on a specimen from the Folsom level (Figure 2.100). The proximal end of a bison radius–ulna can be broken by placing the anterior side on an anvil stone and then hitting the ulna with a hammerstone directly over the proximal interosseous space. The force of a proper blow drives the shaft of the ulna into the radius and produces distinctive breaks. Identical results can be observed on a proximal radius from the Folsom level (Figure 2.101) and a proximal radius–ulna from the Agate Basin level (Figure 2.102). Once the bones are initially fractured in these patterned ways, further fracturing is usually relatively simple. Patterned breakages of this nature can be demonstrated for a number of individual skeletal units.

In bison kill sites from Paleoindian through Late Prehistoric times, many kinds of simple bone tools were produced by breakage (see, e.g., Frison 1974; Reher and Frison 1980). These tools were useful for various butchering opera-

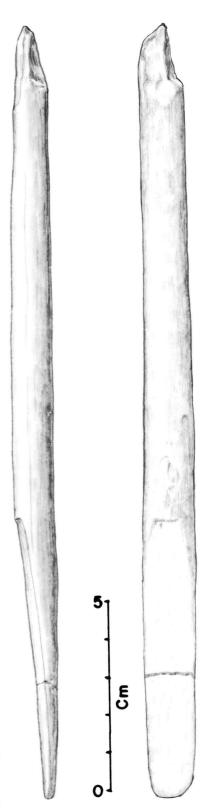

FIGURE 2.99   **Ivory projectile point or foreshaft from the Sheaman site.**

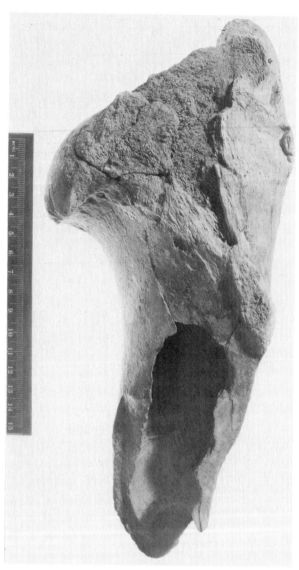

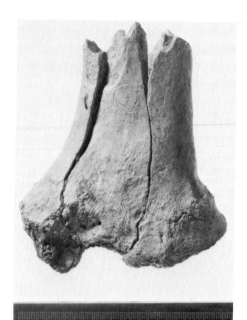

FIGURE 2.101 **Broken bison radius from the Folsom level in Area 2.**

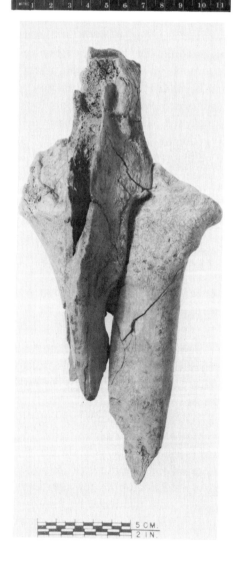

FIGURE 2.102 **Broken bison radius—ulna and possible tool from the Agate Basin level in Area 2.**

FIGURE 2.100 **Broken bison humerus from the Folsom level in Area 2.**

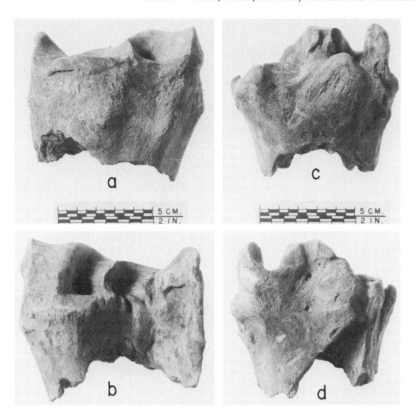

FIGURE 2.103 **Broken bison radius (a, b) and tibia (c, d) from the Folsom level in Area 2.**

tions and probably numerous other tasks. They could be discarded with little or no feeling of loss because of the small amount of time and effort invested in their manufacture. A good example is the proximal radius–ulna from the Agate Basin level (Figure 2.102). Striations and polish on the point suggest deliberate human use.

Although certain kinds of bone may be predictably flaked in a manner somewhat analogous to stone (Bonnichsen 1979:58–60), the spiral-fracturing principle requires special tasks such as grooving, sawing, scraping, and abrading to produce the familiar types of bone tools. There is seldom any question in identifying the toolmarks resulting from these activities. In the case of simple bone tools produced by breakage alone, unequivocal evidence for their true function is often difficult, since they are produced by the same kinds of bone breakage used in butchering and processing. In addition, the evidence of use on working points or edges may be difficult to document in situations where bones are badly deteriorated, as was the case at the Agate Basin site.

There are probably many uses of simple bone tools that have not yet been perceived by archaeologists. The purposes of some bone breakage is not yet well understood. Most such breakage may have been by-products of butchering and processing, but some is likely to have been deliberate, either to produce simple tools or to prepare bone for the production of more sophisticated tools and probably also weaponry. In the Folsom level, for example, a bison radius (Figure 2.103a, b) and a tibia (Figure 2.103c, d) were reduced by pounding nearly to the epiphyses for reasons as yet unexplained.

Another consideration in the study of bone technology is the modification

FIGURE 2.104   **Broken and carnivore-chewed bison metatarsal from the Folsom level in Area 2.**

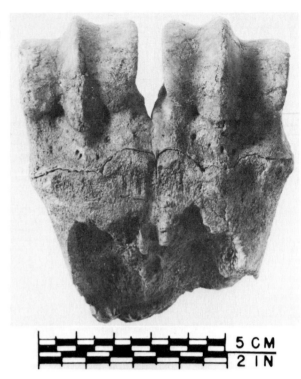

5 CM
2 IN

of bone by animals. Rodents, scavengers, and carnivores break and chew bone in distinctive and patterned ways (see Haynes 1980). It is important that archaeologists be able to distinguish between the results of human and animal bone modification. Carnivores may chew bones to a shape resembling bone butchering tools (see Frison 1978b:Figure 8.7). Carnivore chewing marks may also appear superimposed over human breaks, as can be observed on the distal end of a bison metatarsal from the Folsom level in Area 2 (Figure 2.104). Mistakes in identifying human and animal activities on faunal elements can seriously affect the accuracy of site interpretations.

Cutting marks may be the by-products of butchering, processing, and tool manufacture. Cutting during butchering was usually to sever key muscles or remove flesh from bones. Often a muscle was severed at its point of attachment or where it passed directly over another bone and the cut marks in these cases were made directly on the bone surfaces. In other cases, the cut marks represent tools dragging over bone surfaces during use and had no direct functional relationships to either butchering or processing. All of these kinds of marks may be easily lost through the bone surface deterioration commonly found in archaeological sites.

Bone tools behave in unique ways during use. It was discovered, for example, that chopping with a pointed tool made from a bison tibia produces a polished working edge unless the blows are of sufficient strength to drive off bone chips from the working edge. This provided some basis for interpretation of the polished points on these and other bone tools that had previously been identified as used for scraping or polishing. Paleoindian utilization of bone, antler, and ivory for tools and weaponry is poorly known and understood, largely because of the paucity of evidence. The Agate Basin site, particularly the Folsom level in Area 2, has added some small increments to the data base.

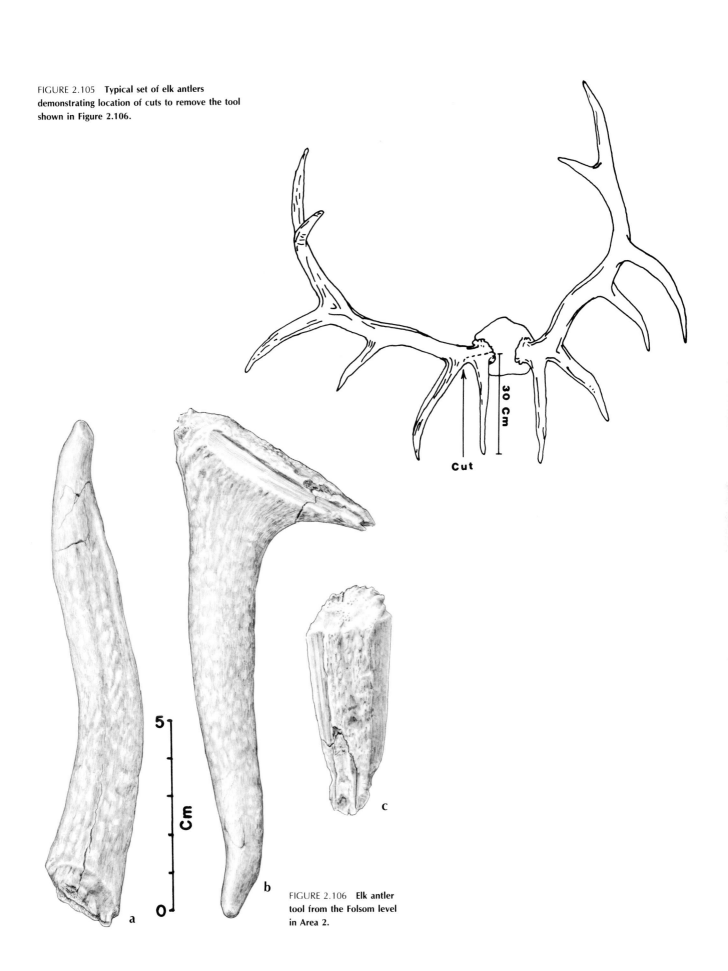

FIGURE 2.105   Typical set of elk antlers demonstrating location of cuts to remove the tool shown in Figure 2.106.

Cut

30 Cm

5

Cm

0

a

b

c

FIGURE 2.106   Elk antler tool from the Folsom level in Area 2.

BONE AND ANTLER ARTIFACTS AND MANUFACTURE TECHNOLOGY FROM THE FOLSOM COMPONENTS

Although only a limited number of bone and antler artifacts were recovered in the Agate Basin site, these are sufficient to indicate a sophisticated and established manufacture technology. Grooving, incising, abrading, chopping, polishing, and drilling processes can be observed on finished artifacts as well as on a small amount of discarded manufacture debris.

Deep longitudinal grooving (as much as 15 mm) can be observed on the main beam of an elk antler in order to remove the first brow tine (Figure 2.105) where only a small amount of softer cancellous material is present (Figure 2.106). The rough burr around the base of the main beam was apparently removed by chopping (Figure 2.106a). The type of tool used in grooving is not known for certain but actual experiments have indicated that a biface, a flake, or a burin-like tool will produce the desired results. The sides of both grooves are flat and straight, indicating skill in the process, unlike the opposite situation where the sides of the grooves are uneven, indicating an inability to use the proper tool in the proper manner.

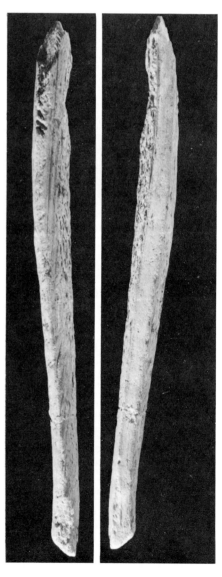

FIGURE 2.107 Distal (left) and proximal ends (right) of a bone projectile point from the Folsom level in Area 2. (Shown actual size)

This tool was from a slightly atypical antler tine in that it is relatively straight and lacks the arcuate shape common to most. Some abrading and polishing of the distal end of the tine is apparent. The attachment area of the tine to the main beam extended several centimeters distally to where it was broken off, and this extension was intentionally constricted slightly (Figure 2.106c) as if to form a means of attachment to something. In two places there are small areas of rodent gnawing but otherwise the artifact is intact. It is believed to be a pressure punch for removing channel flakes on Folsom preforms; speculation as to its method of use is presented in Chapter 3, Section 2.

Deep longitudinal grooving can be observed on bone and on another antler artifact as well. Five items are believed to be parts of bone projectile points (see Frison and Zeimens 1980). Two of these (Figure 2.107) are parts of the same artifact, as can be proven by matching the manufacture grooves; an undetermined but probably small amount of the midsection is missing due to breakage. The break is distinctive and diagnostic of a kind produced in actual use of similar specimens in spearing animals. In these experiments, rapid changes in the angle of entry caused the bone shaft to break. Instead of a single break, a V-shaped piece broke out of the shaft (Figure 2.108) and this appears to have been the case with the Folsom specimen. A distal end (Figure 2.109d) of another bone point was recovered, and it was broken toward the center in a manner identical to that seen on the first specimen.

The manufacture technology for these bone projectile points involved the production of long-bone strips by grooving into long bone, probably bison. The most appropriate long bone for this purpose is the anterior edge of the femur, which provides a strip of the necessary length and straightness. Other long bones, such as a radius or a tibia, might also have been used with some artificial straightening of the strip after removal. Two longitudinal, parallel grooves were required initially, but several other strips could then be removed, each requiring a single groove. A biface functions well as a grooving tool, as has been demonstrated experimentally (see Frison and Zeimens 1980:234–236). Antler strips would also suffice. The one proximal end found (Figure 2.110) is probably of elk antler although its badly deteriorated condition makes an exact determination difficult. This piece was broken in a different manner than the bone pieces.

The two pieces of the nearly complete specimen (Figure 2.107) combine for a total length of 25.2 cm. The extreme tip is missing, as is an undetermined amount from the center, but its total length probably did not exceed 27–30 cm. This is about the maximum length that can be obtained for a bone strip removed from bison long bone, even the somewhat larger subspecies of the late Pleistocene (see Chapter 4, Section 3). The distal end is spirally abraded to form a rounded cross-section. The proximal end retains more of the shape of the original strip of bone, with only a light abrading on the side to reduce its thickness

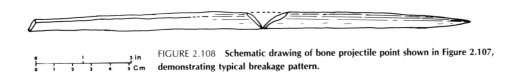

FIGURE 2.108   Schematic drawing of bone projectile point shown in Figure 2.107, demonstrating typical breakage pattern.

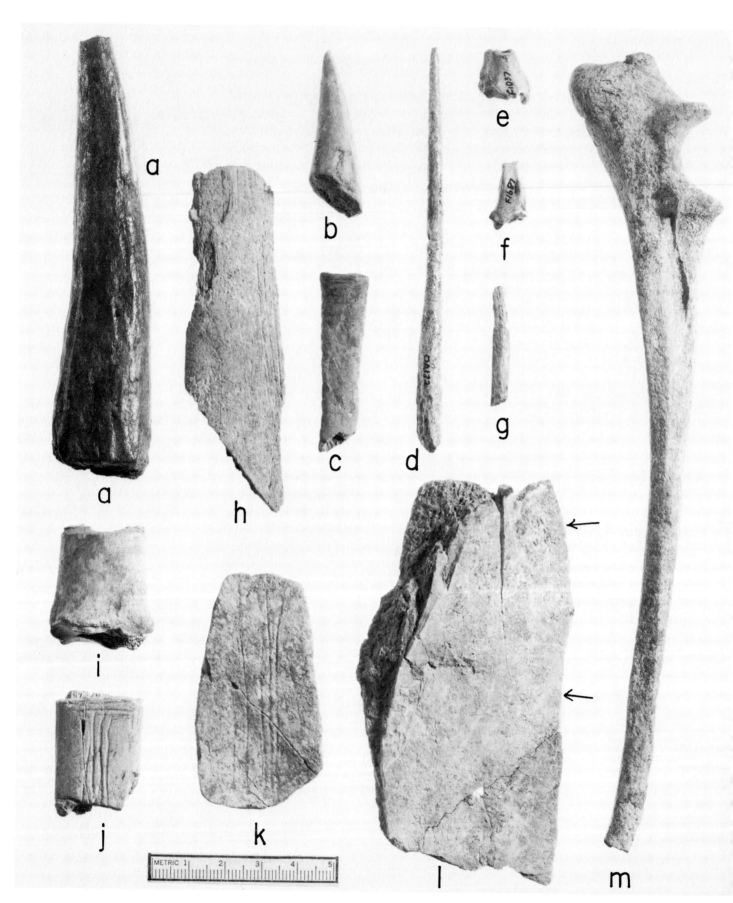

FIGURE 2.109 **Antler from the Hell Gap level in Area 3 (a, b). Worked bone from the Folsom level in Area 2 (d–g, i–m), Area 3 (h), the Hell Gap level in Area 3 (c), and the Sheaman site (i).**

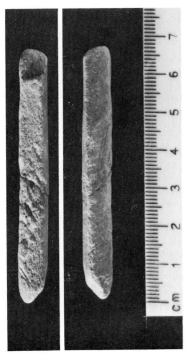

FIGURE 2.110 **Base of antler projectile point from the Folsom level in Area 2.**

from a maximum of 10 mm to 6.1 mm at the base. The base is flat but was deliberately cut off at an angle of about 50° with the longitudinal axis of the artifact. Some deterioration of the outer surfaces may have reduced its dimensions slightly, and in one spot rodent chewing is present. Provenience of this specimen was the vicinity of a nearly complete bison carcass (Figure 2.15), which argues for its function as a projectile point.

On the second bone specimen (Figure 2.109d), the spiral abrading can be observed just forward of the break, which obliterates the longitudinal manufacture groove on one side but not on the other. Severe bone deterioration reduced the diameter of the specimen toward the small end, giving a false impression of its true shape, which probably resembled the distal end of the first specimen. The base of the specimen believed to be antler demonstrates a manufacture technology similar to that of the bone specimens. The base is cut to the same angle and the shank is rectangular in cross section, 5.3 × 8.1 mm (Figure 2.110).

Bone Needles

Sixteen fragments and a nearly complete bone needle were recovered, all but one from Area 2. The nearly complete specimen (Figure 2.111a) is eyed and is missing only the extreme distal end. Another specimen (Figure 2.111b) is broken across the eye. Needle cross-sections vary from nearly round to oval to flattened on one or both sides (see Table 2.1). One of the broken specimens was an extreme tip, so its true cross-section could not be determined. One worked-bone object (Figure 2.109g) is classified as part of a bone needle, but it may be something else. One side is flat; the other is raised in the center to form a distinctly triangular cross-section, with the base 4.8 mm wide and the height 1.9 mm.

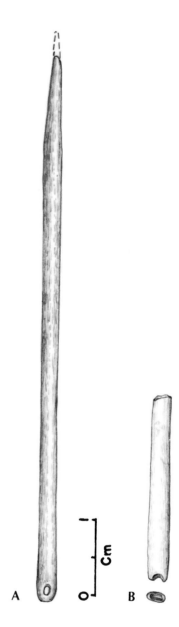

FIGURE 2.111 **Eyed bone needles from the Folsom level in Area 2.**

The bone needles in Area 2 were concentrated in a relatively small area (see Figure 2.16) and were associated with several broken bison scapulae. Although badly deteriorated, grooving marks appear on the blades of several of these scapula pieces. On two specimens (Figure 2.112a, b) straight to slightly curved edges were the result of grooves cut into the bone. On another specimen (Figure 2.109l) the end of a groove about 1.5 mm wide and 3 mm deep remains on a bison scapula fragment and one entire edge of the same specimen resulted from grooving. Deliberate breakage, probably with hammerstone and/or choppers, was apparently part of the process in preparing scapulae for grooving.

The close association between bone needles and grooved scapula pieces suggested that the former were being manufactured from the latter. A fresh bison scapula was obtained and several narrow strips were taken from the thin part of the blade by grooving. The strips were then ground to the shape of the

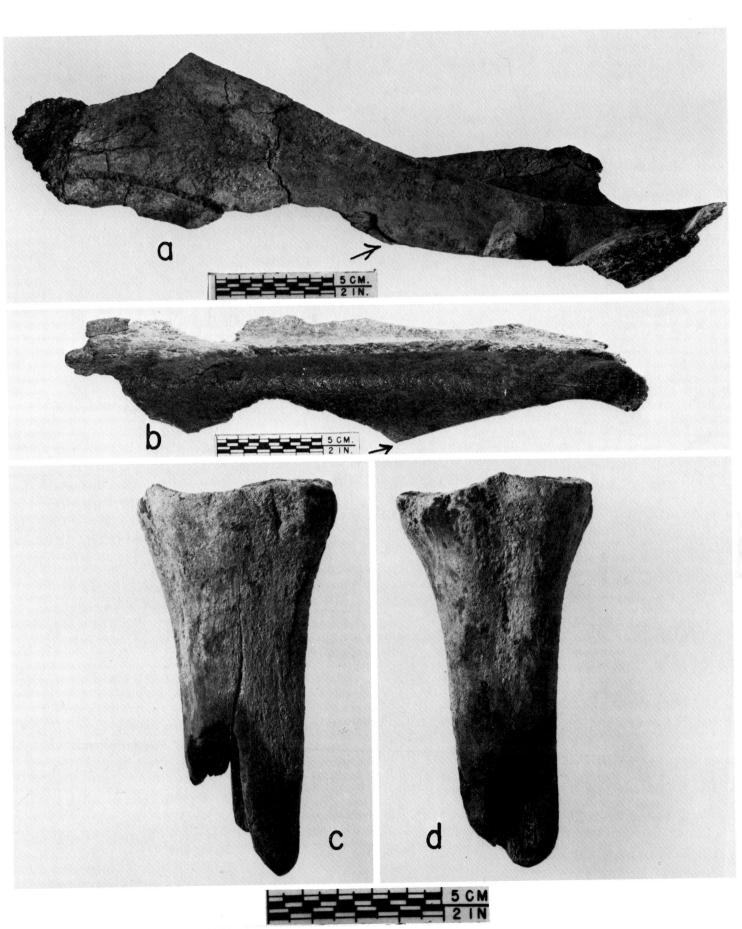

FIGURE 2.112 Cut bison scapulae (a, b) and a bison metatarsal tool (c, d) from the Folsom level in Area 2. Arrows indicate edges formed by grooves.

TABLE 2.1
Folsom Bone-Needle Cross Sections

	Diameter (mm)	
Catalog number	Minimum	Maximum
OA004	1.7	2.5
C3480	1.85	1.9
96552	1.15	1.5
96610	1.3	1.45
C3478	1.3	1.7
C3482	1.9	2.1
96608	1.35	1.7
96612	1.2	1.6
96609	2.1	2.3
C3479	1.1	1.85
C3481	1.25	2.6
C3485	1.25	1.8
C3483	1.15	2.8
C3484	1.5	2.1
OA440	1.4	1.6
F1024	1.9	4.8

needle recovered in the Folsom level. The eye was drilled with a stone flake that was first given a pressure retouch along one edge and then snapped at an angle to form a sharp point. The resulting tool was very similar to one from the Folsom level (Figure 2.21i). It was discovered by experiment that a sharp graver point on a very thin flake (e.g., Figure 2.21f) did not function too well for this purpose although sharp spurs on the corners of ends of working edges on end scrapers (e.g., Figure 2.19k) which are structurally superior to those on a thin flake function well for this purpose.

The bone in the blade of the bison scapula proved to be especially resilient in comparison to rib or long bone and therefore of superior quality for needles. Without the intermediate stages of manufacture between the initial grooving and the finished product, the actual use of bison scapulae for Folsom needle manufacture is speculative, but highly probable.

Miscellaneous Bone Items

The thin, flat bone in the bison scapulae was used for objects other than needles. One piece, irregular in outline (Figure 2.109k) has the edges ground smooth and several lines incised on one side. The opposite side is unaltered. A piece of a bison rib also demonstrates several incised lines, and the end of a transverse cut is visible on one end (Figure 2.109h). Whether this is part of a deliberately made object or a manufacture discard is not known.

Three sections of bison rib of different lengths were made by encircling cuts into the cancellous part of the bone. On one (Figure 2.109j) the cuts were not smoothed, and rough projections were not removed. Two shallow grooves near the transverse cut on one end appear deliberate, as do four irregular longitudinally incised lines on the same side of the rib. The cuts on the end of one of the other two specimens (Figure 2.113b) are more carefully executed, as are the incised lines on one side. On the opposite side is a single, wide, diagonal incised

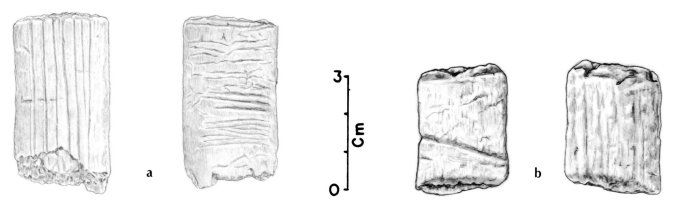

FIGURE 2.113   **Cut and incised rib sections from the Folsom level in Area 2.**

line. One end of the third specimen is damaged. On one side of this specimen are seven incised longitudinal lines; on the opposite side is a complicated pattern of transverse incised lines (Figure 2.113a). The function of these lines is conjectural. They could be decorative, or they could indicate some form of gaming piece. The cancellous bone of one (Figure 2.109j) is missing, which suggests that it might have been part of some kind of foreshaft for the bone projectile points, a viable possibility.

Four specimens of worked bone are fragments of larger items. Each was modified by closely spaced parallel lines etched into one side; the opposite side was smoothed and polished. On one specimen (Figure 2.114a, b) the lines appear to have been sawed into one surface with something like a thin, sharp-edged stone flake. Part of the original edge is relatively sharp. Maximum thickness is 2.3 mm and there is no indication of original size. The three other pieces are similar, but were calcined by intense heat. On one of these (Figure 2.114d), a small, rounded section of the original edge is preserved. The three calcined pieces may be part of the same object. All of these are from the upper Folsom level in Area 3.

Several other miscellaneous items of bone and antler manufacture were recovered in the Folsom level in Area 2. One is a badly deteriorated strip of elk antler 1.2 mm thick (Figure 2.115). It was apparently made first by obtaining a long strip of elk antler from a main beam by using parallel grooves, and then either scraping or abrading it to the desired thickness. The distal end of a fox tibia (Figure 2.109e) and a jackrabbit tibia (Figure 2.109f) were severed by encircling grooves. They may be discarded ends from bone bead manufacture. A

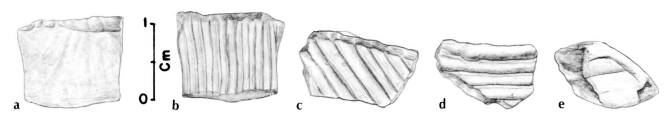

FIGURE 2.114   **Incised bone from the Folsom levels in Area 3.**

5 CM
2 IN

FIGURE 2.115   **Strip of elk antler from the Folsom level in Area 2.**

problematic object was made from the proximal end of a bison metatarsal (Figure 2.112c). It is highly possible that this is a punch similar in function to the elk antler object described previously. The bone was broken in two and a broad, rounded, blunt point was shaped by abrading on the anterior side of the bone. The broken end (17 mm) of a similar point was found nearby. Although it is somewhat deteriorated, its general shape and appearance indicate that it may have been the working end of this same tool or a similar one, and may have broken off in use. It is also possible that the working end of such a tool may have gradually become nonfunctional through continued use, and it was deliberately broken off and the entire end reshaped.

As already mentioned, two pieces of bison rib were driven into the ground at a slight angle, one in the northern part (Figure 2.18) of the Folsom component and another in the southern part, both in Area 2. Each is in an area strongly suspected of being the location of a temporary structure (Figure 2.18). The two ribs might have been pegs used in securing a lodge cover. Both were driven some distance into the ground, although the full extent could not be determined because of the severe deterioration of the bone below the original ground surface.

The derivation of another bone artifact (Figure 2.116), a serrated bone flesher, is questionable, but it is believed to be Folsom. It was found by James Duguid in Area 6, but in a redeposited context. A stock-watering pond had been built in the early 1950s about 225 m down the present arroyo from Area 2. At this point the old buried arroyo is adjacent to the present one and the fill for the earthen dam was taken from the south bank, exposing the deposits in the old arroyo. Prior to the work at the Brewster site in 1959, a serrated bone flesher was found in an exposed dark stratum in the newly exposed area. Several complete bison bone, numerous fragments, and a few small stone flakes were also recovered from the same level in a small test in 1976.

The level in question is probably Folsom since it is in a lower redeposited stratum. It was made on a flat piece of bone from the posterior side of abison tibia. The serrated edge was placed on the end of the bone near the proximal end of the tibia, where the bone thins to about 3.4 mm. On the opposite end the bone is 6.2 mm thick. On the remaining side of the tool, the edge of the bone was rounded for a distance of 9.5 cm; the missing portion of the working edge was probably treated similarly.

A long-bone fragment from the anterior side of the left tibia of a camel from the Folsom level in Area 2 (Figure 2.117) suggests a tool similar to the serrated scraper tool just described. Only a corner of the working edge remains, but several fine serrations are present. This fragment lends some support to the contention that the other serrated scraper tool was indeed redeposited from the Folsom level and that the serrated bone scraper does go back to Folsom times.

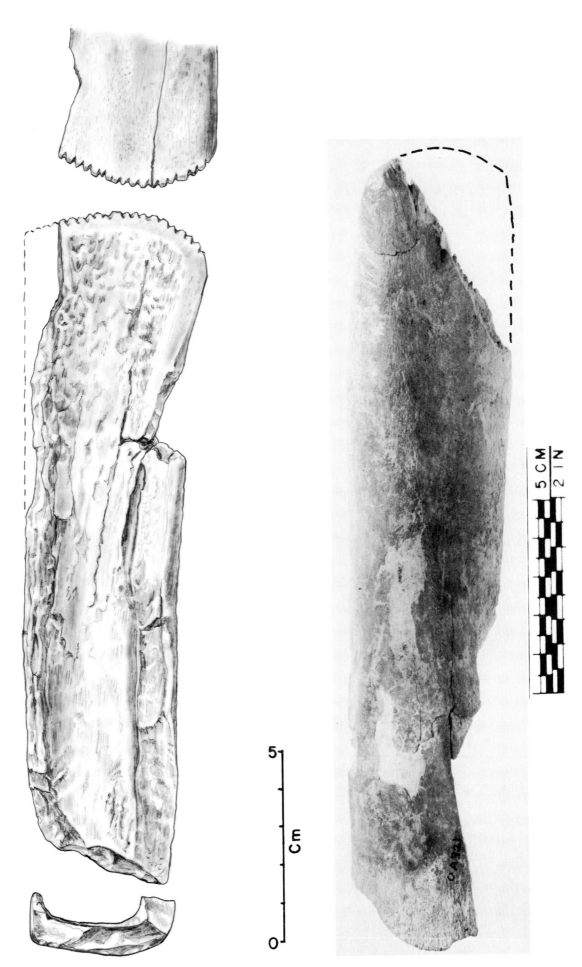

FIGURE 2.116 Serrated bison bone scraper found
redeposited downstream from Area 2 and believed to
be of Folsom origin.

FIGURE 2.117 Broken serrated camel bone scraper
from the Folsom level in Area 2.

FIGURE 2.118 **Bone objects from the Agate Basin levels in Areas 1 (a) and 2 (b).**

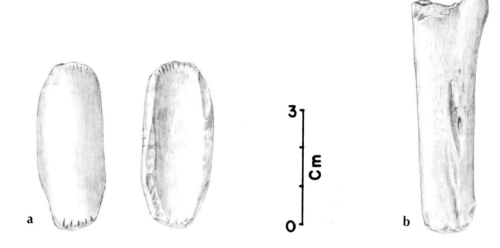

THE AGATE BASIN COMPONENT ARTIFACTS

The Agate Basin level produced very little worked bone. An oval-shaped piece of long bone (Figure 2.118a), probably either deer or pronghorn, was smoothed lightly on the edges and has several notches incised on both sides of both ends. The inside bone surface was smoothed to remove all traces of cancellous bone. This was found in the 1975 excavations in Site 1. Another problematic bone object (Figure 2.118b) is from Area 2 and was made from a piece of unidentified heavy long bone 8.7 mm thick. Part of the inner cancellous bone surface is visible on one side. The edges are rounded and the entire surface except for the base is highly polished. Part of the specimen is missing; a break occurred just forward of a rounded projection on one side. The base of the specimen has the appearance of battering, as if it had been repeatedly hit with a light hammer. In its present condition, its original shape and function are difficult to determine. However, it is strongly suggestive of part of a bone harpoon.

No bison tibia choppers, and only suggestive evidence of what could be considered as other kinds of expedient or fortuitous long-bone tools, were present in any of the Paleoindian components at the Agate Basin site. One exception is the unusually well-preserved radius–ulna unit (Figure 2.102) from the Agate Basin level in Area 2. A few broken long-bone fragments in the Agate Basin level could also have been broken off similar tools during use, but the state of bone preservation in general made this kind of tool-use identification difficult.

THE HELL GAP COMPONENT ARTIFACTS

Scattered around the hearth in the first Hell Gap level were two bison rib fragments that demonstrated transverse cut marks on one end similar to those shown in Figure 2.109h from the Folsom level. These fragments were probably discards of manufacture. The only bone piece that appears to be part of an actual bone artifact is a section of bison hyoid that is cut and polished on one end and has two incised transverse grooves adjacent to the cut (Figure 2.109c). The other end is completely deteriorated, so its original shape or function cannot be determined.

In the same area was a tip of an elk antler tine severed at an angle of about 45° to the long axis of the tine. Removal was by opposing cuts that met in the center so that the face of the cut is nearly flat. The natural curve of the tine was preserved. The tine was ground and polished to accentuate the sharp point. It appears to be a completed artifact, and may have been an atlatl hook (Figure 2.109b). It need only be inserted into a properly prepared hole in the end of an atlatl with the cut face parallel to the posterior surface of the atlatl and secured in place to be functional. Elk antler is a tough, long-wearing material and this piece would have made an excellent atlatl hook.

In the second Hell Gap level was a larger piece of an elk antler that was severed by two deep V-shaped cuts that nearly met in the center (Figure 2.109a). It may have been either a deliberate tool or a discard of manufacture. The end is broken, and there are striations and polish toward the tip. These may have been the result of human tool use or normal day-to-day activities of elk.

THE IVORY OBJECT FROM THE SHEAMAN SITE

An ivory object, probably a projectile point or foreshaft (Figure 2.99) was recovered at the Sheaman site, but no evidence of manufacture technology was present nor were any other ivory objects found either completed artifacts or manufacture debris. A full description of the object is given in the preceding section on the Sheaman site. It is assumed that a strip of ivory, probably mammoth or even possibly mastodon tusk, was obtained by deep grooving similar to that observed on bone and antler objects in the Folsom components. Further shaping was probably by coarse abrading, the final polish by finer abrading, possibly with a fine abrasive material applied with something such as a piece of soft hide.

7.   RAW STONE FLAKING MATERIAL SOURCES

george c. frison

A systematic study of the prehistoric sources, recovery methods, and mechanisms of distribution of stone flaking materials has not yet been realized on the High Plains. The materials are diverse and are scattered over wide areas, much of which has not yet been subjected to even a minimal level of surface reconnaissance. Material from a known source may appear distinctive in texture and appearance from materials from other sources based on small samples. However, when the full range of variation from the various sources is known, the critieria used in separation often lose their diagnostic value. At this time, there is little doubt that many of the larger raw material sources that demonstrate unequivocal evidence of prehistoric exploitation have not yet been documented. Any attempt to relate site materials to actual sources is further complicated by past transport of materials by stream and glacial action, which provided significant amounts of material with relatively little human effort.

All known natural exposures of suitable stone flaking materials demonstrate evidence of prehistoric human exploitation. In many cases, the human effort expended is impressive, considering the level of technology involved. The Spanish Diggings in southeast Wyoming, for example, were described in the early twentieth century (Holmes 1919). Early homesteaders and other whites thought this to be the result of early European explorers looking for precious metals; they were unable to conceive of prehistoric native Americans engaged in this manner of work. However, the evidence indicates that the desire to acquire high-quality raw material was great and resulted in great expenditures of human effort.

The availability of good raw material was certainly greater in Paleoindian times than in later periods. A determination of the beginning date of actual quarrying operations at the Spanish Diggings has not been made, primarily because the methodology to provide such a determination has not yet appeared. Quarry sites do not tend to yield the familiar cultural diagnostics, inasmuch as the final flaked products were completed elsewhere, leaving only early reduction stages at the quarries. Only time will tell whether or not the stone technology evidenced by these early reduction stages differed significantly between Paleoindian and subsequent periods to allow accurate separation.

The nature of quarry sites renders them difficult to investigate with ordinary excavation techniques. In order to follow a buried vein of quartzite or chert, the overburden had to be removed and piled. After removal of the desired material exposed by the first removal of overburden, further exposure is accomplished by backfilling the orginal hole. Over long periods of time, this resulted in badly mixed deposits. In rare cases a single pit was dug and subsequently sealed off, leaving datable materials (see, e.g., Frison 1978b:329–331) and quarrying tools in good context.

The Spanish Diggings are actually exposures of Lower Cretaceous quartzite at the edge of the Hartville uplift; toward the center of the uplift are numerous exposures of older Pennsylvanian chert. The latter exposures demonstrate intensive quarrying on a scale comparable to the quartzite. In addition there are almost innumerable small outcrops and instances of loose material scattered on the surface. The total range of color and texture of the cherts in the Hartville uplift is so large that site-to-source determinations are highly speculative. However, it is very likely that some of the Agate Basin flaking materials came from this source. Figure 2.119 shows the location of the Hartville uplift and other possible sources of Agate Basin site materials.

There is only suggestive evidence at present to indicate that Spanish Diggings quartzite quarries were a source of material for the cultural groups involved at the Agate Basin site. The color and grain size of two quartzite tools are similar to those of Spanish Diggings quartzite, but quartzites of equally fine grain have been discovered at the Clark Ranch quarries about 30 km south of the Agate Basin site.

There are numerous and extensive sources of quartzite both south and east of the Agate Basin site. One of these, known as Flint Hill, is about 30 km directly east of the site in the southern Black Hills near Edgemont, South Dakota. This is

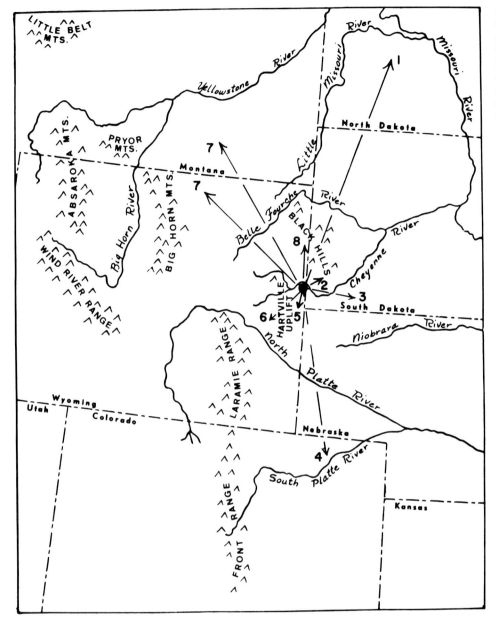

FIGURE 2.119 Suggested sources of raw stone flaking materials at the Agate Basin site. 1: Knife River flint; 2: Flint Hill (quartzite), chert from southern Black Hills; 3: plate chalcedony; 4: Flat Top chert; 5: Old Woman anticline (quartzite); 6: Hartville uplift (chert and quartzite); 7: porcellainite; 8: Morrison formation quartzite.

a large butte capped with a thick stratum of quartzite of varying color and texture. Although the texture of some Flint Hill quartzite appears coarse, it flakes well; similar material appears in Folsom, Agate Basin, and Hell Gap levels at the Agate Basin site. However, it is dangerous at this time to claim Flint Hill as the source of the material, since an equally large source of similar material is present at the Degering Ranch quarries about the same distance (35 km) south of the Agate Basin site; another is located near Hot Springs, South Dakota, about 50 km to the northeast. The ranges of texture and color of quartzite from these sources overlap those from the Flint Hill source. Other unknown quartzite sources are very likely present and any or all could have been familiar to the Agate Basin site cultural groups. There are also significant quantities of locally abundant surface materials. Stream deposits provide small amounts of material, and these are often found at considerable distances from the original sources.

Knife River flint is critical to the interpretation of the Agate Basin site, since this material appears in both Agate Basin and Folsom components. It has been found in a number of quarries in Dunn and Mercer counties, North Dakota, about 523 km (325 miles) north and slightly east of Agate Basin (Clayton *et al.* 1970). Knife River flint is an exceptionally high-quality flaking material with a wide distribution throughout the states and provinces adjacent to and even farther removed from North Dakota. It is distinctive in appearance, and identification based on general appearance is usually considered unequivocal. Whether or not there are other materials that are not readily separable from Knife River flint is a possibility that demands further study. The authors' opinion at this time is that some individual specimens can be questioned, but, in a situation such as in the Agate Basin component at the Agate Basin site, where there are a large number of tools and projectile points, their identification as Knife River flint is correct.

According to Clayton *et al.* (1970:287), Knife River flint is a silicified lignite of Eocene age. These same authors (1970:288) note that silicified fossil trees in Paleocene deposits are nearly identical in color and luster to Knife River flint but that the two can be separated by internal structure. The Folsom component at Agate Basin contains both Knife River flint and silicified wood; the two can be separated only by the tree-ring structure identifiable in the silicified wood.

The source of the silicified wood is difficult if not impossible to resolve at this time. This material is limited in quantity but widespread in occurrence, and variable in quality. A relatively small piece may demonstrate great variation in color and luster with concomitant ranges of quality as flaking material, which indicates why source idenfication is so difficult. Actually, all of the silicified wood in the Folsom component at the Agate Basin site could have resulted from exploitation of a single relatively small core.

Oligocene deposits east of the Black Hills, in South Dakota, contain extensive outcropping of material that is strongly reminiscent of Knife River flint. However, when large samples from both sources are compared, reliable separation is possible on the basis of texture and appearance. The patinas of the two are different; the Oligocene material is more brittle and is of a different flaking quality than Knife River flint. However, quantitative studies are necessary to establish more acceptable criteria for separation. In addition, only preliminary surveys of the archaeological potential of the area east of the Black Hills in South Dakota have been made at this time, so an accurate assessment of prehistoric raw material sources there is not now possible.

Another raw material found in quantity over large areas in Oligocene deposits east of the Black Hills is plate chalcedony. In its natural state, it appears as perpendicular plates .5–3.0 cm thick. In eroded areas these plates collapse into angular pieces. In most cases the plates consist of two separate sheets of light, translucent material weakly cemented together. With careful selection, thin sheets (about 1.0 cm) can be found that are of solid material throughout; only a retouch along a desirable working edge is needed to form a tool. Although only a small amount of this material was used at the Agate Basin site, it was present in Folsom, Agate Basin, and Hell Gap components.

A large part of the drainages of the Tongue, Powder, and Belle Fourche rivers in northeastern Wyoming and southeastern Montana is characterized by landforms and materials resulting from burning of coal beds during past geologic periods. In numerous locations, the resulting heat indurated sedimentary deposits and formed materials regularly used prehistorically for tools and projectile points. At present this material in its various forms is referred to as porcellanite, although in the past it has been referred to as clinker, metamorphosed shale, fused shale, and siltstone. Although somewhat inferior to chert and quartzite, particularly for working edges of tools, in many sites in the Powder River Basin of Montana and Wyoming this material may comprise nearly 100% of flaked stone assemblages. It is plentiful and occurs in a number of colors and textures. Small amounts appeared in the Agate Basin and Hell Gap components at the Agate Basin site.

The Jurassic Morrison formation outcrops widely and produces both chert and quartzite. One of the most common of these is a fine-grained, gray quartzite with excellent flaking qualities. Several flakes and two tools of this material appeared in the Agate Basin component, along with a single projectile point eroding out of the Schultz site. This particular form of quartzite outcrops in many known locations along the eastern foothills of the Bighorn Mountains within 210 km (130 miles) of Agate Basin. Exposures also occur in the Black Hills area, and although their extent is not yet known they seem to be the most likely source for the Agate Basin site materials.

One Folsom projectile point and one large flake of material are of a red chert that, on the basis of color and texture, probably came from the Triassic Spearfish formation in the Black Hills. One outcropping of this material is known about 32 km (20 miles) northeast of Agate Basin in the southern Black Hills. Other occurrences are possible, but the area has been intensively surveyed in the last few years with negative results. There is some evidence of exploitation of surface material at the known source but whether or not this source supplied the material in the Folsom component at Agate Basin cannot be proven at this time. There was, however, no evidence of quarrying.

One end scraper and several flakes in the Agate Basin Folsom component in Area 2 are probably of Flat Top chert, an Oligocene material found in northeastern Colorado about 305 km (190 miles) southeast of Agate Basin. This distinctive chert is a translucent light bluish pink, and contains numerous light-colored spots. It has a waxy luster and flakes well. As with most other materials mentioned here, there may be other sources yet unknown.

Nearly all of the flaking material from the Sheaman (Clovis) site is a high-quality chert varying from nearly transparent to translucent to opaque. Color varies also, and includes a light, clear material with dark inclusions; a light-yellow translucent to opaque material with large dark inclusions; a light-tan to dark-tan material with small black spots and dendritic inclusions; a dark-brown material with darker inclusions, which grades into a banded, multicolored material; a clear, light, translucent material that at first glance appears to be almost black because of the large number of dark inclusions; a green opaque material with complicated dark dendritic patterns throughout; and a number of intergradations of these. The best known source for these materials is the Hartville uplift beginning about 80 km (50 miles) southwest of Agate Basin. A few specimens of a banded quartzite were also found at the Sheaman site. Identical material is found in small amounts in association with a wide variety of cherts in the northern end of the Hartville uplift.

As the name indicates, the Agate Basin site area is the location of scattered nodules of raw material. Fist-sized nodules of translucent white to clear, transparent material with dark inclusions are the most common, although an occasional nodule of darker material is seen. This material was worked into tools and an occasional projectile point, but in general it was difficult to flake successfully.

There are a number of flakes and artifacts that fail to fall into commonly recognized material categories. A visit to any extensive stream deposit containing material of cobble size will yield material of many different kinds and quality, further emphasizing the difficult problems confronting the archaeologist in establishing the sources of stone flaking materials found in archaeological sites.

8. RADIOCARBON DATES

george c. frison

Eighteen radiocarbon dates were obtained from the Agate Basin site and locality. Three of these were collected during the Brewster site investigations (Agogino and Frankforter 1960); the rest were collected by the University of Wyoming–Smithsonian team from 1975 to 1980. Charcoal samples from the Agate Basin level were collected by Bass and Roberts, but none of these were submitted for dating because collectively they constituted a small sample, and because it was believed that a fresh sample would be more likely to yield accurate dates than one stored for nearly two decades in paper bags. The appearance of the charcoal collected by Bass and Roberts in 1961 indicates that charcoal was more plentiful in the southern part of Area 2 toward the old arroyo. Only one bone sample was submitted, and this was from the Sheaman (Clovis) site. The dates are presented in Table 2.2 and are published uncorrected as received from the various laboratories.

Three radiocrabon dates (I-10899, SI-3731, SI-3734) are from charcoal in a redeposited stratum stratigraphically underlying the Folsom components in Areas 2 and 3. Contained also in the stratum are fragments of bison bone, camel bone, and a few flakes and artifacts. None of the artifacts are diagnostic. The three dates are within the presently known range of Clovis, and the bone, charcoal, and artifacts were probably derived from cultural events associated with Clovis.

One charcoal sample was submitted from a hearth in the Folsom level in Area 2 (SI-3733). Another sample (SI-3732) was collected from the top of the Folsom level in Area 3; still another (SI-3730) was from Area 3 in a level between the Folsom and Hell Gap levels. The hearths in the Folsom levels in Area 3 did not yield sufficient charcoal for dating. Agogino and Frankforter (1960) submitted a sample (I-472) from the Folsom level at the Brewster site.

The Agate Basin bone bed in Area 2 contained charcoal associated with burned bone but no defined hearths or fire pits. Enough was collected to submit one sample (RL-557) for dating. A level above the Agate Basin bone bed contained small amounts of redeposited bone, charcoal, and flakes; a very small charcoal sample (RL-738) was submitted. The Hell Gap level in Area 3 contained large amounts of charcoal, most of which was a section of a burned log estimated to have been about 8 cm in diameter. One sample (SI-4430) was submitted. Two other samples (M-1131, O-1252) were submitted from the Brewster site and apparently were from levels above the Folsom level.

One sample (SI-4431) was collected from Area 7 and consists of the combined charcoal from three cultural levels that produced no diagnostic materials. The two remaining samples from the immediate Agate Basin area (SI-4432, RL-1419) were recovered from Archaic period fire pits along Moss Agate Arroyo and were submitted for the purpose of determining the age of the present landforms.

Two charcoal samples from the Sheaman site were submitted. These were from a poorly defined level just above the Clovis component. One sample (RL-1000) was very small; the other one (RL-1241) was adequate. The effects of extreme heat were demonstrated in most of the Clovis level, although not everywhere. Some flakes were destroyed by heat; others were altered in color, yet

TABLE 2.2
Agate Basin Radiocarbon Dates

Laboratory number	Age and date		Cultural affiliation	Site area
I-10899	11,840 ± 130	9890 B.C.	Below Folsom	3
SI-3731	11,700 ± 95	9750 B.C.	Below Folsom	2
SI-3734	11,450 ± 110	9500 B.C.	Below Folsom	3
SI-3733	10,780 ± 120	8830 B.C.	Folsom	2
SI-3732	10,665 ± 85	8715 B.C.	Top of Folsom level	3
SI-3730	10,575 ± 90	8625 B.C.	Between Folsom and Hell Gap	3
SI-4430	10,445 ± 110	8495 B.C.	Hell Gap	3
RL-557	10,430 ± 570	8480 B.C.	Agate Basin	2
I-472	10,375 ± 700	8425 B.C.	Folsom	Brewster
RL-738	10,200 ± 2000	8250 B.C.	Above Agate Basin	2
RL-1241	10,140 ± 500	8190 B.C.	Above Clovis	Sheaman
RL-1000	10,100 ± 2800	8150 B.C.	Above Clovis	Sheaman
RL-1263	10,030 ± 280	8080 B.C.	Bone—Clovis	Sheaman
M-1131	9990 ± 225	8040 B.C.	Agate Basin	Brewster
SI-4431	9750 ± 130	7800 B.C.	Unknown	7
O-1252	9350 ± 450	7400 B.C.	Agate Basin	Brewster
SI-4432	2215 ± 60	265 B.C.	Archaic fire pit	Moss Agate Arroyo
RL-1419	1520 ± 140	A.D. 450	Archaic fire pit	Moss Agate Arroyo

others were not affected. Calcined bone was present, along with bone that demonstrated the results of various degrees of burning. The charcoal dates represent a fire that postdated the Clovis event. As was noted in the earlier section on the Sheaman site, the fire must have been relatively hot and of long duration to accomplish the amount and kind of heat alteration of flakes that occurred. These two dates (RL-1000 and RL-1241) are about 1000 years to recent and probably record a fire postdating the Clovis occupation by that amount of time.

A bone sample (RL-1623) from the Sheaman site consisting of small fragments of bison long bone was also submitted. The fire should not have affected the bone in the Clovis level with regard to dating. However, bone dates from other Paleoindian contexts in the same general region have tended to be unreliable and the errors tend toward the younger side rather than the older. For example, a bone sample from a Cody Complex bison kill component at the Carter/Kerr-McGee site (Frison 1977) in the Powder River Basin to the north of Agate Basin yielded a date of 6950 ± 190 years or 5000 B.C. (RL-737). This date is about 1000 years too recent. However, a date of 10400 ± 400 years or 8450 B.C. (RL-917) was obtained from a charcoal sample from a Folsom component in the same stratigraphic sequence. This is a much more acceptable date. Similar results with attempts to date bone in this area is the rule rather than the exception so that radiocarbon dates on bone are a last resort. It is only fair to point out, however, that the bone and charcoal dates from the Casper Hell Gap site (Frison 1974) were almost identical.

Another consideration in discussing the Agate Basin charcoal samples used in radiocarbon dating is their source. The Folsom sample from Area 2 (SI-3733) was from a hearth of unmistakable cultural origin, and the possibility that any of the charcoal was derived from another source is minimal. The charcoal from the Agate Basin bone bed (RL-557) was collected from well within the bone bed; although not from a well-defined hearth, it did appear to come from a burned area associated with the cultural activities in the bone bed. The charred log in the Hell Gap bone bed (SI-4430) in Area 3 also gave the appearance of having been associated with the cultural activities there. However, the same cannot be claimed for the other Paleoindian radiocarbon samples collected by the University of Wyoming–Smithsonian team in Areas 2 and 3, since they do contain redeposited charcoal. The problem of reliable data gathering and analysis of cultural components on floodplains versus those on terraces of dry arroyos is one that demands intensive study.

chapter three
LITHIC TECHNOLOGY

1. FLAKED STONE TECHNOLOGY AND TYPOLOGY

bruce a. bradley

The flaked stone collection from the Agate Basin site locality has been divided into three groups for the purposes of description and analysis. The first group is from an Agate Basin level, and the second is from a Folsom level directly underlying the Agate Basin level in Area 2. The third group, discussed later in this section, is a Clovis component recovered from the Sheaman site. A small Hell Gap assemblage was recovered, but the tools are not considered here. To facilitate comparative work, this section has been modeled after a study presented by Frison and Bradley (1980) for the Hanson site, a large Folsom site in north-central Wyoming. The same criteria and analytical format have been used. The primary intent is to describe the morphological and technological attributes and characteristics of the retouched artifactual materials. By using the same criteria and analytical format used on the Hanson site it is hoped that direct comparisons may be made.

A standardized Bordes typology has been used for the unifacially retouched artifacts. Each category conforms to the descriptions published by Bordes in *Typologie de Paleolithique Ancien et Moyen* (1961). As in the Hanson site analysis, the non-handaxe bifaces and projectile points were subdivided into additional categories. In addition, the categories of unretouched artifacts, such as Levallois flakes, have been excluded.

PRIMARY TECHNOLOGY

Agate Basin Level

A number of core reduction strategies appear to have been used for the production of flakes and blades from locally available pieces of raw material—primarily clear to nearly opaque chalcedony with small black dendrites and occasional crystal pockets. These strategies verge on opportunism and include a wide range of platform-preparation techniques and the use of multiple platforms and flake-removal surfaces. It is highly likely that the shape, size, and relative homogeneity of the individual pieces of raw material greatly influenced the methods employed to produce usable flakes. Within the sample of 19 cores, bifacially prepared platforms predominate (9 specimens); however, unifacial platforms were also used, either with no platform preparation (1 specimen) or with reduced platform preparation (3 specimens). Two cores exhibited both bifacial and unifacial platforms. On the remainder, platforms were either indiscernible (3 specimens) or dihedral/polyhedral (1 specimen). As to the number of platforms and direction of flake removal, almost every possible combination can be identified. Included are (a) a simple single platform with unidirectional flake removals on 3 specimens; (b) a single platform with multidirectional flake removals on 1 specimen; (c) two platforms with opposed bidirectional flake removals on 2 specimens; (d) two platforms with nonopposed bidirectional flake removals on 1 specimen; (e) multiplatform multidirectional flake removals on 8 specimens, and (f) true disc cores on 2 specimens.

The sequence of flake removal chosen was primarily determined by the attributes of the raw material. This suggests a very loose cultural determination of flaking techniques and methods for the local manufacture of nonspecialized flakes and blades. Several flake-removal sequences were reconstructed from flakes that conjoined to the cores (Figures 2.69d, e; 2.70). One core reduction sequence in particular, reconstructed by the conjoining of a large number of flakes to the original core, warrants an in-depth description.

The original raw material was a small, irregular shaped, stream-rounded cobble of translucent chalcedony with white dotlike quartz inclusions. Similar

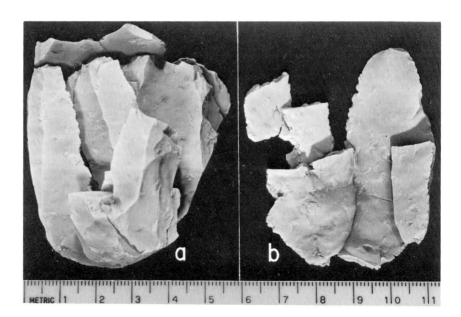

FIGURE 3.1 **Reassembled flakes from a core (a) and reassembled cortex flakes from the same core (b).**

pieces are presently available in the terrace gravels just above the site. First the large end was removed by striking several flakes more or less perpendicularly to the long axis of the nodule. The resultant surface was then used as a platform for the removal of several (6–10) cortical flakes and blades with unifacial platforms prepared by reduction. This process seemingly exhausted the available platform of the desired angle so that platform rejuvenation was necessary for further flake removal. This was accomplished by the removal of two flakes from the platform surface. The first was struck from the center of the flaked surface and hinge-fractured after traveling only about halfway across the platform surface. The second was struck from the edge, removing the entire surface including the hinge-fracture remnant, which produced a usable platform surface and angle. Another 6–10 blades and flakes were then removed more or less perpendicularly to the platform surface. Again the primary platform preparation was achieved through reduction. At this point in the sequence the core surface became fairly flat and the thickness had been greatly reduced; the core was then discarded. At least two of the flakes from this reconstruction had been used as unmodified flake tools (Figures 2.70a–c and 3.1).

Five artifacts specifically identified as cores were recovered from the Folsom level at the Agate Basin site. Material utilized was the same as from the Agate Basin component. One of these cores is discoidal with centripetal percussion flake scars on one surface and marginal flake removals on the opposite face. Two of the remaining cores do not exhibit patterned flake removals and resulted from opportunistic flaking. Both are multiplatformed, and flake removals were multidirectional. Another core is an elongated piece of stone with one end bifacially flaked and the opposite end unifacially flaked. Flake scars run in a bidirectional pattern. This combination of core types closely parallels those from the Hanson site (Frison and Bradley 1980:18–22), although this sample is much too small to allow for relevant comparisons.

Folsom Level

Flake Types.   Only three types of flakes have been recognized within the retouched flake tool assemblage from the Agate Basin site: biface thinning/ trimming, disc, and normal. Complete descriptions of these type categories may be found in the Hanson site monograph (Frison and Bradley 1980:24–27). Table 3.1 lists the tool types by flake types utilized for both Agate Basin and Folsom levels. Little difference is seen overall between the two levels in the types of flakes chosen for different types of tools, aside from a preference for biface reduction flakes for borer manufacture in the Folsom assemblage. No such preference was found in the Agate Basin component; an equal number of borers were made on biface reduction flakes and on normal flakes.

Even the percentages of flake types retouched into all tool types are almost the same for the Agate Basin and Folsom levels. These have been calculated as follows: normal, 39% Agate Basin to 37% Folsom; disc, 4% Agate Basin to 0% Folsom; biface reduction, 44% Agate Basin to 52% Folsom; unclassified 14% Agate Basin to 11% Folsom.

Platform Preparation.   Another feature of flakes that may indicate differences in production technology from one assemblage to another is the manner

TABLE 3.1
Agate Basin and Folsom Level Tool Types by Flake Types

Tool type	Normal		Disc		Biface		Unclassified	
	AB	F	AB	F	AB	F	AB	F
8	1	0						
9	3	7			3	5	2	0
10	3	2			2	1		
11	2	0			1	1		
12	1	0			0	4		
13			1	0	5	2		
15	0	1			7	1	1	0
16	0	1			1	0		
17	1	0			2	0		
19	1	0			0	1		
21					2	0		
22	1	0	1	0	1	0		
23	0	1	2	0	0	1		
26							1	0
28	2	0						
29	1	0						
30	13	9			0	2	1	1
31	4	0			2	1	2	1
33					2	0		
34	3	1			3	11	1	1
35					1	3		
39					5	4	1	2
42	2	2			3	1	1	0
43	0	1			2	0	1	1
44	0	1						
54								
62	2	1			3	0	3	2

[a] AB, Agate Basin; F, Folsom.

of platform preparation. This may include one or a combination of preparation techniques on each flake. The following platform attributes were recorded in this study: plain, dihedral, polyhedral, faceted, ground, and reduced. Table 3.2 lists these and all observed combinations by flake type for both the Agate Basin and Folsom levels. There is no apparent difference between the platform-preparation techniques in the two levels. Both show the entire range of combinations from plain (unprepared) through faceted, reduced, and ground (complex preparation). One can therefore draw the conclusion that platform preparation was normally employed during reduction sequences and that several techniques were used in a selective manner.

To get an idea of the relative uses of these techniques, their percentages may be calculated. This is done by occurrence rather than by flake count; that is, a flake with a faceted, reduced, and ground platform is counted as one occurrence in each category. In the Agate Basin level we find 29% faceting, 32% reducing, and 39% grinding, in the Folsom level, 41% faceting, 22% reducing, and 37% grinding. The only difference of any significance is that the Folsom level materials show more faceting, whereas tools in the Agate Basin level exhibit more

TABLE 3.2
Agate Basin and Folsom Level Platform-Preparation Types by Flake Types

Platform-preparation attributes	Normal		Disc		Biface		Unclassified	
	AB	F	AB	F	AB	F	AB	F
Plain	4	4	2	0	1	1		
Plain, reduced	3	1			2	0		
Plain, ground					3	0	1	0
Plain, reduced, ground	2	0			3	1		
Dihedral	2	1	1	0	3	0		
Dihedral, reduced	1	0			1	0		
Dihedral, ground	0	1						
Dihedral, reduced, ground	1	0						
Polyhedral	1	1			0	1		
Faceted	1	1			0	1		
Faceted, reduced					2	2		
Faceted, ground	3	1			7	8		
Faceted, reduced, ground	1	3			6	3		

[a] AB, Agate Basin; F, Folsom.

platform reduction. This percentage of faceting in the Folsom level compares favorably to the percentage for the retouched flakes from the Hanson site (Frison and Bradley 1980:27). From these observations and calculations it is possible to conclude that no substantial difference in primary and secondary flaking technology are apparent between the Folsom and Agate Basin assemblages from the Agate Basin site.

SECONDARY TECHNOLOGY

Unifacial Retouch. The examples of unifacial retouch seen on the tools from the Agate Basin site appear to have resulted from a direct percussion technique. Some of the fine retouch used to produce the small borer tips may have resulted from a pressure technique; however, it is not possible to be certain of the technique used since even the relatively fine retouch observed on the ends of some end scrapers has been reproduced experimentally with direct percussion.

Bifacial Retouch and Thinning. Bifacial retouch and thinning were restricted to the production of bifaces and projectile points; the two categories are considered separately here. Most of this involved marginal areas where force was applied either by direct percussion or by pressure.

Biface Manufacture Technology

AGATE BASIN LEVEL

All of the non-projectile-point bifaces recovered from the Agate Basin level fall within production sequences 1 through 3 observed at the Hanson site (see Frison and Bradley 1980:31–42). These categories represent initial biface shaping and thinning but do not include extensive and/or refined biface thinning. Of the 15 specimens in this study, 7 are Category 1 bifaces. Three are in Category 2, and 5 are in Category 3.

Two of the Category 1 bifaces (Figures 2.72e and 2.73f) are simply large, flat flakes that were flaked bifacially around the margins with noninvasive selective percussion flaking. All three of the Category 2 bifaces recovered are distal fragments. Little additional information is evident because of their fragmentary condition (e.g., Figure 2.73a). Of the five Category 3 bifaces found, four are fragmentary. All but one were made from local Agate Basin chalcedony (e.g., Figure 2.73b) and probably were originally intended to be made into projectile points. Breakage and abandonment were caused most often by material flaws but occasionally by flaking mistakes. The fragmentary specimen shown in Figure 2.72a is very likely of a coarse, red Flint Hills, South Dakota, quartzite; it has a unifacial beveled retouch along one distal margin, indicating that it had been prepared for use in its present stage of manufacture. One of the chalcedony specimens (Figure 2.72b) is similar. This retouch also occurred on some of the Category 3 bifaces at the Hanson site (Frison and Bradley 1980:33) and in the Agate Basin–Hell Gap level in the Carter/Kerr-McGee site (Frison 1977). It seems quite likely that all of the Category 2 and 3 bifaces were used during the butchering and processing of bison. The Category 1 bifaces may also have served a utilitarian function; however, the fact that they were made from locally available material could explain their presence without a definite functional intention. There is no direct evidence that any of these bifaces served primarily as cores.

FOLSOM LEVEL

As was the case for cores, the sample size for Folsom level bifaces is quite small (eight specimens) and does not allow direct comparisons with larger assemblages. One Category 1 biface in two pieces (Figure 2.25h) and another Category 1 fragment, along with two Category 2 fragments and one Category 3 fragment, appear to be manufacture discards. A single Category 3 biface (Figure 2.25b) has an abrupt beveled retouch along one distal/lateral margin, indicating that it was intended for use. Unfortunately, the distal end is missing and exact edge-to-longitudinal-axis angles could not be determined. This specimen does compare favorably with one from the Hanson site (Frison and Bradley 1980:Figure 21c, d).

Two pieces recovered form the midsection of a Category 5 biface (Figure 2.25a) showing fine, sharp marginal retouch. These pieces probably represent the remains of a specifically produced biface knife. Once again this type of artifact was found at the Hanson site (Frison and Bradley 1980:39–40). Another biface is an exhausted core that was modified slightly to form a biface tool (Figure 2.25g). In both Agate Basin (Figure 2.72c, d) and Folsom (Figure 2.25e) assemblages there were fragments of plate chalcedony with bilateral retouch that could conceivably be regarded as bifaces, since the necessity of biface thinning was eliminated by the natural configuration of the raw material.

Projectile Point Manufacture Technology

The stages of fluted point manufacture evidenced in Folsom level artifacts recovered at the Agate Basin site very closely parallel those of the Hanson site (Frison and Bradley 1980:45–52) and are as follows:

FOLSOM FLUTED POINTS

Stage 1: Blank Manufacture and Selection. One artifact (see Figures 2.79l and 3.2a) is a medium-size, flat, hinge-fractured biface flake that had been

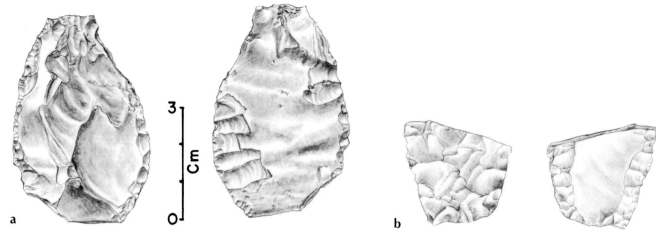

FIGURE 3.2 **Folsom projectile point preform (a) and a broken Folsom preform (b).**

marginally retouched and partially bifacially pressure flaked before it was discarded. The platform end of the flake would have been the proximal end of the preform and the hinge fracture would have become the distal end of the preform. Abandonment was apparently caused by the presence of a small crystal pocket near one proximal corner that probably would have interfered with further flaking and/or flute removal.

Stage 2: Initial Shaping and Thinning.   One preform base fragment retains evidence of the initial shaping and thinning process on one face. The other face had progressed through Stage 6 and had broken at that point (Figures 2.26w and 3.2b). Initial shaping was accomplished with careful percussion bifacing that produced a smooth, regular surface.

Stage 3: Pressure Shaping and Thinning.   No examples recovered exhibited evidence of this stage of manufacture. Two pieces were recovered at the Hanson site and are illustrated in that report (Frison and Bradley 1980:46; Figure 28a, b).

Stage 4: Specialized Flaking of One Side.   No examples of this stage of manufacture were recovered, although several preforms flaked to further stages exhibit remnants of this stage (Figure 2.26d, m). Two specimens are illustrated in the Hanson site report (Frison and Bradley 1980:Figure 28c, d).

Stage 5: Channel-Flake Platform Preparation.   The base of a preform that was broken during the attempt to remove the first channel flake was recovered (Figure 2.26v). The platform had not detached and the preform was broken by a heavy bend break, probably because of insufficient support during loading. The resulting preform fragment shows the method of platform isolation and preparation by faceting, reducing, and grinding.

Stage 6: Channel-Flake Removal.   Evidence of the initial channel-flake removal attempt was seen on nine preforms and preform fragments (Figure

FIGURE 3.3 **Reassembled broken Folsom preform.**

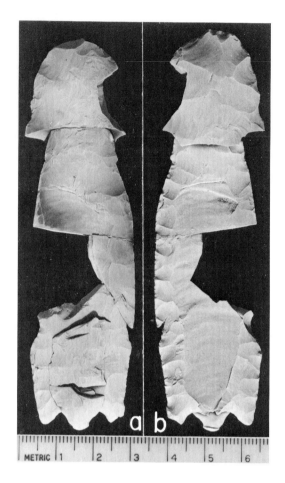

2.26a, b, d, f, m, p, s, w, x). In all cases the channel-flake removal truncated regular shaping pressure-flake scars and in no case did it truncate any finely flaked margin retouch. The majority of these fluting attempts were successful in that the preforms were further flaked. Only one (Figures 2.26w and 3.2b) was definitely broken and discarded at this stage of manufacture. Parts of the first channel flake (Figure 2.26q, r) on one specimen (Figure 2.26p) were recovered. When the flake is replaced in its channel on the preform, there is about 3.5 mm between striking platforms of the first and second channel flakes (Figure 3.3).

Stage 7: Specialized Pressure Shaping and Thinning of Second Face. One complete preform (Figure 2.26m) and one midsection (Figure 2.26d) were abandoned after Stage 9 failures but retained good evidence of Stage 7 attributes. Both exhibit flake scars resulting from regularly spaced and removed pressure flakes meeting at the long axis of the preform. These flake scars demonstrate relatively deep negative bulbs of applied force along the margins, producing a hollow-ground effect. The complete preform was discarded after unsuccessful channel-flake removal, and the midsection piece was discarded after preform collapse during the second channel-flake removal attempt. Part of the first channel was recovered (Figure 2.26e).

It should be noted that the lateral margins of Folsom preforms were very thin after this pressure flaking, and no evidence of edge beveling as a means of platform production was observed. Platform preparation appears to have been selective, tending to utilize a platform-reduction technique.

Stage 8: Channel-Flake Platform Preparation. No preforms recovered retained the second channel-flake platform, nor could any second channel flakes recovered be replaced in channel-flake scars on preforms.

Stage 9: Channel-Flake Removal. Six preforms and fragments were discarded after the completion of Stage 9. It is interesting to note that four preforms could easily have been retouched into functional and what would be considered acceptable projectile points, based on the attributes of those that were completed (Figure 2.26a, f, s, x). These specimens will be individually described at the end of this section.

Three fragments resulted from breakage during the removal of the second channel flake (Figures 2.26d, f; 3.4) and three preform tips exhibiting evidence of flutes on both faces were found (Figure 2.26a, j, o). Part of the channel flake on one of these (Figure 2.26j) was recovered, which demonstrates the situation whereby a second channel flake executes an *outre passe* through to the opposite preform face. All of these preform tip fragments were blunt to rounded and were thickest at the end, which probably contributed to the breakage during the second channel-flake removal. Tip-beveling is not present; they were instead bifacially abruptly flaked and lightly abraded. It is possible also that intentional tip-snapping as proposed by Judge (1973:169) was performed in some cases, although this process has not been conclusively demonstrated. Personal experimental attempts have shown that it is much more difficult to break a preform at the termination of the shortest flute than to retouch down to it. Most experimental attempts at tip-snapping have resulted in breakage well down into both flutes, leaving a basal piece too small to retouch into an acceptable projectile point. There are also a substantial number of Folsom points that are not fluted all the way to the tip on both sides, yet retain long flutes. The *outre passe* (Figure 2.26j) would obviously have ruled out tip-snapping.

Stage 10: Postfluting Retouch. Only one basal point fragment that included postfluting marginal and basal retouch was found (Figure 2.26h). The retouch is bifacial irregular, and fairly abrupt; it does not invade the flutes on

FIGURE 3.4 **Part of a Folsom preform broken during removal of the second channel flake.**

either side. In addition, two basal fragments from the Brewster site (Figure 2.41a, c) have invasive lateral margin retouch extending into the edges of the channel-flake scars. Heavy lateral edge grinding also occurs on all of these specimens. The manufacturing sequence follows the same process observed at the Hanson site (Frison and Bradley 1980:Figure 32). One Folsom base (Figure 2.41b) was found by James Duguid in Area 2 shortly after the Bass and Roberts investigations in 1961. This specimen demonstrates invasive lateral margin retouch extending into the edges of the channel-flake scars. It was made from a distinctive opaque reddish chert; a few flakes of the same material are in the Area 2 Folsom component. Although exact provenience data are lacking, it seems reasonable to assign this specimen to the Agate Basin Area 2 Folsom assemblage.

It can be demonstrated beyond any doubt that projectile point manufacture was part of the site activities in the Folsom component in Area 2. Unfinished specimens are extremely valuable in revealing details of the manufacture process. A description of a number of these projectile point preforms ensues. This will aid not only in understanding the manufacture process but also in comparing specimens from other sites, such as the Hanson site (Frison and Bradley 1980) and Lindenmeier (Wilmsen and Roberts 1978).

One seemingly successfully fluted preform was discarded without final retouching. Although no features of Stages 1–5 of manufacture remain, the sequence is inferred. Stage 6 removed a flake that ran about two-thirds the length of the preform and terminated in a step fracture. A narrow area of a previously removed flute remains on the right side of this flute. It seems that a channel flake was removed but not deemed adequate so another platform was set up and a second channel flake removed from the same face. Stage 7 was then undertaken using an evenly spaced nonserial selective pressure-flaking sequence. The channel-flake removal on the second face eliminated any evidence of the Stage 8 procedure. Stage 9 resulted in what must be considered a highly successful channel-flake removal. The bulb and fracture release are slightly skewed to the left but the entire flute expanded nicely and removed a flake with nearly parallel sides. It traveled the entire length of the preform and removed only a very small portion of the distal end with an *outre passe* fracture. This channel must be considered almost perfect. The platform was removed with a "lipped" fracture initiation, leaving the proximal end with the desired knife edge. A few selected flakes were then removed from the distal end, removing a small portion of the overshot fracture. No other retouch was done. No edge grinding is present.

It is very difficult to understand why this preform was not finished into a projectile point. As far as I can tell it meets all of the expected standards of even the best Folsom points known from actual site material. Only a short period of time and a small amount of effort would have been necessary to complete it (Figures 2.26x, 3.5, and 3.6).

Another specimen is a large preform fragment (Figure 2.26f) that was abandoned for projectile point manufacture after Stage 9 resulted in its being shortened by an overshot channel-flake removal. This channel flake began with an evenly expanding configuration and traveled about half the length of the preform before it expanded to the margins, producing the *outre passe* fracture.

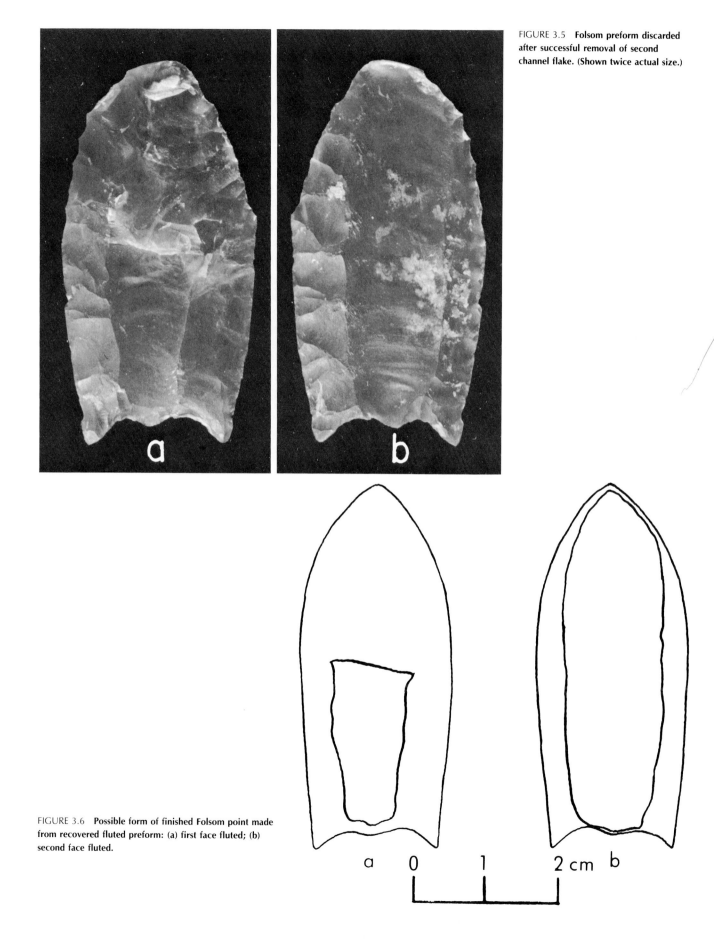

FIGURE 3.5   Folsom preform discarded after successful removal of second channel flake. (Shown twice actual size.)

FIGURE 3.6   Possible form of finished Folsom point made from recovered fluted preform: (a) first face fluted; (b) second face fluted.

This apparently shortened the preform too much for it to be readily reworked into a projectile point. The lateral edges and distal end were then denticulated with opposed bevel flaking. This presumably was done to produce a usable tool but no convincing evidence of use is present. One preform "ear" is missing, but at what point it was broken off is not clear.

Another preform (Figure 2.26m) is quite interesting in that a series of successive fluting failures is apparent on one side. Stages 1 through 4 are inferred, and Stages 5 and 6 seem to have been repeated three times; each time only a small short and/or narrow channel flake was removed. At this point Stages 7–9 were completed, with the Stage 9 channel flake being very narrow and short. The preform was then discarded. It is not at all clear why a fluting attempt was made on the second side when the first was so poorly accomplished. As found, this preform, though poorly fluted, could have readily been transformed into a functional projectile point within the range of observed acceptability at some other Folsom sites (Frison and Bradley 1980; Wilmsen and Roberts 1978).

One large preform (Figure 2.26s) was discarded after Stage 9 had been completed. Stages 1–8 seem to have been normally completed, with the initial channel-flake removal having been particularly successful. The Stage 9 flake removal ended in a deep hinge fracture as the flake entered an area of relatively coarse material. Even with this apparent flaw, the preform could have been readily retouched into an entirely acceptable, functional Folsom point. It seems obvious also that a knowledgeable flint knapper would have predicted the results of the Stage 9 channel-flake removal.

A preform midsection (Figure 2.26d) once again demonstrates the standard point-production sequence. It broke during or immediately after the Stage 9 channel-flake removal. Of particular interest are the large size of the piece, its regularity, and the width of the first channel removal; also, it was made from a coarse-grained quartzite. This is one example of among many from the Agate Basin and Hanson sites of successful flutes on tough or coarse materials, and provides evidence contrary to Crabtree's conclusion (1966:9) that "the raw material had to be of high quality (obsidian or heat-treated chert or chalcedony)."

A fragmented Folsom point preform (Figures 2.26p, q, r; 3.3) exhibits the most interesting and perplexing manufacture sequence and breakage of all of the Agate Basin Folsom component specimens. A large Knife River flint preform was completed through Stage 5. Stage 6 produced a channel flake that traveled the entire length of the preform and removed a small portion of the distal end by an *outre passe* fracture (Figure 3.7a). Stages 7 through 9 were then completed, with the second channel-flake removal terminating just short of the new distal end of the preform that resulted from the overshot fracture of Stage 6 (Figure 3.7b). At this point the normal sequence was interrupted. Instead of simply retouching it to make a projectile point that was fluted almost to the tip, the knapper reflaked the initially fluted side with specialized pressure shaping and thinning (Stage 4). A channel-flake platform was prepared and a channel flake was successfully removed, terminating just before the distal end (Figure 3.7c). Once again, instead of retouching the preform to make a projectile point, the knapper broke it into several pieces with a sharply focused radial break originating in one of the channel-flake scars. Although a radial break may occur during

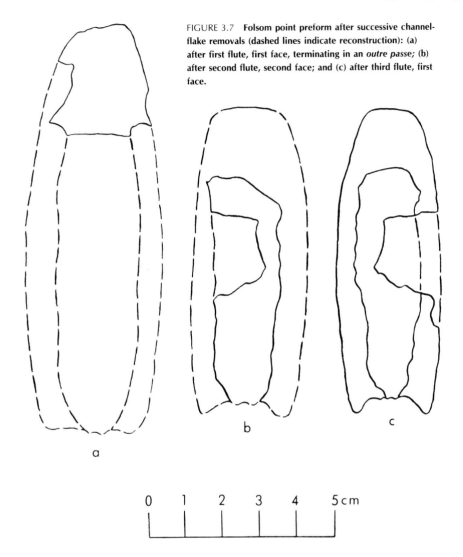

FIGURE 3.7 **Folsom point preform after successive channel-flake removals (dashed lines indicate reconstruction): (a) after first flute, first face, terminating in an *outre passe*; (b) after second flute, second face; and (c) after third flute, first face.**

0   1   2   3   4   5 cm

flaking, the sharp focus of the fracture initiation of this break indicates that the preform was struck a forcible blow near the center of one of the channel-flake scars. This break most likely resulted from intention rather than error. If this preform had been completed to a projectile point it would have been one of the better Folsom points ever known to have been produced. Possible reasons for its incompletion will be discussed subsequently.

The final preform to be described (Figures 2.26a and 3.8) again varied in manufacture sequence and standard morphology. It is quite small and noticeably asymmetrical. Stages 1–5 of manufacture are inferred and Stage 4 seems to have been incomplete. The initial channel-flake removal is mostly obliterated by a subsequent channel on the same side of the point. Only a small amount of the flake scar remains along the right side of the preform. At this point the preform was given an asymmetrical retouch, and Stages 7 through 9 were completed. The final channel-flake removal traveled the length of the preform and removed a small portion of the tip with an *outre passe* fracture. Some retouch was then performed on one side of the tip; however, none was on any other part of the

FIGURE 3.8 **Fluted Folsom preform reworked into a tool.**

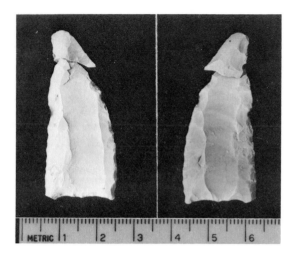

preform. This retouch accentuated its asymmetrical form, and was very likely done to produce or maintain a tool edge although no definite evidence of tool use is present.

Once again we do not know why the flaking process was continued. The specimen is smaller than most of the recovered completed Folsom points, but it could easily have been flaked into a functional projectile point that would have been within the range of variation of known specimens.

UNFLUTED POINTS   Two projectile points that were not prepared or fluted by means of the process just described were recovered from the Folsom level. The first (Figure 2.26c) exhibits irregular selective pressure-flake scars with shallow and narrow base-thinning flakes on both sides. A selective retouch around the entire point was then done and it was finished with light, lateral, basal margin grinding. Technologically and typologically this projectile point exhibits characteristics reminiscent of Clovis points from the western United States. It is also highly similar to a reworked fluted point recovered from the Hanson site (Frison and Bradley 1980:Figure 33).

The second unfluted projectile point (Figure 2.26g) is simply a biface thinning flake that has been bifacially and selectively pressure retouched to form a Folsom projectile point. Areas of both the dorsal and bulbar surfaces of the original flake blank are still visible and the pressure flaking seems to have been done intentionally, leaving areas on the point that resemble flutes. This technology was also noted at the Lindenmeier site (Wilmsen and Roberts 1978). Basal margin grinding supports the conclusion that this was a completed projectile point.

AGATE BASIN PROJECTILE POINTS   Agate Basin-style projectile points (Frison 1978a; Roberts 1951, 1961a; Wormington 1957) were recovered in large numbers from the Agate Basin level in Areas 1 and 2. A total of 133 points and fragments are included in this study. An additional 37 pieces are classified as Hell Gap; Agate Basin or Hell Gap; possibly Agate Basin; possibly Hell Gap; and those specimens too fragmentary to identify. Three technological observations were made for each point or fragment, including (a) the technique of the initial shaping (percussion, pressure, or absent); (*b*) the technique of final surfacial shaping (pressure or absent); and (*c*) the technique of final margin shaping (pressure or absent). Not surprisingly, the most common combination for the Agate Basin points was as follows: no visible initial shaping flake scars, pressure shaping and thinning, and marginal pressure retouch. There are, however, a significant number of Agate Basin points that retain some evidence of the initial shaping technique, which was in all but one instance percussion flaking. Workmanship and care in flaking are, for the most part, very good to excellent, but occasional poorly flaked points do exist.

There seems to have been a generalized reduction system that may be divided into only three stages of manufacture, which correspond to the three technological subdivisions just described. When visible percussion shaping and thinning were done in an evenly spaced selective sequence to produce very regular longitudinal and lateral preform cross-sections, the pressure flaking following was mostly a surface-regularizing process, with occasional thinning taking place especially at the tips and bases. This pressure flaking tended to be shallow and ran to the longitudinal axis at about 90°. It was evenly spaced and carefully executed. No instances of serial flaking were observed, and all flaking was basically selective. This was also true of the marginal pressure retouch, which was mostly bifacial and somewhat abrupt. On some specimens this retouch invaded the surface almost to the center. Although these projectile points are relatively thin, the emphasis seems to have been placed on regularity—especially of the longitudinal cross-section and lateral margins. Great care was taken in all stages of manufacture and flaking mistakes were rare. Lateral margins and bases were mostly lightly smoothed by abrasion from the base to about the point of maximum width.

Only the two unfluted projectile points (Figure 2.26c, g) and the single fluted base (Figure 2.26h) represent completed points from this stratigraphic unit. The specimen recovered by Duguid (Figure 2.41b) should probably be included. The first two were complete, but the last two were broken with simple bend breaks. No evidence of reuse of projectile points can be claimed for the Folsom level.

Projectile Point Use and Reuse

FOLSOM LEVEL

AGATE BASIN LEVEL

It is quite evident that many of the Agate Basin projectile points were reworked and/or reused before abandonment. This evidence is observable in the outline morphology, abrupt changes in longitudinal cross-sections, and variations in flaking styles and regularity. Outline morphology was proposed in a study by Peterson (1978) as a means of identifying reworked Agate Basin projectile points. Point plotting of the artifacts on a rectangular grid system was used and outlines and degrees of lateral margin convergence were determined. An archetype of an Agate Basin point was described, based on the ratio of breadth to length and the ratio of lateral margin grinding length to point length. Variations from this expected model were then explained as different types of projectile point reworking. This general approach was modeled after the work done by Bradley (1974) on the Casper site Hell Gap points; however, the point-plotting system was devised by Peterson. His conclusions were that all available fragment types of sufficient size (bases, midsections, and tips) were reutilized, with basal fragments predominant. This approach does indeed allow one to make statements about reuse of Agate Basin points; however, the conclusions all rest on the existence of an original Agate Basin point in outline form. This assumption has not been adequately tested and variations in initial acceptable point forms have not been established.

The projectile points with adequate provenience data from the Agate Basin level in Area 2 are what is accepted as the Agate Basin type with very few exceptions. One (Figure 2.54a) is a true Hell Gap type; another (Figure 2.52g) demonstrates a slight shoulder reminiscent of the Hell Gap type. All other provenienced Hell Gap type projectile points were from a proven Hell Gap component (see, e.g., Figures 2.56m, t; 2.83a–f).

The specimen shown in Figure 2.54a was the only Hell Gap projectile point recovered in situ in the Agate Basin bone bed, and it may be intrusive. If it is not intrusive, the range of outline variation in the points from the Agate Basin level is quite extreme—from the Hell Gap type point at the wide end of the range to the long, narrow Agate Basin points at the other, with virtually a continuum between them. it is unlikely that all of this variation can be explained by reworking.

The identification of projectile points that have been reworked is based on observations of major changes in longitudinal cross-sections and flake scar patterns. Features considered to indicate reworking include these: (*a*) an abrupt change in thickness along the longitudinal cross-section (Figure 3.9b); (*b*) irregular flake scar patterns truncating normal regular flake scar patterns (Figure 3.9d); (*c*) abrupt changes in outline form (Figure 3.9d); and (*d*) remnants of breaks (Figure 3.9e). These features are often found in combinations, which

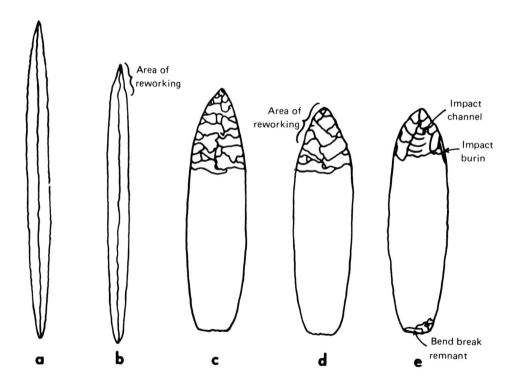

FIGURE 3.9 Normal Agate Basin point, side view (a); reworked tip of Agate Basin point, side view (b); normal Agate Basin point, flake scar pattern (c); reworked tip of Agate Basin point, flake scar pattern (d); and reworked Agate Basin point with remnant breaks (e).

provides an even stronger case for reworking. Much of the suspected reworking is demonstrated by the removal of pressure flakes that are qualitatively different from the initial shaping and retouch pressure-flake scars. They tend to be deeper, more abrupt, and less carefully spaced. In addition, fine edge retouch is lacking in most cases.

This presents the possibility that the reworking of projectile points was done either by persons other than the original producer, or by the original producer under unfavorable circumstances. There is physically no reason why reworking could not have been accomplished with the same skill and care as shown in the original point, so other explanations must be sought. The circumstances may reflect a number of sociocultural possibilities. Craft specialization is one such possibility; perhaps only certain individuals produced the highly refined projectile points, either because of special skill or because of their religious position or status. Another possibility is that the points were produced under highly controlled religious circumstances in order to increase their functional capabilities in a hunt. If either of these situations occurred, it is unlikely that every family and/or band would include a specialist or the necessary religious person to make or remake broken points to the required physical and/or religious specifications. It is also probable that virtually every individual within these groups would possess the necessary skills to undertake basic flaking processes up to and including bifacial projectile point reworking.

The analysis of the projectile points and fragments from the Agate Basin level resulted in evidence that 62% were not reworked and 38% were reworked. Of the pieces that showed signs of reworking, 37% were base fragments with reworked tips, and 34% were tip fragments with reworked bases; 3% were reworked along an edge, 15% were midsection fragments reworked on the base and tip, and 11% were reworked all over.

Two categories of projectile point damage have been recorded: use-damage and breaks. The use-damage category includes the various types of breaks that may be assumed to have occurred through use, as on impact. The break category lists the various morphological break combinations that may have been caused either in a use or a nonuse situation. Three areas of the projectile points were examined for use-damage: tip, sides, and base. Damage to tips was seen as generalized impact, impact burin, impact channel, and simple crushing. Damage to the edges of the points was in the form of irregular, deep, abrupt flake removals. Damage to the bases was in the form of burin spall removals. Of these types of damage, all may occur during impact; however, breaks due *specifically* to impact made up a total of 49% of all types of use-damage (see Table 3.3).

Nine different subdivisions of the break category have been recorded: bend, constrained bend, radial, *outre passe,* perverse, radial bend, flaw, "shear," and unknown. Of these only perverse and flaw breaks are specifically manufacture breaks. The rest could have occurred at any stage of manufacture or use of the projectile points. A tabulation of the break types by point types is given in Table 3.4. All of the manufacture breaks occurred on pieces classified as of unknown projectile point type. This strongly indicates that this group of artifacts would more properly have been classified as bifaces, specifically as blanks or preforms.

Projectile Point Use-Damage and Breaks

AGATE BASIN LEVEL

TABLE 3.3
Projectile Point Use-Damage by Point Type

Damage		Projectile point type						
Area	Type	Agate Basin	Hell Gap	Agate Basin/ Hell Gap	Agate Basin?	Hell Gap?	Unknown	Total
Tip	Simple impact	25	3	1		1	1	31
Tip	Impact burin	12						12
Tip	Impact flute	11	1	1			1	14
Tip	Crush	11	1		1			13
Side	Flaking	25	3	2	1	1		32
Base	Burin	10	2					12
Total		94	10	4	2	2	2	114

Overall, the evidence indicates that the majority of the projectile points were broken during use as projectile points, and not as knives or other tool types.

FLAKE TOOL TYPOLOGY

As was mentioned earlier, the system used to classify tools in this study is the same as that employed for the Hanson site assemblage (Frison and Bradley 1980). A modified Bordes typology is used in order to allow direct comparisons between the Agate Basin site and Hanson site assemblages. Although the criticism has been advanced that this system does not describe the "character" of the tool assemblage, this problem may be overcome by a thorough examination of the listing of tool types by flake types (Table 3.1) and the illustrations.

TABLE 3.4
Break Types by Projectile Point Types[a]

Break type	Projectile point type						
	Agate Basin	Hell Gap	Agate Basin/ Hell Gap	Agate Basin?	Hell Gap?	Unknown	Totals
Bend	40	4	5		1	4	54
Constrained bend	40	6	4				50
Radial bend	7		2				9
Radial	8		1			1	10
Perverse						3	3
"Shear"			1				1
Outre passe	1						1
Flaw						3	3
Unknown	7	1	2	1	1		11
Totals	103	11	15	2	2	11	142

[a]Counts do not equal number of artifacts but represent the number of breaks present (e.g., a midsection fragment has at least two breaks).

TABLE 3.5
Agate Basin Site Flake Tool Type Counts

Tool type	Agate Basin level	Folsom level
8	1	0
9	8	12
10	6	3
11	3	1
12	1	4
13	6	2
15	8	2
16	1	1
17	4	0
19	1	1
21	2	0
22	3	0
23	2	2
26	1	0
28	2	0
29	1	0
30	16	12
31	10	2
33	2	0
34	7	13
35	1	3
39	6	6
42	6	3
43	3	2
44	0	1
54	1	0
62	8	0
Total	110	73

Agate Basin Level

Eighty-eight retouched flake tools have been included in this study. Table 3.5 lists the tool type counts. By far the largest percentage of tools falls in the Bordes types 9–19, 21–23, and 30–31. These describe the types usually referred to as side scrapers, transverse scrapers, and end scrapers, respectively. The remaining tools are fairly evenly distributed among types 34–35 (borers), 39 (raclettes), 42–43 (notches), and 54 and 62 (other). Although the total number of artifacts studied was 88, 110 tool classifications were counted. This resulted because 11 of the 88 artifacts were considered multiple tools, and each tool type occurrence was counted separately. A listing of the multiple-tool combinations for the Agate Basin assemblage is given in Table 3.6.

Folsom Level

Fifty-seven retouched flake tools were used in this study of the Folsom assemblage. After classification it was found that 36% were types 9–19 (side scrapers), 3% were types 21–23 (transverse scrapers), 19% were types 30–31 (end scrapers), 22% were types 34–35 (borers), and the remainder were types 39 (raclettes), 42–43 (notches), and 44 (beak). Including the multiple tools, 73 tool classifications were made. A list of the Folsom multiple tools is given in Table 3.7.

TABLE 3.6
Multiple-Tool Combinations: Agate Basin Level

Tool type number	Type name	Catalog number	Figure number
31/42	Atypical end scraper/double notch	96045	2.66o
10/31/34	Single convex side scraper/atypical end scraper/typical borer (2)	OA269	2.65b
19/30	Convergent convex side scraper/typical end scraper	11309	2.63f
10/35/43	Single convex side scraper/atypical borer/denticulate	OA270	2.63c
33/43	Atypical burin/denticulate	96079	2.63b
9/43	Single straight side scraper/denticulate (inverse)	55	2.64h
31/34/42	Atypical end scraper/typical borer/notch	39	2.71n
30/42	Typical end scraper/notch	11305	2.71k
31/34	Atypical end scraper/typical borer (inverse)	11289	2.71t
26/30	Abrupt retouch side scraper/typical end scraper	11304	2.71m
30/34	Typical end scraper/typical borer	11273	2.66t, 2.67c
10/34	Single convex side scraper/typical borer	96096	2.61e

TABLE 3.7
Multiple-Tool Combinations: Folsom Level

Tool type number	Type name	Catalog number	Figure number
34/35	Typical borer/atypical borer	96558	2.21m
9/34	Single straight side scraper/typical borer	OA189, 30	2.23b
34/35	Typical borer/atypical borer	96589	2.19p
34/39	Typical borer/raclette	OA296	2.19t
11/34	Single concave side scraper/typical borer	OA026	2.21g
9/30	Single straight side scraper/typical end scraper	OA276	2.19h
		96426	2.19l
		OA045	2.19c
10/30	Single convex side scraper/typical end scraper	OA191	2.21x
10/30/42	Single convex side scraper/typical end scraper/typical notch	OA061	2.19d
13/30/42	Double straight-convex side scraper/typical end scraper/typical notch	96597	2.19i
16/23	Double concave side scraper/convex transverse scraper	OA123	2.19b
9/23/31	Single straight side scraper/convex transverse scraper/atypical end scraper	OA305	2.22a

At this point in the analysis it is interesting to compare the tool typologies of the Agate Basin and Folsom levels. These comparisons are of the greatest value when made by general type category rather than by individual type category.

The percentages of side-scraper types are almost identical in the two levels. This similarity is even evidenced, although not as strongly, in the flake types chosen for manufacture. Transverse scrapers were found in small quantities in both levels, with the greatest number coming from the Agate Basin level. This may be the result of a greater occurrence of disc core flakes that were trimmed into tools. By definition the only difference between side and transverse scrapers is the location and relative size of the retouched edge to the flake axis. If a disc core flake is chosen as a scraper flake-blank a transverse type is most likely to result. It is therefore unlikely that the greater occurrence of transverse scrapers in the Agate Basin assemblage is anything other than a product of technological variation.

The percentage of end scrapers is slightly larger in the Agate Basin level than in the Folsom level. The difference, however, is not enough to indicate significant variations in either site function or tool use patterns. The greatest amount of variation in the tool type assemblages between the two levels is seen in the percentage of borers represented; 7% in the Agate Basin level and 23% in the Folsom level. This seems to indicate a major difference in either site function or tool use patterns.

The remaining tool categories contain too few pieces to be readily compared. However, the number of tool type categories represented is greater in the Agate Basin level than in the Folsom level. This may indicate a greater range of acceptable tool variation in Agate Basin times, or it may simply be a function of the number of tools found. Further speculative statements seem unwarranted, unless the necessary supportive evidence can be accumulated.

One other aspect of tool manufacture that may be compared is the number and type of tools produced as multiple-tool artifacts. Within the Folsom assemblage, 13 multiple-tool artifacts were counted, with 3 having three tool edges and 10 being a combination of two edges. This represents 22.8% of all retouched flakes. The Agate Basin assemblage included 12 multiple-tool ar-

TABLE 3.8
Comparative Flake Tool Count and Percentages

| | Hanson site | | Agate Basin site | | | |
| | | | Folsom level | | Agate Basin level | |
Types	Number	%	Number	%	Number	%
Nos. 9–19, 21–23: side and transverse scrapers	88	47	28	40	46	41
Nos. 30, 31: end scrapers	58	31	14	20	26	24
Nos. 34, 35: borers	29	16	16	23	8	7
Other	12	6	12	17	30	27
Totals	187	100	70	100	110	99

tifacts with 3 having three tool edges and 9 having two. This represents 13.6% of the retouched-flake count. Conclusions from this difference are difficult to determine, and once again discussion becomes speculative. It may be that multiple-tool artifacts were more acceptable during Folsom times or that different site functions are represented in the two levels.

One way to help answer these questions is to define Folsom and Agate Basin assemblages based on data from other sites. At present this is difficult to do, because of the lack of comparable data from other sites. One site that has

TABLE 3.9

Dimensions and Indices of Projectile Points Recovered from the Agate Basin Site (1975–1980)[a]

Point number	Point type[b]	Total length (mm)	Blade length (mm)	Maximum width (mm)	Maximum thickness (mm)	Stem length (mm)	Angle of basal convergence (degrees)	Maximum length / Maximum width	Blade length / Maximum width	Maximum width / Blade thickness	Blade / Stem length	Reworking	Raw material[c]	Figure number
96060	AB	85.2[d]	36.6	23.1	8.8	48.6	14.5	3.69	1.58	2.62	.75	?	H	2.53o
96107a	AB	83.7[d]	46.2	23.0	7.8	37.5	14.5	3.64	2.01	2.95	1.23	No	K	2.52d
11307	AB	74.0	36.8	18.6	6.1	37.2	13.0	3.98	1.98	3.05	.99	No	K	2.52i
35008a	AB	78.6	23.4	25.0	9.0	55.2	9.0	3.14	.94	2.78	.42	Tip	Q	2.51m
96228	AB	57.8	22.5	21.0	6.9	35.3	14.5	2.75	1.07	3.04	.64	?	K	2.52f
96085	AB	80.5	35.8	23.8	7.8	44.7	9.0	3.38	1.50	3.05	.80	Tip	H	2.53n
96221	AB	88.0	47.0	20.2	6.5	41.0	7.5	4.35	2.33	3.11	1.15	No	H	2.53m
96118a	AB	—	63.0	26.0	7.2	—	8.0	—	2.42	3.61	—	No	K	2.52c
98605	AB	89.2[d]	43.5	26.2	7.5	45.7	12.5	3.40	1.66	3.49	.95	No	K	2.52k
35003a	AB	79.4	34.4	27.0	7.4	45.0	12.5	2.94	1.27	3.65	.76	Base	Q	2.51e
96042	AB	—	46.0	24.5	6.8	—	7.5	—	1.88	3.60	—	No	H	2.53p
35006a	AB	—	63.0	21.0	6.1	—	8.0	—	3.00	3.44	—	No	K	2.51b
11317	AB	141.0	83.6	21.9	7.0	57.4	9.5	6.44	3.82	3.13	1.46	No	K	2.51g
35002a	AB	81.5[d]	49.5	24.2	7.6	32.5	13.0	3.37	2.05	3.18	1.52	No	K	2.51a
35011a	AB	61.1	20.1	17.0	6.7	41.0	10.0	3.59	1.18	2.53	.49	Overall	H	2.51j
35004a	AB	54.0	18.8	19.8	7.3	35.2	10.5	2.72	.94	2.71	.53	Tip, base	H	2.51h
96076	AB	49.0[d]	14.0	18.0	6.0	35.0	5.0	2.72	.78	3.00	.40	Tip, base	Q	2.54o
35001a	AB	186.5[d]	126.7	25.6	7.7	—	—	—	4.94	3.32	—	Tip	H	2.59a, b
96205	AB	68.3[d]	41.5	18.0	6.3	26.8[d]	14.0	3.79	2.30	2.86	1.54	Overall	K	2.52g
96231	HG	—	—	30.8	6.5	—	18.5	—	—	4.74	—	No	Q	2.83b
96603	HG	58.3	29.3	25.0	7.0	29.0	14.0	2.33	1.17	3.57	1.01	No	C	2.54a
35009a	AB/HC	62.0	28.0	23.5	6.2	34.0	16.0	2.64	1.19	3.79	.82	No	Q	2.51k
OA051	AB	69.3	33.3	16.2	6.1	36.0	11.5	4.28	2.06	2.66	.93	No	K	2.52h
35010a	AB	84.6[d]	42.6	25.0	7.3	42.0	15.0	3.38	1.70	3.42	1.01	No	M	2.51i
96000 11291, 96602, 11294	AB	55.0[d]	16.0[d]	18.0	7.7	39.0	9.0	3.05	.89	2.34	.41	Tip	H	2.54b
11294	AB	130[d]	107	19.0	5.5	23.0[d]	—	6.84[d]	5.63	3.45	—	No	K	2.52a
11319	AB	69.5	22.5	24.0	7.0	47.0	12.0	2.90	.94	3.43	.48	Tip, base	K	2.55a
11332 96237,	AB	—	53.8	22.4	4.9	—	12.0	—	2.40	4.57	—	No	K	2.55b
96601	AB	112.2	46.2	26.0	8.0	66.0	6.5	4.31	1.78	3.25	.70	No	K	2.52b
OA059	C	39.1	23.9	19.0	5.4	15.2	—	2.06	1.26	3.52	1.57	No	H	2.26c
OA112	F	39.5	18.2	19.3	3.9	21.3	—	2.05	.94	4.95	.85	No	H	2.26g
OA151	HG	81.5[d]	75.0	31.8	7.4	—	—	—	.53	4.29	—	No	Q	2.83a
OA140	HG	49.8[d]	42.7	29.8	7.9	—	—	—	1.43	3.77	—	Yes	Q	2.83c
508,082[e]	AB	102	56.0	23.3	6.9	46.0	11.0	4.37	2.40	3.37	1.20	No	H	2.56j
508,073[e]	AB	99.7[d]	—	26.2	7.5	—	6.0	—	—	3.49	—	Tip	K	2.56a
OA060	AB	73.1[d]	—	20.9	6.9	36.7	8.5	—	—	3.02	—	Yes	H	2.53q
508,092[e]	HG	61.2	31.3	23.2	6.7	29.9	7.5	2.63	1.34	3.46	1.04	Blade	Q	2.56t
508,074[e]	AB	74.1[d]	—	22.7	7.7	47.3	12.5	—	—	2.94	—	Blade	H	2.56b
508,081[e]	AB	68.8[d]	43.5	24.9	6.7	—	—	—	1.74	3.71	—	No	Q	2.56i
508,083[e]	AB	78.3[d]	—	22.1	7.1	41.5	9.5	—	—	3.11	—	No	H	2.56k
OA176 OA458, 96094, 96094a	AB	187.0[d]	—	28.5	8.1	86.0	13.0	—	—	3.51	—	No	K	2.59c, d

[a]Includes Folsom, Agate Basin, and Hell Gap levels.
[b]AB, Agate Basin; HG, Hell Gap; C, Clovis; F, Folsom unfluted.
[c]K, Knife River flint; H, Hartville uplift chert; Q, local quartzite; C, chert of unknown source; M, Morrison formation quartzite.
[d]Incomplete measurement.
[e]Smithsonian, 1961.

been investigated and analyzed in a comparable manner is the Hanson site (Frison and Bradley 1980), as has been mentioned earlier. Although several time periods are represented in the locality, a sealed Folsom deposit was found and partially excavated. Table 3.8 lists the counts and percentages of tool types by general category for the Hanson and Agate Basin sites.

PROJECTILE POINT TYPOLOGY

Folsom Level

Only four projectile points that are considered to have been completed were recovered. These include a small Clovis point (Figure 2.26c) (Haury 1953; Wormington 1957), the bases of two fluted Folsom points (Figures 2.26h and 2.41b) (Frison and Bradley 1980; Roberts 1935; Wilmsen and Roberts 1978; Wormington 1957), and a pseudofluted Folsom point (Figure 2.26g) (Wilmsen and Roberts 1978). All of these specimens fall within the range of the described types and more elaborate descriptions need not be made here. Comments about their technological features were made earlier.

Agate Basin Level

Two distinct projectile point styles have been recovered from this level: Agate Basin and Hell Gap. A number of points intermediate between these styles have also been found. These are separated into Agate Basin/Hell Gap (falls within the range of both types), Agate Basin? (identification uncertain but closest to Agate Basin), Hell Gap? (identification uncertain but closest to Hell Gap), and unknown (too fragmentary to classify). To illustrate the range of size, shape, and resulting indices of several measurable specimens, a chart of the continuous variables has been included (Table 3.9).

THE SHEAMAN SITE

Clovis Biface Technology

Certain aspects of Clovis biface technology may be observed on bifaces from the Anzick (Lahren and Bonnichsen 1974) and Simon (Butler 1963) sites in Idaho and the San Jon site in New Mexico (Roberts 1942). The nature of the raw material form is not obvious, but the size of the bifaces and the area of

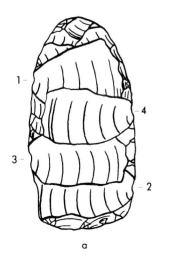

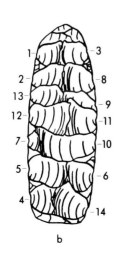

FIGURE 3.10 **Stylized Clovis biface thinning sequences: (a) alternate opposed biface thinning including frequent *outre passe* flakes as in Figures 3.11 and 3.12. (b) opposed diving biface thinning, with hinge-fracture flakes very common.**

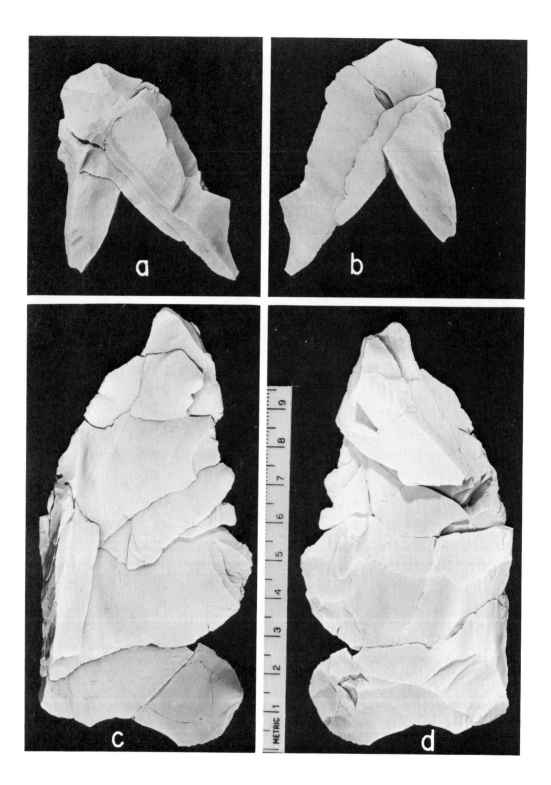

FIGURE 3.11 Reassembled biface reduction flakes from the Sheaman (Clovis) site.

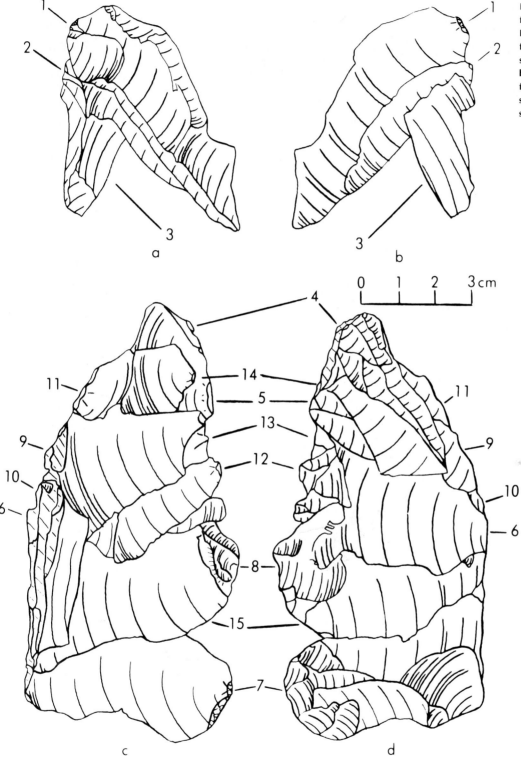

FIGURE 3.12 Reassembled flakes from the Clovis biface shown in Figure 3.11: (a) dorsal surface of flakes from first face; (b) bulbar surface of flakes from first face; (c) bulbar surface of flakes from second face; (d) dorsal surface of flakes from second face. Numbers indicate sequence of manufacture.

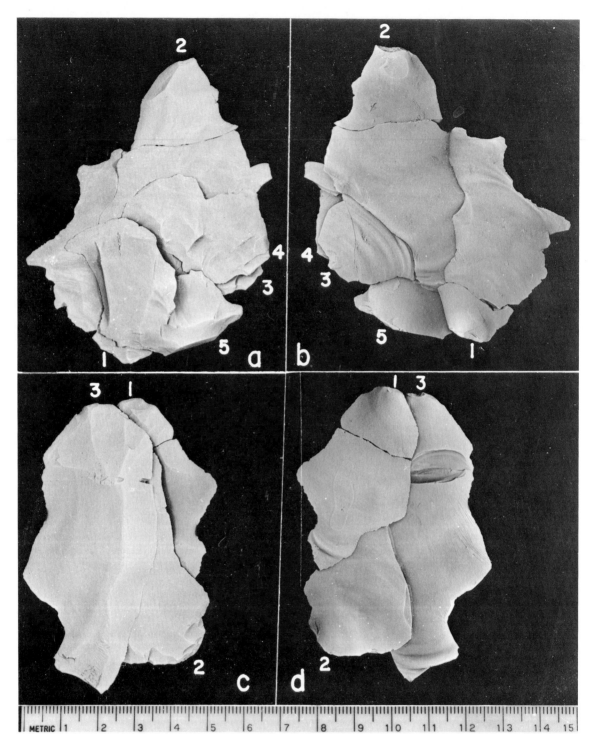

FIGURE 3.13 **Reassembled Clovis biface reduction flakes from the Sheaman site. Numbers indicate sequence of flake removal.**

retained cortex on some of them indicate that they were not made from large flakes. Initial shaping and thinning included the removal of large percussion thinning flakes in a patterned sequence, designated *alternating opposed biface thinning*. This involved the removal of a large flake from a margin near either end of the biface. Another flake was then removed from the opposite margin near the other end, but from the same face. The next step removed another large flake from the original margin, but again from the same face. This was placed between the first two flake removals. If additional thinning was needed, one or more additional flakes were removed from the center area of the biface. In this manner a single face of a biface was regularly thinned with the removal of only a few large flakes (Figure 3.10). Individual flake platform preparation was used and flakes traveled most of the way across the biface, in many cases terminating as *outre passe* flakes.

This specific pattern was not always followed, but it is seen in a majority of cases and seems to constitute a specifically Clovis biface production process. As the thinning progressed and the biface became narrower and regularized, a new type of thinning flaking was employed. This change of method occurred near the end of the flaking sequence and allowed for maximum thinning without the danger of *outre passe* flake production. It is designated *opposed diving biface thinning* flake removals. It was accomplished by the removal of a sequence of flakes from one margin on one face with intentional hinge-fracture terminations at or near the midline of the biface. These flake scars were then met, and most of the hinging removed, by the removal of a series of thinning flakes from the opposite margin. Although this process allows maximum thinning, when it is done on the same face more than a couple of times surface regularity becomes hard to maintain and flaking errors tend to be compounded.

Only one biface was recovered from the Clovis level in the Sheaman locality at the Agate Basin site. Along one margin of the biface the percussion flaking scars were obliterated by pressure flaking, and the method of final thinning is no longer obvious. It was possible, however, to observe the Clovis biface thinning sequence from a series of conjoined biface thinning flakes. A series of conjoined flakes from a single biface are the most informative (Figures 2.96, 3.11, and 3.12). This sequence illustrates the initial alternating opposed biface thinning described earlier. In this case, instead of individual large flakes, somewhat smaller pairs of flakes were normally struck.

This biface production (Figure 3.12) began with the removal of flake 1 from the right margin of the first face. A second, smaller flake, flake 2, was then removed from almost the same place. It is possible that this was accidentally struck during the follow-through stroke of flake 1. An overlapping flake, flake 3, was then removed from the left margin. At this point the biface was turned over and the remaining flakes were removed from the second face. This sequence was begun by the removal of flakes 4 and 5 from near the distal end and from the left margin, as seen in Figure 3.12. Next, flake 6 was struck from the right margin near the center of the biface (this flake was not recovered). Flakes 7 and 8 were then removed from the left margin from near the proximal end, advancing toward the center. Flakes 9, 10, and 11 were then removed from the right margin, this time from the distal end.

The reconstructible sequence ends with the removal of flakes 12, 13, 14,

FIGURE 3.14   **Reassembled Clovis biface reduction flakes from the Sheaman site. Numbers indicate sequence of flake removal. (Actual size.)**

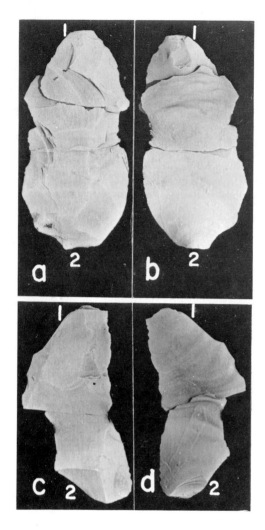

and 15 from the left margin. The first three were struck in sequence from the distal center of the biface, advancing toward the distal end. Flake 15 was removed from the proximal center of the biface. Even with the large number of *outre passe* flake productions, the width of the central area of the biface was only reduced from 5.5 cm to 4.6 cm. This indicates that substantial biface thinning was achieved using this method.

In addition to this biface reduction sequence, two other flake sequences were conjoined that illustrate the alternating opposed biface thinning process (Figure 3.13). The opposed diving flake biface thinning method is illustrated by two conjoined flake sequences (Figure 3.14).

2. FLUTING OF FOLSOM PROJECTILE POINTS

george c. frison and bruce a. bradley

The reason for the fluting seen in Folsom projectile points has been the subject of much speculation. It was an innovative process, and the technology involved required an extensive knowledge of the properties of the stone flaking materials, the necessary tool assemblage, and a considerable amount of skill on the part of the flint knapper. Speculations on how the channel flakes were removed have occupied the thoughts of Paleoindian archaeologists for over half a century. Evidence from the Agate Basin site gives an indication of what might have taken place.

An elk antler artifact (Figures 2.105 and 2.106) recovered from the Folsom level in Area 2 at the Agate Basin site is the first brow tine of a large mature male elk (*Cervus elaphas*) and is believed to be a tool used in the process of fluting projectile points. The tine was removed by deep grooving and chopping. The antler may have been from a freshly killed animal, or it may have been recently shed; either would have provided maximum strength. The artifact was found in close association with Folsom projectile point preforms representing about every stage of manufacture, as indicated by the various kinds of breakage that occurred during the process.

The deep longitudinal grooves made to remove the antler tine from the main antler beam were carefully placed so that the plane formed on the tool by the two opposing cuts is at right angles to the tip end of the longitudinal axis of the antler tine. This end was carefully abraded and polished to form a dull, rounded point with a small central depression. Although any straight elk antler tine might have been modified for use, a brow tine—and the first one in particular—is most suitable because of its relative robustness. Ideally the antler should be straight and require little or minimal tip alteration. Although it might be possible to obtain an antler that has a natural shaft/tine suitable for use as a fluting tool most antlers would need to be cut to obtain the correct angle, and this was the case with the archaeological specimen. It was taken from a slightly atypical antler, in that most brow tines are too curved to provide the proper strength. However, a study of several hundred modern elk antlers indicates that about 5% do demonstrate at least one relatively straight brow tine.

PROPOSED METHOD OF USE

The T shape of the recovered antler tine suggested it was a tool operated by chest pressure in much the same way as proposed by Crabtree (1966). This method has been successfully employed by Bradley for several years (Hole and Heizer 1973), using an unmodified elk antler that had a natural T-shaped tine/beam juncture. This antler functioned both for fluting bifacial preforms and for producing pressure blades from cores. The only problem encountered was that not enough consistently and slowly loaded force could be attained to remove channel flakes with the smooth bulbar surfaces observed on most archaeological Folsom points. Experiments with indirect percussion proved to be only partially satisfactory. Various forms of leverage, primarily modeled after methods devised by J. B. Sollberger (1977), were also used experimentally. These techniques allowed the consistent removal of channel flakes with smooth bulbar surfaces.

In order to answer some of the questions regarding its function, an experimental copy of the elk antler tool was produced. Although many elk antlers were available, careful selection was necessary to find one with a tine that closely resembled the prehistoric one. Upon selection of a satisfactory antler, the first brow tine was cut from the beams of the antler so that the angle between the cut end and tip approximated the angle on the Folsom elk antler tool. Several Folsom-style preforms were made by Bradley, a grooved log support was constructed, and attempts were made to remove channel flakes from the preforms using the antler with chest pressure. The results were minimally acceptable. Channel flakes were removed but they were short and tended to bounce and form irregularly.

It was decided that more and better controlled force was needed. A simple leverage device was devised by the authors. It allowed the loading of a much greater force with consistent and slow application (Figure 3.15). The experimental elk antler tine in a simple lever system proved effective as a preform fluting tool. Several preforms have been fluted to or almost to the tip using a variety of raw materials, including a tough, coarse-grained quartzite. The preform is placed vertically in a log support that has a slot cut from it through which the channel flake falls upon removal. The elk antler tine tip is then placed on the prepared platform at an angle slightly less than 90°. The lever is fit into a notch in a log buried vertically in the ground in front of the log preform support. The angles are adjusted and the platform contact checked. When everything is deemed correct, slow force is applied downward to the end of the lever. When

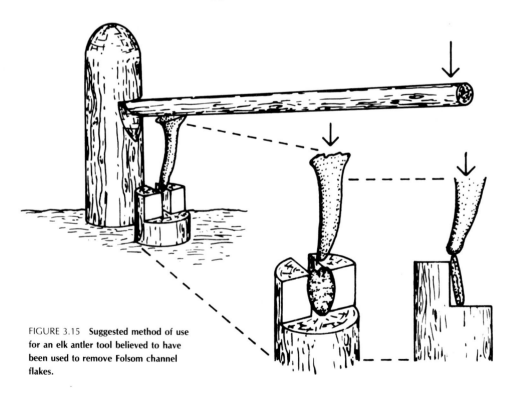

FIGURE 3.15 Suggested method of use for an elk antler tool believed to have been used to remove Folsom channel flakes.

the force of the antler against the platform produces enough pressure to initiate fracture, the channel flake is removed. In experiments, as in archaeological situations, channel flakes usually fragment. The only complete channel flake recovered is from the Folsom level in Area 3 (Figure 3.16).

After several channel-flake removals, the experimental antler tip became indented at the location where the platforms had contacted it. At first this was an advantage because it helped keep the antler tip from slipping off the platform. Eventually, however, the indentation became too deep and the area of contact with the platform was too large, making fracture initiation and control difficult. At this point the antler tip needed to be ground down to reduce the depth of the indentation. Eventually this process removed the hard outer layer of antler and reached the soft interior cancellous tissue. The antler was then no longer functional and had to be abandoned. However, the experimental tool was an antler shed from an immature animal and the dense outer part of the antler was much thinner than it would be on a mature one. Also, the experimental tool was not as robust as the Folsom tool.

A bone tool that is functionally similar to the elk antler tool was made on a relatively small bison metatarsal, probably one from a yearling female. The bone was broken when fresh across the diaphysis at a point where the cross section of the bone is nearly rectangular. However, in a cross-sectional view, one corner protrudes slightly more than the others; this is where the bone is thickest (10.2 mm). The shaft of the bone was broken so that this corner extends longitudinally beyond the others and a rounded blunt point was formed on the end (Figure 2.112c, d). This tool would function in the same manner as the elk antler tool. In fact, a short piece of long bone was broken on one end and the opposite end was prepared in a manner identical to that seen on the end of this tool. It may have been a point of a similar tool, or even the point of this same tool broken earlier.

The elk antler and bison metatarsal tools do not answer all of the questions concerning the technological process of fluting Folsom points. There may have been alternative means of applying pressure and holding the preform. It is possible, also that the recovered antler and bone tools were used as indirect percussion tools. In this case, however, it appears more likely that some means of continuous, increasing pressure was applied to dislodge the channel flakes.

There are also many questions concerning the reasons for fluting Folsom points. Arguments can be made that the flutes provide a superior means of hafting. On the other hand, not all Folsom points were fluted and the unfluted varieties can be hafted successfully. In addition, there is no satisfactory evidence to indicate that fluting improved their lethal qualities.

An argument can be made that the fluting process was an art form or was performed in the realm of ritual. It does seem to have been a wasteful process, considering the number of preforms destroyed in the fluting process. Other preforms appear to have been discarded only because of inferior flutes, although poorly fluted Folsom points have been recovered in kill sites, and well-fluted preforms were on occasion abandoned. Other projectile points were given the appearance of fluting, but in reality were nothing more than thin, flat flakes on which a flaking process was applied to produce an outline form.

Conclusions drawn from experiments are not to be used as proofs. On the

FIGURE 3.16 **A complete Folsom channel flake recovered in Area 2.**

FIGURE 3.17   **Folsom point made by Bradley from Spanish Diggings quartzite. Flutes were removed by a tool and method illustrated in Figure 3.15.**

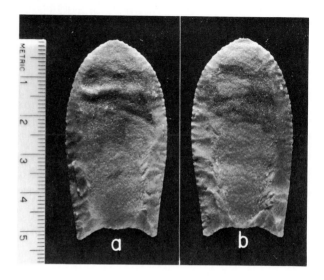

other hand, experimental applications can provide the analyst with some means of judging the possibilities and limitations imposed on tool use. The process of fluting Folsom projectile points using this means of channel-flake removal consistently gives results that are difficult if not impossible to distinguish from those of the Folsom knappers (Figure 3.17).

chapter four
FAUNAL STUDIES

1. ANALYSIS OF POSTCRANIAL BISON REMAINS

george m. zeimens

Precise analyses of disarticulated, fragmentary, and scattered bones are essential to interpretations of archaeological sites. Bone distribution, toolmarks on bones, and patterns of bone breakage are all artifacts of cultural activity. The skeletal elements are also fossils that contain morphological data pertinent to the biological and population structures of the animals, both of which may directly reflect certain aspects of the environment at the time of the cultural event. In this section the bison postcranial skeletal elements from the Agate Basin kill site will be analyzed, in order to describe and explain various activities, and to describe the animals involved in those activities. These data will contribute to the overall analysis of the event or series of events that took place at the site.

METHODOLOGY

During excavation the bones were left in place until they had been stabilized with preservatives and plotted on the site map. Matrices surrounding the bones were washed through a fine (1 mm mesh) water-screen in order to, as near as possible, realize total recovery. Large intact blocks of matrix were washed through the screen when the conditions were such that dissection with tools would have damaged both bone and artifacts. Field identification of many of the elements was tentative, and positive identification was sometimes possible only after the specimens had been cleaned in the laboratory. Individual bones and bone fragments were numbered sequentially during removal. Articulated units were assigned single numbers and were usually placed in plaster jackets for transport. As each bone was cleaned in the laboratory it was identified and counted, and breaks and other observable marks were noted. Individual examination of each specimen in the laboratory resulted in the identification of some possible tools and many nonbison bones that were not recognized as such in situ.

In order to achieve consistency, the writer examined each bone element. Identification was aided by the comparative collections at the University of Wyoming. These collections contain material from numerous archaeological sites as well as modern skeletons of known age and sex. A good comparative collection is indispensable to this kind of study, and serious problems are encountered in attempts to use inadequate comparative collections or to substitute non-*Bison* specimens. For example, the epiphyseal fusion rates published by Koch (1935:371–376) and by Duffield (1973:133) are based on rates established mainly from European bison (*Bison bonasus*), and are not directly applicable to the American bison. The proximal end of the radius apparently begins to fuse in the fourth year in the European animals but is already fused at the end of the first year in New World animals.

Unfortunately, the University of Wyoming collections do not yet contain all the specimens of known age needed to determine the full range of fusion rates. In the herds that specimens are drawn from, most of the male calf crop is butchered before the animals are 2 years old, and only the healthiest females are kept for breeding stock. The mortality rate is low among these young, hardy animals and, consequently, very few have become available for the collections. However, the age gap in the collections did not seriously hinder this study, since very few immature postcranial bones were preserved well enough to allow comparison of the area of the epiphyseal juncture or other aspects of bone growth and development.

All measurements taken during the studies were obtained with three instruments: a pair of sliding calipers, an osteometric board, and a 2000-ml graduated cylinder. Only one instrument of each type was used throughout, to reduce error. The measurements were taken by four people, and each was responsible for taking only certain measurements; again, to minimize error, each measurement was taken twice. With these restrictions it is reasonable to assume that the degree of error was held to ±1 mm and ±5 ml. These metric data were used to compare the sizes of the bones with *Bison* from other sites, as well as to attempt to determine the age and sex of individuals.

The minimum number of individuals (MNI) for each bone bed was obtained by simply counting the bones. The highest frequency of any single element was used to derive the MNI. Many more animals may have been present than are indicated, but because of poor bone preservation and, in particular, loss of much of the site through erosion and looting, more accurate estimates could not be obtained by this or any other method of determining MNI. Although the MNI is not considered to be an accurate representation of the total number of animals involved here, it can be used to determine the relative numbers of animals (i.e., many animals as opposed to few animals). This is important when considering the relative size of the human population involved, relative amounts of meat obtained, and animal-procurement methods.

Natural attritional factors that alter bone assemblages have been the subject of many studies (see Binford 1978; Bonnichsen 1973; Myers *et al.* 1980), from which it becomes obvious that all the factors determining the condition of bones as they are found in archaeological sites are not easily ascertained or quantified. The poor condition of the bone, especially from the Hell Gap and Agate Basin levels, severely limited this study. There are several probable explanations for this poor preservation. Two factors of attrition that affected the bone were the large quantity of clay in the soil and the heaviness of the overburden. The expansion and contraction of the clay, combined with the weight over long periods of time, broke and distorted the bone to the extent that much of its usefulness for this kind of analysis was lost. Preservation in the Folsom level was noticeably better than in the other levels, even though these bones were buried deeper. The Folsom level contained more sand and less clay, and the bones were not as greatly affected by the elastic properties of the soil; nor were the bone surfaces as badly deteriorated.

The surfaces of the Agate Basin level bones were so poorly preserved that most cut marks were obliterated; cut marks could be determined with certainty on only two bones from the Hell Gap level. The Folsom level bones were similarly affected, but to a lesser extent, so that cut marks did remain on numerous specimens. In all levels the epiphyseal surfaces of the unfused bones from immature animals were badly deteriorated, so that this aging criterion was severely limited. This deterioration is probably due to some unknown aspect of the soil chemistry.

Predators had some effect on the bone from all levels. Carnivores and scavengers chew, break, and eat bones in a relatively systematic manner, producing breakage patterns that are becoming better understood and more readily identified (Haynes 1980). Their actions also affect bone distribution; if this is not recognized, taphonomic analysis can be seriously affected. One need only observe large dogs attacking a cow or buffalo carcass, or coyotes tearing apart a deer or antelope, to realize how much carnivores may alter both the morphology and distribution of bones. Eagles and other large raptors may also have had an effect on the bone beds at some archaeological sites. Eagles alone feeding on carcasses as large as antelope and deer can completely disarticulate the carcasses within a few hours and scatter them over large areas.

Carnivores also swallow large bone fragments, which are redeposited later in their feces. It is suspected that several small, polished bone fragments found in the bone beds at Agate Basin have gone through the digestive tract of a large carnivore. If this is true, the fragments may have been ingested elsewhere and later deposited in the bone beds after the cultural event occurred. A mustelid such as a badger is capable of dragging large bones or portions of a large animal some distance. Rodents feed on carcasses and modify bones by gnawing and can thereby rearrange at least smaller bone elements. Porcupines are notorious for doing this. However, scavenger and carnivore activity is relatively scarce at the

Agate Basin site, although unmistakable canine marks were found on the broken end of a distal metacarpal from the Agate Basin bone level and rodent gnawing was obvious about the edge of the glenoid fossa on a scapula from a partially articulated bison cow in the Folsom level.

Other attritional factors that may have affected the bone are also difficult to quantify. It is likely that some of the evidence for the primary cultural activities (i.e., killing and butchering) was altered or obscured by subsequent activities such as camping, bone tool manufacture, and meat storage and retrieval. It could not be determined how long the bones were exposed to the sun and other elements of weather before they became completely buried. Bones that remained unskinned, if any of these were present, were probably affected less by weather than those that were completely exposed. Also, it could not be determined how deeply the bone beds were buried during the various cut-and-fill cycles of the arroyo system.

The extent of breakage before bones are buried also affects the rate of deterioration. Apparently, when marrow cavities became filled with clay, bones fragmented much more than those that remained empty. Root action and burning may also have affected the bone beds to varying extents. Roots were present in some of the bone beds at the time of excavation, and evidence of former root systems was present in nearly all of the cultural levels. Some burned bone fragments were present in all levels. However, only when burned bone fragments were found in and around hearths could the burning be associated with cultural activity.

Another factor that seriously affected the site was the digging done by artifact collectors, and a good share of the site was negatively affected in this way. Backdirt piles contained large numbers of bones, none of which could be used during this analysis since they were badly fragmented and their provenience could not be determined. On the positive side, however, it must be remembered that the bone beds were in the bottom of a steep-sided arroyo that was aggrading through time. In this situation spring runoff and heavy rains would have been silt and debris laden and would have tended to cover the bone beds rapidly, thereby enhancing preservation and discouraging the activities of carnivores.

It is impossible to determine to what extent the data have been altered by all of the factors listed. Carnivores and scavengers altered the bones and poor bone preservation subsequently changed what remained. Bones of least density have suffered the greatest deterioration and it is those bones—bones mainly from immature animals—that provide the most meaningful data for such sensitive studies as aging and population dynamics. Being aware of all this leaves no doubt that the distribution of the bone at the time of excavation was only partly the result of prehistoric cultural activity. Because of these limiting factors, many aspects of the cultural events at the site remain obscure, and cultural interpretations are consequently limited.

BUTCHERING: GENERAL CONSIDERATIONS

Three classes of data were considered in the butchering analysis: cuts and breaks, presence or absence of bone elements, and bone articulations and distribution. Cuts of human origin were preserved best in the Folsom level and to a lesser extent in the Hell Gap levels. The Agate Basin level bone was too badly deteriorated for cut marks to remain. The causes of bone breakage were also unclear on much of the Agate Basin bone. Observations on the presence or absence of particular bone elements were affected most by the small sample size and by the extreme deterioration, which made identification difficult. Most complete bones were identifiable, but larger fragments that would have been easy to identify under more favorable conditions of preservation were not so in this case. Since much of the bone was fragmented, poor bone preservation also affected the determination of the exact number of any given bone found at the site.

Bone distribution and breakage patterns are believed to represent both primary and secondary butchering as well as very limited manufacturing and use of bone tools. For the purposes of this study, *primary butchering* is defined as those initial activities (skinning, dissecting, stripping, marrow extracting) that took place immediately upon the death of the animals to prepare them for immediate consumption, transportation, or storage. *Secondary butchering* is defined as any further processing that took place beyond the primary phase, such as retrieval from storage, drying, removal of tendons, and preparation for cooking. Obviously it is sometimes difficult to draw the line between primary and secondary butchering.

Prehistoric methods of primary butchering are now fairly well understood because large bodies of comparative data are available from numerous kill sites, from numerous experiments that replicate those data (see Frison 1970:8–25; 1974:26–60; 1978b:301–328), and from analysis of extensive historical accounts (see, e.g., Wheat 1972). However, accurate interpretations of primary butchering are difficult to achieve from bone bed analysis, in part because of the attrition factors mentioned earlier, and in part because secondary butchering destroys much of the evidence for primary butchering.

Very few investigators have concerned themselves with the problems of prehistoric meat transportation or storage, and no known experiments have focused on these problems. Using ethnographic analogy is perhaps the best way available to investigate prehistoric secondary butchering processes. Binford's (1978) study of the Nunamuit Eskimo is oriented specifically toward the problems of butchering, storage, and distribution of the faunal remains. This analysis makes extensive use of Binford's observations. Caution, of course, must be used in transposing recent observations thousands of years into prehistory.

The future will undoubtedly see more intensive studies, with differing emphases, of animal kill sites and related camp sites and processing areas. It is possible that several bodies of extant data may be reevaluated with the problems of meat storage and secondary butchering processes in mind. Some experimentation with meat storage would undoubtedly be helpful in providing more meaningful observations on secondary butchering processes.

BUTCHERING EVIDENCE

The Folsom Level

The main evidence for butchering in the Folsom level consists of a few cut marks and breaks. Evidence for skinning is present on two metatarsals, both from large, mature animals. One of these consists of the distal two-thirds with a complete epiphysis. The outer layer of the bone is deteriorated, but a total of 47 cuts are visible on the dorsal surface from the nutrient foramen up to about midshaft along both sides of the vascular groove. The cuts vary in length from 2.5 to 10 mm and were apparently produced with a thin, sharp-edged stone tool. Some of the cuts are almost perpendicular to the long axis of the bone; others veer off at almost a 45° angle. Seven cuts on the posterior side run perpendicular to the long axis and extend to the anterior surface.

The other metatarsal consists of the broken proximal and distal ends, which were discovered 1 m apart and then matched together. Again the outer layer is deteriorated somewhat, but a small group of five short, transverse cuts remain on the anterior portion of the lateral side at the center of the shaft, and three similar cuts are visible on the midline of the anterior surface halfway between the shaft center and the proximal end. These kinds of cuts have been reproduced experimentally by skinning, but may also be produced by scraping of the bone (see Binford 1978:153).

Deep indentations are present on the second specimen on the lateral side just above the shaft center near the broken ends. These were probably produced at the time the metatarsal was broken by a blunt instrument, such as a bone or stone chopper. The marks could also have been produced by a person grasping one or both ends of the bone and smashing the shaft against an anvil stone. The resultant break extends in a spiral fashion in two directions from the center of the shaft. This type of break was present on 80% of the metatarsals and 50% of the metacarpals. Its purpose may have been to disarticulate the distal portion of the foot, or to extract marrow, or both. Skinning the metatarsals and metacarpals could have been an initial step in primary butchering, or it could have been done secondarily. The hide could have been removed from both elements during the initial skinning process, or it could have been cut above the proximal ends of the metapodials, in which case the metatarsals and metacarpals with the remaining parts of the feet could have been separated from the carcass and both hide and marrow removed later. Whatever the method of skinning, marrow extraction would probably have been done relatively soon after the primary butchering, since bone marrow apparently becomes putrid if stored in the bone, even if storage is by freezing (see Binford 1978:152, 468). One immature metatarsal was broken and carnivore chewing marks appear around the resulting edges (Figure 2.104).

Many long-bone shaft fragments were present in the Folsom component. These probably resulted from both primary and secondary butchering; some may be debris from tool manufacture. On three of these fragments are cut marks. One of these fragments (Figure 4.1) is from the lateral side of a distal left femur and resulted from a long, spiraling break. One edge is scalloped from depressed fractures, which suggests that a series of blows from a large, blunt instrument was necessary to produce the desired break. A series of cut marks along the edge of the supracondyloid fossa probably represents cutting for meat stripping during primary butchering. The other two specimens with cut marks are small long-bone fragments, probably fragments of the same femur. One cut (Figure 4.2, bottom) seems too deep to have resulted from normal muscle stripping, but no other explanation is readily apparent. A similar deep cut mark appears on the dorsal surface of a rib (Figure 4.2, top).

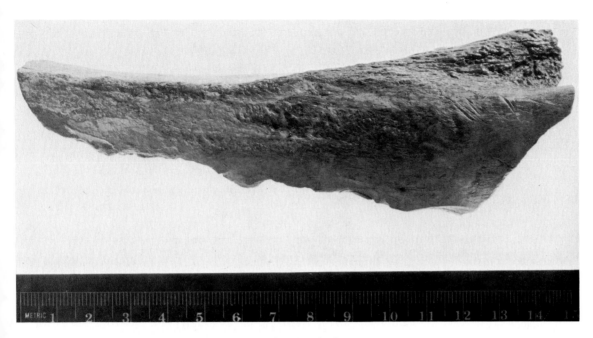

FIGURE 4.1 Broken bison femur with butchering marks from the Folsom level in Area 2.

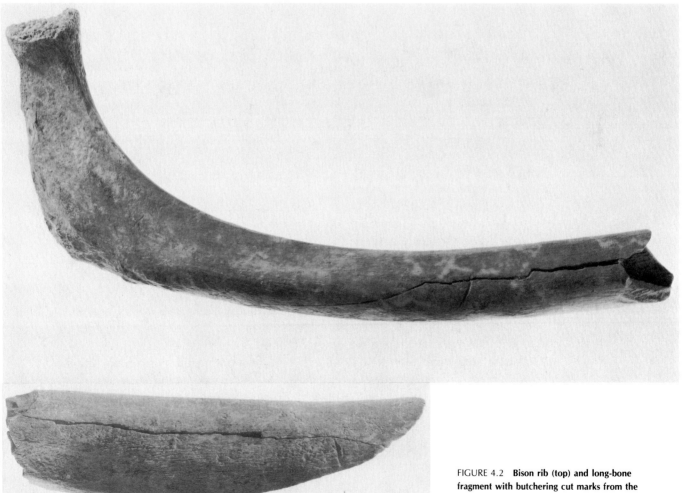

FIGURE 4.2   Bison rib (top) and long-bone fragment with butchering cut marks from the Folsom level in Area 2.

Two kinds of breaks are common at the proximal end of Folsom level humeri. One occurred between the center of the shaft and the deltoid tuberosity (Figure 2.100). This is the most common break and its purpose was probably to gain access to the marrow cavity. The second type occurs on the neck or head. Here depressed fractures from heavy blows often are present around the edge of the break. This break may have been for disarticulation of the upper leg, meat stripping, or for the manufacture of tools (cf. Frison 1970:30–33; 1974:38–40, 50–57; Frison *et al.* 1976:48). One specimen demonstrates carnivore chewing marks that probably occurred after it was removed in butchering. Both kinds of breaks required the use of heavy choppers or hammerstones. Distal breaks on humeri were usually near the end of the shaft (Figure 4.3). The humerus of a bison calf (Figure 4.4) demonstrates considerable carnivore chewing. The proximal end was scalloped, apparently by a carnivore hooking a canine tooth over the rim of the shaft after the head was removed and then prying chunks of bone loose. The distal end was chewed also; apparently the carnivores favored immature bones.

Femora and tibiae were usually broken near the center of the shafts, but were also occasionally broken close to both ends of the shafts (Figure 2.103c, d). Breaking these bones near the center of the shafts would seem to be a more efficient way to get to the marrow cavities, so perhaps the alternate method was deliberate and intended to preserve the long portions of the shafts for use in manufacturing tools or other bone items. One tibia was chopped completely through the condyles. This break was probably for disarticulation of the patella and associated ligaments for meat stripping. This specimen demonstrates light carnivore chewing around the edges and into the cancellous bone exposed by breakage.

Radii are easily broken to gain access to the marrow cavity. The posterior side may be smashed close to the proximal end after the ulna is removed, or the ulna may be smashed and driven into the radius. One proximal radius from the Folsom level demonstrates this (Figure 2.101), as does a possible bone tool from the Agate Basin level (Figure 2.102).

Several vertebrae also bear cuts and breaks. Longitudinal cuts low on the base of the dorsal spine are common and were made with sharp tools (Figure 4.5). One thirteenth and one fourteenth thoracic vertebra demonstrate cuts near or between the articular processes. These were probably made for the purpose of disarticulating the vertebral column. The dorsal spines are often broken just above the base. It appears that the loins were cut as low as possible on the spine and then stripped upward far enough to allow the spines to be broken or chopped off. After breakage, the dorsal portion of the spine was carried away with the meat. The lateral processes of thoracic vertebrae were also often broken close to the ends, presumably to release muscles and facilitate stripping of meat. Light carnivore chewing can be identified also at the same location on two specimens.

The heads of ribs often remained attached to the vertebrae. The ribs were normally chopped off at the distal ends and were subsequently snapped off near the neck. The distal ends, costal cartilage, and sternal bones are conspicuously absent in the bone beds and were probably carried away as a single unit. The

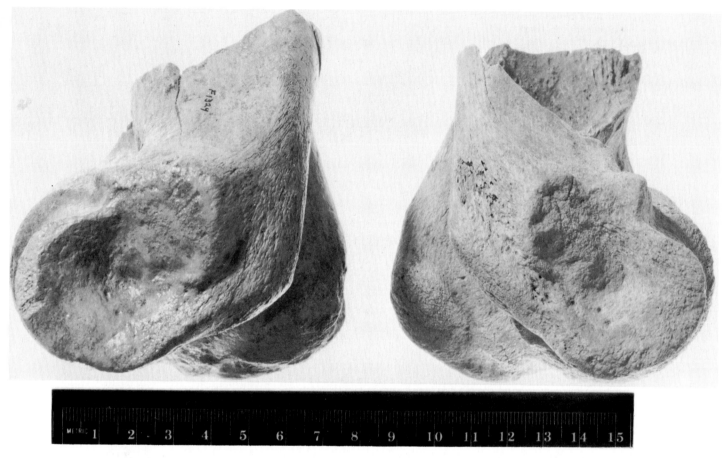

FIGURE 4.3   Butchered bison humerus from the Folsom level in Area 2.

heads were apparently snapped by the method described by Frison (1974:45) at the Casper Hell Gap site, and ethnographically by Binford (1978:53) for the Nunamiut Eskimo. This method of snapping the ribs by means of a sharp upward lift after separation from the costal cartilages has been proven to work well in actual butchering experiments with bison. It produces a distinctive break that so far has not been produced experimentally in any other manner.

The Folsom level contained several articulated units. One unit consists of a left distal humerus, proximal radius, and proximal ulna. These are heavy, robust bones, apparently from an old male. Bone surfaces are relatively well preserved but no cut marks are visible. The humerus is broken near the distal end. The radius is broken just below midshaft and displays a spiral break along the medial side, which extends upward and terminates near the proximal end. The shaft of the ulna is broken at the interosseous space and the olecranon was broken off, leaving only the articular portion of the bone (Figure 4.6). A heavy hammerstone would have been necessary to produce these breaks. The ulnar breaks were probably to loosen ligaments so muscles could be stripped; the

FIGURE 4.4 Bison calf humerus with carnivore damage from the Folsom level in Area 2.

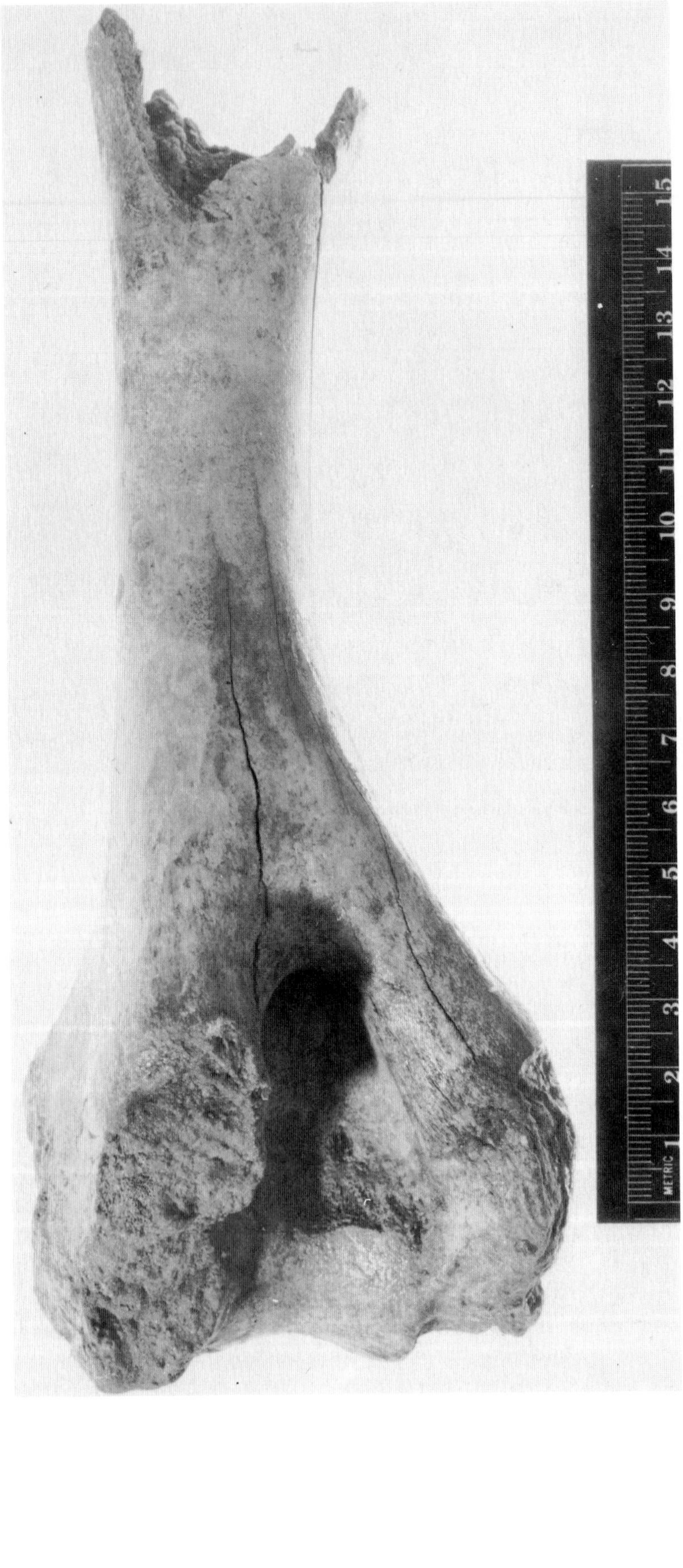

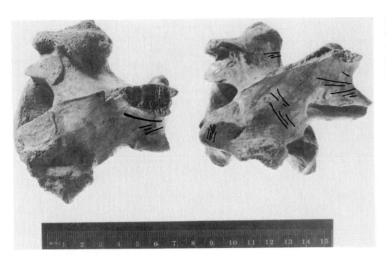

FIGURE 4.5 **Bison thoracic vertebrae with butchering marks from the Folsom level in Area 2.**

other breaks, to gain access to the marrow cavities. This particular unit probably resulted from primary butchering activities. No olecranon processes were found; they may have been removed from the area along with the meat.

Another articulated unit consists of the anterior portion of a cow 5–6 years old. This articulation consists of the skull, both mandibles and proximal hyoids, all 7 cervical vertebrae, the first 10 thoracic vertebrae, 11 left ribs, and the entire left front leg (Figure 2.15 top). The cranial cavity was entered on the left side through the temporal fossa. Breakage extends from the eye orbit, through the zygomatic process and lacrimal, through the coronoid process of the mandible, then on through the parietal and squamous bones (Figure 4.7). The break extends to the rear of the skull and provided entry directly into the center of the cranial cavity to the brain. Depressed fractures from chopping tools are visible along the edge of the break and leave little doubt that the skull was opened intentionally. Tool marks and cuts on the lateral side of the left mandible (Figure 4.8) suggest that the skull was at least partially skinned. In addition, cuts on the lingual sides of both mandibles along the diastema suggest that the tongue was removed. Similar cuts were present on at least three other mandibles from the Folsom level, including both mandibles from a calf.

The cow was lying on its left side, indicating that it was turned over after the skull was opened. The only other butchered bone found with this unit is the scapula. Here, the acromion and spine were broken off, presumably for stripping meat. The extraction of the brain, removal of the tongue, and breaking of the scapula, along with the missing portions of the cow, are regarded as evidence for primary butchering. That the remaining bones in the unit are unmarked and unbroken (bone surface preservation was good) suggests that they were not butchered. This evidence may support the idea that this was part of a frozen meat cache. If the cow was on the bottom of a frozen meat pile and became frozen to the ground, it could have been difficult to retrieve the animal when the pile was reopened. The butchered side of the animal may also have been deliberately placed at the bottom of a meat pile in order to prevent good meat from freezing to the ground.

This, of course, is mostly conjecture, but ethnographic data provide us with a good analogy (Binford 1978:59). The Nunamiut Eskimo apparently had a

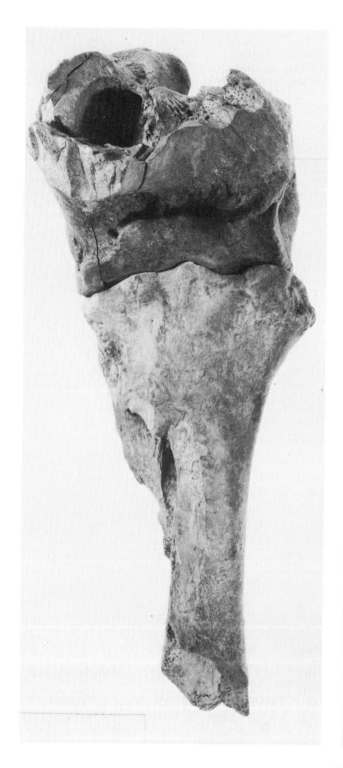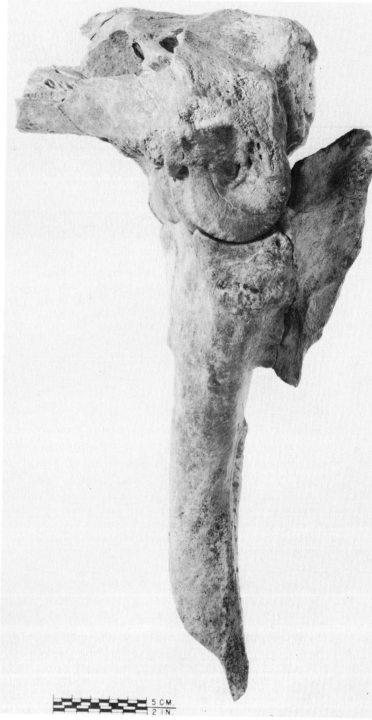

FIGURE 4.6 Butchered humerus and radius–ulna from the Folsom level in Area 2.

FIGURE 4.7 **Female bison skull from the Folsom level in Area 2.**

FIGURE 4.8 **Bison mandible from the skull shown in Figure 4.7, demonstrating cut marks that are presumably from butchering.**

problem with the bottom portion of a cache freezing to the ground. In the situation where this was observed, the portions of the animal that were abandoned by the Eskimo were almost identical to those represented by the cow unit in the Agate Basin Folsom component.

Binford (1978:460) reports that "a heavy-handed butchering" technique was applied during secondary butchering of frozen meat, but no evidence for this kind of butchering was present on the cow unit. The evidence does suggest, however, that portions of the unit were abandoned, possibly for the reason just presented, or for some as yet undetermined reason. An alternative possibility is that the unit represents a surplus of meat that was not used. However, the intense butchering performed on the other bones in the level does not support this.

Several smaller articulated units were found near the cow and may have originated from that animal. These include one pelvic unit, which contained both innominates, the sacrum, and all five lumbars; a unit that contained a right humerus, radius, ulna, and carpals; and one entire right hind leg. Disarticulated bones in the pile with the hind leg were two additional complete femora, one complete tibia, one partial front foot (first, second, and third phalanges and sesamoids), three rib shaft fragments, one lumbar vertebra, and one fifth thoracic vertebra. Other than being disarticulated from the main animal these units bear no evidence of butchering, but poor bone preservation would not have allowed cut marks to have been preserved. If these bones are units that were retrieved from a meat cache, the fact that they are not broken might be explained by again referring to the Nunamiut example where rancid marrow was carefully avoided (Binford 1978:152, 468).

The Agate Basin Level

As already mentioned, very little butchering evidence was retrievable from the Agate Basin level because of the extremely poor preservation. Deterioration was advanced to the extent that in some cases even articulations were difficult to determine with certainty. Primary butchering seems to have been largely obscured by secondary butchering. Few bones were saved from Area 1 of the site, which very likely was the main kill area, so it was not possible to compare the bone breakage and distribution from Area 1 with those from Area 2.

The bone from Area 2 appears to be distributed around two or three central piles (see Figure 2.44). The bones comprising these piles may represent elements discarded when meat caches were opened. The bones scattered outside of the area of the central piles may reflect secondary butchering that took place after the caches were opened and regular withdrawals were being made. Foot units were the most common articulated units in the Agate Basin level and usually consisted of either the proximal metapodial with varying elements of the carpals or tarsals remaining attached, or the distal metapodial with phalange and sesamoid elements attached. Approximately 65% of both the metacarpals and metatarsals were broken at the center of the shafts. Of these metapodial units, 27 were metatarsals and only 6 were metacarpals. There is no known explanation for this difference in frequency between the two, but it may reflect a different method of handling the front and hind legs during early stages of primary butchering. It is also possible that units were disarticulated from the main carcass elsewhere and were brought into this area for marrow extraction, since metatarsals do contain slightly more marrow than the metacarpals.

The other articulated units were located near the centers of the main bone concentrations. They include one skull with 5 cervicals, two units containing the first 4 cervicals, one unit with 5 cervicals and the first 4 thoracics, three units of 2 thoracics and 2 ribs, one unit with 5 thoracics, one unit containing 13 thoracics and 13 ribs, a sacrum with 5 lumbars, a group of 5 ribs, a group of 7 ribs, three distal tibiae and tarsals, one distal radius with carpals, metacarpal, and phalanges, and one entire left hind leg. It could not be determined to what degree these reflect either primary or secondary butchering practices.

The Hell Gap Level

The Hell Gap level postcranial bone sample is small and poorly preserved, so that little evidence is left with which to analyze butchering techniques. However, one cervical vertebra demonstrates evidence of breaking the ventral, lateral, and dorsal processes, and a dorsal spine has a series of horizontal cuts near the base. One first rib of a young animal was chopped off at the distal end. One humerus from a young individual demonstrates a spiraling break near the distal end. One left distal metacarpal contains a spiraling break that originated near the center of the shaft. The metacarpal also bears a series of short cut marks on the dorsal surface near the medial side, similar to those found on the Folsom level metatarsals described earlier.

Articulations in the Hell Gap level were ambiguous. The level appeared to contain a central pile of heavily butchered bone around which smaller, broken elements were scattered. The bottom of the pile contained a number of bones, some articulated and some not, that suggest a unit similar to the cow unit in the Folsom level. The entire Hell Gap bone bed was under several meters of overburden, and items such as skulls were flattened. However, the unit in question consists of a skull, seven cervicals, six thoracics, and possibly four ribs and a scapula. No butchering evidence such as cut and chopping marks was discernible because of the advanced deterioration of the bone. Although the evidence is not as well defined here as in the Folsom level, both primary and secondary butchering is suggested. It seems likely that the pile represents a frozen meat cache that was opened.

BONE COUNTS, MNI, AND RELATED OBSERVATIONS

The bone count (Table 4.1) indicates that a minimum of 9 individuals were present in the Folsom level. The MNI was derived from the atlas vertebra; however, the bones recovered represent only about 35% of the total number of bones that would be present from the death of 9 animals. The Agate Basin level MNI was determined to be 75 animals based on right metacarpals, and only about 20% of the total possible bones from that level were present. The Hell Gap level contained a minimum of 8 individuals based on the left scapula count, and only about 10% of the total number of bones possible from this number of animals were recovered. It must be remembered that parts of the bone beds in all three components were not preserved; however, the absence of certain bones may reflect butchering practices.

TABLE 4.1
Agate Basin Site Bone Count

| | Levels | | |
	Hell Gap	Agate Basin	Folsom
Vertebrae			
Cervical			
1	2	15	9[a]
2	3	17	7
3	2	1	3
4	2	1	2
5	2	2	6
6	1	4	2
7	1	7	5
Thoracic			
1	1	4	5
2	1	2	5
3	1	2	5
4	1		4
5	1		2
6	1		4
7			1
8			3
9			2
10			3
11			1
12			2
13			3
14			2
Lumbar			
1		5	4
2		2	3
3		2	4
4		4	4
5		6	3
Sacrum		6	5
Caudal		6	14
Sternum		2	2

	Left	Right		Left	Right		Left	Right	
Rib									
1				3	6		3	2	
Scapula	8[a]	6		19	21		3	1	
Humerus	3			21	27		7	3	
Radius				34	35		7	4	
Ulna				18	14		5	1	
Carpals									
2+3				30	38		3	6	
4				19	33		5	5	
Radial				27	32		4	6	
Intermediate				25	18		4	5	
Ulna				14	23		6	4	
Accessory[b]				19				8	
Metacarpal	1			63	75[a]		7	8	

	Front	Rear	Unknown	Front	Rear	Unknown	Front	Rear	Unknown
Phalanges									
Proximal	4	2	2	135	186	61	36	10	
Medial[b]			7			326			48
Distal[b]			8			165			25

(continued)

TABLE 4.1 (*Continued*)

	Front	Rear	Unknown	Front	Rear	Unknown	Front	Rear	Unknown
Sesamoids[b]									
Proximal		2			120				44
Distal					39				10

	Left	Right		Left	Right		Left	Right	
Pelvis	1	1		4	10		6	7	
Femur				17	16		6	4	
Patella	1	1		16	19		5	6	
Tibia	1	1		30	23		6	6	
Tarsals									
Astragalus	5	1		49	44		4	10	
Calcaneus	5	2		45	44		1	7	
1				1					
2+3	2			26	25		3	4	
c+4	4			42	42		1	4	
Lateral malleolus				14	12		4	4	
Metatarsal				63	53		4	7	

[a]Element used to determine MNI.
[b]Side undetermined.

Few fetal bones were recovered. Part of a fetal pelvis, two scapulae, and a calcaneus were found in the Folsom level, and a humerus was found in the Agate Basin level. These specimens were compared with modern specimens of known age. One Folsom level fetus specimen compared favorably with a 7–8 month specimen; another appeared to be near full term. The Agate Basin level specimen compares favorably with the fetus of 7–8 months development. Insufficient fetal material was recovered to provide worthwhile interpretations, although many specimens should have been present, assuming a normal breeding season. Absence of fetal material could reflect differential preservation or, more likely, removals for consumption.

Sterna, caudals, patellae, and olecranon processes of the ulna were all absent. Sternal bones were probably removed with the brisket. The patella and olecranon may have been removed to loosen muscle attachments and subsequently taken to a processing area. Caudals may have been taken with the hide; the almost total absence of these elements suggests that the animals were skinned and the hides taken to another location.

Pete (Bison Pete) Gardner, a longtime Wyoming owner and operator of a commercial bison herd, has collected data on the weights of freshly skinned bison hides. His figures indicate that a green, mature bull hide may weigh as much as 250 lb, and that green yearling hides average about 125 lb. A few weeks of drying will reduce the weight by about 35%. This would indicate that in the Agate Basin level alone at least 7000 lb of green hides were present.

Young animals are underrepresented in the bone beds. Again, this may reflect differential preservation and/or processing. It is also possible that the younger animals were allowed to escape. A few young animals are present but their deaths could have been accidental. Experiences in handling modern bison herds have demonstrated that if a mixed herd is confined in tight quarters, several young animals will soon be killed by the milling herd. Binford (1978:86) observed that the Nunamiut do not kill calves to be used as food. Sometimes calves are selectively killed for their tender hides, and in these instances the Eskimo feed the carcasses to the dogs. One can also speculate that at Agate Basin young animals were not killed because of the hunters' conservation ethics. However, at this time there is no satisfactory explanation for the disproportionate number of young animals in the site.

There are ways to estimate the weight of the meat that was removed from the animals, but since the bone beds are not complete, and the Agate Basin component may represent more than a single event, a calculation of the quantity of meat obtained would not be reliable for any given kill event. Therefore, it would not provide a reliable basis for calculating the size of the prehistoric human groups or the length of time they might have survived on the meat obtained. However, some method of meat preservation and storage was necessary.

Even though the deteriorated condition of the bone at the Agate Basin site would not allow reconstruction of the entire butchering process, enough data were present to suggest that butchering at the Agate Basin site did not differ greatly from other Paleoindian or even Late Prehistoric period sites. Except for the method of opening the cranial cavity, the descriptions of butchering at the Late Prehistoric Glenrock site (Frison 1970) probably provide a satisfactory model for butchering at Agate Basin. Cuts and breaks appear at approximately the same points and seem to have been made with the same types of tools. In addition, we do know that the same tool types were present at both sites, which were separated 10,000 years in time.

The observations made during this study provide no basis to challenge the statement that butchering typology may never serve as a chronological or cultural indicator (Frison 1974:27). The main difficulty with identification of differences in butchering practices is that too many variables exist that cannot be controlled. Variation from one site to the next may be the result of different weather conditions, number of animals killed, time of year, landforms involved, and many other factors.

POPULATION STRUCTURE AND BIOLOGICAL CONSIDERATIONS

The postcranial bones at the Agate Basin site provided only minimal information about the age and sex of the bison populations. Aging of immature animals proved difficult because few bones from immature animals revealed satisfactory preservation at the epiphyseal juncture. Size comparisons of the immature bones present were also difficult because of the bones' fragmentary condition. Attempts at sexing the animals were moderately successful but only to the point of establishing some general trends. Nearly all of the bones suitable for measurement were from mature animals, with maturity being determined by fusion of the epiphyses. However, the exact age of fusion of certain elements such as the distal ends of the metapodials and proximal ends of the phalanges has not yet been determined. The only immature bones included in the analysis were astragali, which, because of their structure, are difficult to age correctly.

TABLE 4.2

Metacarpal Lengths for the Agate Basin and Horner Sites (Mature Animals)

Length (mm)	Agate Basin site			Horner site	
	Folsom	Agate Basin	Hell Gap	U.W.[a] area	Princeton area
195					1
196		1			
197					1
198		1			1
199		1		1	2
200				1	1
201					1
202		3		1	
203				1	
204		1			
205	1			3	
206		1			1
207		2			
208		1		3	
209		1		3	2
210		1		2	
211	1	2		2	
212	1	2	1	5	1
213		5		4	2
214		2		6	1
215				3	1
216		3		5	1
217	2	1		2	3
218		4		2	2
219		3		2	
220		7		4	
221				1	1
222	1	4		3	
223		1		2	
224		1			
225		1			1
226				3	
227		2			
228				1	
229		2			
230	1				
231					
232		1			
233					
234					
235		2			
236					
237					
238					
239					
240					1

[a]U.W. = University of Wyoming.

TABLE 4.3

Metatarsal Lengths for the Agate Basin and Horner Sites (Mature Animals)

Length (mm)	Agate Basin site			Horner site	
	Folsom	Agate Basin	Hell Gap	U.W.[a] area	Princeton area
240					
241					
242					
243					
244					
245		1			
246					
247					
248		1		1	
249		1			1
250					
251					
252				1	
253		1		2	
254		3			
255		1		2	
256					
257				5	
258		1			
259	1	1		1	
260	1	1			
261		4		4	
262				4	
263		2		1	
264		2		3	
265		4		1	
266		1		1	
267		2			
268				5	
269		1		3	
270		2			
271					
272		3		1	
273				2	
274		1		1	
275		5		2	
276		1			
277					
278		1			
279					
280					
281					
282		1			
283		1			
284				2	
285					
286					
287					
288					
289					
290					

[a]U.W. = University of Wyoming.

TABLE 4.4
Astragalus Volumes[a]

Site	Volume (cm³)		N
	Mean	Range	
Folsom	127.96	90–175	27
Agate Basin Folsom level	115.00	100–170	7
Agate Basin	111.41	80–160	78
Agate Basin Hell Gap level	110.00	105–115	3
Casper	108.40	75–155	57
Olsen–Chubbuck	105.76	80–150	46
Horner (U.W.[b] area)	100.05	70–140	94
Horner (Princeton area)	94.36	65–140	86
Finley	115.13	80–140	37
Hawken	98.85	65–125	35
Buffalo Creek	86.53	60–130	98
Vore	80.83	55–110	54
Glenrock	72.99	50–110	122

[a]Data from Frison 1978b.
[b]U.W. = University of Wyoming.

Only certain skeletal elements were selected for measurements: metapodials, astragali, and proximal or first phalanges. These were chosen because they were most numerous, they were the best preserved, and they are major weight-bearing bones and consequently should reflect animal size. However, sample sizes were small, especially from the Folsom and Hell Gap levels, and may not be representative of the actual population. Included for comparison are measurements of the Horner site (Jepsen 1953) metapodials and volumes of the Horner site astragali. The Horner bone sample is still being studied and the phalanges have not yet been measured. If the present data are correctly interpreted, two bison populations are represented in the Horner sample—one around 9000 years of age (identified as the Princeton area component) and the other about 10,000 years of age (the University of Wyoming area component). Comparison of the size of certain Agate Basin skeletal elements with those from several other sites indicate that the bison of around 10,000 years ago were larger than the modern form, but little other taxonomic data can be derived from postcranial material (Tables 4.2–4.4). The size differential in terms of actual animal weight is not known.

Metapodials

Metapodial measurements were taken from the Paleoindian components at the Agate Basin site and comparative data were used from two components at the Horner site. The number of individual specimens from which at least one measurement could be obtained included 25 from the Folsom level, 168 from the Agate Basin level, 2 from the Hell Gap level, 113 from the older Horner component, and 30 from the younger one (Tables 4.5 and 4.6). This metapodial analysis follows a similar analysis by Bedord (1974:199–240) for the Casper site. Bedord experimented with 13 measurements, but was only able to demon-

TABLE 4.5
Metacarpal Measurements

	Mean (mm)	Range (mm)	N
M1: Maximum length			
Agate Basin site			
Hell Gap level	212.00	—	1
Agate Basin level	216.00	196–235	38
Folsom level	216.29	205–230	7
Horner site			
U.W. area[a]	214.00	199–227	60
Princeton area	207.04	195–240	24
M2: Transverse width of proximal end			
Agate Basin site			
Hell Gap level	79.00	—	1
Agate Basin level	75.50	54–92	54
Folsom level	74.82	63–86	11
Horner site			
U.W. area[a]	76.03	66–89	57
Princeton area	71.41	58–84	17
M3: Transverse widths at shaft center			
Agate Basin site			
Hell Gap level	48.00	—	1
Agate Basin level	47.25	38–58	36
Folsom level	48.14	42–54	7
Horner site			
U.W. area[a]	45.38	36–52	52
Princeton area	43.37	35–53	19
M4: Transverse width at distal end			
Agate Basin site			
Hell Gap level	75.00	69–81	2
Agate Basin level	78.17	69–92	65
Folsom level	82.18	71–96	11
Horner site			
U.W. area[a]	78.59	67–88	59
Princeton area	76.74	64–89	19

[a]U.W. = University of Wyoming.

TABLE 4.6
Metatarsal Measurements

	Mean (mm)	Range (mm)	N
M1: Maximum length			
Agate Basin site			
Hell Gap level			0
Agate Basin level	264.71	242–283	35
Folsom level	259.50	259–260	2
Horner site			
U.W. area[a]	264.39	252–284	44
Princeton area	249.00	—	1
M2: Transverse width of proximal end			
Agate Basin site			
Hell Gap level			0
Agate Basin level	58.19	46–71	46
Folsom level	57.00	53–60	5
Horner site			
U.W. area[a]	59.16	50–68	50
Princeton area	53.67	49–57	3
M3: Transverse width at shaft center			
Agate Basin site			
Hell Gap level			0
Agate Basin level	36.53	32–46	30
Folsom level	37.67	37–39	3
Horner site			
U.W. area[a]	36.80	28–43	40
Princeton area	33.00	—	1
M4: Transverse width at distal end			
Agate Basin site			
Hell Gap level			0
Agate Basin level	69.90	54–81	68
Folsom level	70.63	66–74	8
Horner site			
U.W. area[a]	69.98	60–77	48
Princeton area	69.00	66–72	2

[a]U.W. = University of Wyoming.

strate positive results by use of the first 4. Consequently, only those 4 measurements were used during this study. These include

M1   Maximum length
M2   Transverse width of the proximal end
M3   Transverse width at the center of the shaft
M4   Transverse width of the distal end

Bedord concluded that the most reliable method of obtaining sex data was by use of a simple bivariate technique where a ratio derived by the formula $M3/M1 \times 100$ was plotted against M4 on a scattergram. Clusters of the higher values of the ratio are considered to indicate males; the lower, females. Only the Agate Basin level contained a large enough sample for this technique to be applied, and then only 32 metacarpals and 24 metatarsals yielded all the neces-

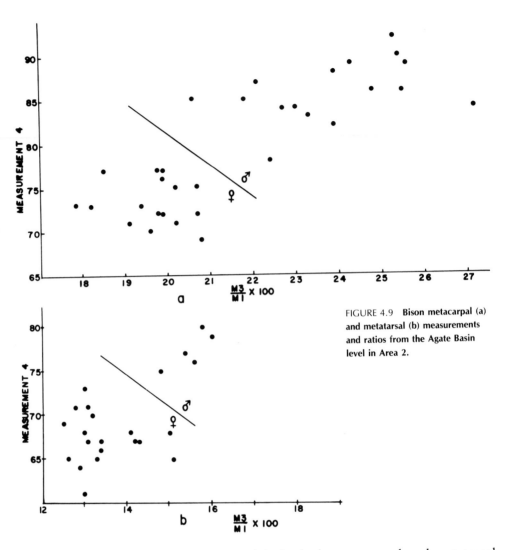

FIGURE 4.9 **Bison metacarpal (a) and metatarsal (b) measurements and ratios from the Agate Basin level in Area 2.**

sary measurements. Clusters occurred in both the metacarpal and metatarsal samples. If properly interpreted, the metacarpals are equally divided into male and female categories (Figure 4.9a). Six of the metatarsals fall into the male category and 18 fall into the female category (Figure 4.9b). These data represent only the measurable specimens, which are a small sample of the MNI, and some unknown sample of the true population. However, the results are similar to those arrived at using astragali and phalanges.

Astragali   The methods used to measure the astragali were the same as reported from the Casper site (Zeimens and Zeimens 1974:245–246). Seven specimens were from the Folsom level, 78 from the Agate Basin level, 3 from the Hell Gap level, 94 from the older Horner component, and 86 from the younger one. No attempt was made to age the astragali before they were measured, and the only measurement taken was volume. The only component from Agate Basin that produced a significant sample was the one from the Agate Basin level. When the volumes from the Agate Basin level are plotted on a histogram, a quadrimodal distribution appears, which is interpreted to reflect both age and sex (Figure 4.10). The

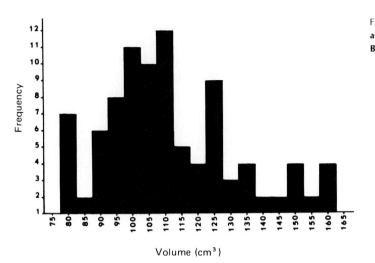

FIGURE 4.10 **Volumes of astragali from the Agate Basin level in Area 2.**

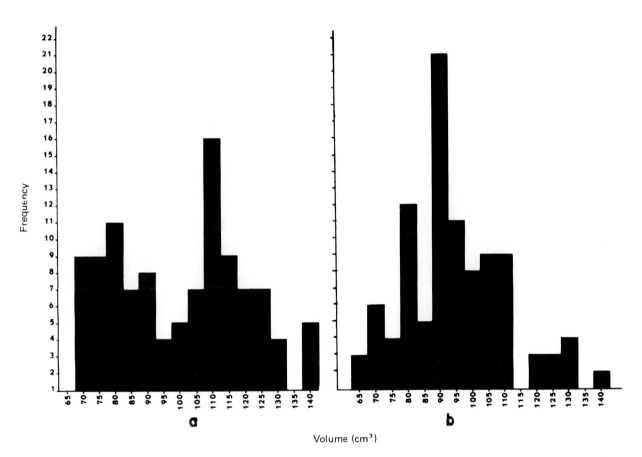

FIGURE 4.11 **Volumes of astragali from the Horner site: University of Wyoming area sample (a) and Princeton area sample (b).**

peak with the highest values probably represents older males; the next highest, younger males and robust females; another, near mature and mature females; and the lowest, immature animals of both sexes. Mature males account for 10.2% of the sample or 5.3% of MNI if paired. Immature males and robust females yield a high estimate of 21.7% and a low estimate of 12%; females,

58.9% and 30.6%; and immature animals, 8.9% and 5.3%. In this case where the smaller specimens were measured, the seven specimens believed to be immature do not seem to be representative. In a normal population this category should contain the majority of individuals if the sample represents a catastrophic death assemblage (see Reher 1970:53; 1974:118). Males also appear underrepresented, although this may reflect cultural practices to compensate for the natural behavior of bison during handling. Male bison tend to congregate away from the cows and calves during most of the year and are detrimental to driving the animals at any time; they may have been deliberately excluded from procurement events. Males are also underrepresented in the Horner site astragali samples (Figure 4.11).

Phalanges   Bison phalanges have been largely neglected by archaeologists. They have been traditionally lumped (fronts, rears, lefts, rights, laterals, and medials) together as proximal, medial, and distal bone counts. Even in rare instances where the proximal elements were measured they were still lumped as though they represent one element of the animal, when in actuality they represent eight separate elements (Agenbroad 1978:55; Lorrain 1968:129). Lumping these elements would be analogous to lumping metacarpals with metatarsals and would produce a skewed bone count.

Of the phalanges, the first or proximal elements were the most numerous at Agate Basin and suffered the least amount of deterioration through natural causes. The proximal phalanges from the Folsom and Agate Basin levels were analyzed in an additional effort to ascertain the sexual composition of the sample and to provide a means of comparison of the relative size of the animals with other populations. Only two specimens from the Hell Gap level were measurable so they were excluded from the analysis. Pathologies occur frequently on phalanges and are believed to result from bone breakage. The pathologies are manifest as unnatural lumps or changes in the angle of the long axis of the bone and prevent accurate measurements. As a result, only mature, complete, and normal specimens were measured.

Well-preserved anterior proximal phalanges are easily distinguishable from posterior ones. However, poorly preserved or pathological specimens are often difficult to separate. Anterior specimens are shorter, wider, and generally more robust than posterior ones. The articular groove or sulcus that extends vertically down the center of the base is more U shaped at both ends on the anterior specimens, and narrower and more V shaped on the posterior ones (Duffield 1973). Anterior specimens are distinguishable from posterior specimens using these visual criterial, and may also be distinguished metrically by use of an index derived from the following formula:

$$\text{Width of proximal end/length} \times 100$$

When the derived index is 51 or more, the specimen is anterior; when the index is 50 or less, the specimen is posterior. This index, first used by Empel and Roskosz (1963) to ascertain sex in European bison, was found here to distinguish front phalanges from rear but has no proven value for determining sex on American bison.

TABLE 4.7
Phalange Measurements

Level	Type	Mean	Range	N
M1: Maximum length (mm)				
Agate Basin	Front	72.80	66–81	69
	Rear	74.36	67–85	73
Folsom	Front	74.29	68–84	14
	Rear	74.50	72–79	6
M2: Transverse width of proximal end (mm)				
Agate Basin	Front	40.25	35–47	67
	Rear	35.35	31–42	71
Folsom	Front	40.93	36–50	14
	Rear	36.50	36–38	6
M3: Transverse width of distal end (mm)				
Agate Basin	Front	39.45	33–47	69
	Rear	34.96	30–41	77
Folsom	Front	40.77	37–49	13
	Rear	36.0	35–38	6
M4: Volume (cm³)				
Agate Basin	Front	57.82	40–85	71
	Rear	48.61	35–75	79
Folsom	Front	62.50	45–100	14
	Rear	51.66	45–55	6

Determining right and left sides of the proximal phalange may be accomplished but the techniques have not been perfected. When placed on a flat surface with the ventral side down they will "rock like a table with one short leg" (Dottrens 1946). When rocked from the base toward the head (proximal to distal), they rock either to the left or right of the long axis. In preliminary experiments with elements of known anatomical position, those that rock to the left are from the left foot and those that rock to the right are from the right foot. The front laterals sometimes rock only very slightly and pathological specimens may not rock at all. Dottrens first used this rocking technique to distinguish laterals from medials and it was used later by Duffield (1970) to attempt to distinguish fronts from rears. However, on American bison this technique appears to distinguish lefts from rights also. More comparative material of known anatomical position is needed before the technique can be perfected. For this study the proximal phalanges were separated into fronts and rears only. Studies in progress may allow similar differentiation of medial and distal phalanges.

After separating the phalanges as described, measurements were taken in order to separate males from females. The Folsom level produced 20 measurable specimens, the Agate Basin level produced 150, and the Hell Gap level produced none, so only the Agate Basin sample was considered large enough to be meaningful (Table 4.7). Four measurements were taken. These are Measurements 1, 2, and 3 described by Lorrain (1968:126), and volume. They are referred to here as

M1	Maximum length
M2	Transverse width of proximal end
M3	Transverse width of distal end
M4	Volume

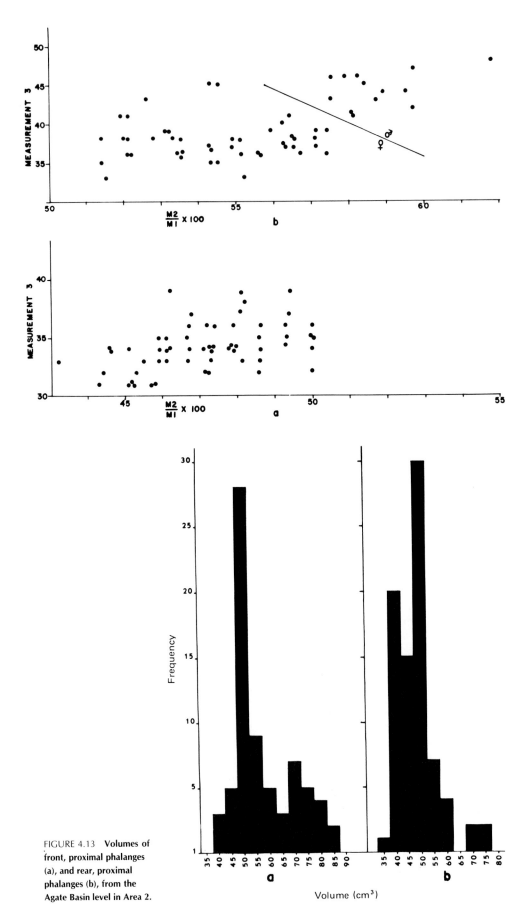

FIGURE 4.12 **Rear, proximal phalanges (a), and front, proximal phalanges (b)—measurements and ratios from the Agate Basin level in Area 2.**

FIGURE 4.13 **Volumes of front, proximal phalanges (a), and rear, proximal phalanges (b), from the Agate Basin level in Area 2.**

M1 was taken by placing the specimens ventral side down on an osteometric board. M2 and M3 were taken with sliding calipers at the widest points on the bone. M4 necessitated boiling the bones in paraffin before they were submerged in a graduated cylinder containing water to measure displacement, basically the same method used to measure the astragali. Ratios were then calculated and the results were plotted on scattergrams.

Measurements for the rear phalanges failed to produce clusters (Figure 4.12a). There is no present explanation for this unless great variation is present in rear phalanges. However, a distinctive cluster on the high range of the values for the anterior phalanges did emerge (Figure 4.12b). The cluster is interpreted to represent males, which constitute 22.4% of the sample. Volumes were plotted on a histogram and both fronts and rears produced bimodal distributions. Volumes were taken even when some pathologies were present; 25.3% of the anterior phalanges sample fell into the male category (Figure 4.13a). By contrast, only 5% of the sample of rear phalanges fell into this category (Figure 4.13b). No explanation of these discrepancies can be given, although many possibilities exist. At this time, the best suggested procedure would be to acquire a large sample of phalanges from known anatomical positions in order to be able to make more positive statements concerning some of the data discussed.

SUMMARY

In summary, the butchering process is divided into two categories of activity, here designated primary and secondary butchering. Division between the two is not always clear and can vary from one site to another. However, primary butchering concerns the attention given to an animal soon after it is killed to prepare it for immediate consumption, salvage nonfood parts of the carcass, and/or prepare it for transport. Secondary butchering includes a wide range of activities that concern preparation of the meat for consumption after cooling or after being taken to storage, and salvage of further items such as tendons, hooves, horns, and bones for nonfood use.

Bone deterioration and secondary butchering or processing destroyed much of the evidence of primary butchering in the Agate Basin component in Area 2. In addition, it is not known if this bone bed is the actual kill location. It probably is not; the evidence from Area 1 of the site might have provided some solution to this, but this evidence is unfortunately not extant. The best guess at this time is that the bone bed in Area 2 is close to a kill area. The animals were probably killed nearby and reduced to units that could be more easily moved. The units were then piled and frozen, and most of the butchering evidence remaining in Area 2 resulted from the processing of these units.

The butchering evidence does suggest a process that was present on the High Plains from Paleoindian times until European influence in protohistoric times. Most variation results from the unique conditions that existed for each site. This introduced so many variables and so few can usually be accurately determined from site data that butchering procedures normally remain unclear. However, the content of tool kits argues for similar butchering methods throughout the known time span of High Plains prehistory. The tool assemblage in Folsom, Agate Basin, and Hell Gap components are similar and they are in turn similar to those of later time periods.

Information on population dynamics from postcranial bison material from the Agate Basin site was severely limited by inadequate samples and poor bone preservation. There is a definite need to pursue the study of postcranial material so that reliable means of aging and sexing animals is possible. Positive identification of all phalanges is needed so that the archaeologist can distinguish right from left, and front from rear feet. These kinds of data may appear trivial but small inaccuracies rapidly multiply and adversely affect the final analysis.

2. BISON DENTITION STUDIES
george c. frison

PROBLEMS OF LARGE HERBIVORE SURVIVAL

The life span of a large, grazing herbivore depends to a large extent on how long its teeth can withstand the continual attrition caused by mastication of grasses and other food plants. Herbivore teeth are well designed to gather and break up the fibers of grasses, but in so doing they wear away at a surprisingly fast rate. Once a flaw appears in the tooth row, the rate of tooth deterioration increases and the intake of food is impaired. The trend is irreversible and the result is death. Poor grass and severe winters, common occurrences on the High Plains, hasten the process. The life of a bison, for example, can be nearly doubled by artificial winter feeding of high-protein concentrates, which slows the rate of tooth wear significantly. Bison may survive part of the winter on willows the diameter of a man's thumb and coarse wild ryegrass that grow along river bottoms, but prolonged diets of such roughage result in excessive tooth wear and adversely affect animal condition.

The first lower molar (M_1) is where the problems of old age usually begin for buffalo and other large grazers. M_1 is the first permanent tooth to come into wear and it is also the first to wear out. At about 7 years of age for the bison of Paleoindian times, the prefossette of M_1 wore down to the extent that the enamel area of the anterior crescent was greatly decreased. The efficiency of the tooth in masticating food was thereby decreased, resulting in increased wear on the occlusal surfaces of the two remaining molars. By 9 years of age, serious breakdown of M_1 was usually evident and M_2 was beginning to go the same route. After 2 or 3 more years of inadequate intake of winter feed as a result of bad teeth, the animal was weakened and was then likely to become a victim of predators in late winter or early spring. Spring and early summer, with lush feed, offered a short reprieve to old animals that avoided death or starvation during the previous winter, and a series of open winters could add a year or so to the life span.

SYSTEMATICS OF TOOTH ERUPTION

Tooth eruption in mammals is systematic. As a result, the age of an animal—a bison, cow, sheep, or horse, for example—can be determined from the stage of tooth eruption. After the eruption cycle is completed, less accurate age determinations can be made on the stages of tooth wear or deterioration. There is good reason for the livestock operator to look into the mouth of an animal purchased. Few remain in the business long who are unable to determine an animal's age and future promise from the condition of its teeth.

Fortunately, for both the animals and the livestock operator, the incisor teeth are probably the most reliable age indicators. It is relatively easy to get a good view of the incisors but more difficult to obtain a good view of the molars. Unfortunately for the archaeologist, however, the incisor teeth do not always remain in place. The anterior part of the mandible deteriorates relatively quickly and the incisor teeth are often lost, especially in Paleoindian deposits of greater age. Consequently, most of our observations on eruption and wear are derived from the molar teeth (Frison and Reher 1970).

Tooth eruption has been questioned as a sensitive enough age determiner for use by archaeologists in seasonality studies (e.g., Brumley 1973:18–19). However, the greatest limitation of this method would seem to be the requirement of valid samples of young animals in a population. The method is particularly adaptable to catastrophic events, such as a large bison kill as represented at the Casper site (Frison 1974), the Hawken site (Frison *et al.* 1976), and the Agate Basin component at the Agate Basin site.

Tooth wear in the age-groups beyond maturity is not as sensitive a seasonality determiner as the combination of wear and eruption in the younger groups. Kurtén (1953, 1964) earlier demonstrated the utility of the method for age-grouping in fossil populations, as have Reher (1970, 1973, 1974); Frison *et al.* (1976), and Frison (1978a). Perhaps the most convincing evidence of systematic tooth eruption in bison is from large numbers of animals butchered from modern herds (see, e.g., Frison 1978a:45). In one case a sample of nearly 200 mandibles was obtained, representing animals butchered at about 1.7 years of age. All demonstrate closely similar eruption of M_1 and M_2. These came from a large herd (about 700) living on the open range, with males and females allowed free association throughout the year.

Since the systematic nature of tooth eruption is well demonstrated from known-age animals in present-day herds, there should be no reason to deny its application to fossil animal populations such as those in archaeological site assemblages. As has been mentioned in the preceding section, the late Pleistocene bison were larger than the modern form, but there is no reason to suspect that the systematics of tooth eruption differed among the various subspecies even though there has been a gradual decrease in size in bison from Late Pleistocene to historic times.

The sensitive changes in molar tooth eruption for a bison calf can be readily observed. At birth, the fourth deciduous premolar (dP_4) is fully erupted and M_1 is still well below the alveolus. At 1 month of age light wear can be detected on dP_4 and M_1 is barely visible behind dP_4. The entire mandible has increased in size considerably, compared to its size at birth. At about 2 months, the anterior part of M_1 is showing above the alveolus. At between 3 and 4 months, the posterior part of M_1 is above the alveolus (Frison 1978a:44–45). At 5–6 months, M_1 is well above the alveolus but not yet in wear. Olsen–Chubbuck (Wheat 1972) provides a good example of calves at this age (Frison 1978a:46);

so does the Glenrock Buffalo Jump (Frison 1978a:46; Reher 1970). At about 7 months, wear is present on both sides of the anterior section of M_1 although the wear on the posterior slope may be light. At about 8–9 months, the anterior half of M_1 and also the anterior part of the posterior section is in wear. M_2 is still below the alveolus but is visible, as demonstrated by calves from the Hawken site (Frison 1978a:49; Frison *et al.* 1976). At 10–11 months, both anterior and posterior sections of M_1 are in wear but M_2 has not erupted above the alveolus.

These data demonstrate that from birth until 11 months of age, M_1 increases in length from below the alveolus to its maximum length. In quantitative terms, this represents an average increase of usually between 21 and 25 mm in the larger late Pleistocene bison, allowing for the normal size differences in a population. The same systematics can be applied to M_2 and M_3 as demonstrated in the Hawken site sample (Frison 1978a) for animals in the younger age-groupings. Beyond Age-group 4 (see next section), the seasonality determinations become increasingly less accurate but annual groupings are still possible.

The upper teeth are every bit as reliable age indicators as the lower ones. In fact, in the process of aging animals at two sites, Hawken (Frison *et al.* 1976) and the Big Goose Creek site (Frison, Wilson, and Walker 1978), Wilson independently aged the bison using the upper molars. The results were identical with those obtained using the lower molars, which was done by the writer. Eruption and wear patterns coincide, and it is simply a matter of gaining the necessary familiarity with either the upper or lower teeth, whichever offers the best sample. However, because of the structure of the bison skull, the mandibles stand a much higher probability of preservation.

For the purposes of the archaeologist, aging of animals not only gives the age but also imparts information as to the time of year the animal was killed, provided it was born during the normal birthing season. Therefore, to obtain reliable seasonality determinations a valid sample of an animal population is necessary, since for any given individual there is a certain probability that it was born outside the normal birthing period. However, the normal birthing season for large herbivores on the High Plains is predictable within close limits and follows a yearly pattern. For bison it begins in the early spring with the appearance of an occasional calf, and slowly builds to a peak, declining as it began. Valid samples of the animal population taken at any point in time will demonstrate this feature in the tooth eruption schedules of the young animals.

Large prehistoric animal kills, or any events that resulted in instantaneous death assemblages, provide the necessary sample if adequate preservation of the remains occurred. Cultural activities often adversely affected these kinds of assemblages but taphonomic methods are now able to allow for the effects of butchering and processing, and permit increasingly meaningful interpretations from death assemblages resulting from human animal-procurement activities.

The tooth sample from Area 2 in the Agate Basin bone level was minimally sufficient for aging studies, using all available materials recovered during the 1961 and 1975–1979 excavations. Only the lower dental elements were used since mandibles were the better preserved and greatly outnumbered the maxillary units. Sixty-six partial to complete mandibles comprise this Agate Basin sample. Metric and visual determinants were taken from the molar teeth, which have been proven to demonstrate more reliable eruption schedules than the premolars.

Any discussion of bison tooth eruption and tooth wear requires some standardized means of description. The two processes are separate and directly opposed. One standard measure of tooth eruption used here and by others (see Frison *et al.* 1976; Reher 1970, 1973, 1974) is the maximum enamel height at the metaconid measured from the base to the top of the enamel on the anterior, lingual section of each of the three molar teeth. This is referred to as *metaconid height*.

A method of describing wear on the occlusal surfaces was developed during the analysis of the Hawken site bison (Frison *et al.* 1976:38–39). Crompton and Hiiemae (1969) illustrated a selenodont tooth with some numbered wear facets but their purpose was to demonstrate the evolutionary aspects of primitive mammalian teeth as they modified into the selenodont condition. Their treatment of tooth wear surfaces was inadequate for an exhaustive description of selenodont tooth wear surfaces without modifications that might conflict with future numbering they might undertake. Consequently a descriptive device (Figure 4.14) was developed. To this point, at least, it appears to be adequate. However, its usefulness is limited largely for animals up to the age of maturity, because afterward the occlusal surfaces tend to flatten for their entire length (see, e.g., Figure 4.25) and lose their former configuration of ridges and valleys (see, e.g., Figure 4.19).

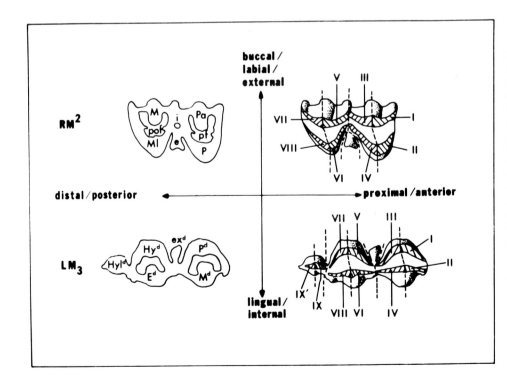

FIGURE 4.14 **Descriptive aids for the discussion of bison dental morphology and wear. Upper left: right M² (worn), showing cusps and fossettes. e, endostyle; i, interfossette; M, metacone; Ml, metaconule; P, protocone; Pa, paracone; pf, prefossette; pof, postfossette. Upper right: right M² (lightly worn) showing numbering of wear facets referred to in text. Numbers increase in posteriad direction. Lower left: left M₃ (worn), showing cusps. Eᵈ, entoconid; exᵈ, exostylid; Hyᵈ, hypoconid; Hylᵈ, hypoconulid; Mᵈ, metaconid; Pᵈ, protoconid. Fossettes as in RM². Lower right: left M₃ (lightly worn) showing numbering of wear facets referred to in text. Numbers increase in posteriad direction. Directional terminology for teeth is shown at termini of the four cardinal axes: alternatives reflect the varying usage of different authors. Other terms are also available, and are used in specialized contexts (Frison *et al.* 1976).**

Based on tooth eruption and wear, there were 12 age-groups of animals in the Agate Basin component bone bed in Area 2. One age-group (No. 10) is apparently missing, and some animals may have lived beyond 12 years but were either not represented or not identified in the sample. Beyond Age-group 5, the groupings became rather tentative, and are based on tooth wear alone. The age-groups and the criteria used for their determination are presented subsequently. Tooth facet wear refers to Figure 4.14. Butchering activities and bone deterioration left few complete mandibles. Consequently, the illustrations of specimens in the various age-groups deal mainly with the details of eruption and wear of molar teeth.

Age-group 1: .8–.9 years. Five specimens. All deciduous premolars are in wear. Wear is seen on facets I–VIII on M_1. M_2 is unerupted but visible in the opening behind M_1 just below the level of the alveolus. M_3 is in the early bud stage and is totally enclosed behind M_2 (Figures 4.15 and 4.16). None of the recovered specimens have deciduous incisors in place. Figure 4.15 is from the Folsom level and is presented at this time because it is the only calf mandible complete enough to demonstrate the entire sequence of tooth development at approximately .9 years of age.

Age-group 2: 1.6–1.8 years. Six specimens. All deciduous premolars are in place. M_1 is now fully erupted and has been reduced in length by several millimeters through wear. M_2 is erupted and there is considerable variance in wear. On one specimen (Figure 4.17) there is light wear only on facets I and II; on another the wear is extended to facets V and VI (Figure 4.18). M_3 is not erupted but is visible in the opening behind M_2, still below the level of the alveolus. The fourth permanent premolar has not yet pushed above the level of the alveolus.

Age-group 3: 2.6–2.9 years. Ten specimens. P_2 and P_3 are usually in place and show little wear. Either dP_2 or dP_3 or both may still be in place but are soon to be lost. The dP_4 is still in wear but P_4 is pushing it upward and it is visible well above the alveolus (Figure 4.19). M_1 and M_2 are in full wear and the exostylid on M_1 is either beginning or is actually in wear. M_3 is erupted and varies from no wear on any facets (Figure 4.20a) to wear on facets I and II (Figure 4.20b) and even light wear on facets III and IV. The hypoconulid is still below the level of the alveolus but it is visible (Figure 4.20a).

Age-group 4: 3.6–3.9 years. Eleven specimens. P_2 and P_3 are in wear; dP_4 may rarely be in place but is usually gone. Light wear is present on P_4. Wear on M_3 varies. Usually it is present on facets I to VIII, with none on the hypoconulid. Wear may be light on facet VII with none on facet VIII on the one extreme (Figure 4.21b) and light wear may be present on the hypoconulid on the other extreme (Figure 4.21a). Exostylid on M_2 is not yet in wear.

Age-group 5: 4.6–4.9 years. Eight specimens. All permanent premolars and molars are in place and in full wear. Hypoconulid on M_3 is in wear but on some specimens the enamel is separated from the remainder of the tooth (Figure

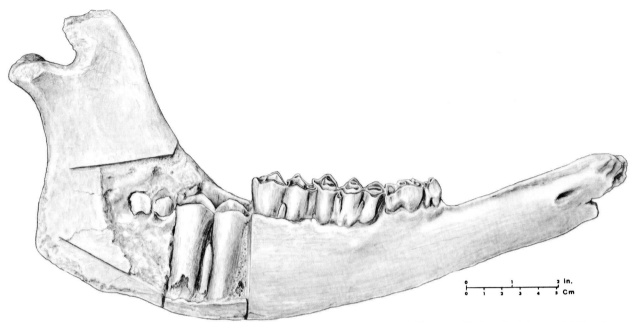

FIGURE 4.15 **Age-group 1. Bison mandible from the Folsom level in Area 2.**

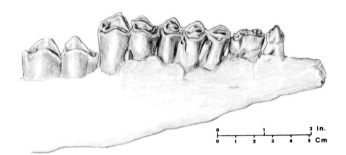

FIGURE 4.16 **Age-group 1. Bison mandible from the Agate Basin level in Area 2.**

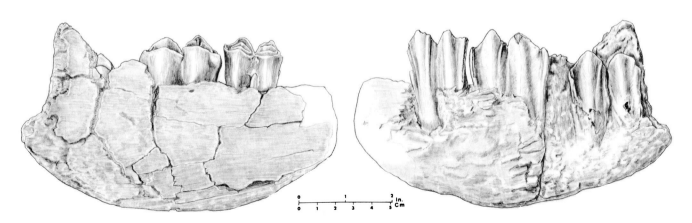

FIGURE 4.17 **Age-group 2. Partial bison mandible from the Agate Basin level in Area 2.**

FIGURE 4.18   **Age-group 2. Partial bison mandible from the Agate Basin level in Area 2.**

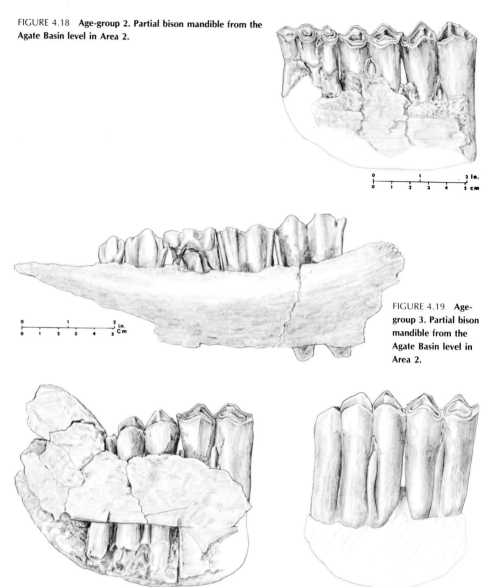

FIGURE 4.19   **Age-group 3. Partial bison mandible from the Agate Basin level in Area 2.**

FIGURE 4.20   **Age-group 3. M_1's and M_2's from the Agate Basin level in Area 2.**

4.22). On others, however, wear has advanced so that the enamel on the hypoconulid joins the enamel on the remainder of the tooth on both lingual and buccal aspects (Figure 4.23). Exostylid on M_2 is usually just ready to come into wear. On one specimen, the fourth incisor (I_4) is erupted and ready to begin wear (Figure 4.23).

Age-group 5 represents mature animals. There are animals represented in all of the first five age-groups, suggesting a wider range of ages than is normally found in an instantaneous procurement event. Even so, these are discrete age-groups with no intermediate specimens.

Age-groups of animals beyond maturity are based on tooth wear, which is less systematic than tooth eruption. M_1 may break down earlier on one animal

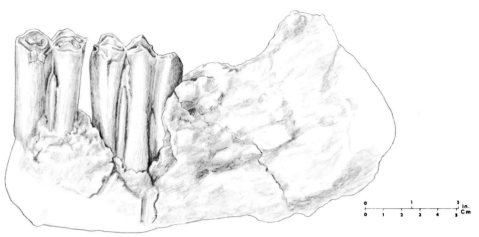

FIGURE 4.21   **Age-group 4. M₁'s and M₂'s from the Agate Basin level in Area 2.**

than on another, which can give the individual animal a year or more shorter life span. Even so, at least seven more age-groups are proposed.

Age-group 6: 5.6–5.9 years. Ten specimens. Wear continues but no deterioration of M_1 is evident. The enamel line at the base of the M_1 metaconid is nearly to the level of the alveolus. The exostylid on M_2 is in wear (Figure 4.24).

Age-group 7: 6.6–6.9 years. Eleven specimens. The enamel line of M_1 is above the alveolus but that of M_2 is at the alveolus or just below. The prefossette on M_1 is reduced in size, allowing noticeable cupping of the dentine between it and the outside enamel. Occasionally there is a slight breakdown of the outside enamel of M_1 adjacent to P_4 (Figure 4.25). The exostylid on M_3 is now either coming into or is already in wear (Figure 4.26a). Note the congenital absence of P_2 on the specimen in Figure 4.25. The character of the molar occlusal surfaces is changing rapidly at this age; they are beginning to flatten out over the entire tooth row.

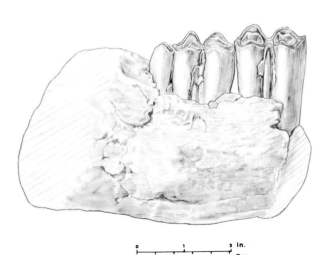

FIGURE 4.22   **Age-group 5. M₁ and M₂ from the Agate Basin level in Area 2.**

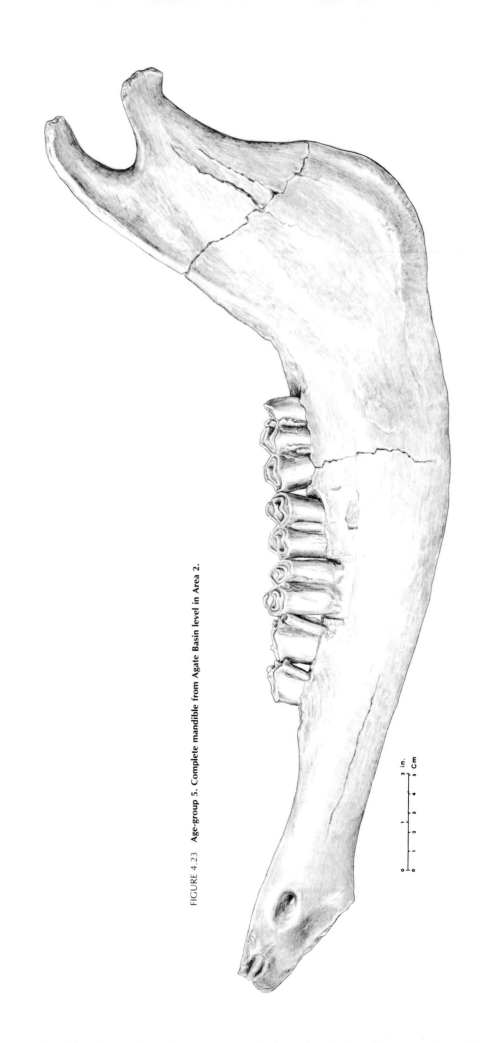

FIGURE 4.23 Age-group 5. Complete mandible from Agate Basin level in Area 2.

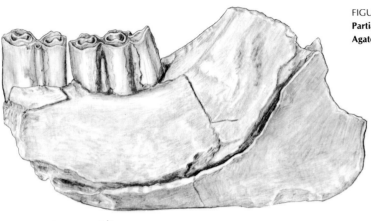

FIGURE 4.24 **Age-group 6. Partial mandible from the Agate Basin level in Area 2.**

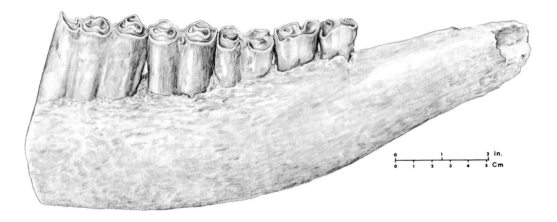

FIGURE 4.25 Age-group 7. **Mandible from the Agate Basin level in Area 2. Note congenital absence of P$_2$.**

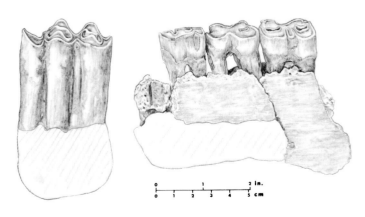

FIGURE 4.26 **M$_3$ in Age- group 7 (left) and a specimen that may be in Age-group 9. Both are from the Agate Basin level in Area 2.**

Age-group 8: 7.6–7.9 years. Three specimens, proposed only on the metaconid height of M_3's. From other assemblages we know that the prefossette of M_1 may be worn away and the base of the enamel on the metaconid of M_2 is at the level of the alveolus. Considerable variation in the wear on M_1 is present in this age-group and it is no longer a reliable age indicator.

Age-group 9: 8.6–8.9 years. Three specimens. On one specimen the enamel at the metaconid of M_1 is gone. The prefossette is worn away and the postfossette nearly so. M_2 is well worn, with the prefossette nearly gone. The enamel level of M_2 is above the level of the alveolus. On one specimen, both M_1 and M_2 are reduced in height but the occlusal surface is nearly flat and continuous across P_4; M_1 and M_2 and the other teeth are missing. This group is based largely on the metaconid height of M_3. One specimen may be in this age-group (Figure 4.26b), and demonstrates clearly the condition whereby P_4, M_1, and M_2 are still intact even though the enamel height is low and the enamel level protrudes well above the alveolus level.

Age-group 10: 9.6–9.9 years. No specimens. From other assemblages we know that the enamel base of M_3 is now at the level of the alveolus and that the condition of M_1 and M_2 may vary greatly.

Age-group 11: 10.6–10.9 years. One specimen, proposed on the basis of a single M_3. The enamel level of M_3 is above the alveolus and the height of the tooth is greatly reduced.

Age-group 12: 11.6–11.9 years. One specimen, proposed on the basis of a single mandible with M_2 and M_3 intact. M_2 is nearly gone; only 9 mm of enamel is left on the metaconid. M_3 is reduced to less than 20 mm of enamel at its metaconid. M_1 is worn below the level of the alveolus, with only root stubs remaining. It is extremely doubtful that an animal in this condition could survive another winter. By late fall, its only remaining occlusal surface with any potential for breaking grass fibers would be a further reduced M_3.

Determination of Seasonality and Rates of Tooth Attrition

If the bison calving season peaked around late April or early May as at present, the Agate Basin bison were killed during the period from around early January until late March. A larger sample would undoubtedly have provided a closer determination of seasonality. It is unfortunate indeed that a large area of the site was looted and that the bone collected in the 1942 excavations was not saved. A better representation of the first three age-groups in particular would have strengthened the study. Also needed is the bone assemblage from Area 1 in order to determine its relationship to Area 2. The small number of ageable mandibles from Area 1 do appear, however, to fall in the same time of year as those from Area 2.

Some ideas on the rates of attrition of bison teeth can be derived from a study of the Agate Basin component bison teeth. Table 4.8 presents the average enamel heights of all molar teeth in the 12 age-groups proposed. On the basis of these data, the average yearly attrition on M_1's was 6.5 mm; on M_2's, 6.0 mm,

TABLE 4.8
Agate Basin Level: Average Metaconid
Height of Bison Molar Teeth (millimeters)

Age-group	M_1	N	M_2	N	M_3	N
1	55.3	3				
2	50.2	5	69.2	4		
3	42.3	6	60.6	8	68.1	9
4	39.5	2	58.0	7	65.6	9
5	30.3	6	49.9	6	58.4	8
6	23.5	2	41.8	5	53.8	9
7	16.1	3	32.1	7	46.9	11
8	18.0	1	32.0	1	41.5	3
9			11.5	2	35.5	2
10						
11					25.0	1
12			9.0	1	20.0	1

and on M_3's, 5.3 mm. These appear to be relatively high rates of attrition. The average yearly attrition for M_1 on mature animals for the Casper site Hell Gap bison was 4.2 mm. However, the yearly M_1 tooth attrition of about 5.3 mm for the Hawken site bison (Frison 1978a) approaches that of the Agate Basin site bison. The Hawken site is about 4000 years later in time than Agate Basin and contained bison intermediate in size between the late Pleistocene and modern forms.

A Late Plains Archaic (Late Middle Prehistoric period) bison kill dated at around 2200 years B.P. demonstrated an annual attrition on M_1's of 5.98 mm (Clark and Wilson 1981). This value is quite close to that for the Agate Basin bison. Average yearly attrition for M_1's of mature Late Prehistoric period bison at the Glenrock and Wardell sites (Reher 1970, 1973) was 3.2 and 3.3 mm, respectively. The reasons for these widely differing rates of wear are not yet understood.

Whatever the underlying causes for differences in bison tooth wear from site to site and between time periods, the results indicate a shorter life span for the late Pleistocene–early Holocene bison than for the bison of the Late Prehistoric period. At the Glenrock and Wardell bison kill sites, 15 or 16 age-groups were proposed, compared to 11 or 12 at the Casper and Agate Basin sites.

Another noticeable feature of the Agate Basin bison is their lack of tooth anomalies compared to those observed at the Casper site (Wilson 1974). One Agate Basin mandible (Figure 4.25) demonstrates a congenital lack of P_2, but otherwise the Agate Basin mandibles are noticeably free of defects. Environmental stress has been suggested as the underlying cause for this condition at the Casper site, but the nature of this is pure speculation at this time. Whatever the answer, it would appear that the late Pleistocene–early Holocene bison were undergoing some kind of stress that resulted in exceptionally heavy tooth wear.

Population Structure

The Hawken site is mentioned regularly in this discussion for several reasons even though it is not a Paleoindian bison kill. The Hawken site bison are an intermediate form, measurably smaller than the bison of Paleoindian times but larger than the modern form. In addition, a large sample of ageable material was recovered. Also, bison procurement at the Hawken site embodied the principle of arroyo entrapment of animals, which is believed to have been employed at the Agate Basin site. With these attributes it is regarded as having produced a body of data that can be compared with the Agate Basin site.

Although much of the Agate Basin bone bed was destroyed, it is unlikely that the addition of mandibles lost would change the population structure significantly. The present sample was taken from large areas of the bone bed and should be a valid population sample unless cultural activities resulted in a nonrandom distribution of mandibles, which is a possibility. Since the mandibles were badly deteriorated and broken from both weathering and processing, it is difficult to associate pairs, so each mandible is treated as a single animal. However, in at least three cases (one each in Age-groups 3, 6, and 7) right and left mandibles probably came from the same animal.

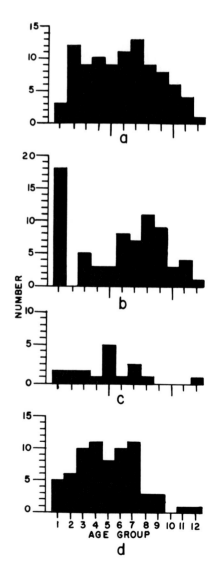

FIGURE 4.27 Population structure of bison from the Hawken site (a), the Casper site (b), the Hell Gap level at Area 3 (c), and the Agate Basin level in Area 2 (d).

One unresolved problem in the taphonomics of large, communal bison kills is the lack of sufficient animals in the younger age-groups. This is true for the later time periods as well as those of the Paleoindian. Examples include Casper (Reher 1974), Olsen–Chubbuck (Wheat 1972), Hawken (Frison *et al.* 1976), Wardell (Reher 1973), and Glenrock (Reher 1970). At the Casper site, calves were better represented than in any of the other kills mentioned but Age-group 2 was missing and Age-groups 3, 4, and 5 were significantly underrepresented (Figure 4.27b). At the Hawken site calves in particular and all of the remaining immature age-groups to a lesser extent were underrepresented (Figure 4.27a). At the Late Prehistoric period Glenrock Buffalo Jump (Reher 1970) and the Wardell site (Reher 1973) calves were poorly represented as were yearlings and 2-year-olds.

One common explanation for these phenomena is that young animals were channeled into a different butchering and processing procedure than were the older animals. This may be so but it remains to be proven. The same conditions prevailed in the sample from the Agate Basin component in Area 2, where both the youngest and oldest age-groups are underrepresented. The age structure (Figure 4.27d) is not what is expected for a catastrophic kill event that should represent the composition of a normal herd at a given point or short space of time. We must assume unexplained events between the biocoenose and the thanatocoenose in prehistoric communal bison kills.

The sex makeup of the Agate Basin sample is even more difficult to determine because there are few mandibles complete enough to provide the necessary measurements. One measurement that has been proposed as a reliable sex indicator is the mandible width, described as the vertical distance between the alveolus and the base of the mandible directly below M_3. The underlying principle is that the larger overall size of the males compared to females will be reflected in the size of the mandibles. Results from several kill sites demonstrate a bimodal distribution (see Reher 1970, 1973, 1974). At the Casper site, mandibles where widths were less than 83 mm were classified as female whereas those greater than 86 mm were classified as male (Fig. 4.28b). The small measurable sample from the Agate Basin component shows a similar distribution (Figure 4.28a). The one mandible with a height of 85 mm certainly represents a male, and the one of 80 mm height is very likely also a male, since it was taken from Age-group 4 and was not yet fully mature. Extreme deterioration of the bone at the Agate Basin site compared to the Casper site may have resulted in all mandi-

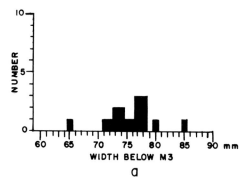

a

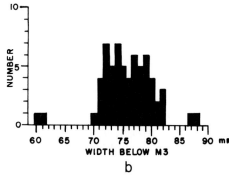

b

FIGURE 4.28 Mandible measurements for the Agate Basin component (a) and the Casper site (b).

ble measurements from the Agate Basin site being 2 mm or so less than the measurements from the Casper site.

Another phenomenon not yet fully explained in many large communal bison kills is what appears to be a shortage of mature males. One exception is the Hawken site, which yielded 8 measurable mature male skulls out of an estimated 100 animals and fragments of at least 13 others. At the Casper site about the same total number of animals were recovered and only 4 mature male skulls were included. It is possible that male–female ratios in bison kill sites can be explained by their behavior in procurement situations.

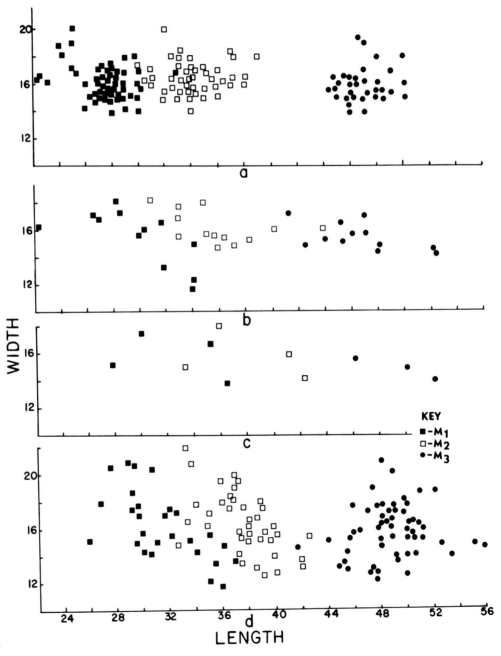

FIGURE 4.29 Length–width measurements of M_1(■), M_2(□), and M_3(●) for the Casper site (a), the Hell Gap component (b), the Folsom component (c), and the Agate Basin component (d) at the Agate Basin site.

Reher (1974:117, 121) used mandible width measurements along with length–width ratios of M_1 to demonstrate a quantifiable size difference between the late Pleistocene bison and the present-day form. Length–width measurements of all molar teeth for the Agate Basin component bison (Figure 4.29d) indicate slightly longer molars (2–3 mm) than those of the Casper site bison (Figure 4.29a). M_1 is slightly wedge-shaped, decreasing in length gradually as the tooth wears and becomes shorter. M_2 shows the same tendency, but M_3 maintains about the same length throughout its life. All teeth are slightly wider toward the base and this is reflected in tooth widths of the older animals. The Casper site teeth do demonstrate a somewhat tighter width grouping but this is because the Casper site measurements represent maximum tooth width. The Agate Basin site measurements, in contrast, represent the occlusal surface width, which changes as the animal increases in age.

THE HELL GAP COMPONENT

The limited extent of the one known Hell Gap bone bed suggests a bison-procurement effort much smaller than the one in the Agate Basin component. It very likely represents a single event. Bone preservation was slightly better than in the Agate Basin component although the pressure from overburden compressed and badly distorted the skulls. Arroyo cutting subsequent to the Hell Gap kill removed part of the bone bed to the north but its limits were reached in all other directions (Figure 2.81). The mandible sample is smaller than the one from the Agate Basin component but still a number of age-groups can be defined:

Age-group 1: .6–.7 years. Two specimens, none complete. On one, dP_3 and dP_4 are in place and in wear. Facets I–IV of M_1 demonstrate wear, with only light wear on facets V and VI. The deciduous premolars were recovered but not in place, and all demonstrate wear. The other specimen consists of dP_4 and M_1 only. The latter has wear on facets I–IV and only very light wear on facets V and VI.

Age-group 2: 1.6–1.7 years. Two specimens, both incomplete. M_2 demonstrates wear on facets I–IV but facets V–VIII are badly damaged; even so, light wear can be seen on facet V. This is an exceptionally large M_2. The M_1 specimen is in full wear but the exostylid is about 6.5 mm below the occlusal surface.

Age-group 3: 2.6–2.7 years. Two specimens. In both cases butchering damage has made determination of age difficult. On one, the mandible was broken so that M_3 was dislodged and pushed downward, giving the impression it had barely erupted above the level of the alveolus. However, closer examination revealed very light wear on cusps I and II of M_3, which would require it to be more fully erupted in order to oppose M^3. All other eruption and wear stages indicate an animal about 2.6–2.7 years of age; dP_4 is just above the alveolus and the exostylid of M_1 is just ready to begin wear. The other specimen in this age-group consists of a single M_3. A few mandible fragments that may represent the opposite side of the first specimen are also present.

Age-group 4: 3.6–3.7 years. One specimen, represented by a single M_2 with metaconid height of 58 mm and the exostylid still well below the occlusal surface.

Age-group 5: 4.6–4.7 years. Six specimens. Four of these are almost certainly paired, although butchering and weathering damage is heavy. These are nearly mature animals. All permanent premolars and molars are in place and in wear. The hypoconulid on M_3 demonstrated light wear, and the exostylid on M_2 was usually in wear or very nearly so.

Age-group 6: 5.6–6.7 years. One specimen is probably in this age-group, but it seems to have been an unusually small animal. M_3 is missing but wear on the remainder of the teeth strongly suggests this age-group, although all teeth are extremely small. The occlusal surface is in good condition and the exostylid of M_2 is in full wear but remains separate from the remainder of the tooth. One relatively low M_1 length–width measurement expresses the diminutive size of this single specimen (Figure 4.29b) in the Hell Gap sample. Two specimens of comparable size were present in the Casper site sample (Figure 4.29a), indicating that relatively small animals are to be expected in these late Pleistocene–early Holocene bison populations.

Age-group 7: 6.6–6.7 years. Three specimens. The enamel base of M_1 is above the alveolus but that of M_2 is still below. The prefossette on M_1 is noticeably smaller, and cupping of the anterior part of M_1 and posterior part of P_4 is evident. The exostylid on M_3 is just coming into wear.

Age-group 8: 7.6–7.7 years. One specimen. The enamel level on M_2 is at the level of the alveolus, and the exostylid on M_3 is in wear. A definite pathological condition is evident, since the anterior part of P_4 and all of P_3 have not worn normally; both are about 7 mm higher than the molar tooth row. P_2 is missing. This probably reflects some problem with the upper premolars that has apparently produced more than normal wear on M_2 and M_3.

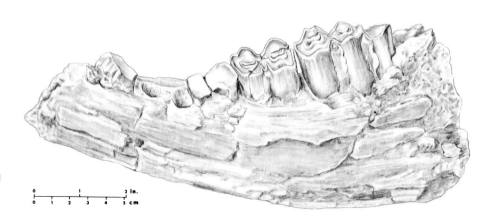

FIGURE 4.30 **Badly worn and deteriorated mandible from the Hell Gap component at the Agate Basin site.**

TABLE 4.9
Hell Gap Level: Average Metaconid Height of Bison Molar Teeth (millimeters)

Age-group	M_1	N	M_2	N	M_3	N
1	55.0	2				
2	49.0	1	68.5	1		
3	45.0	1	66.0	1	74.1	2
4			58.0	1		
5	34.7	3	51.0	5	58.1	6
6	16.5	1	35.0	1		
7	19.0	2	32.3	3	45.3	3
8	17.0	1	26.0	1	36.0	1
12			11.0	1	22.0	1

Extreme Old Age: Estimated 11–12 years. One specimen. P_4 is missing. M_1 is worn to the alveolus. Both fossettes of M_2 are gone but 11 mm of enamel remains at the metaconid and M_3 is still in good condition (Figure 4.30). This mandible is regarded as that of an old animal, but a pathology could have resulted in early breakdown of the tooth row in the vicinity of P_4 and M_1. It is difficult, if not impossible, to place this specimen in an age-group with any feeling of confidence.

Although the sample is small, the animals from the Hell Gap component form tighter age-groups than those from the Agate Basin component. It is proposed that they were killed sometime around the middle or latter part of December. The sample is too small to establish a true population structure (Figure 4.27c), and butchering on the mandibles was too destructive to determine the sex of the animal from mandible width below M_3. The length–width ratios of the molar teeth (Figure 4.29b) demonstrate a close approximation to those from the Casper site, and they are also noticeably smaller than the Agate Basin sample (Figure 4.29d). Tooth wear on the Hell Gap bison was high (see Table 4.9), as was the wear on the teeth of the Agate Basin bison. Noticeable among the Hell Gap specimens were two M_3's in Age-group 3, probably from the same animal, with metaconid heights of over 74 mm, which is unusually high.

THE FOLSOM COMPONENTS

Folsom-age bone beds were found stratigraphically beneath the Agate Basin component in Area 2 and also beneath the Hell Gap component in the original Brewster site area (Area 3). There was a concentration of skulls in the Brewster site area, according to the investigators (Agogino and Frankforter 1960), but only two were considered to be recoverable. No mandibles or lower teeth were mentioned in the report. None were found in the small amount of extant faunal material from the original investigation in the Brewster site area, or any of the later excavations.

The Folsom bone bed in Area 2 contains the skeletal remains of a nearly complete female and a calf along with partial remains of seven other animals.

The time of year of the kill is strongly indicated by three animals. The first is the calf, which is probably around .9 years or 11 months old as determined by tooth wear on facets I–VIII of M_1. M_2 is not yet erupted and M_3 is represented by tiny buds developing and totally enclosed behind M_2 (Figure 4.15). As expected, the upper teeth demonstrate the same age.

A small amount of fetal material was present from two individuals—one close to full term, the other a month or so younger. Though not conclusive due to the small sample size, this is highly suggestive of a late winter or early spring kill date. The female is in Age-group 5 (fully mature), with I_4 coming into wear. Four other mandibles and fragments are in the older age-groups and are insufficient in number for a meaningful determination of the structure of the population from which the animals were taken. Length–width measurements of molars (Figure 4.29c) indicate sizes comparable to those of the Agate Basin component specimens.

Present also in the Folsom component in Area 2 were the partial remains of at least four pronghorn (*Antilocapra americana*). These were probably killed elsewhere and have no connection with the arroyo as a trap. They were probably introduced into the cultural level through normal site activity and are treated in another section.

THE AGATE BASIN COMPONENT IN SITE AREA 1

In 1975, when the writer began excavations in Area 1, only the spoil-dirt piles remained; almost nothing was left in situ. Nevertheless, the spoil-dirt piles were screened in order to recover any remaining bone.

It is very likely that the bone data from Area 1 would have provided a better understanding of the cultural activities associated with the bison procurement. To the best of our knowledge Area 1 contained only a pure Agate Basin component. Pictures taken during the 1942 excavation reveal large amounts of bone (see Figures 1.7 and 2.1), and the spoil-dirt piles mentioned produced a large number of complete long bones demonstrating no evidence of butchering, in direct contrast to the bone assemblage recovered in the bone bed in Area 2.

At least two other observations suggest that Area 1 might have been an actual kill location: (*a*) a high concentration of projectile points as demonstrated by the earlier collections and (*b*) the presence of complete or nearly complete articulated animals, as is strongly suggested by earlier accounts. The projectile points from the Area 1 excavations are extant and there is a reasonably accurate eyewitness account of one nearly complete bison and numerous large articulated sections. The authors are well aware of the dangers encountered in the use of eyewitness accounts and the use of material lacking good context, so these statements regarding Area 1 must be considered as somewhat conjectural.

R. E. Frison, whose efforts first brought the Agate Basin site to the attention of Frank H. H. Roberts, told the senior author that he saw a nearly complete skeleton of an animal in Area 1 when he worked at the site with Roberts in 1942. He described the animal as being in a normal reclining position on its belly, with hind feet extended anteriorly and placed slightly to one side and front legs with radii–ulnae extended anteriorly and metacarpals and front feet extended posteriorly. He said that the long bones and axial skeleton were removed

FIGURE 4.31 **Rear bison feet in situ in Area 1.**

during excavation, but the feet were deliberately left in place for future reference. He also said that when he first viewed the original exposure of bone in the arroyo bank, the bone was highly visible. Large quantities of bone were scattered downslope to the arroyo bottom, suggesting that Area 1 was probably only a remnant of a much larger bone bed.

Excavations in 1975 did support these earlier claims of a bison skeleton in Area 1. The rear feet of a bison were found in situ (Figure 4.31) and in about the position and location described. The front feet were no longer in place; they were probably removed by artifact hunters subsequent to the work in 1942. The presence of the complete or nearly complete animal along with numerous complete long bones from the spoil-dirt piles strongly suggests a different set of activities than in Area 2, but unfortunately this all must be highly speculative.

Several loose teeth and mandible fragments were recovered among the other bones from Area 1 in 1975, and some of these provide evidence of the time of year during which the animals were killed. Sixteen molars and four premolars, both uppers and lowers, are from animals less than 4 years of age and allow age determinations. They are separated into age-groups as follows:

Age-group 1: Five specimens. A complete M_1 should be in the .6 year range. Eruption is nearly complete, with a metaconid height of 55.5 mm, and wear of facets I and II is just beginning. Wear on another M_1 is present on facets I–VIII, indicating an age around the .9 year stage. Wear on an upper M^1 matches this .9-year-old specimen, and two upper P^4's compare with animals in the .6–.9 year range.

Age-group 2: Five specimens. One M_2 demonstrates wear on facets I–VI but only light wear on facets VII and VIII, and represents an animal in the 1.8–1.9 year range. Three are M_1's with wear suggesting a 1.6–1.9 year spread. A broken M_3 is also in this age-group.

Age-group 3: Five specimens. Three M_1's have the exostylid either in wear or just coming into wear. One P_4 and dP_4 are in this age-group. One M_3 has light wear on facets I and II. Age spread is 2.6–2.9 years.

Age-group 4: Two specimens. One M_2 has the exostylid just coming into wear and an M_3 has wear on facets I–VIII, with only a trace of wear on the hypoconulid or facet IX. These are almost certainly within a 3.5–3.9 year age spread.

Although this sample is small, the writers feel that it is indicative of animals that were killed in winter or early spring, during the same months that the animals in the Agate Basin component in Area 2 were killed. On the other hand, there is nothing to establish a direct relationship between Areas 1 and 2. If Area 1 were the actual kill for the animals processed in the Agate Basin component in Area 2, it would be expected that some broken projectile points and tools from one area would match those from the other. This was not the case, even though the number of lithic artifacts from both areas was large, raw materials were similar, and both were Agate Basin components.

THE SHEAMAN SITE CLOVIS COMPONENT

Three teeth from the Sheaman site Clovis component are suggestive of the season of occupation, but make up too small a sample for there to be certainty. Two of the teeth are the dP_2 and dP_3 premolars, intact in a mandible; these are from a young calf. Light wear is evident on the crown of P_2, but not enough to have worn through the enamel layer. It is suggested that this calf was less than a month old.

The third tooth is an M_1 from a slightly older calf. Although the surrounding bone is missing, a comparison of the height of the tooth enamel with that of other specimens of known age indicates that the tooth was probably erupted above the level of the alveolus and was probably from an animal .1–.25 year old. If these two specimens are indicative of the normal calving period, the Sheaman Clovis site could have been a late spring–early summer occupation.

3. BISON TAXONOMY

george c. frison

It is an established fact that, as an animal population, the late Pleistocene bison were larger and possessed different horn structures than present-day bison. This leads directly into the problem of taxonomy, even though it is of less interest to the anthropological archaeologist than the cultural aspects of a site. The history of bison taxonomy has been adequately discussed by Wilson (1974, 1975, 1978), who used the earlier work of others and his own observations on specimens from a number of sites in an attempt to develop a more rational approach to Holocene bison taxonomy. His conclusions derive mainly from a large body of evidence suggesting that the late Pleistocene bison did not suffer complete extinction, and that modern bison did not derive from a separate and distinct evolutionary line, a position held to be true earlier.

Wilson's line of reasoning, based on a larger and better controlled data base than those of earlier observers, indicates that the late Pleistocene bison did indeed form the gene pool out of which the later bison evolved. During the Holocene, a gradual shrinking in size of the bison occurred, probably due to natural selection resulting from changing environments. This trend may have accelerated slightly during the Altithermal period, from about 8000 to 5000 years ago. These ideas contrast with those of Skinner and Kaisen (1947), who felt that two sympatric species, *Bison antiquus* and *Bison occidentalis*, were present on the Central and Southern Plains with no intermediate forms. However, Skinner and Kaisen did describe a form (*B. antiquus figginsi*) that could have been interpreted as an intermediate form. Animals killed at the Casper site dated at 10,000 years B.P. represent taxonomically both *B. antiquus* and *B. figginsi* as described by Skinner and Kaisen, so the concept of intergradation between *B. antiquus* and *B. occidentalis* can be supported.

Pursuing Wilson's line of reasoning further, he proposes that Skinner and Kaisen's two species (*B. antiquus* and *B. occidentalis*) were not sympatric but allopatric, and also contemporaneous. Because of a clinal depression to the south through time, *B. occidentalis* tended to lag *B. antiquus* over much of the Plains. If Wilson's (1975, 1978) reasoning is correct, *B. antiquus* and *B. occidentalis* could not have existed as separate species and were valid only at a subspecific level. Their proper designations would be *B. b. antiquus* and *B. b. occidentalis*; the present form is *B. b. bison*.

The observable differences between *B. b. antiquus* and *B. b. occidentalis* are in the deflection of the horn-cores, orbital protrusion, and cranial breadth of male skulls. Wilson's interpretation of the extant data is that "*antiquus*" forms were present in the early Holocene in the Northern Plains and "*occidentalis*" forms gradually moved south through time into the Central and Southern Plains. The exact rate of progression for this trend is not known, but there is evidence for intergradation of the two forms at the Casper site 10,000 years B.P. (Wilson 1974), as we have seen, and a definite "*occidentalis*" present in the Black Hills of Wyoming and South Dakota 6500 years B.P. (Frison *et al.* 1976).

One of the salient problems of bison taxonomy has been that of sexual dimorphism. The bison bone from the first excavation at Agate Basin was discarded because it was identified as modern bison and therefore considered of little value, since large samples of modern bison were already available. The significant size difference between males and females and the tendency for prehistoric hunters to trap nursery herds were not realized at that time, so that female skulls of the late Pleistocene and early Holocene, being within the range of males of modern bison, were thereby wrongly identified.

The preponderance of nursery herds in Paleoindian kill sites makes it necessary to develop a method of subspecific determination based on female as well as male skulls. Wilson (1978:14–16) has demonstrated clearly that cranial measurements can be used reliably to differentiate between fossil and modern bison and also to determine sex, provided the age of the animals is known. It is hoped that this methodology will be improved upon so that it can be used for accurate subspecific determinations as well.

Unfortunately, skulls are comparatively rare. Many of both sexes were destroyed to varying extents in the butchering process. Skulls also deteriorate rapidly compared to long bones, and they do not become buried as quickly or as easily as long bones because of their size and shape. A separation between the late Pleistocene and modern bison can be demonstrated by measurements of individual skeletal elements (see, e.g., Bedord 1974; Frison 1978b:283–287; Zeimens and Zeimens 1974), but these measurements do not separate "*antiquus*" and "*occidentalis*," so that the problem of taxonomy in bison is largely that of obtaining adequate samples of reliable taxonomic determiners, at this point, skulls. The data from large kills by humans, because these are catastrophic in nature, result in large numbers of animals, and can be closely dated. Unfortunately, the behavioral characteristics of the hunters in butchering and processing, together with the deteriorating effects of the elements, generally tend to limit severely the number of reliable determiners that can be recovered.

Given the small number and poor condition of the skulls from the Agate Basin component, it is difficult to do more than speculate on subspecific identification. One young male skull (Figure 4.40a) demonstrates mostly characteristics of the southern or "*antiquus*" form, with a suggestion of some intergradation of the northern or "*occidentalis*" form. The one female skull (Figure 4.40b) is too incomplete; also, the horn-cores demonstrate pathological tendencies, which make any identification difficult. The standard measurements of the two skulls are presented in Table 4.15.

Four skulls, two male and two female, were recovered from the Hell Gap component in Area 3. Measurements for these are in Table 4.15. They are regarded as "*antiquus*," although they were all compressed by pressure of the overburden. Skulls F2332 and F1478 (Table 4.15) were subjected to both vertical and right-angle pressures, since they were on the rising slope of the arroyo bank. They are herein referred to *B. b. antiquus*, although F2332 (Figure 4.41a) may demonstrate some "*occidentalis*" characteristics.

Agogino and Frankforter (1960) recovered two skulls from the Folsom component in Area 3 (Brewster). Only one of these was available for measurement (Wilson 1974:163 and Table 4.15). Agogino and Frankforter regarded this as *B. antiquus*, although Wilson (1974:160) felt that the specimen demonstrated a clear indication of some aspects of the northern (*occidentalis*) phenotype. The mature specimen from the Folsom component in Area 2 is female. Its horn-cores are missing (Figure 4.7), allowing only limited metric determinations (Table

4.15). The deteriorated condition of the exterior of the skull made it impossible to determine whether the horn-cores were broken off deliberately by the hunters or accidentally in the trapping process, or if some pathology was present.

4. BISON PROCUREMENT
george c. frison

In terms of bison procurement, the Agate Basin site was merely the focal point of an event whose success required the intense effort and cooperation of a number of persons. The operation would have varied somewhat from one time to another and was determined by several factors, including the topography, vegetative cover, weather, time of day, and the day-to-day idiosyncrasies of bison behavior. More than the immediate site locality was involved; conditions several kilometers distant could have an effect on the outcome of any given buffalo drive. The historic period is used here to depict conditions in Folsom, Agate Basin, and Hell Gap times with respect to bison activities. There is a possibility of error in doing this, since the animals were a different subspecies and some vegetation differences may have existed, particularly during Folsom times.

During spring and summer in the Agate Basin area, with grass knee high as far as the eye can see, the problems of winter survival seem far removed. However, heavy snow and cold temperatures later in the fall bring the realization that it will be nearly half a year before green grass returns. During this period the bison would expend nearly all their efforts in finding enough food to survive the blizzards and below-zero temperatures of winter.

Bison is the only species of large grazing animals to survive through the Pleistocene to the present on the High Plains, except for the significantly smaller pronghorn. Their survival is testimony that they have mastered the techniques of grazing during the winter. In deep snow they do not paw for feed as many other grazers do. Rather they use their large heads like snowplows, pushing snow to one side to expose the grass. When they are full, they simply lie down until hunger forces them through the same cycle again. Domestic range cattle run a far distant second to bison when it comes to winter survival on the High Plains.

Several thousand generations of *Bison* and subspecies have lived on the High Plains during late Pleistocene and Holocene times. Their responses to winter conditions were developed through intense natural selection during this time. The importance of such things as the location of and access to feed and water are obvious to the casual observer, but many more subtle aspects must be considered in evaluating a piece of country as a buffalo range. For example, topography and wind direction determine what areas will be exposed for grazing in times of deep snow. Snow melts from sandy soils and southern exposures before the northern slopes. "Breaks"—the rough, dissected areas adjacent to stream valleys—provide protection during severe storms, as do brush thickets in stream valleys. During extremely bad winters, the brush thickets may be the only food available. The Paleoindian hunter, knowing that he would ultimately corral and kill bison at the Agate Basin site, was totally familiar with the country. Consequently, he knew about where the animals would be and the likelihood of performing a successful drive after observing conditions on any given day.

If conditions in Paleoindian times were similar to those during the last hundred years, the drainage of the Cheyenne River around the southwestern part of the Black Hills in present-day Wyoming and South Dakota was excellent bison country. The combination of open rolling country, river and arroyo bottoms, river breaks, and timbered foothills provided ideal year-round food and shelter. Fall and early winter storms would have moved the scattered herds of animals and concentrated them along the river bottoms of the Cheyenne River. Later on in the year, as the river bottoms were grazed and tramped out, deepening ice and snow cover would have made it difficult to reach the remaining grass. The animals would then have begun to move out into tributaries such as Moss Agate Creek, grazing the arroyo bottoms until the feed there was depleted or no longer available as the result of deep or crusted snow. Their attention would then have turned to the windswept ridges. During this period, the hunters could have hazed a herd of the proper size into the arroyo, which with some modification formed a trap at the Agate Basin site. There were probably enough animals concentrated in this area of the Cheyenne River in winter so that the failure to trap one herd would have left sufficient numbers for the process to be repeated with a different herd.

This is the way in which the present-day bison would utilize the Agate Basin area if there were no fences or domestic livestock to offer competition for feed. Once the Agate Basin arroyo filled with sediments in post–Hell Gap times, it would no longer have served the purpose of a trap, and another site would have been selected. Bison hunters in later time periods apparently favored other areas and/or different procurement methods.

PRESENT-DAY BISON   Evidence from the Agate Basin site indicates that Paleoindian use of the location was for the purpose of winter bison procurement in order to provision the cultural group. The object of the procurement effort, the late Pleistocene bison, was a large, wild, grazing animal whose behavior was probably not too far removed from that of its modern counterpart, which narrowly escaped extinction during the nineteenth century. Fortunately, extinction was averted and there are sizable herds today that allow meaningful observations on their day-to-day behavior. In addition, a number of buffalo raisers have been engaged in the business long enough to acquire more than a superficial level of expertise with the animals.

The accoutrements used in handling buffalo reflect the differences between them and range cattle. Bison fences are higher; corrals and working pens are stronger. A squeeze gate designed for cattle needs some modification for bison because the latter are quicker, and they lack the relatively broad shoulders of domestic cattle. In addition, the bison is still further away from domestication and will not calmly accept the constraints of a squeeze gate. As a result, they never stop struggling until completely exhausted and often seriously hurt themselves. The skeletons of present-day buffalo reflect this innate wildness. Few older animals lack extensive damage to bones, particularly ribs, neural spines, pelvis, and horns. A buffalo cow in a present-day herd was butchered because of extreme old age and consequent failure to produce a calf. Crippled in a rear leg while being run through a chute, the cow was still able to function well enough for several years as a breeding animal. During butchering it was discovered that the head of the femur was broken off and had grown into the acetabulum, leaving no connection to the distal part of the bone. Still the muscles had developed to the extent that the animal had limited use of the leg and was able to keep up with the herd with little difficulty. The neural spine on each thoracic vertebra had been broken and healed also, reducing the height of the hump by several centimeters. On another female the right ilium and left ischium had been broken and healed. Similar and even worse conditions are the rule rather than the exception.

Bison do not always react well to being driven with horses. Several owners of large herds have abandoned the use of horses for motor vehicles. The bison are less wary of a person in a pickup truck than one on a horse. The trucks usually have metal wings and heavy bumpers that can force the animals to move. On a horse, one stands a strong chance of being pushed to one side or trampled. When handling bison in or out of a corral, one must be alert and able to react quickly, and one must expect the unexpected. Inadequate fences or gates can be destroyed if bison are pushed beyond certain levels of stress. It is easy to understand the carnage reported in historic bison pounding situations, where the animals caused about as much damage to themselves as the hunters were able to inflict. Any person or persons who happened to stand in the way of a group of bison when they were in this frenzied condition could expect the worst.

To nonparticipant observers such as the archaeologist and historian, it is easy to regard the driving, trapping, and killing of bison as similar to hunting by pursuit. However, constraining the animals injects an entirely different set of parameters for the hunters to cope with, and greatly increases the dangers involved. The hooves and horns of bison are sharp; the bison can travel at high rates of speed, and will not always change course to avoid an obstacle the size of a human being. This is particularly true when they suddenly realize that the way to open country is blocked by an impenetrable barrier such as a fence, a box canyon, a precipice, or the steep sides of a parabolic sand dune. Their immediate and usual reaction upon perceiving such a situation is to reverse their course and charge full tilt in the only direction they know freedom lies, which is the direction from which they came.

This particular facet of bison behavior is probably the one that worked to the greatest advantage of the hunter, provided it was properly exploited. A single animal or a small group (not more than 6 animals) that approaches a barrier can reverse direction and, unless there is a gate that can be closed, the pursuing hunters can do little to stop them. By adding more animals, and since bison follow a lead animal, the larger herd (for example, 30 animals) will be strung out for a distance. In this situation, the leader will reverse direction, followed immediately by those directly behind it (lead animals are almost without exception older females). The animals at the rear (the drag) will not be able to react in time. They will be moving forward at full speed, and the lead will be moving in the opposite direction at full speed. The result is a short period of confusion. This is the moment that the hunters had to take advantage of if they did not have a corral or other restraining feature. The hunters then prolonged the period of confusion by using spears, darts, or arrows or whatever weaponry they had. Once the animals became confused, they were no longer capable of resuming their course toward freedom and were then just as apt to charge each other or the walls of the arroyo as to attempt to return in the direction from which they came.

LANDFORMS AND CORRALS AS PALEOINDIAN BISON TRAPS

In large in situ bone beds, like Agate Basin, some part of the original land surface on which the bone bed was deposited is preserved. Usually a small, undisturbed segment provides a basis for the reconstruction of larger segments. It has been determined, for example, that at Olsen–Chubbuck (Wheat 1972) animals were driven at right angles into a narrow, steep-walled arroyo. At the Casper site (Frison 1974) the animals were driven into the constraining walls of a parabolic sand dune (Albanese 1974). At the Hawken site (Frison *et al.* 1976) the animals were driven up the bottom of an arroyo until a natural barrier and steep banks formed a trap. In all three cases, the landform involved was determined from small remnants.

Identification of the landform used in bison procurement is of great importance because its effectiveness in terms of animal behavior can then be determined, and manpower requirements can be judged, telling us something about the size of the human group involved. The writers feel that most arroyo traps such as Hawken and Agate Basin and sand dune traps such as at Casper were probably not capable of totally restraining the animals. Instead, they were designed to restrain the animals long enough for the hunters to take advantage of the animals' confusion. Many other, more subtle strategies may have been added. For example, two or three persons with a hide or other simple barrier across the arroyo or the opening of a sand dune or corral would be sufficient in most cases to prevent the escape of animals in a highly confused state. Artificial fences very likely enhanced the natural qualities of the landforms at both Casper and Hawken, with the expenditure of very little human effort in relationship to the economic benefits resulting from obtaining a large number of bison at a predetermined location.

In some bison-procurement sites such as Jones–Miller (Stanford 1978) and Horner (Jepsen 1953; and more recent unpublished work by the writer), there were no landforms present that would have aided appreciably in constraining animals, so an artificial structure such as a corral with diverging fence lines may have been used. There seems no reason to deny the Paleoindian the ability to build and maintain a corral capable of holding bison, since hunters of the Late Archaic Besant cultural complex were accomplishing this with a similar basic technology in the same general area (see Frison 1970). Although Besant does suggest a highly sophisticated level of prehorse bison procurement, there is nothing to suggest a lower level of sophistication among the Paleoindian. Evidence for corral posts is lacking at both Jones–Miller and Horner, but a substantial corral capable of holding bison does not require posts if the building logs are large enough and are properly anchored together. It is extremely unlikely that the lack of the required natural landform would negate the use of a location that was of exceptional value for bison procurement if alternative locations were not extant.

First-hand knowledge and familiarity with the day-to-day behavior of bison allows investigators to evaluate many other proposed methods of procurement. The bogging of bison as a procurement method is based mostly on conjecture and a refusal to concede prehistoric man his true hunting ability. Bison clearly enjoy bogs and will wallow in them belly deep to graze and/or fight flies on a hot day. Bogs do little to impede the progress of a healthy animal, although they do trap the weak and sick ones. When someone tries to drive bison into a bog, they usually refuse to cooperate. The same is true of ice. Bison will wander out on an ice-covered stream or pond and may even break through the ice. On the other hand, trying to drive the animals across ice can be a frustrating experience.

Bogs should not be confused with what are commonly referred to as buffalo wallows, which are shallow depressions that filled with water. Buffalo rolled in these to the extent that the wallows became larger and deeper. In some areas wallows are still features of the landscape and may contain water during parts of the spring and summer. They may be up to 40 m in diameter and over 1 m in depth, and many were enlarged in historic times by livestock operators for use as stock-water reservoirs. As many of these wallows dried up in summer, they became dust wallows that were then as much of an attraction to the bison as when they contained water.

The other aspect of killing an animal in a bog is that it is almost impossible to butcher an animal and remove the meat from the bog without ruining it. The knowledgeable hunter first chases an animal, bison or otherwise, out of the bog and then kills it. The Paleoindian was an accomplished hunter, and possessed the skills and weaponry to take animals under conditions imposed by the hunter, rather than by the animals.

The use of snowdrifts and bodies of water as a regular means of constraining bison in order to kill them also seems unlikely, unless sufficient manpower was available to remove the animals immediately. An animal as large as a mature bison with all four feet extended into a snowbank is extremely difficult to extract, as is one lying in water of any depth. As in the case of the bog, strong, healthy animals are unlikely to become trapped in snowdrifts. If one did, the intelligent hunter would first try to let the animal extract itself under its own power and then kill it, which would save much effort on the hunter's part.

Late in the winter and in early spring, weaker animals may have become trapped in deep snow to be killed relatively easily, particularly under conditions of crusty snow where the heavier animals break through and the hunters do not. However, such weakened animals were the natural prey of other predators, which would have offered competition to the human hunters. Animals of this nature would probably have been used by human groups in times of real food shortages but not under normal circumstances, since the food they provided

FIGURE 4.32   **Present-day analog of an arroyo bison trap.**

would have been definitely inferior to that from healthy animals. It should be emphasized once more that the Paleoindian was an accomplished hunter and could use this knowledge and ability to the disadvantage of the animals.

Using studies of taphonomics and paleolandforms, and observations on the behavior of present-day bison, we conclude that in Paleoindian times the arroyo containing the Folsom, Agate Basin, and Hell Gap components was wider and deeper, and the sides were steeper than at present. Fewer large tributary arroyos existed. This contrasts sharply with the arroyo today, which is shallow, has gently sloping banks, many tributaries, and a wide, flat bottom covered with a heavy stand of grasses. The arroyo banks in Paleoindian times were probably high and steep enough to hold the bison, and some natural knickpoint may have formed a barrier or at least a partial obstruction that was modified with logs to form a trap. The bison were probably driven up the arroyo into the trap rather than stampeded over the bank as was probably the case at the Olsen–Chubbuck site (Wheat 1972). The configuration of the old Agate Basin arroyo would not have allowed an Olsen–Chubbuck type of procurement operation.

However, several arroyos close to the present-day Agate Basin site are of the proper configuration to serve as bison traps (Figure 4.32). The arroyo bottoms regularly develop knickpoints (Schumm and Hadley 1957) as a result of the normal processes of erosion. Their usefulness as animal traps depends on their configuration from one time to another and they may change form rapidly as a result of spring runoff and summer thunderstorms.

There is no clue at the present time as to the number of years the Agate Basin site was used for bison procurement. The presence of Folsom, Agate Basin, and Hell Gap components with bone beds in situ is suggestive of continuity through a long period of time. However, the components are in what was then an arroyo bottom, and consequently any given component was subject to destruction by normal yearly flooding, even though the general trend for the period was one of aggradation. Whether the site was used annually, periodically, or only at times when a combination of conditions fortuitously resulted in the presence there of sufficient bison to allow communal hunting is not known. There must have been alternative locations that were favorable, since as we have seen rainfall and consequently the amount of grass vary significantly over short distances on the Plains. Only the presence of bison in the Agate Basin site locality can be regarded as a reason for its attraction to human groups in the winter. It was apparently decided to spend the winter close to the frozen meat piles rather than move them to a more suitable location for human habitation.

THE AGATE BASIN SITE AS AN ARROYO TRAP

5. CULTURAL MODIFICATION OF BONE FROM PRONGHORN (*ANTILOCAPRA AMERICANA*) AND OTHER SMALL MAMMALS

danny n. walker

The pronghorn bone at the Agate Basin site was probably from animals killed away from the site and brought in for use as food. Extensive cultural modifications were present on all the pronghorn material recovered. Modifications presumably resulted from the complete butchering and breakage of the bone for maximum utilization of the food resource. A minimum of four individuals of pronghorn were present in the Folsom faunule, based on either four occipitals or four right humeri.

Breakage patterns within the pronghorn remains recovered from the Folsom fanule are very similar in appearance to those seen in the 212 individuals from the Eden–Farson site (Frison 1971) in southwestern Wyoming, which has been dated at 230 ± 100 years B.P. (Frison 1978b:61). Carcass processing at the two sites appears quite similar, despite the age and cultural affiliation differences. Minor differences in bone treatment are present, but these may be a result of sample size. The similarity in the patterned breakage on the bone in the two sites suggests similar butchering processes. There is a very limited sequence of steps that are most efficient in butchering an animal of this size, and the possible variations in the sequence described by Frison (1971) would account for any differences between the two sites.

Bone surfaces were moderately eroded, and only a few cut marks remained. These were on the anterior medial surface of a scapula neck, the posterior lateral side of four distal humeri, the distal end of two tibiae, the anterior midshaft of one radius (Figure 4.33d), and the left lateral surface of one atlas. All these marks probably reflect defleshing of the bones during processing.

Most butchering evidence consists of breakage either from initial dismemberment of the carcass or from marrow processing. Initial processing breaks were seen on the distal tibiae (Figure 4.34c–g), four proximal metatarsals—each with at least one depressed fracture 1–2 cm from the proximal end (Figure 4.34a,b)—and the midsection of a radius shaft (Figure 4.33d). Marrow-processing breaks are probably those on two scapulae, five distal humeri (Figure 4.33e–i), two proximal radii, and one proximal ulna. The absence of proximal humeri and tibiae and distal femora probably reflects breakage beyond recognition during marrow processing, a feature also noted by Frison (1971).

For the most part, skulls and mandibles were also treated in the manner of the Eden–Farson material. Again, cut marks were difficult to discern on the skull material because of the eroded bone surface. Faint traces of cut marks could be seen on one maxilla. Maxillae and mandibles were identical in breakage to those at Eden–Farson, and one fairly complete mandible was recovered. One point at which the Agate Basin sample differed from Eden–Farson is the presence of the occipital condyles. The remains of the Eden–Farson skulls con-

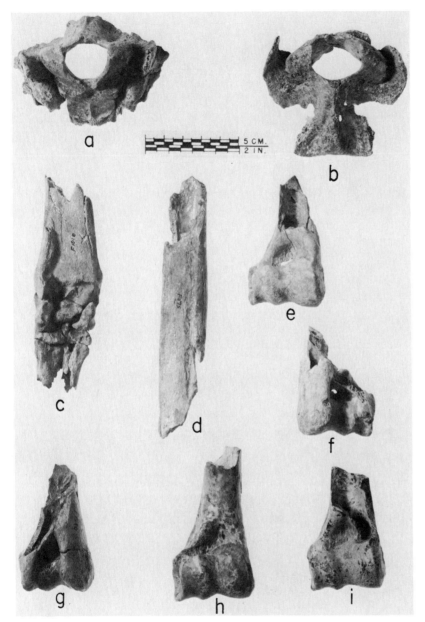

FIGURE 4.33 **Butchered pronghorn bone from the Folsom level in Area 2.**

tained only maxillae and horn-cores, whereas four occipital condyles were re-covered at Agate Basin (Figure 4.33a,b), an apparent difference in the processing at the two sites.

Three types of butchering units—carpal units (Figure 4.33c), tarsal units (Figure 4.34a, b), and vertebral units—are represented among the Agate Basin bones. These same units were among the most common units at Eden–Farson. The tarsal and carpal units were also the more common units found at the Big Goose Creek site (Frison, Wilson, and Walker 1978), where mountain sheep and white-tailed deer were processed in an apparently similar manner. These two units are to be expected in nearly all types of processing sites, because they provide little flesh and the marrow yield is low. Following separation of these

FIGURE 4.34 (a–g) Butchered pronghorn bone from the Folsom level in Area 2. (h) *Camelops* first phalange from below the Folsom level in Area 3.

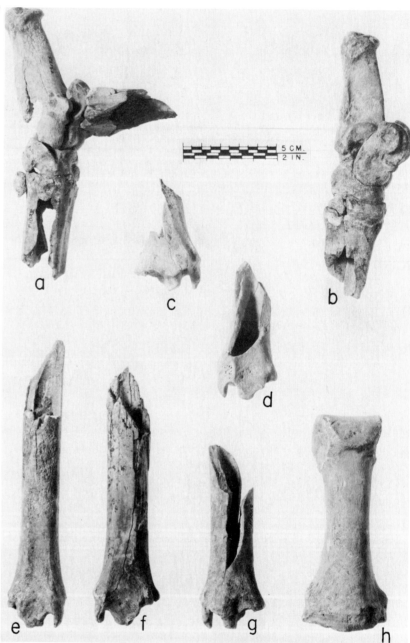

units from the metapodials and the lower limbs, they provide convenient hand-holds for stripping the muscle from the rest of the leg. Skinning marks present on the Eden–Farson (Frison 1971:265) units were not visible on the Agate Basin specimens, again probably because of the eroded surface of the bone. The Agate Basin and Hell Gap faunule pronghorn were apparently butchered in the same manner, although interpreted from a much smaller sample.

There are presently three pronghorn processing sites with a known sample size sufficient to propose valid hypotheses for processing techniques and se-quences. The Eden–Farson site (Frison 1971) has already been mentioned. The second is a site on the upper Missouri River in Montana known as the Lost

Terrace site (Davis 1976; Davis and Fisher n.d.); a minimum of 25 animals were processed there during an Avonlea occupation. White (1952) discussed butchering evidence on the remains of 31 pronghorn from 39FA83 in Angostura Reservoir, South Dakota, and proposed a sequence for the butchering of the animals at that site. Other reports on pronghorn processing (Brumley 1975; Cleveland 1976; Deaver and Greene 1978; Eakin 1979; Lyman 1978) suffer from the small sample sizes involved. Valid processing sequences cannot be determined from the remains of two or three animals. Therefore, no sequence of steps can be proposed for the processing of the Agate Basin pronghorn.

Pronghorn procurement at Agate Basin had to have been different from that proposed for bison. Although communal procurement of pronghorn has been recorded both archaeologically and ethnographically (Davis and Fisher n.d.; Egan 1917:238–241; Frison 1971; Regan 1934:54; Steward 1938:33), trapping procedures were vastly different from those used for bison (Frison 1978b: 251–257), since the behavior of pronghorn is not conducive to arroyo trapping. The Agate Basin pronghorn specimens were probably killed during an individualized hunt, the exact technique of which is unknown. Ray (1932:82) states that among the Sanpoil of eastern Washington, pronghorn were more successfully hunted by individuals; no more than two men hunted together, and the usual technique was "still-hunting" near a watering place. Steward (1938) documents driving animals past hidden archers, attracting animals to a hidden hunter by taking advantage of their curiosity ("flagging"), and the use of disguises consisting of a pronghorn head and skin. Any of these methods may have been used by the Agate Basin hunters.

Butchering and/or processing marks were seen on bones from four other species found at the site—wolf, domesticated dog, fox, and jack rabbit. Similar marks may have been present on bones of other species, but the deterioration of bone surfaces would have destroyed the evidence.

Two depressed fractures (one medial and one lateral) were present on the wolf humerus shaft (U.W.A. F1169; U.W.A. indicates the specimen is in the University of Wyoming Anthropology collection); cut marks were present on the distal end. The tibia (U.W.A. F1865) appears to have had both ends broken off, but the bone surface is too highly eroded to state this positively. The left humerus (U.W.A. F1418) has had both articular ends chewed off by other carnivores.

The ulna from domesticated dog (U.W.A. F1719) exhibits an extensive series of cut marks (Figure 2.109m) along the top of the olecranon process. These marks probably resulted from cutting the olecrani ligament during disjointing of the forearm. The surface of the radius recovered from the Clovis occupation at Sheaman (U.W.A. E1075) was too highly eroded for the preservation of any cut marks.

The fox femur shaft (U.W.A. F2137) exhibits a series of cut marks on the proximal end, apparently from either defleshing the femur or attempting to disjoint the femur from the acetabulum. The distal tibia (U.W.A. F1037) appears to be a remnant of the grooving and snapping bone bead technique (Figure 2.109e). This technique of bone bead manufacture is common in Plains archaeology and consists of carving a groove around the bone and then breaking the bone (Frison, Wilson and Walker 1978).

A jack rabbit tarsal and distal tibia unit (U.W.A. F1042) appears to be a remnant of removing the foot from the hind leg. Similar breakage was seen on the tibiae found in Rabbit Bone Cave near Cody, Wyoming (Stuckenrath and Mielke 1972). Breaking the tibia at this point is the easiest way to remove the foot.

6. EARLY HOLOCENE VERTEBRATE FAUNA

danny n. walker

Hoffmann and Jones (1970) presented a comprehensive review of the then known information on the late-glacial (13,000–10,500 B.P.) distributions of mammals on the Northern Plains. They stated that the region "has not yet yielded faunas from this period, and interpretations of faunal and climatic shifts must be based on indirect biogeographic evidence [p. 363]." The little biogeographic information present at that time indicated that either a boreal woodland or a cold loess steppe and tundra environment, shifting in location in response to local climatic conditions, was likely in the region. The steppe or savanna areas were probably restricted to a limited area just east of the Rocky Mountains and the Wyoming Basin, according to Hoffmann and Jones' prediction.

The late Pleistocene (full-glacial) fauna from the Wyoming area has become much better known since 1970 (Figure 4.35) and appears to support Hoffmann and Jones' hypothesis of either steppe or savanna conditions during the late-glacial period. Studies by the University of Wyoming (Frison and Walker 1978; Madden 1978; Shaw and Frison 1979; Walker 1974, 1977, 1982; Walker and Frison 1980; Zeimens and Walker 1974) and the Universities of Kansas and Missouri (Adams 1979; Chomko 1978, 1979; L. D. Martin *et al.* 1977, 1979; L. D. Martin and B. M. Gilbert 1978) have added to the late Pleistocene fauna as it was summarized by Anderson (1974). Table 4.10 lists the presently known extinct or no longer locally extant members of this late-glacial fauna. Some of the latter are still found in Wyoming but not in the vicinity of the sites where they were found. At least 50 additional mammalian species recorded from these sites are extant in the site vicinities (Anderson 1974:Table 1).

Because of the increased knowledge of the fossil fauna, it is now possible to begin evaluating the regional environment of the Northwestern Plains during the late-glacial (13,000–10,500 B.P.) and Pre-Boreal (10,500–9140 B.P.) periods. Frison and Walker (1978) have proposed the presence of an arctic steppe–savanna (Matthews 1976) for north-central Wyoming during this period. Gilbert *et al.* (1978) and Chomko (1978, 1979) analyzed faunas from the northern Bighorn Mountains of Wyoming and compared them with Guthrie's (1968a, 1968b) work in the Alaskan refugium. As a result, they proposed a similar steppe–tundra environment for the area. The same faunas were present in both

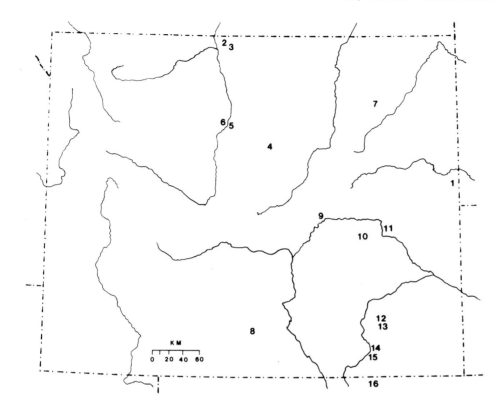

FIGURE 4.35 **Major late Pleistocene sites in Wyoming and adjacent states that contain extinct taxa or taxa no longer extant in the vicinity of the sites. Locations of other sites may be found in Anderson (1974). 1: Agate Basin. 2: Natural Trap Cave. 3: Prospects Shelter. 4: Little Canyon Creek Cave and Bush Shelter. 5: Colby Mammoth Kill. 6: Worland gravel pit. 7: Carter/Kerr-McGee. 8: Union Pacific Mammoth. 9: Casper. 10: Little Box Elder Cave. 11: Douglas *Ovibos* locality. 12: Bell Cave. 13: Horned Owl Cave. 14: C & M gravel pit. 15: Monolith gravel pit. 16: Chimney Rock Animal Trap.**

areas (Alaska and Wyoming) at that time and essentially the same floral components have been proposed for both reconstructions (Guthrie 1968a, 1968b; Matthews 1976; Marlow, this volume, Chapter 5, Section 3). Both the Alaskan and Wyoming late Pleistocene reconstructions agree with Hoffmann and Jones' (1970) idea that steppe or savanna biotas were in the Wyoming Basin during the late-glacial period.

Gilbert *et al.* (1978) further proposed a change from this steppe–tundra to a more grassland-like condition between 14,000 and 11,000 B.P. from the evidence at Natural Trap Cave. These faunal and vegetational changes in extreme north-central Wyoming occurred at a time when evidence elsewhere indicates a global change in climate and environment (Bryson 1974). Data from seafloor cores collected worldwide (CLIMAP 1976:1134) show a stable period reflected by the seafloor fauna from 24,000 to 14,000 B.P. After 14,000 B.P. conditions began approaching those of today. Natural Trap Cave, the Colby Mammoth Kill (Frison 1976; Walker and Frison 1980), and Chimney Rock Animal Trap (Hager 1972) are Wyoming sites that are dated from this period. Shifts in the faunal compositions as indicated at Natural Trap Cave in particular demonstrate evidence for the change to grassland conditions. Other late Pleistocene sites in the area (e.g., Bell Cave, Chimney Rock Animal Trap, Little Box Elder Cave, Little Canyon Creek Cave) do not have the necessary stratigraphic or radiometric controls to detect these changes. It is known that the Holocene record (post-10,000 B.P.) can be separated from the Pleistocene record at these sites and others by an essentially extant, modern fauna. However, some Holocene range changes may have occurred.

TABLE 4.1

Presently Extinct or No Longer Extant Late Pleistocene Mammals from Wyoming Archaeological and Paleontological Sites

	Little Box Elder Cave	Bell Cave	Horned Owl Cave	Chimney Rock Animal Trap	Little Canyon Creek Cave	Bush Shelter	Natural Trap Cave	Prospects Shelter	Laramie and Platte River gravel terraces	Colby site	Agate Basin si
Order Insectivora											
Microsorex hoyi	X										
Order Rodentia											
Ochotona princeps	X	X	X	X	X	X	X	X			
Dicrostonyx torquatus	X	X			X	X	X	X			
Microtus pennsylvanicus	X	X			X	X		X			
Microtus xanthognathus								X			
Phenacomys intermedius	X	X	X		X	X		X			X
Clethrionomys gapperi					X	X					X
Lagurus curtatus	X	X	X		X	X	X	X			X
Order Carnivora											
Canis lupus	X	X		X			X	X			X
Canis dirus[b]							X				
Ursus arctos	X			X							
Arctodus simus[b]	X						X	X			
Gulo gulo	X	X		X			X				
Mustela nigripes	X			X	X						
Martes nobilis[b]	X	X		X	X		X				
Panthera leo atrox[b]	X			X			X		X		
Miracinonyx trumani[b]					X		X				
Order Perissodactyla											
Equus conversidens[b]	X	X					X		X	X	
Equus sp.[b]	X	X	X				X	X			
Order Proboscidea											
Mammuthus sp.[b]							X		X	X	X
Order Artiodactyla											
Antilocapra americana	X	X	X	X			X	X	X	X	X
Platygonus compressus[b]											X
Navahoeoceros[b]	X										
Camelops cf. *hesternus*[b]	X	X	X				X	X	X	X	X
Hemiauchenia sp.[b]	X										
Bison bison ssp.[b]	X	X		X		X	X	X	X	X	X
Symbos sp.[b]	X				X		X	X			
Ovibos moschatus									X		
Ovibovini indet.[b]	X	X			X						
Oreamnos americanus	X	X	X		X						
Ovis canadensis catclawensis[b]	X	X			X	X	X	X			

[a]Species still found within the state are no longer in the site vicinity.
[b]Extinct taxon.

Graham (1979) has synthesized paleoenvironmental data and his study indicates that the steppe–savanna predicted for Wyoming was also widespread over much of the Southern and Central Plains. The deciduous and coniferous woodlands most studies had previously suggested (Wells 1970; H. E. Wright 1970) were not apparent in the vertebrate record. Graham believes that extensive riparian zones were present along most streams and rivers as a result of increased moisture, but upland areas were generally restricted to a grassland environment. The Wyoming studies discussed in this section support Graham.

Only the Casper site in Wyoming contains an extinct species other than *Bison* dated later than Clovis (post-11,200 B.P.), prior to the present study. The Casper site, a Hell Gap cultural complex *Bison* kill site, contains a single, immature individual of *Camelops* (Frison, Walker, Webb, and Zeimens 1978). Unfortunately, most of the post-11,000 B.P. sites are megafaunal kill sites and attempts to recover a microfauna from which climatic interpretations can be made have been unsuccessful. The Agate Basin site is an exception to this rule.

Excavations at the Agate Basin site during 1978 and 1979 revealed a Folsom component with 23 species of vertebrates and a minimum of 15 species of invertebrates (Evanoff, this volume, Chapter 5, Part 6). Previous excavations in the Agate Basin component had resulted only in a collection of *Bison*. Several of the species from the Folsom component (mainly microvertebrates) occur in restricted ecological niches today and may be used to propose a paleoenvironmental reconstruction of the Folsom period of northeastern Wyoming, at least for the immediate vicinity of the Agate Basin site. Other Folsom sites on the Northwestern Plains—the Hanson site (Frison 1978b; Frison and Bradley 1980), the Carter/Kerr-McGee site (Frison 1977), and the Lindenmeier site (Roberts 1935; Wilmsen and Roberts 1978)—have not provided suitable fauna for paleoenvironmental reconstruction. Bone preservation at the Hanson site was poor and only an occasional non-*Bison* bone was recovered. The Carter/Kerr-McGee site is a multicomponent *Bison* kill site but only *Bison* bones were recovered from the Folsom level. Twelve species of mammals were recovered at Lindenmeier (Wilmsen and Roberts 1978:Table 5), all of which range over a wide variety of ecological zones. In contrast, the faunule recovered from the Folsom level at the Agate Basin site contains five species of micromammals that today occupy restricted ecological zones and should provide valuable information as to the distribution of late-glacial mammals on the Northwestern Plains. The regional environment during that time also can be defined more precisely.

THE MODERN ENVIRONMENT

Detailed climatological data are not available for the immediate Agate Basin site area, but records are available for six locations within 75 km (Becker *et al.* 1977; Becker and Alyea 1964a, 1964b). Temperature, precipitation, and average frostfree days for these six locations are presented in Table 4.11. These values are for the 30-year period 1931–1960 and most likely reflect little of the conditions present during the late-glacial and Pre-Boreal periods. Dillon (1956) produced hypothetical precipitation patterns for North America during the Wisconsin glaciation and proposed that northeastern Wyoming had less than 25 cm of rain per year and a mean July temperature of approximately 6.6°C less than at present. With a maximum July temperature of 7.2°C needed for the maintenance of an ice cap (Dillon 1956), the area around the Agate Basin site would have had close to glacial conditions. Although the fauna from Agate Basin supports Dillon's conclusion in part, climatic reconstructions based on the small mammals indicated that the regional climate was not quite as severe as predicted by Dillon's model.

Prior to the present investigation, no detailed studies of the extant mammalian fauna of northeastern Niobrara County had been conducted. Numerous museum collecting parties have visited the Black Hills (Turner 1974:8–10), but their emphasis was on the Black Hills proper, not the surrounding prairie or shortgrass region. The region to the southwest of the Black Hills, under consideration here, was especially neglected. Turner (1974:Table 29) considered the Black Hills mammalian fauna to consist of 70 species, 11 of which have not yet been verified as occurring in the Black Hills. Turner's report emphasized faunal origins and the faunal list was restricted to the area delimited by the distribution

TABLE 4.11
Climatic Data for the Agate Basin Site Area

	Locality							Predicted Late-glacial[a]
	Dull Center	Kirkley	Lusk	Morrisey	Newcastle	Spencer	Average	
January temperature[b] (°F)								
Minimum	8	12	13	11	13	5	10	−10
Mean	24	24	25	26	24	18	24	4
Maximum	36	34	36	36	35	32	35	15
July temperature[b] (°F)								
Minimum	55	55	52	58	58	58	56	36
Mean	73	76	71	74	74	74	73	53
Maximum	89	86	86	91	89	89	88	68
Monthly precipitation[c] (inches)								
Minimum	.3	.5	.5	—	.4	.4	.4	7.0–10.0
Mean	2.3	3.1	2.8	—	2.6	2.4	2.6	
Maximum	12.3	16.9	15.0	—	13.6	13.7	14.3	
Frostfree days[d] (32°F frost)	125	115	117	—	137	—	124	

[a]From Dillon 1956.
[b]From Becker and Alyea 1964a.
[c]From Becker and Alyea 1964b.
[d]From Becker et al. 1977.

of the Jurassic Sundance formation, which outcrops in a circular pattern around the Black Hills.

Discounting bats and those species of mammals restricted to boreal or deciduous forest areas (a minimum of 20 km from the Agate Basin site), 37 species of mammals can be expected near the site area (Table 4.12). Six of these were not verified in the Black Hills (Turner 1974), but their normal habitat is a plains or grassland environment rather than upland forest. In fact, two of the latter species (northern grasshopper mouse, *Onychomys leucogaster,* and black-tailed jack rabbit, *Lepus californicus*) were collected during the summer of 1979 in the Agate Basin site area. Table 4.12 lists those mammals either collected or observed within a 5-km radius of the site during 1978 and 1979. Thirteen of the expected grassland species not observed have been extirpated from the region by the activities of man (Table 4.12). Four species expected in a grassland biota were not observed or collected. Thus Turner's records and field observations in 1978 and 1979 define modern grassland–steppe forms present in the area today fairly well. The modern fauna is indicative of a sagebrush–steppe biota with only six species of boreomontane or cordilleran affinities present. All of these have been known to range into grassland areas and their presence near the Agate Basin site is no surprise.

The faunal remains from two localities in the Agate Basin site area form the basis of what is here named the Agate Basin local fauna. It is late-glacial/Pre-Boreal in age based on radiometric dates from the various levels of the site and is divided into four faunules. The majority of the material from the Clovis faunule was recovered from the Sheaman site Clovis component (48NO211). The remainder of this faunule was recovered from levels below the Folsom component at the Agate Basin site (48NO201) dated at 11,450 ± 110 years B.P. (SI-3734).

TABLE 4.12
Modern, Extant Mammalian Fauna at the Agate Basin Site

Known regional fauna[a]	Grassland species expected at Agate Basin	Observed and/or collected 1978–1980	Extirpated
Widespread species			
Castor canadensis			
Peromyscus maniculatus	X	X[b]	
Ondatra zibethicus	X	X[c]	
Erethizon dorsatum			
Canis latrans	X	X[d]	
Canis lupus	X		X
Vulpes vulpes	X	X[d]	
Ursus americanus	X		?
Ursus arctos	X		X
Procyon lotor			
Mustela frenata			
Mustela vison			
Taxidea taxus	X	X[c]	
Mephitis mephitis	X	X[d]	
Felis concolor	X		X
Felis rufus		X[d]	
Cervus elaphus	X		X[e]
Odocoileus hemionus	X	X[c]	
Odocoileus virginianus	X	X[d]	
Antilocapra americana	X	X[c]	
Bison bison bison	X		X
Steppe species			
Lepus townsendii	X	X[d]	
Spermophilus tridecemlineatus	X	X[b]	
Cynomys ludovicianus	X	X[d]	
Perognathus fasciatus	X	X[b]	
Perognathus hispidus	X		
Reithrodontomys montanus	X[f]	X[d]	
Microtus ochrogaster	X	X[b]	
Vulpes velox	X[f]		X
Mustela nigripes	X		
Spilogale putorius	X[f]		X
Great Basin species			
Eutamias minimus	X	X[c]	
Sonoran species			
Sylvilagus audobonii	X	X[c]	
Lepus californicus	X[f]	X[c]	
Spermophilus spilosoma	X[f]		
Dipodomys ordii	X	X[b]	
Reithrodontomys megalotis	X	X[d]	
Onychomys leucogaster	X[f]	X[b]	
Deciduous forest species			
Sylvilagus floridanus			
Sciurus niger			
Peromyscus leucopus			
Urocyon cinereoargenteus			?
Boreomontane species			
Sorex cinereus	X	X[d]	
Tamiasciurus hudsonicus			
Glaucomys sabrinus			
Clethrionomys gapperi			
Microtus pennsylvanicus		X[d]	

(continued)

TABLE 4.12 (Continued)

Known regional fauna[a]	Grassland species expected at Agate Basin	Observed and/or collected 1978–1980	Extirpated
Zapus hudsonius			
Martes americana			X
Mustela erminea			
Gulo gulo			X
Felis lynx			X
Cordilleran species			
Sorex nanus		X[d]	
Sylvilagus nuttallii			
Marmota flaviventris			
Thomomys talpoides	X	X[d]	
Neotoma cinerea	X	X[d]	
Microtus longicaudus		X[d]	
Ovis canadensis	X		X

[a]Turner 1974.
[b]Trapped within 2 km of Agate Basin.
[c]Observed within 5 km of Agate Basin.
[d]Owl pellet remains or "pickups" within 5 km of Agate Basin.
[e]Reintroduced.
[f]Presence not verified in the Black Hills proper by Turner (1974) but should be expected in the surrounding grasslands.

The Folsom faunule is the largest from the site and has been dated at 10,789 ± 120 years B.P. (SI-3733) and 10,665 ± 85 years B.P. (SI-3732). The Agate Basin faunule is dated at 10,430 ± 570 years B.P. (RL-557) and the Hell Gap faunule is dated at 10,445 ± 110 years B.P. (SI-4430). The last three faunules were recovered from levels containing their respective cultural components.

Previous investigations at the Agate Basin site resulted in the identification of only two species of mammals other than *Bison*. Agogino and Frankforter (1960:105–106) reported *Bison* from the Agate Basin faunule and "bones of one elk and several bison" from the Folsom faunule. Roberts (1961a:126) reported *Bison* and bones "from one of the Cervidae" from the Agate Basin level. Bass (1970:21) reported that the majority of the bones recovered from his excavations were *Bison* but "a few undoubtedly represent one of the Cervidae." He also recorded "a few jackrabbit bones" from the Agate Basin occupation. None of the non-*Bison* faunal material mentioned could be located for this study and is not included in the following discussion.

A total of 28 taxa of vertebrates are presently known from all faunules of the Agate Basin local fauna. These include 1 amphibian, 1 reptile, 3 birds, and 23 mammals (Table 4.13). Four taxa (*Mammuthus* sp., *Camelops* sp., *Platygonus compressus*, and *Bison b. antiquus*) are extinct; 5 taxa (*Clethrionomys gapperi*, *Phenacomys intermedius*, *Microtus pennsylvanicus*, *M. longicaudus*, and *Lagurus curtatus*) have not been reported for the modern fauna from the immedaite vicinity; and 2 taxa (*Canis lupus* and *Cervus elaphus*) have been extirpated by the activities of Euro-American settlers (Long 1965; Turner 1974). At least 15 taxa of invertebrates (all Gastropoda) have also been recovered from the Folsom faunule. A discussion of these taxa is presented in Chapter 5.

Table 4.13
Vertebrate Members of the Agate Basin Local Fauna, MNI, by Faunule

	Clovis	Folsom	Agate Basin	Hell Gap
Cf. *Rana pipiens*		3		1
Snake		1		1
Centrocerus urophasianus		1		
Turdus migratorius				1
Cf. *Hylocichla*				1
Sorex cinereus				2
Sylvilagus cf. *nuttallii* or *audobonii*	1	1		1
Lepus cf. *townsendii* or *californicus*		2		
Spermophilus tridecemlineatus		3		
Thomomys talpoides		5	1	1
Perognathus cf. *fasciatus*				1
Peromyscus maniculatus		2		>7
Clethrionomys gapperi		2		
Phenacomys intermedius	1	3		1
Microtus pennsylvanicus	2	8		9
Microtus longicaudus	2	17	1	18
Lagurus curtatus		2	1	1
Canis latrans		1		
Canis lupus		2	1	
Canis sp.	1	1		
Vulpes vulpes		1		
Mephitis mephitis		1		
Mammuthus sp.	1			
Platygonus compressus		1		
Antilocapra americana	1	4	2	1
Camelops sp.	1[a]	1		
Cervus elaphus		1		
Bison bison antiquus	1	9	75[b]	8

[a]Found below Folsom level in Area 3 in noncultural context.
[b]Count is University of Wyoming collection only.

The fauna was recovered by two processes. The first, which resulted in the collection of the larger forms, involved normal archaeological excavation techniques. The second involved the water-screening of materials from the cultural levels by a technique adapted from Hibbard (1949) utilizing fine screens and water under low pressure. The two methods complemented each other and resulted in a high level of recovery of both faunal and cultural material.

It is readily apparent (Table 4.13) that each of the four cultural components is not equally represented in the fauna. Several factors may have been responsible. First, only a small section (about 45 m²) of the Sheaman site Clovis level remained; the rest was lost to erosion, gully formation, and previous excavation. Over 70% of the Clovis component at the site was water-screened but little microfaunal material was present. The entire volume of the Folsom component at the Agate Basin site was water-screened and the largest microfaunal sample was recovered. The Agate Basin component was water-screened, but very little faunal material other than *Bison* was present. This may reflect the fact that the Folsom level was a camp and activity area whereas the Agate Basin component appeared to be more a kill and processing area. The Hell Gap occupation area was very small (about 40 m²). Eighty percent of this area was covered by a *Bison* bone bed, and only a sample was water-screened. The remaining part of the excavated area appeared to be a camp activity area associated with at least two hearths. These deposits were water-screened and all of the Hell Gap microfauna came from this area. The small area and the high density of microfauna recovered indicate the possibility of cultural utilization of these smaller forms. The absence of microfauna in the Clovis and Agate Basin faunules is not due to collecting techniques; rather, the fauna was either not present or not preserved.

The minimum number of individuals (Table 4.13) was determined by counting the most common element of each species from the individual faunules. In addition, if immature animals or very old animals were represented by another element, these were added to the minimum number of individuals.

SYSTEMATIC DESCRIPTIONS   Abbreviations used in subsequent discussions of the faunal members are as follows: M, molar; P, premolar; C, canine; and I, incisor. The abbreviation *cf.* is used in the sense of "showing affinities toward."

CLASS AMPHIBIA
Order Anura
FAMILY RANIDAE
Genus cf. *Rana*—Frog

Geologic Range of Genus: Miocene to Recent in North America (Romer 1966:364).

Geographic Distribution: The ranid frogs are widespread in North America east of the western edge of the Great Basin (Stebbins 1966:70–77).

Habitat: Most species frequent springs, creeks, rivers, ponds, canals, and reservoirs where there is permanent water and aquatic vegetation (Bernard and Brown 1978:88–91; Stebbins 1966:75–76).

Material: Four humeri (U.W.A. F1057, F1080, F1162), one pubis (U.W.A. F1065), and numerous vertebrae (U.W.A. F1058, F1079, F1087, F1141, F1161) were recovered from the Folsom faunule. Two humeri (U.W.A. F1216, F1455) and two vertebrae (U.W.A. F1468) were found in the Hell Gap faunule.

Discussion: This material is provisionally referred to this genus on the basis of size and general similarity to recent specimens of *Rana pipiens* in the U.W.A. comparative collection.

CLASS REPTILIA
Order Squamata
FAMILY UNIDENTIFIED—SNAKE

Material: Three vertebrae (U.W.A. F1114) were found in the Folsom faunule and four vertebrae (U.W.A. F1218, F1467) were found in the Hell Gap faunule.

Discussion: The fragmentary nature of the specimens made definite assignment to a family impossible. They are closer in appearance to the Colubridae than the Viperidae, two of the families occurring in the site area today.

CLASS AVES
Order Galliformes
FAMILY TETRAONIDAE
Genus *Centrocerus*

Centrocerus urophasianus—Sage Grouse

Geologic Range of Species: Pleistocene to Recent in North America (Brodkorb 1964: 334).

Geographic Distribution: The sage grouse is found throughout the western United States (Robbins *et al.* 1966:84).

Habitat: This grouse is normally found in sagebrush areas. It summers in the foothills and winters on the plains, although it is present year-round in the Powder River Basin. Its principal food is sagebrush (Robbins *et al.* 1966:84).

Material: One proximal ulna (U.W.A. F1007) and one proximal coracoid (U.W.A. F1194) were recovered from the Folsom faunule.

Discussion: The sage grouse is quite common in the area today. Marked sexual dimorphism is present in the species (Hargrave 1972) and the Folsom specimens were the size of female grouse in the U.W.A. comparative collections. The ulna was found near one of the postulated Folsom lodge structures and its presence may be due to cultural activity.

Order Passeriformes

FAMILY TURDIDAE

Genus *Turdus*

Turdus migratorius—Robin

Geologic Range of Genus: Pleistocene to Recent in North America (Romer 1966:378).

Geographic Distribution: The robin is widespread in North America south of the polar regions (Robbins *et al.* 1966:230).

Habitat: This bird is most commonly seen near human habitations today (Robbins *et al.* 1966:230), but may be found in a wide variety of local habitats where trees and/or shrubs provide suitable cover.

Material: One humerus (U.W.A. F1260) lacking the extreme proximal end was recovered from the Hell Gap faunule.

Discussion: This specimen was one of five bird bones recovered from the small water-screened area of Hell Gap occupation, and the specimens may be related to cultural activity. All appear slightly burned and came from the same restricted location within the site.

FAMILY TURDIDAE

Genus cf. *Hylocichla*—Thrush

Geologic Range of Genus: Pleistocene to Recent in North America (Romer 1966:378).

Geographic Distribution: Several species of this genus occur throughout North America (Robbins *et al.* 1966:232), although none winter in the northern portion of the United States.

Habitat: Most members of this genus occur in woodland habitats (Robbins *et al.* 1966:232).

Material: One proximal ulna (U.W.A. F1222), one distal ulna (U.W.A. F1224) (from opposite sides), and one proximal humerus (U.W.A. F1225) were found in the Hell Gap faunule.

Discussion: All three specimens were recovered from the Hell Gap occupation and appear slightly burned. Their presence may be due to cultural activities.

Order unidentified

Material: Two cervical vertebrae (U.W.A. F1085, F1223), one first phalange (U.W.A. F1041), and two fragmentary humeri (U.W.A. F1476, F1477).

Discussion: One vertebra and the phalange are from the Folsom faunule. They are within the size range of the grouse identified from that faunule and may eventually be referable to the sage grouse. The second vertebra was from the Hell Gap faunule and is the size of the small Turdidae forms recorded for that faunule; it may be referable to one of those species. The two humeri are from the Hell Gap faunule and were broken; morphological characteristics needed for identification were missing. They are the size of the other Turdidae species from the faunule.

CLASS MAMMALIA
Order Insectivora
FAMILY SORICIDAE
Genus *Sorex*

Sorex cinereus—Masked Shrew

Geologic Range of Species: Middle Pleistocene (Kansan) to Recent in North America (Hibbard 1958:12).

Geographic Distribution: The masked shrew is widely distributed in the United States and most of Canada (Hall and Kelson 1959:26). Two subspecies occur in suitable habitat over the entire state of Wyoming (Long 1965:518).

Habitat: This shrew prefers moist, open areas near water but often is found on dry forest floors in the eastern United States (Hall and Kelson 1959:25). In Wyoming, the species is most numerous in montane habitats (Long 1965:517). Banfield (1974:9) reports humidity may be a restricting factor in their distribution. Ground cover consisting of leaves, stumps, decayed logs, and herbaceous vegetation also appears to be a factor in its distribution.

Material: Two left mandibles (U.W.A. F1252, F1253) were recovered from the Hell Gap faunule.

Discussion: As with most of the Hell Gap faunule small vertebrates, these mandibles appear burned and are possibly related to cultural activity.

Order Lagomorpha
FAMILY LEPORIDAE
Genus *Sylvilagus*

Sylvilagus cf. *nuttallii* or *audobonii*—Cottontail Rabbit

Geologic Range of Genus: Lower Pliocene to Recent in North America (Romer 1966:396).

Geographic Distribution: Both possible species of cottontail are widely distributed in western North America (Hall and Kelson 1959:261, 267). These two species and *S. floridanus* (eastern cottontail) occur in Wyoming (Long 1965:542, 545).

Habitat: *S. nuttallii* and *S. audobonii* occur throughout the Upper Sonoran and Transition life zones in Wyoming (Nelson 1909:199), with *S. nuttallii* occurring in wooded or brushy areas and *S. audobonii* frequenting the plains or relatively open country (Hall and Kelson 1959:264).

Material: A single scapula (U.W.A. E1086) was recovered from the Clovis faunule at the Sheaman site. A left maxilla with P^4 (U.W.A. F1091), two partial tibiae (U.W.A. F1687, F2120), one distal humerus (U.W.A. F1717), and two burned and broken thoracic vertebrae (U.W.A. F1178) were found in the Folsom faunule. One lower premolar (U.W.A. F1219) and a calcaneus (U.W.A. F1217) were found in the Hell Gap faunule.

Discussion: Most modern identifications of cottontails are made on indistinct pelage characters or local site habitat, both of which are normally impossible to determine in an archaeological context. Complete skulls are also used for osteological identifications, but even these are not always sufficient (Hall 1951:122). Postcranial elements are almost impossible to separate. If during the early Holocene at the Agate Basin site (as proposed later), the local area contained an understory of low shrubs, the cottontail remains may be *S. nuttallii*. This also assumes that the ecological preferences of the two species have not changed in the past 10,000 years.

One of the distal tibiae from the Folsom faunule appears to be either a bone bead or bone tube manufactured by use of the groove and snapping technique. This technique is fairly common in post-Paleoindian periods (Frison, Wilson, and Walker 1978). This tibia from the Folsom faunule indicates that the technique was present over 10,800 years in North America.

Genus *Lepus*

Lepus cf. *californicus* or *townsendii*—Jack rabbit

Geologic Distribution: Late Pleistocene (Wisconsin) to Recent in North America (Hibbard 1958:21).

Geographic Distribution: The jack rabbit is widespread over the western plains and mountain area of North America (Hall and Kelson 1959:271–288). The white-tailed jack rabbit (*L. townsendii*) has a statewide distribution in Wyoming (Long 1965:549). The black-tailed jack rabbit (*L. californicus*) occurs only in the southeastern plains area of the state, although it is presently expanding its range north and west (Long 1965:547, 552).

Habitat: Both the black-tailed and white-tailed jack rabbit normally inhabit the open prairie regions of the state, although the white-tailed may be found in the Transition life zone (Nelson 1909:78) or woodland areas bordering meadows and pastures as well as alpine tundra (Bernard and Brown 1978:18).

Material: One pelvis (U.W.A. F1008), one calcaneus (U.W.A. F1031), one distal metapodial (U.W.A. F1040), one tarsal unit consisting of distal tibia, calcaneus, and astragalus (U.W.A. F1042), one radius (U.W.A. F1043), one proximal ulna (U.W.A. F1046), and two ulnar carpals (U.W.A. F1048, F1052) were recovered from the Folsom faunule.

Discussion: The postcranial elements of these two species of jack rabbit do not exhibit distinct morphology. These Folsom faunule specimens are larger than any in a series of six recent jack rabbit specimens in the U.W.A. comparative collections, but the size variation in the two forms is unknown. The Agate Basin specimens are much too large to be confused with the snowshoe hare (*L. americanus*), which is unknown in the region today (Turner 1974: 150–151).

Based on the presence of two left ulnar carpals, there are at least two jack rabbits from the Folsom faunule. The tarsal unit apparently represents a lower foot that was removed from the leg. The isolated calcaneus was burned and recovered along the edge of the postulated northeast lodge structure. It is probable that all specimens relate to cultural activity.

Order Rodentia

FAMILY SCIURIDAE

Genus *Spermophilus*

Spermophilus tridecemlineatus—Thirteen-lined Ground Squirrel

Geologic Range of Species: Middle Pleistocene (Illinoian, possibly Kansan) to Recent in North America (Hibbard 1970:419–430).

Geographic Distribution: This small ground squirrel is found throughout the plains and prairie regions of North America (Hall and Kelson 1959:346). Four subspecies occur in Wyoming and cover all but the western one-fifth of the state (Long 1965:578). *S. tridecemlineatus* is the only ground squirrel found near the Agate Basin site today, although *S. spilosoma* (the spotted ground squirrel) is of unverified occurrence in the region (Turner 1974:151).

Habitat: The thirteen-lined ground squirrel is a classic grassland species, normally found in tall grass or brushy contacts between tall grass and herbaceous vegetation in Montana (Hoffmann and Pattie 1968:39) but also in shortgrass prairie in Iowa (Bowles 1975). The species was found throughout the shortgrass and sagebrush areas near the Agate Basin site in 1979. Its presence in the more open areas at Agate Basin is probably due to a lack of competition with other species of ground squirrels.

Material: One left mandible with P_4, M_1, and M_2 (U.W.A. F1089), one left mandible with unerupted P_4 and alveolus for M_1–M_3 (U.W.A. F1090), one left mandible fragment with P_4–M_1 (U.W.A. F1164), and one right mandible with P_4–M_3 (U.W.A. 1689) were recovered from the Folsom faunule.

Discussion: The thirteen-lined ground squirrel is a burrowing animal and is commonly intrusive into archaeological site levels (W. R. Wood and D. L. Johnson 1978). The four mandibles listed all exhibited the same color and general appearance as the nonintrusive specimens of other species. Other specimens of this ground squirrel were collected but are not listed. They are regarded as intrusive because of an appearance or color change in the bone. No definite cultural modifications could be seen on the specimens, although all were recovered from near a postulated lodge.

FAMILY GEOMYIDAE

Genus *Thomomys*

Thomomys talpoides—Northern Pocket Gopher

Geologic Range of Species: Late Pleistocene (Wisconsin) to Recent in North America (Hibbard 1958:14).

Geographic Distribution: This species of pocket gopher is common in the western United States (Hall and Kelson 1959:438–439) and its range includes all of Wyoming (Long 1965:600–612).

Habitat: *Thomomys talpoides* is found in a wide variety of habitats, including desert valleys, rugged desert ranges of mountains, semiarid plains, mountain forest meadows, and above timberline (V. Bailey 1915:23–25).

Material: One left mandible (U.W.A. F1045), one maxilla with left P^4–M^1 and right P^4–M^1 (U.W.A. F1051), one left mandible with I–M_1 (U.W.A. F1064), one left P_4 (U.W.A. F1071), one left mandible with P_4 (U.W.A. F1072), one right mandible with P_4 (U.W.A. F1073), one left mandible with P_4–M_1 (U.W.A. F1078), one left mandible with I–M_2 (U.W.A. F1086), and one cranium with complete dentition (U.W.A. F1073) were recovered from the Folsom faunule. One left mandible with P_4 (U.W.A. F1193) was recovered from the Agate Basin faunule. Two humeri (U.W.A. F1220, F1221) and one lower premolar (U.W.A. F1234) were found in the Hell Gap faunule.

Discussion: Pocket gophers are notorious for being intrusive in archaeological sites (W. R. Wood and D. L. Johnson 1978). Some additional specimens recovered from the site were not listed because they appeared to be intrusive. The color and appearance of the cataloged specimens are identical to those of clearly nonintrusive bone in the site. No cultural modifications were observed on any of the gopher material.

FAMILY HETEROMYIDAE

Genus *Perognathus*

Perognathus cf. *fasciatus*—Olive-backed Pocket Mouse

Geologic Range of Species: Late Pleistocene to Recent (A. E. Wood 1935:78).

Geographic Distribution: This pocket mouse is found over the Northern Plains area of North America (Williams and Genoways 1979) and is known from the eastern three-quarters of Wyoming (Long 1965:614).

Habitat: The grassland plains and desert areas of the western United States are the normal habitat for pocket mice. They are usually not found in mountainous areas (Osgood 1900:11). In eastern Wyoming, this species appears to prefer sites with a low, closely spaced vegetation pattern (Maxwell and Brown 1968).

Material: A single left mandible with P_4–M_2 (U.W.A. F1254) was found in the Hell Gap faunule.

Discussion: *Perognathus fasciatus* is one of three species of *Perognathus* found in eastern Wyoming (Long 1965:613–618). The specimen is easily separated from *P. hispidus* by its smaller size. *P. flavus* also occurs in eastern Wyoming but is very rare (Long 1965:613–618). *P. flavus* and *P. fasciatus* are very similar in tooth morphology, but the Hell Gap faunule specimen appeared closer to *P. fasciatus*, however.

FAMILY CRICETIDAE

Genus *Peromyscus*

Peromyscus maniculatus—Deer Mouse

Geologic Range of Species: Late Pleistocene (Wisconsin) to Recent in North America (Hibbard 1968:17–18).

Geographic Distribution: This mouse is widespread in North America (Hall and Kelson 1959:614–615). Two subspecies occur in Wyoming (Long 1965:630).

Habitat: The deer mouse occurs in widely different local habitats; swamps, watercourses, upland prairies, rocks, cliffs, and arid desert regions are all inhabited by this species (Osgood 1909:26).

Material: One left mandible with M_1 (U.W.A. F1447) was found in the Clovis faunule at the Agate Basin site. Two right mandibles with M_1–M_3 (U.W.A. F1038, F1163) and one left mandible with M_1 and M_2 (U.W.A. F1200) were found in the Folsom faunule. One right mandible with M_1 and M_2 (U.W.A. F1235), one left mandible with M_1–M_3 (U.W.A. F1236), one left mandible with M_1 and M_2 (U.W.A. F1466), ten edentulous right mandibles and two edentulous left mandibles (U.W.A. F1213, F1457, F1470) were recovered from the Hell Gap faunule.

Discussion: The deer mouse is one of the most abundant small mammals living in the area today. Over 50% of the rodents recovered during collecting activities in 1979 were *P. maniculatus*. It was found in the dry sagebrush–grass community as well as in the tall grass in the gully below the site.

Genus *Clethrionomys*
Clethrionomys gapperi—Red-backed Vole

Geologic Range of Species: Pleistocene (Nebraskan) to Recent in North America (Repenning 1980:Figure 1).

Geographic Distribution: The red-backed vole is most commonly found in the boreal forest of the Rocky Mountains and northern North America (Hall and Kelson 1959:715). In

FIGURE 4.36 **Microtine teeth from the Agate Basin site. All specimens are from the Folsom faunule except B, which is from the Hell Gap faunule. (A) U.W.A. F1157, *Microtus pennsylvanicus* left M_1 and M_2; (B) U.W.A. F1237, *M. pennsylvanicus* right M_1 and M_2; (C) U.W.A. F1155, *M. pennsylvanicus* right M_1 and M_2; (D) U.W.A. F1069, *M. pennsylvanicus* left M_1 and M_2; (E) U.W.A. F1154, *M. pennsylvanicus* right M^2; (F) U.W.A. F1139, *M. pennsylvanicus* right M^2; (G) U.W.A. F1149, *Lagurus curtatus*, left M_1 and M_2; (H) U.W.A. F1129, *L. curtatus* left M_1; (I) U.W.A. F1150, *L. curtatus* left M^3; (J) U.W.A. F1152 *L. curtatus* right M^3; (K) U.W.A. F1146, *Microtus longicaudus* right M_1 and M_2; (L) U.W.A. F1145, *M. longicaudus* right M_1 and M_2; (M) U.W.A. F1102, *Clethrionomys gapperi* left M_1–M_3; (N) U.W.A. F1103, *C. gapperi* left M_1; (O) U.W.A. F1084, *C. gapperi* right M_1; (P) U.W.A. F1125, *C. gapperi* left M^1; (Q) U.W.A. F1125, *C. gapperi* left M^2; (R) U.W.A. F1101, *C. gapperi* left M_2; (S) U.W.A. F1153, *Phenacomys intermedius* left M_1; (T) U.W.A. F1100, *P. intermedius* left M^1; (U) U.W.A. F1092, *P. intermedius* left M_1; (V) U.W.A. F1130, *P. intermedius* left M^3 (heavily worn).**

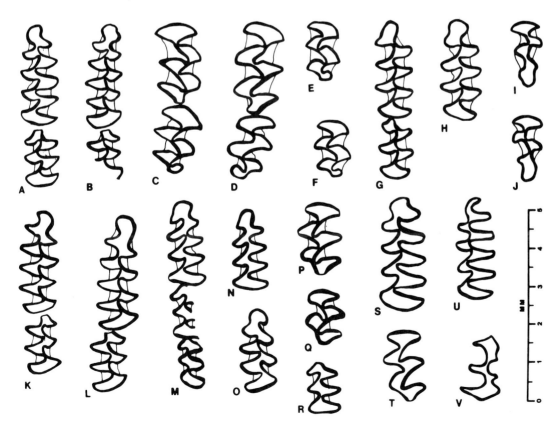

Wyoming, the species is found in all mountainous regions of the state, including the Black Hills (Long 1965:643).

Habitat: Historically, the red-backed vole has been considered a typical coniferous forest species (Hoffmann and Pattie 1968:41), but it has been reported from several other habitats, including birch and aspen woodlands and brushy riparian habitats, woodpiles, fallen logs, or low-spreading branches of creeping juniper (Bernard and Brown 1978:53; Turner 1974:105–106).

Material: One left M_2 (U.W.A. F1101; see Figure 4.36R), one left M_1 (U.W.A. F1103; Figure 4.36N), one right M_1 (U.W.A. F1084; Figure 4.36O), one left mandible with M_1–M_3 (U.W.A. F1102; Figure 4.36M), and one left maxilla with M^1 and M^2 (U.W.A. F1125; Figure 4.36P–Q) were recovered from the Folsom faunule.

Discussion: The red-backed vole does not occur in the site area today. Turner (1974:108) lists numerous records for the Black Hills, all within the boreal cap above 1400 m elevation. The local site environment is entirely different from any recorded for *Clethrionomys*.

Genus *Phenacomys*

Phenacomys intermedius—Heather Vole

Geologic Range of Species: Middle Pleistocene (Nebraskan) to Recent in North America (Guilday and Parmalee 1972:170; Repenning 1980:Figure 1).

Geographic Distribution: This species is found only in the Canadian and Hudsonian life zones of boreal North America (Hall and Kelson 1959:719). *Phenacomys* is found in the mountainous regions of the south and western portions of Wyoming (Long 1965:647) and is not recorded for the Black Hills (Turner 1974:149).

Habitat: Guilday and Parmalee (1972:170) reported that the species shows a preference for open, dry, coniferous forests. Armstrong (1972:234) reported that *P. intermedius* had been captured in a wide variety of habitats in Colorado, including lodgepole and ponderosa pine forests, stream-bank communities and among willows in rank grasses.

Material: One maxilla with right M^1 (U.W.A. F1446) was recovered from the Clovis faunule at the Agate Basin site. Three left M_1's (U.W.A. F1092, Figure 4.36U; F1099; F1153, Figure 4.36S), one right M_1 (U.W.A. F1093), two left M_3's (U.W.A. F1133), one left M^1 (U.W.A. 1100, Figure 4.36T), and one heavily worn M^3 (U.W.A. F1130, Figure 4.36V) were recovered from the Folsom faunule. One left M^2 (U.W.A. F1458) and one left M_2 (U.W.A. F1459) were recovered from the Hell Gap faunule.

Discussion: The heather vole is not recorded from the area today. The closest known locality for the species is the southern Laramie Range in Albany County, approximately 250 km to the southwest. The species has been recovered from five late Pleistocene–early Holocene sites on the west slope of the Bighorn Mountains, including the Medicine Lodge Creek site from a level dated at 9590 B.P. (Walker 1975:76–77). It is also known from three late Pleistocene–early Holocene sites in the northern Laramie Range. The species is not recorded from either area today and clearly was more widespread during the late Pleistocene–early Holocene in Wyoming.

Genus *Microtus*

Microtus pennsylvanicus—Meadow Vole

Geologic Range of Species: Middle Pleistocene (Kansan) to Recent in North America (Repenning 1980:Figure 1).

Geographic Distribution: This wide-ranging vole is found throughout the northern half of North America (Hall and Kelson (1959:725). In Wyoming, two subspecies occur—one in the northeastern corner of the state, the other in the western quarter (Long 1965:648).

Habitat: Bailey (1900:20) places the species in marshes and damp, grassy places. In the Black Hills, the meadow vole occurs from the boreal cap, down through the Transition zone and into the arid plains where there are suitable riparian habitats. The species appears to have the greatest range of environmental tolerances of any member of the genus (Turner 1974:115), but is usually considered an indicator of colder climates (Hibbard 1956).

Material: One left (U.W.A. E1081) and one right (U.W.A. E1082) M_1 were recovered in the Clovis faunule at the Sheaman site, and one right M^2 and left M^3 (U.W.A. F1443) were found in the Clovis faunule at the Agate Basin site. Three left mandibles with M_1 (U.W.A. F1067, F1111, F1156), one left mandible with M_1 and M_2 (U.W.A. F1157, Figure 4.36A), four left M_1's (U.W.A. F1063, F1068, F1075, F1083), one left maxilla with M^1 and M^2 (U.W.A. F1069, Figure 4.36D), one right M_1 (U.W.A. F1062), one right maxilla with M^1 and M^2 (U.W.A. F1155, Figure 4.36C), one left M^2 (U.W.A. F1139, Figure 4.36F), and two right M^2's (U.W.A. F1154, F1199) were recovered from the Folsom faunule. One left mandible with M_1 (U.W.A. F1239), six left M_1's (U.W.A. F1240, F1472), one right mandible with M_1 and M_2 (U.W.A. F1155, Figure 4.36B), one right mandible with M_1 (U.W.A. F1238), four left M^2's (U.W.A. F1241, Figure 4.36E; F1461), two right M^2's (U.W.A. F1242), three right M_1's (U.W.A. F1471, F1452), and one left mandible with M_1 and M_2 (U.W.A. F1451) were recovered from the Hell Gap level.

Discussion: The meadow vole was not found in the immediate area during trapping activities in 1979, although it was recovered from owl pellets 5 km south of the site. This species of vole is normally found in a much more mesic habitat than is seen at the site today. It thus appears that the area was probably fairly mesic during the early Holocene.

Genus *Microtus*

Microtus longicaudus—Long-tailed Vole

Geologic Range of Species: Late Pleistocene (Wisconsin) to Recent in North America (Hibbard 1958:17).

Geographic Distribution: This vole occurs widely in the western United States and Canada (Armstrong 1972:240). It is known in suitable montane habitat throughout Wyoming with a disjunct population in the Black Hills. Only a single subspecies is known from Wyoming (Long 1965:653–656).

Habitat: The habitat of the long-tailed vole is generally montane areas (Long 1965:654), but in the Black Hills the species has been known to inhabit riparian areas along streams that descend into the Transition zone (Turner 1974:108–109).

Material: Two right M_1's (U.W.A. E1083, E1084) and one left M_1 (U.W.A. E1085) were recovered from the Clovis faunule at the Sheaman site. Two left mandibles with M_1 and M_2 (U.W.A. F1055, F1066), two left mandibles with M_1 (U.W.A. F1144, F1147), ten left M_1's (U.W.A. F1056, F1059, F1097, F1112, F1120, F1136, F1143, F1187, F1192, F1197), three right mandibles with M_1 and M_2 (U.W.A. F1053, F1128, F1145, Figure 4.36L), four right mandibles with M_1 (U.W.A. F1054, F1095, F1146, Figure 4.36K; F1148), and ten right M_1's (U.W.A. F1060, F1061, F1082, F1096, F1122, F1126, F1132, F1142, F1198, F1203) were recovered from the Folsom faunule. One left mandible with M_1 (U.W.A. F1441) and one right mandible with M_1 (U.W.A. F1442) were recovered from the Agate Basin faunule. One left mandible with M_1 and M_2 (U.W.A. F1474), two left mandibles with M_1 (U.W.A. F1247, F1475), seven left M_1's (U.W.A. F1250, F1453), three right mandibles with M_1 and M_2 (U.W.A. F1243, F1244, F1246), three right mandibles with M_1 (U.W.A. F1245, F1248, F1454), and eleven right M_1's (U.W.A. F1249, F1473) were recovered from the Hell Gap faunule.

Discussion: *M. longicaudus* was the most common microtine recovered in each faunule at the site. The dental patterns of *M. longicaudus* and *M. montanus* (the montane vole) are identical and the two species generally are only separable by population mean size differences, *M. longicaudus* being slightly larger. *M. longicaudus* was identified in the fauna by the shape of the infraorbital foramen preserved on two of the maxillae as defined by Hall and Cockrum (1953:413–426). The infraorbital foramen on these specimens was not constricted posteriorly, thus showing the *M. longicaudus* shape. The *M. montanus* shape is abruptly constricted posteriorly and no maxilla was referable to *M. montanus*. All mandibles were referred to *M. longicaudus* by association with the maxillae and lack of any other evidence indicating the presence of *M. montanus*.

Most of the specimens from the Folsom level were recovered from water-screening concentrate near the two eastern postulated lodge structures. All appear burned to some extent, but the possibility of cultural utilization of the Folsom level rodents is unknown. The abnormally high concentration of small rodents found in the Hell Gap level has better possibilities for cultural utilization but, again, definitive proof is lacking. This species of vole is not found in the site vicinity today, although it is recorded for the Black Hills. Its presence indicates a more montane-type or mesic environment during the early Holocene.

SUBFAMILY MICROTINAE—VOLE

Material: Two right M^1's (U.W.A. E1076), one left and one right M^3 (U.W.A. E1077, E1078), one left mandible with fragmentary M_1 and M_2 (U.W.A. E1079), and one maxilla with right and left M^1 and M^2 (U.W.A. E1080) were recovered from the Clovis faunule at the Sheaman site. One fragmentary left M_1 (U.W.A. F1444) was recovered from the Clovis faunule at the Agate Basin site. Three fragmentary left M_1's (U.W.A. F1170, F1190), three fragmentary right M_1's (U.W.A. F1081, F1088, F1089), five M_3's (U.W.A. F1081, F1121, F1127, F1134, F1140), seven left M^1's (U.W.A. F1076, F1088, F1098, F1113, F1131, F1188, F1196), three right M^1's (U.W.A. F1088, F1135, F1138), four right M_2's (U.W.A. F1081, F1201), two left M_2's (U.W.A. F1081, F1118), two left M^3's (U.W.A. F1134), one maxilla with right M^1 and M^2 (U.W.A. F1167), one maxilla with left M^1 (U.W.A. F1123), one maxilla with right M^1 (U.W.A. F1158), one maxilla with right M^1, left M^1 and M^2 (U.W.A. F1159), one maxilla with right and left M^1 and M^2 (U.W.A. F1166) and twenty-four fragmentary isolated teeth (U.W.A. F1160, F1191) were recovered from the Folsom faunule. Three left M_2's (U.W.A. F1226, F1463), eight right M_2's (U.W.A. F1227, F1463), fourteen left M_1's (U.W.A. F1233, F1450, F1464, F1465), eleven right M^1's (U.W.A. F1232, F1450, F1464, F1465), seven left M^2's (U.W.A. F1232), three right M^2's (U.W.A. F1230), eight left M^3's (U.W.A. F1228, F1448, F1462), seven right M^3's (U.W.A. F1229, F1448, F1462), seven edentulous maxillae (U.W.A. F1214, F1456), three edentulous mandibles (U.W.A. F1215, F1469), and several unidentifiable fragments of teeth (U.W.A. F1251) were recovered from the Hell Gap faunule.

Discussion: Because of a lack of association of these specimens with diagnostic teeth, they are referred here to the subfamily only. Based on the absence of any other species of *Microtus* with the M^2 pattern shown by *M. longicaudus* (i.e., *M. montanus*), those specimens listed with M^2's are probably referable to either *M. longicaudus* or *Lagurus curtatus* (discussed subsequently). The M^2 of *M. pennsylvanicus* is highly diagnostic and cannot be confused with that of any other microtine. The remainder of the teeth (M^1, M^3, M_2, M_3, and fragmentary M_1) could belong to *M. longicaudus*, *M. pennsylvanicus*, or *Lagurus*.

Genus Lagurus

Lagurus curtatus—Sagebrush Vole

Geologic Range of Species: Late Pleistocene (Wisconsin) to Recent in North America (Hibbard 1970; Repenning 1980: Figure 1).

Geographic Distribution: The sagebrush vole is found only in the western United States (Hall and Kelson 1959:752). In Wyoming, the species is found in the central, western, and southern portions of the state, mainly from the Transition zone (Long 1965:661).

Habitat: The sagebrush vole is generally limited to or closely associated with various species of sagebrush (*Artemisia* spp.), or areas of sagebrush mixed with other shrubs (Armstrong 1972:245; Johnson *et al.* 1948; Hoffmann and Pattie 1968:41).

Material: One left mandible with M_1 and M_2 (U.W.A. F1149, Figure 4.36G), one right M_1 (U.W.A. F1124), one left M_1 (U.W.A. F1129, Figure 4.36H), two left M^3's (U.W.A. F1150, Figure 4.36I; F1151), and one right M^3 (U.W.A. F1152, Figure 4.36J) were recovered from the Folsom faunule. One left mandible with M_1 and M_2 (U.W.A. F1440) was recovered from the Agate Basin faunule. One left M_1 (U.W.A. F1460) was recovered from the Hell Gap faunule.

Discussion: The sagebrush vole was not a major member of the early Holocene microtine community at the site. In fact, environmental reconstructions (discussed subsequently) based on the fauna indicate that although this vole must have been present on the uplands, it was probably rare in the arroyo bottom. The species is not found in northeastern Niobrara County today.

Order Carnivora
FAMILY CANIDAE
Genus *Canis*
Canis latrans—Coyote

Geologic Range of Species: Pleistocene (Kansan, possibly earlier) to Recent in North America (Nowak 1979:73–82).

Geographic Distribution: The coyote is found throughout North America west of the Appalachian Mountains (Hall and Kelson 1959:845) but is expanding its range eastward (Bekoff 1978). Two subspecies occur in Wyoming (Long 1965:673).

Habitat: The habitat of the coyote is extremely varied, ranging from desert to above timberline (Hoffmann and Pattie 1968:55).

Material: One fragmentary cervical vertebra (U.W.A. F1725), one complete cervical vertebra (U.W.A. F1212), and one left femur (U.W.A. F1009) were recovered from the Folsom faunule.

Discussion: Only one individual is represented here. The specimens were almost identical in size to those of a recent coyote from Fall River County, South Dakota. No suggestions of cultural modifications or use were apparent on the specimens.

Genus *Canis*
Canis lupus—Gray Wolf

Geologic Range of Species: Pleistocene (Illinoian) to Recent in North American (Nowak 1979:93–102).

Geographic Distribution: The gray wolf was formerly widespread over much of North America, but is extirpated from much of its former range (Hall and Kelson 1959:849). Three subspecies formerly occurred in Wyoming, but the wolf now is apparently completely extirpated from the state (Long 1965:675–668; J. Weaver 1978).

Habitat: The wolf was formerly found in all habitats from the arctic tundra to hot deserts (Hoffmann and Pattie 1968:55).

Material: One shaft of a right humerus (U.W.A. F1169), one left tibia shaft (U.W.A. F1865), one atlas (U.W.A. F1625), one axis (U.W.A. F1626), one immature metacarpal (U.W.A. F1853), one left humerus (U.W.A. F1418), and one left scapula (U.W.A. F1427) were recovered in the Folsom faunule. One proximal scapula (U.W.A. B1154) was recovered from the Agate Basin faunule.

Discussion: This material was almost identical in size with a large gray wolf skeleton in the U.W.A. comparative collection. Based on epiphyseal union, the humeri, tibia, scapula, atlas, and axis are from a mature animal; the metacarpal is from an animal less than 1 year old, so there are a minimum of two individuals from the Folsom level. Because of the eroded bone surface on the Agate Basin faunule specimen, no cultural modifications could be seen. A discussion of butchering of the Folsom faunule species is given earlier in this chapter (Section 5).

Genus *Canis*
Canis sp.—Medium-sized Canid

Material: One radius (U.W.A. E1075, Figure 4.37b) was found in the Clovis faunule at the Sheaman site. One ulna (U.W.A. F1719, Figure 2.109m), one left maxilla (U.W.A. F2138, Figure 4.38), one right I^2 (U.W.A. F1034) and the posterior quarter of a cranium (U.W.A. F1480) were found in the Folsom faunule.

Discussion: All of this material is midway in size between wolf and coyote (Figure 4.37b). Similarly sized specimens from other sites in Wyoming have been identified as domesticated wolf-dog hybrids (Walker 1980; Walker and Frison 1979, 1982).

The maxillae is described by Walker and Frison (1982). Comparative measurements of the cranium and maxillae are presented in Table 4.14. The atlas, axis and cranium, while not found together, do form a unit and appear to be from the same individual. Based on the visual characteristics and comparisons of the postcranial material, there is a strong possibility that this canid material from the Folsom faunule represents an early population of domesticated

FIGURE 4.37 **Canid radii: (A) modern wolf (*Canis lupus*); (B)**
U.W.A. E1075 from the Clovis faunule at the Sheaman site; (C)
Roberts Buffalo Jump (Witkind 1971); (D) Wardell (Frison 1973);
(E) Big Goose Creek (Frison, Wilson, and Walker 1978); (F)
modern coyote (*Canis latrans*). Note the size similarity of the
Sheaman specimen to other prehistoric specimens.

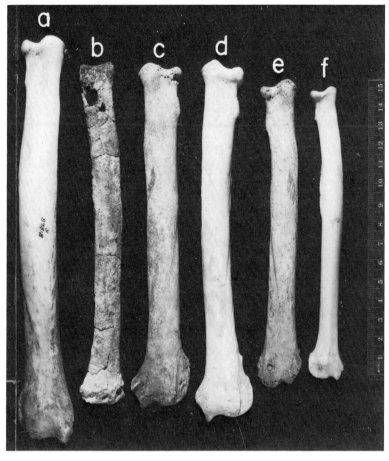

canids in North America, similar to those described by Walker and Frison (1982). This is in spite of the fact the skull measurements of wolves and the domesticated canids appear to strongly overlap, on a one-by-one basis. Walker and Frison (1982) demonstrated that discriminant function analysis of complete skulls was needed in order to separate the two groups because of their genetic closeness. Butchering marks on the postcranial bones are discussed earlier in this chapter (Section 5).

Genus *Vulpes*

Vulpes vulpes—Red Fox

Geologic Range of Species: Late Pleistocene (Wisconsin) to Recent in North America (Hibbard 1958:18).

Geographic Distribution: The red fox is found over most of North America north of Mexico (Hall and Kelson 1959:856). Two subspecies occur in Wyoming today (Long 1965:679).

FIGURE 4.38 ***Canis* sp. (U.W.A. F2138) maxilla from**
the Folsom faunule.

Table 4.14

Selected Measurements of Prehistoric Domesticated Dogs, Modern Wolves and the Folsom Faunule Canid[a]

Measurement		Domesticated Canid	Modern Wolf	Folsom Canid
Basion–Synsphenion	N	13	18	
	Min.	51.5	53.0	59.0
	Max.	64.9	64.3	
	$\bar{\chi}$	56.6	58.8	
	σ	4.0	3.0	
Diameter of Auditory Bullae	N	11	18	
	Min.	23.4	24.3	27.0
	Max.	28.7	28.7	
	$\bar{\chi}$	26.0	26.4	
	σ	1.6	1.2	
Greatest Mastoid Breadth	N	14	18	
	Min.	71.2	72.3	80.7
	Max.	86.1	83.6	
	$\bar{\chi}$	78.7	78.4	
	σ	4.4	3.8	
Breadth Auditory Meatus	N	13	18	
	Min.	70.0	72.1	79.2
	Max.	82.8	83.1	
	$\bar{\chi}$	77.2	76.8	
	σ	4.2	3.6	
Breadth Occipital Condyles	N	14	18	
	Min.	40.6	42.6	48.9
	Max.	52.0	51.9	
	$\bar{\chi}$	46.0	46.8	
	σ	3.2	2.9	
Breadth Paroccipital Processes	N	11	18	
	Min.	53.2	54.9	61.7
	Max.	66.3	67.8	
	$\bar{\chi}$	60.1	61.2	
	σ	4.0	3.6	
Breadth Foramen Magnum	N	13	18	
	Min.	20.3	19.3	21.4
	Max.	24.3	24.2	
	$\bar{\chi}$	22.6	21.5	
	σ	1.4	1.5	
Zygomatic Breadth	N	11	19	
	Min.	124.9	121.9	151.0
	Max.	148.1	149.5	
	$\bar{\chi}$	132.6	132.0	
	σ	12.3	7.8	
Height Occipital Triangle	N	12	18	
	Min.	50.1	52.0	58.7
	Max.	64.3	62.5	
	$\bar{\chi}$	58.1	58.2	
	σ	4.0	2.9	
Length P[4]	N	13	19	
	Min.	22.6	21.5	23.4
	Max.	27.0	27.5	
	$\bar{\chi}$	24.3	24.7	
	σ	1.1	1.4	

(*continued*)

TABLE 4.14 (*Continued*)
Selected Measurements of Prehistoric Domesticated Dogs, Modern Wolves and the Folsom Faunule Canid.[a]

Measurement		Domesticated Canid	Modern Wolf	Folsom Canid
Maximum Breadth P⁴	N	14	19	
	Min.	10.7	12.2	12.3
	Max.	15.1	15.6	
	$\bar{\chi}$	13.5	13.8	
	σ	1.2	1.0	
Minium Crown Breadth P⁴	N	13	19	
(between roots)	Min.	9.3	8.4	8.9
	Max.	11.4	11.8	
	$\bar{\chi}$	10.1	10.2	
	σ	0.6	0.8	
Length M²	N	12	19	
	Min.	7.5	7.5	8.1
	Max.	9.1	9.7	
	$\bar{\chi}$	8.3	8.4	
	σ	0.6	0.6	
Breadth M²	N	12	19	
	Min.	11.0	10.3	11.6
	Max.	13.8	15.5	
	$\bar{\chi}$	12.1	12.5	
	σ	0.9	1.2	

[a]Measurements in millimeters from von den Driesch (1976).

Habitat: This fox, primarily an inhabitant of wooded regions, is generally absent from open areas of the Great Plains (Armstrong 1972:260), although an active den was found in a shortgrass community near Gillette, Wyoming (Clayton Marlow, personal communication, 1980). This present distribution in the Powder River Basin is a recent phenomenon.

Material: One distal tibia (U.W.A. F1037) and one femur shaft (U.W.A. F2137) were recovered from the Folsom faunule.

Discussion: Only two specimens of the red fox were recovered from the site; however, both exhibit cultural modifications. These are discussed earlier in this chapter (Section 5).

FAMILY MUSTELIDAE

Genus *Mephitis*

Mephitis mephitis—Striped Skunk

Geologic Range of Species: Late Pleistocene (Wisconsin) to Recent in North America (Hibbard 1958:19).

Geographic Distribution: This species of skunk has been recorded over most of North America (Hall and Kelson 1959:1935). It occurs statewide in Wyoming (Long 1965:702).

Habitat: Forest edges, open woodland, brushy grassland, and riparian vegetation are the most common areas where the striped skunk can be found today (Bernard and Brown 1978:67; Hoffmann and Pattie 1968:56).

Material: One right mandible with roots of P_4 and M_1 (U.W.A. F1003) was found in the Folsom faunule.

Discussion: This specimen is completely burned, which explains the broken and missing teeth. No signs of cut marks or other cultural modifications were apparent. However, the fact the specimen was burned does indicate the possibility of cultural usage.

Order Proboscidea

FAMILY ELEPHANTIDAE

Genus *Mammuthus*

Mammuthus sp.—Mammoth

Geologic Range of Genus: Early (?Nebraskan) to late Pleistocene (Wisconsin) or early Holocene in North America (Maglio 1973:61–66).

Geographic Distribution: Mammoth remains are widespread across North America (Maglio 1973:61–66).

Habitat: The mammoth was apparently a grazing form, associated with Pleistocene grasslands (Tikhomirov 1958).

Material: One fragment of tusk (U.W.A. E1052) was recovered from the Clovis faunule at the Sheaman site.

Discussion: The species is represented in the fauna strictly because of cultural activity. The tusk fragment has been fashioned into a projectile point, identical to others found in contemporary deposits in Montana (Lahren and Bonnichsen 1974) and elsewhere (Hester 1972:117; Sellards 1952:33). The specimen is described by Frison and Zeimens (1980).

Another unpublished record of *Mammuthus* is also known from the area. This specimen, an isolated lower third molar, is associated with the first terrace above Lance Creek, 4 km south of Mule Creek Junction and 17 km southwest of the Agate Basin site. The exact age of the terraces along Lance Creek are unknown, but a minimum age of late Pleistocene is suggested by the presence of the mammoth tooth. Correlations between the Lance Creek deposits and the Moss Agate Arroyo deposits cannot be made directly.

Order Artiodactyla

FAMILY ANTILOCAPRIDAE

Genus *Antilocapra*

Antilocapra americana—Pronghorn

Geologic Range of Species: Late Pleistocene (Wisconsin) to Recent in North America (Hibbard 1958:22).

Geographic Distribution: Historically, the pronghorn was found throughout western North America (Sundstrom *et al.* 1973:10). In Wyoming, it is found statewide in suitable habitats (Long 1965:717).

Habitat: This species occurs in the open plains areas at all elevations, and is normally associated with sagebrush or saltbush and grass communities (Sundstrom *et al.* 1973:20).

Material: One proximal left metatarsal (U.W.A. E1026) was found in the Clovis faunule at the Sheaman site. One fragmentary right maxilla with full dentition (U.W.A. F1004), one complete left mandible with full dentition (U.W.A. F1005), one fragmentary right mandible with M_1 and M_2 (U.W.A. F1180), two right ascending rami (U.W.A. F1209, F1835), four occipitals (U.W.A. F1001, Figure 4.33a; F1179; F2113, Figure 4.33b; F2154), one right distal tibia (U.W.A. F1015, Figure 4.34g), three left distal tibiae (U.W.A. F1002, Figure 4.34d; F1013, Figure 4.34c; F1014, Figure 4.34f), one left distal humerus (U.W.A. F1680, Figure 4.33g), four right distal humeri (U.W.A. F1012, Figure 4.33f; F1682, Figure 4.33i; F2028, Figure 4.33h; F2121, Figure 4.33e), one radius shaft (U.W.A. F1175, Figure 4.33d), one left pelvis unit (pelvis, fragmentary proximal femur, and fragmentary proximal tibia, U.W.A. F2116), one left foreleg unit (proximal metacarpal, all five carpals, and distal radius, U.W.A. F1016, Figure 4.33c), and three rear leg units (proximal metatarsal and all tarsals, U.W.A. F1507, Figure 4.34b; proximal metatarsal, fused central and fourth tarsal and fused second and third tarsal, U.W.A. F1022, Figure 4.34a; right distal tibia, calcaneus, and astragalus; U.W.A. F2152) were recovered from the Folsom faunule. In addition, there were numerous other butchered and broken bones, all from the Folsom faunule (U.W.A. F1010, F1011, F1017, F1021, F1023, F1027–F1030, F1032, F1035, F1036, F1044, F1047, F1049, F1050, F1104–F1110, F1176, F1177, F1181–F1186, F1195, F1204–F1206, F1503, F1506, F1508, F1509, F1533, F1535, F1541, F1543, F1594, F1595, F1598, F1601, F1603, F1678, F1679, F1681, F1683–F1686, F1789, F1791, F1836, F1851, F1854, F1873, F1878, F1880, F2008,

F2023, F2024, F2061, F2062, F2130, F2133, F2161). The Agate Basin faunule produced one distal tibia (U.W.A. B0995, Figure 4.34e), one fused second and third tarsal (U.W.A. F1207), one distal femur epiphysis (U.W.A. 0047F), one fragmentary thoracic vertebra (U.W.A. B1341), one astragalus (U.W.A. F1259), one fragmentary second phalange (U.W.A. F1258), and one patella (U.W.A. F1256). An astragalus (U.W.A. F2224) and a carpal unit (radial, medial, and ulnar, U.W.A. F2239) were found in the Hell Gap faunule.

Discussion: Extensive cultural modifications were present on all the pronghorn material recovered. Modifications presumably resulted from the complete butchering and breakage of the bone for maximum utilization of the food resource. A minimum of four individuals of pronghorn were present in the Folsom faunule based on either the four occipitals or four right humeri.

FAMILY TAYASSUIDAE

Genus *Platygonus*

Platygonus compressus—Flat-headed Peccary

Geologic Range of Species: Late Pleistocene (Sangamon to Wisconsin) (Hibbard 1970: 426–430) to early Holocene (this report) in North America.

Geographic Distribution: Widespread in North America, from New York to California and Michigan to Mexico during the Wisconsin (C. E. Ray *et al.* 1970:92).

Habitat: Historically, this form of peccary has been proposed as a warm-climate or interglacial indicator (Hay 1923:216; Lundelius 1967:297), but new data and distribution records indicate that the species inhabited a wide range of habitats, including periglacial conditions near the base of melting glaciers (Eshelman *et al.* 1972; C. E. Ray *et al.* 1970: 91–92). The species appears to have been adapted to more open country or plains conditions rather than forested areas (Guilday *et al.* 1971:290–307).

Material: One mandibular condyle (U.W.A. F1417) was recovered from the Folsom faunule.

Discussion: This specimen represents the first record of *Platygonus compressus* from Wyoming. It is also the first known North American record of the species in definite association with human activity (Guilday *et al.* 1971:282). *Platygonus* was apparently associated with cultural material and a date of 10,000 ± 175 years B.P. at Levi Shelter, Texas (Alexander 1963), but the exact relationships between the artifacts and bone remains were not defined. The Agate Basin specimen is charred and was recovered from an extensive activity area on the south side of the Folsom occupation at the Agate Basin site. No definite cut or butchering marks were on the specimen but the breakage is suggestive of forceful removal from the skull.

This is also the most northwestern record of *Platygonus* in the Plains. Corner (1977:84) presented late Pleistocene records for south-central Nebraska. G. E. Lewis (1970) reported the recovery of four possibly early Holocene (Scott and Lindvall 1970) skulls and associated postcranial material from Denver, Colorado. Stanford (1979) reported another record of the species from eastern Colorado dating between 29,000 and 12,000 B.P. Most records of this species are farther east or south than any of the foregoing specimens.

This specimen from Agate Basin also represents the youngest occurrence of the species to date. Its association with the Folsom occupation at Agate Basin provides a date of between 10,500 and 10,800 B.P. for the species. The association between the Levi Shelter date and the *Platygonus* specimen from that locality would indicate that date to be a minimum for the stratigraphic level and the specimen may be much older. The Welsh Cave peccaries and associated fauna were dated at 12,950 ± 550 years B.P. (Guilday *et al.* 1971:260). A minimum date of 10,790 ± 150 years B.P. was obtained on the Ann Arbor, Michigan herd (Eshelman *et al.* 1972:246) but these authors believed that "the date . . . may be 2,000 to 4,000 years too young," based on stratigraphic evidence. Similarly, the date of 11,900 ± 750 years B.P. for the Mosherville, Pennsylvania, specimen is also regarded as too young (C. E. Ray *et al.* 1970:84). Finch *et al.* (1972) reviewed several other late Pleistocene–early Holocene occurrences, but again, all appear older than the Agate Basin specimen.

FAMILY CERVIDAE

Genus *Cervus*

Cervus elaphus—Wapiti or American Elk

Geologic Range of Species: Late Pleistocene (Wisconsin) to Recent in North America (Hibbard 1958:21).

Geographic Distribution: The wapiti was distributed over the northern United States and southern Canada (Hall and Kelson 1959:1002) until 1800. In Wyoming, the form is now restricted to mountainous regions (Long 1965:711), although it occasionally wanders into basin areas.

Habitat: The wapiti was known to have occupied deciduous and conifer forests, brushlands, and grasslands historically, but may have been most abundant in grasslands, open woodlands, and forest edges (Hoffmann and Pattie 1968:67).

Material: One brow tine (U.W.A. OA010) and one cut antler strip (U.W.A. OA117) were recovered from the Folsom faunule.

Discussion: This is the earliest Wyoming record of the extant form of wapiti. The tine had been fashioned into a tool and is described in detail elsewhere (Chapter 2). The antler strip is approximately 30 cm long, 1 cm wide, and 2 mm thick. Its use and/or function is problematic. Wapiti was also reported by Agogino and Frankforter (1960) from their excavations of the Folsom occupation at the Agate Basin site. An unsuccessful attempt was made to locate this material in connection with the present study.

FAMILY CAMELIDAE

Genus *Camelops*

Camelops sp.—American Camel

Geologic Range of Genus: Early Pleistocene (Blancan) (Webb 1965:33) to early Holocene (Frison, Walker, Webb, and Zeimens 1978) in North America.

Geographic Distribution: This extinct genus of camel has been found in Pleistocene deposits over much of western North America (Webb 1965).

Habitat: *Camelops* was apparently a grassland form (Frison, Walker, Webb, and Zeimens 1978; Guthrie 1968a; Webb 1965).

Material: One first phalange (U.W.A. F1255) was recovered from the Clovis faunule at the Agate Basin site. One left medial, anterior tibia (U.W.A. OA321) fragment was found in the Folsom faunule.

Discussion: The first phalange was recovered from a level containing redeposited cultural material below the Folsom occupation in the extreme western portion of the Agate Basin site. The phalange exhibits rodent chewing but no definite cultural modifications (Figure 4.34h). The tibia fragment from the Folsom faunule has been fashioned into a tool with a serrated edge; however, most of the working edge has been broken from the remainder of the tool. *Camelops* has been found in three other Wyoming locations in a cultural context (Frison 1976; Frison, Walker, Webb, and Zeimens 1978; Walker and Frison 1980).

FAMILY BOVIDAE

Genus *Bison*

Bison bison cf. *antiquus*—Bison

Geologic Range of Subspecies: Late Pleistocene (Wisconsin) to early Holocene in North America (Hibbard 1958:22; Wilson 1974:133).

Geographic Distribution: *B. b. antiquus* has been reported in numerous Pleistocene and early Holocene deposits in central and western North America (Hibbard 1958:22; Wilson 1975).

Habitat: The habitat requirements (open or semiopen grassland areas) of this extinct subspecies of *Bison* were probably fairly similar to those of the recent plains subspecies, *B. b. bison* (Graham 1979).

Material: Skulls of mature males (U.W.A. F2332, Hell Gap, Figure 4.41a; F1478,

FIGURE 4.39 *Bison b. antiquus* skulls from the Folsom faunule: (a) male; (b) calf.

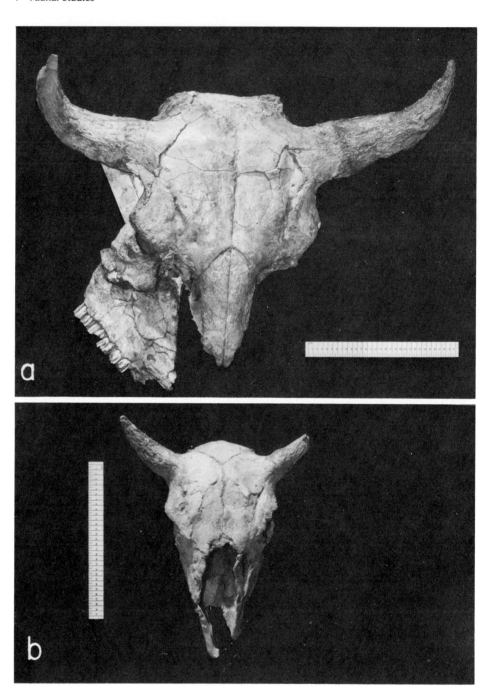

Folsom, Figure 4.39a; B1574, Agate Basin, Figure 4.40a); mature females (U.W.A. 0109F, Hell Gap, Figure 4.41b; 0209F, Hell Gap, Figure 4.41c; F0006, Agate Basin, Figure 4.40b; F1479, Folsom), and a calf (U.W.A. F1518, Folsom, Figure 4.39b) were recovered. Postcranial material was recovered from all occupation levels at the site as well. Detailed counts and descriptions of this postcranial material can be found earlier in this chapter (Section 1).

Discussion: The largest sample of *Bison* bone from the site is from the Agate Basin faunule in Area 2 with a minimum of 75 animals recovered during the University of Wyoming excavations. This figure is incomplete because several other episodes of excavations (both professional and nonprofessional) have occurred in this level. Estimates including all excava-

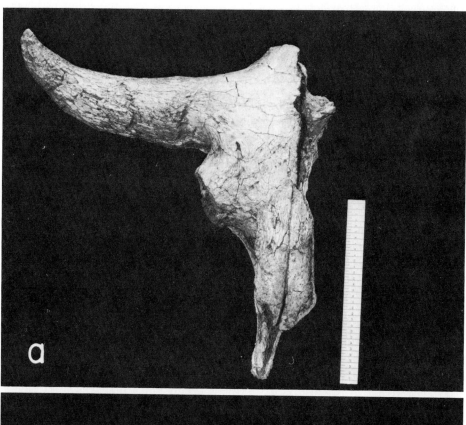

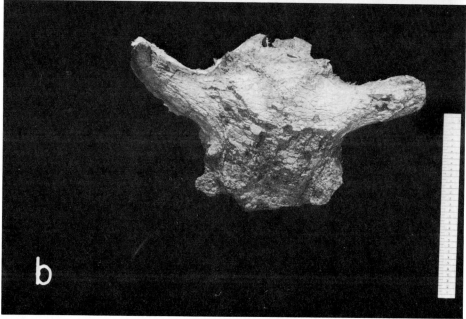

FIGURE 4.40 **Bison b. antiquus** skulls from the Agate Basin faunule: (a) male; (b) female.

tions indicate that remains of as many as 200 animals may have been originally present in the Agate Basin faunule. The other cultural levels in Areas 2 and 3 contained up to 9 animals (Table 4.13).

Wilson (1974:160, 163, 165) presented information and measurements of a single female skull from the Folsom level excavations conducted by Agogino (Agogino and Frankforter 1960:105–106). The latter authors assigned the specimen to *Bison antiquus*. This identification later was confirmed by Wilson (1974:160). Table 4.15 presents a standard series of measurements (Skinner and Kaisen 1947) on all skulls excavated from Agate Basin after

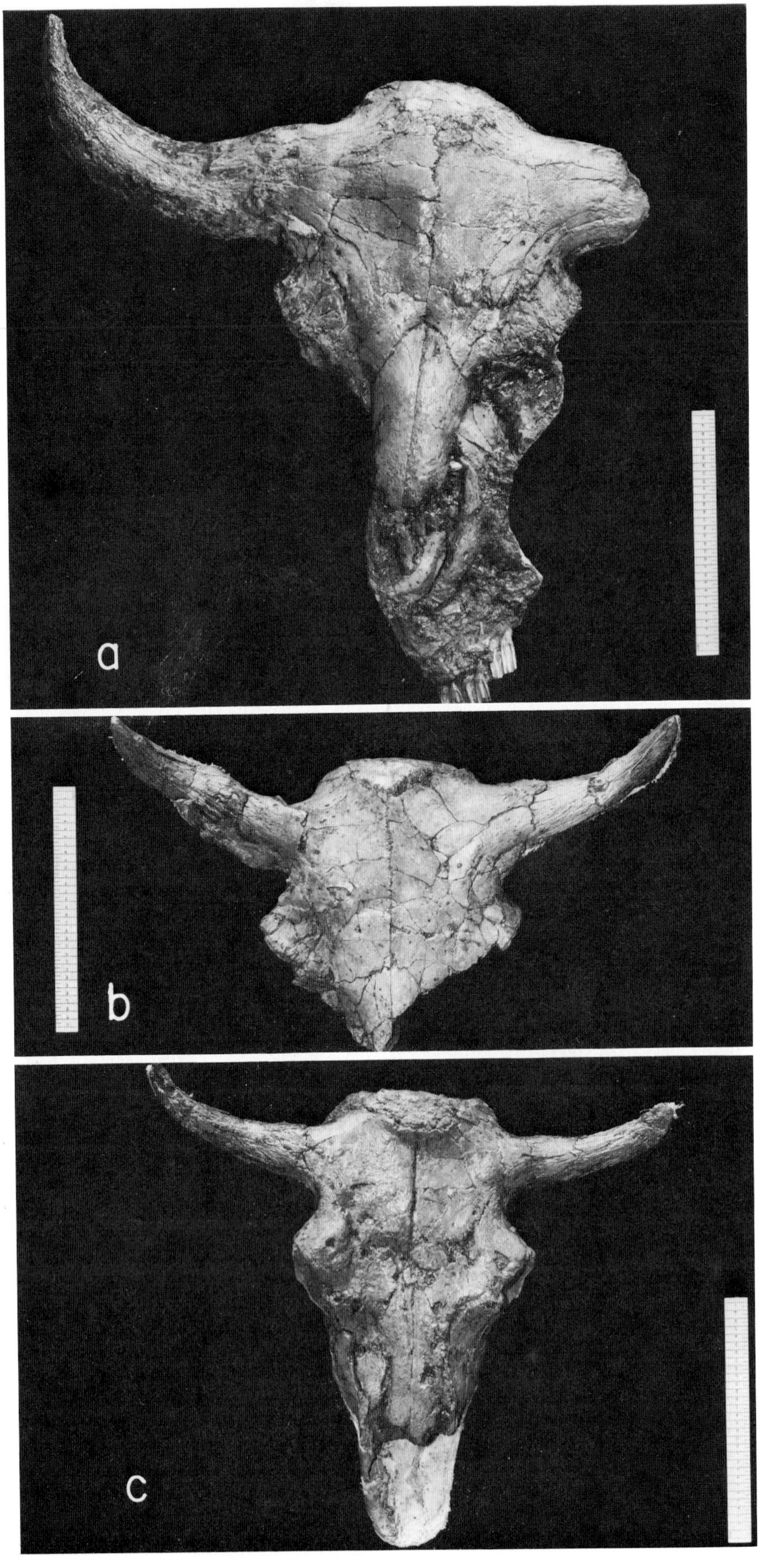

FIGURE 4.41 *Bison b. antiquus* skulls from the Hell Gap faunule: (a) male; (b, c) females.

TABLE 4.15
Comparative Measurements of Adult *Bison* Skulls from the Agate Basin Local Fauna[a] (millimeters)

Standard measurement[b]	Male			Female				
	F2332 (HG)	B1574 (AB)	F1478 (F)	0209F (HG)	0109F (HG)	F0006 (AB)	F1479 (F)	Agogino[b] (F?)
1. Spread of horn-cores, tip to tip	960	890	780	662	620			675
2. Greatest spread of cores on outside curve	990	914	800	663	624			685
3. Core length on upper curve, tip to burr	350	270	270	230	210			205c
4. Core length on lower curve, tip to burr	425c	360	314	275c	235			240c
5. Length, tip of core to upper base at burr	293	270	236	208	185			190c
6. Vertical diameter of horn-core		98					59	70c
7. Circumference of horn-core at base		345c						217
8. Greatest width at auditory openings								290
9. Width of condyles			144		113			
10. Depth, occipital crest to top of foramen magnum					77	96		
11. Depth, occipital crest to lower border of foramen magnum					122	127c		
12. Transverse diameter of horn-core	126c	115	108	100	61	66		66
13. Width between bases of horn-cores	295	246	280	234	200	195		220
14. Width of cranium between horn-cores and orbits	365	294	325	259	226	227		265
15. Greatest postorbital width	400c	340	366	334	298	238c		
16. Anterior orbital width at notch	315c	240	265		230			
17. Width of skull at masseteric processes above M^1			135		195			
18. Rostral width at maxillary–premaxillary suture					130			
19. P^2–M^3, alveolar length			168				165	
20. M^1–M^3, alveolar length			102				106	
O–P Length, occipital crest to tip of premaxilla	650c	570c			545		535c	
F–P Basilar length, foramen magnum to tip of premaxilla							354c	
O–T Length, occipital crest to tip of nasals	540	400	515		425			
O–N Length, occipital crest to nasal–frontal suture	300	260	280		198			157c
M–P Length, beyond P^2 to tip of premaxilla							151	
N–T Length of nasals	238	230	228		222			
21. Angle of posterior divergence of horn-core	87°	88°	72°	63°	80°			75°
22. Angle of proximal horn-core depression	10°	11°	9°		10°			0°
Index of horn-core curvature	145	133	133	132	127			126c
Index of horn-core compression		85						106c
Index of horn-core proportion		78c						94.5c
Index of horn-core length	96	92	83	89	93			93c
Index of orbital protrusion	91c	86	86	78	76	95c		

[a]HG, Hell Gap faunule; AB, Agate Basin faunule; F, Folsom faunule.
[b]From Wilson 1974.
[c]Measurement estimated because of damage at measurement point.

Wilson's analysis. This table also demonstrates that the latter specimens support the *antiquus* identification. The entire population can be referred to that subspecies, although an occasional character of *B. b. occidentalis* appears (Frison, this volume, Chapter 4, part 3).

EARLY HOLOCENE ENVIRONMENT OF THE NORTHWESTERN PLAINS

The use of micromammals recovered from archaeological sites to reconstruct paleoenvironments has become a common practice. Grayson (1981) has provided an excellent review of the many problems associated with this practice. This author is in agreement with Grayson in that the use of the presence or absence of species in a local fauna is a more acceptable method for reconstructing paleoenvironments than relative abundance methods. The biases that may occur by methods of accumulation, process of deposition, recovery techniques, and so on inject too much variability into analyses using relative percentages of species. Basing the presence of a specific habitat on a single species can be just as dangerous. However, if several species having similar habitat requirements are recovered together, a more positive reconstruction is possible. Such was the case in the present study with the various faunules of the Agate Basin local fauna.

A comparison of the modern fauna (Table 4.12) and the Folsom faunule of the Agate Basin local fauna (Table 4.13) indicates that although some of the species associated with the Folsom faunule are also members of the modern steppe or grassland fauna, four montane or mesic rodents (*Microtus longicaudus,* long-tailed vole; *M. pennsylvanicus,* meadow vole; *Clethrionomys gapperi,* red-backed vole; and *Phenacomys intermedius,* heather vole), and one steppe form (*Lagurus curtatus,* sagebrush vole) were present in the region as well. The addition of these species indicates that the local environment during deposition of the fauna was much different from the modern situation.

As was noted earlier in the chapter, the early Holocene Moss Agate Arroyo was steep-walled and flat-bottomed, and had few major tributaries within 2 km of the Agate Basin site. Away from the arroyo, the surrounding uplands were generally flat, but exhibited a gently rolling topography (see Albanese, this volume, Chapter 5, Section 1). The modern arroyo is different from this early Holocene arroyo. The arroyo walls slope gently and are more or less continuous with the bottom; the arroyo is over 100 m wide in places. Numerous tributaries are also present near the site area. The modern arroyo bottom contains a lush vegetation community consisting of tall to medium grasses, wild roses, and sagebrush. The bottom is fairly wet during the spring runoff or following a summer downpour, but it soon dries and becomes firm.

Only two species of rodents were found in the arroyo during 1979: the deer mouse (*Peromyscus maniculatus*) and the prairie vole (*Microtus ochrogaster*). In the uplands away from the site, the vegetation consists of sagebrush, prickly pear, and several types of shortgrass. Four Sonoran or steppe mammalian species were found in the uplands: *Onychomys leucogaster* (northern grasshopper mouse), *Dipodomys ordii* (kangaroo rat), *Spermophilus tridecemlineatus* (thirteen-lined ground squirrel), and *Perognathus fasciatus* (olive-backed pocket mouse). The deer mouse was also present in the upland sagebrush areas and was captured almost twice as often as all other species combined.

It is not known exactly how much the presence of a modern stock pond has affected the small-mammal population at the site area. Trapping around the perimeter of the pond revealed that both the prairie vole and deer mouse were present, with the deer mouse outnumbering the prairie vole by over 2 to 1. Immediately downstream below the dam, the situation was reversed. Here the prairie vole outnumbered the deer mouse by almost 10 to 1. Thus the situation below the dam, where the vegetation was less varied, probably reflects more the natural habitat before construction of the dam, with the prairie vole competitively excluding the deer mouse. The dam has provided a more varied habitat allowing the deer mouse to compete with the prairie vole. Competitive exclusion between these two genera has been demonstrated from several controlled experiments (Grant 1970, 1971, 1972) and one record of exclusion has been found experimentally between the deer mouse and the prairie vole (Whitaker 1967). However, soil studies (Reider, this volume, Chapter 5, Section 2) suggest that present conditions below the dam are not indicative of those of the early Holocene. This also is demonstrated by the habitat requirements of the microfauna recovered from the site.

The combined presence in the Folsom faunule of the long-tailed, heather, red-backed, and meadow voles indicates that the arroyo bottom was much more mesic but not saturated during late-glacial time. The more diverse late-glacial fauna indicates that the modern flora has deteriorated in its composition from an extensive grass and forb community in the bottom of the arroyo around 10,780 B.P. to the more xeric adapted plants of today. Soil studies have also suggested that the arroyo bottom was more moist at the time of the Agate Basin occupation (Reider, this volume, Chapter 5, Section 2). A mesic meadow soil association was present over the entire arroyo floor in the vicinity of the Folsom occupation. The presence of the ranid frogs in the Folsom level is further evidence that relatively mesic conditions were present. Presently these frogs are found only around the pond at the site. An examination of the invertebrate members of the Folsom horizon resulted in an identification of genera whose ecological requirements also fit this reconstruction. Forms that were present require moist conditions but no extensive bodies of standing water (La Rocque 1970).

In addition to the grasses and the forb understory in the Folsom arroyo, the habitat requirements of the red-backed and heather voles, and possibly the long-tailed vole (Findley 1951), indicate that trees were also present in the arroyo bottom. *Lagurus curtatus* (sagebrush vole), *Centrocerus urophasianus* (sage grouse), and *Antilocapra americana* (pronghorn), all of which are closely associated with various types of sagebrush, indicate sage-covered uplands. The low numbers of sagebrush voles in each faunule does show a lack of sagebrush cover close to the arroyo. The absence of the sagebrush vole in the modern fauna indicates that it was not able to survive in the area during the remaining parts of the Holocene and retreated south and west of the area to more favorable habitats. Despite extensive sagebrush cover in the site area today, largely the result of overgrazing by livestock and attempted farming of land during the 1920s and 1930s, the sagebrush vole has apparently not had enough time to reinvade this optimum sagebrush habitat.

A probable vegetational reconstruction for the Folsom time period, based on these micromammal associations, might include the following species as dominants in the arroyo bottom: *Poa pratensis* (Kentucky bluegrass), *Poa ampla* (big bluegrass), *Deschampia caespitosa* (tufted hair grass), *Agropyron trachycaulum* (slender wheatgrass), *Carex* spp. (several species of sedges), *Rosa* sp. (wild rose), *Populus tremuloides* (quaking aspen), *Symphoricarpos occidentalis* (western snowberry), *Geranium richardsonii* (wild geranium), and *Artemisia tridentata vaseyana* (mountain big sagebrush) (Clayton Marlow, personal communication, 1979). Such vegetative and small mammal associations have been recorded in more montane and/or mesic habitats in the region. Several other forms of vegetation also would be present, but probably as subdominants. Studies concerning the vegetative associations of small mammals conducted approximately 160 km south (Maxwell and Brown 1968) and 560 km west

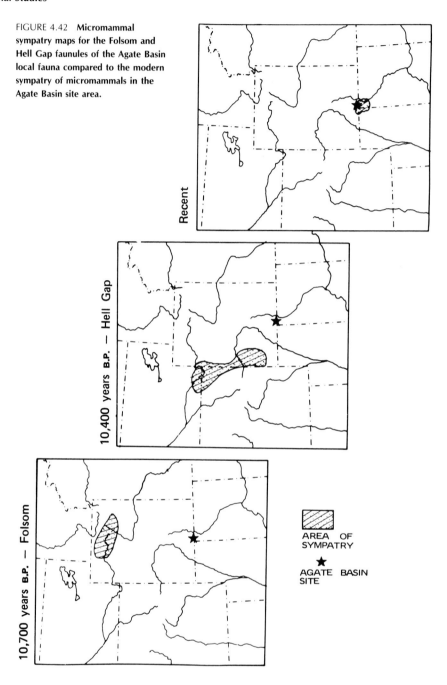

FIGURE 4.42 Micromammal sympatry maps for the Folsom and Hell Gap faunules of the Agate Basin local fauna compared to the modern sympatry of micromammals in the Agate Basin site area.

(Findley 1951) also tend to support the foregoing reconstruction. Although some of the grass species appear to be different, the genera are identical.

Four to five hundred years later, during the occupation by the Hell Gap people, conditions appear to have deteriorated to something similar to the modern situation. The arroyo was still steep-walled and flat-bottomed but the loss of the red-backed vole and the addition of the olive-backed pocket mouse indicate that the wet meadow covering the bottom was starting to dry out, with the probable loss of the shrub and small tree understory. The presence of the shrew, robin, and thrush indicates that some ground cover was still present. The deer mouse population began to increase, but the two mesic voles (meadow and long-tailed) were still dominant. The addition of the olive-backed pocket mouse to the fauna at this time substantiates the hypothesis for the deterioration of the local environment. This species is mainly found in shortgrass areas (Jones 1953) and almost never in a wet bog-type situation.

The area of sympatry (an area of overlapping modern ranges of the micromammals from a fauna) is shown in Figure 4.42 for the Agate Basin site Folsom and Hell Gap faunules, and the modern fauna found at the Agate Basin site today. The Folsom area of sympatry indicates that a micromammal association similar to the Folsom faunule can be found today in the coniferous forest region of northwestern Wyoming. A comparison of climatic data from modern recording stations in the area of sympatry (Table 4.16) and from near Agate Basin (Table 4.11) indicates that January and July mean temperatures are 9°F and 13°F colder, respectively, than in the Agate Basin region today (Table 4.11). There is a .2 inch increase in precipitation and 90 fewer 32°F frostfree days than presently recorded around Agate Basin.

The Hell Gap area of sympatry reflects a shift to the south and east of the area of Folsom sympatry. This is primarily due to the addition of a steppe species, *Perognathus fasciatus,* to the fauna and the loss of a boreal form, *Clethrionomys gapperi.* This indicates a probable reduction in the overall amount of boreal-type cover in the area of the site. This area of sympatry in northwest Colorado and south-central Wyoming, though still containing major coniferous forest areas, also includes a major portion of the sagebrush–grassland region of the southern Wyoming Basin. Modern climatic data for this area of sympatry are presented in Table 4.17. A comparison of this modern data with the data in Table 4.11 from the Agate Basin site area shows that January mean temperatures in the area of sympatry average 5°F colder than

TABLE 4.16

Climatic Data for the Folsom Faunule Micromammal Area of Sympatry

	Locality					
	Dubois	*Kendall*	*Pinedale*	*Big Piney*	*Sunshine*	*Average*
January temperature[a] (°F)						
Minimum	− 9	− 2	− 3	− 6	6	− 3
Mean	22	12	12	9	21	15
Maximum	34	26	26	25	35	29
July temperature[a] (°F)						
Minimum	43	37	41	39	44	41
Mean	62	57	60	59	61	60
Maximum	80	75	80	79	76	78
Monthly precipitation[b] (inches)						
Minimum	.3	1.1	—	—	.4	.6
Maximum	1.5	2.0	—	—	3.0	2.2
Annual precipitation[b] (inches)	9.4	17.0	—	—	17.1	14.5
Frostfree days[c] (32°F frost)	50	17	34	—	—	34

[a]From Becker and Alyea 1964a.
[b]From Becker and Alyea 1964b.
[c]From Becker *et al.* 1977.

TABLE 4.17
Climatic Data for the Hell Gap Faunule Micromammal Area of Sympatry

	Locality											
	Craig, Colo.	Rangley, Colo.	Meeker, Colo.	Jensen, Utah	Bonanza, Utah	Vernal, Utah	Dixon, Wyo.	Encampment, Wyo.	Centennial, Wyo.	Fox Park, Wyo.	Saratoga, Wyo.	Average
January temperature[a] (°F)												
Minimum	2	4	5	2	8	4	3	10	12	4	8	6
Mean	17	18	27	17	20	17	18	22	22	15	20	19
Maximum	33	33	36	29	34	29	32	34	32	27	33	32
July temperature[a] (°F)												
Minimum	47	54	46	51	57	51	46	47	47	36	48	48
Mean	67	74	66	73	75	70	66	64	62	54	66	67
Maximum	86	93	85	93	93	89	84	82	77	72	84	85
Monthly precipitation[a,b] (inches)												
Minimum	.8	.5	1.0	.5	.4	.5	.7	.8	—	1.0	.4	.7
Maximum	1.5	1.3	1.8	.9	1.1	.9	1.3	1.8	—	1.7	1.3	1.4
Annual precipitation[a,b] (inches)	13.5	8.8	16.2	7.7	8.4	8.0	12.6	14.5	—	16.7	9.3	11.6
Frostfree days[c] (32°F frost)	—	—	—	—	—	—	87	97	81	20	87	74

[a]From U.S. Weather Bureau 1964, 1965; Becker and Alyea 1964a.
[b]From Becker and Alyea 1964b.
[c]From Becker et al. 1977.

at the Agate Basin site today, July mean temperatures are 6°F colder, and there is 2.7 inches less precipitation in south-central Wyoming and northwest Colorado than there is at the Agate Basin site. There are 50 fewer 32°F frostfree days in the area of sympatry, as compared with the modern climatic data from Agate Basin.

These modern climatic data for recording stations within the two areas of sympatry give an indication of what climatic conditions may have been during the late-glacial and Pre-Boreal periods of northeast Wyoming, based on the major assumption that we can extrapolate from modern climatic data. These modern data should not be considered as absolute for either occupation but they represent a possible climatic regime (Semken 1980).

It is apparent that the modern climatic data for the two sympatry areas are not identical. The yearly temperatures were warmer during the Hell Gap occupation than during Folsom times and there was an associated longer frostfree period. The main difference in climatic conditions between the two faunules is the 2.5-inch decrease in yearly precipitation. With the colder Folsom temperatures shown by the Folsom sympatry, the effective moisture may have been equal to or even greater than it is at present. The higher temperatures and decreased precipitation associated with the Hell Gap faunule indicate that although overall conditions were cooler than at Agate Basin today, it was probably much drier than the Folsom sympatry indicates—that is, there was a greater evapotranspiration rate. This evapotranspiration rate was probably not as high as that today at Agate Basin. Based on these sympatry comparisons, during the late-glacial and Pre-Boreal periods in northwest Wyoming, year-round temperatures could have been cooler than today, associated with a greater effective amount of moisture and a major decrease in the number of frostfree days.

If these data are considered indications of the climate during the Folsom and Hell Gap occupations at Agate Basin, one point is obvious: Almost half of the difference between glacial and modern times was reached by the time of Hell Gap occupation. This is within a period estimated at around 400 years. I do not interpret this as a "sudden" change in conditions from Folsom to Hell Gap, to be necessarily followed by an equally sudden, more gradual change to modern conditions. Rather, this may have been one of a series of short-term but sharp changes in climatic conditions over the Holocene (Wendland 1978:273–287). A comparable situation may have occurred after the Little Ice Age 200 or 300 B.P. A micromammal sample under investigation (the River Bend site) from this time period may or may not be used as a model to substantiate this idea of short-term climatic changes at the end of the Pleistocene and over the Holocene.

Despite the extensive water-screening, almost no micromammals (Table 4.13) were recovered from either the Clovis or Agate Basin levels and therefore no areas of sympatry could be ascertained for these faunules. Microforms were not preserved in these two cultural levels, if they were ever present. The differences in the types of occupations may be relevant. Other excavations have revealed that a much more varied fauna is expected in a camp site association than in a kill site (Frison, Wilson, and Walker 1978). However, sizable numbers of microvertebrates have been recovered from *Bison* kill site bone beds at Cherokee Sewer (Semken 1980) and Jones–Miller (Rawn n.d.). Their absence here remains unexplained.

Archaeological excavations at the Agate Basin site have resulted in the collection of an extensive vertebrate fauna, mainly from the Folsom and Hell Gap cultural horizons. At least 11 of these mammalian species are present in the fauna as a result of the cultural activities at the site. The bison and pronghorn were the two species most extensively utilized, mainly for food. Tools and/or decorative items were manufactured from bones of the following species: cottontail rabbit, red fox, mammoth, pronghorn, wapiti, and bison. Cut and/or butchering marks also appear on wolf and medium-sized canid bones. No definite indications of cultural modifications or usage could be seen on the various micromammal, bird, reptile, or amphibian remains; they may all occur naturally in the site.

A comparison of this local fauna with the modern fauna shows that four large mammals are extinct and five micromammals no longer occur in the immediate site area as a result of the apparent lack of suitable habitat. The extinction of *Mammuthus* occurred between Clovis and Folsom times; *Camelops* became extinct between Folsom and Hell Gap times; *Platygonus compressus* became extinct between Folsom and Agate Basin times. The fourth (*Bison b. antiquus*) lingered until early Altithermal times (Frison *et al.* 1976).

Comparing the Folsom faunule with the Hell Gap faunule demonstrates the loss of one boreomontane species (*Clethrionomys gapperi*) and the addition of one steppe species (*Perognathus fasciatus*) sometime between Folsom and Hell Gap times. The change in the area of sympatry for the micromammals from the Folsom to Hell Gap faunules is due to the addition of *Perognathus fasciatus* to the fauna. The modern range of *Clethrionomys* overlaps the Hell Gap sympatry as presented. The loss of the three remaining boreomontane micromammals

SUMMARY

(*Microtus longicaudus, M. pennsylvanicus, Phenacomys intermedius*) and one steppe species (*Lagurus curtatus*) occurred following the Hell Gap occupation.

Microvertebrates have provided the best evidence for environmental and ecological reconstructions for the site area during the early Holocene of northeastern Wyoming. These data provide evidence that the seemingly abrupt climatic changes noted previously for the end of the Pleistocene in Wyoming (Frison, Wilson, and Walker 1978; Walker 1975) were not as sudden as they first appeared to be. The Agate Basin local fauna has shown that these changes were more gradual, probably occurring over several thousand years. An arctic steppe–savanna (Guthrie 1968b; Matthews 1976) has been proposed for the Northwestern Plains (Wyoming) during the full-glacial and late-glacial periods (Frison and Walker 1978; Gilbert *et al.* 1978). Gilbert *et al.* (1978) and Chomko (1979) have also demonstrated that there was an environmental change in the area between 14,000 and 11,000 B.P. A tundra-type biome gave way to more of a grassland biome through the loss of the tundra members of the faunal community. The Folsom and Hell Gap faunules of the Agate Basin local fauna shows a continuation of this environmental change to an environment even more similar to the modern type. Progressively lesser amounts of tall grasses, and more shortgrass types, as well as a more extensive sagebrush community, are recorded.

chapter five
PALEOECOLOGICAL STUDIES

1. GEOLOGIC INVESTIGATION
john albanese

The geologic interpretations presented in this section are based primarily on field studies carried out at intervals during the period 1974–1980. The distribution of Quaternary sediments was mapped by use of a plane table and alidade. A total of 94 m (310 feet) of geologic profile trenches were dug with a backhoe machine. Stratigraphic sections were measured both in backhoe trenches and in areas excavated for archaeological purposes. Sediment samples collected at 12-cm intervals from five measured sections were examined under the binocular microscope. Mechanical analyses of sediments that are presented by Reider in Section 2 of this chapter were used as supplemental data.

METHOD OF INVESTIGATION

The Agate Basin site lies on the southwestern margin of the Black Hills uplift. The climate is semiarid and the vegetation is typical of a sagebrush–grass biome. The physiography in this portion of the Black Hills and the adjoining portion of the Powder River Basin is characterized by linear, ephemeral stream valleys that alternate with bedrock ridges trending northwest–southeast. These ridges are usually capped by alluvial deposits of Pleistocene age.

The Agate Basin–Brewster site complex lies at the head of the valley of a fifth-order (scale 1:24,000) ephemeral stream, Moss Agate Creek, at an elevation of 1085 m (3560 feet). The stream drains to the southeast and traverses a

GENERAL GEOLOGIC SETTING

FIGURE 5.1 **Map of the Agate Basin site locality showing Q₂ channel.**

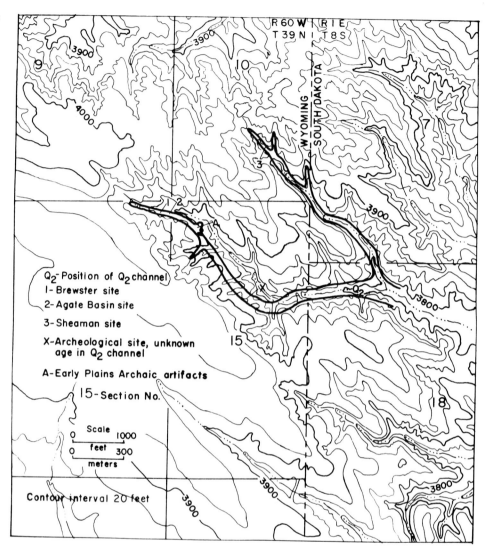

valley locally called Moss Agate Arroyo. In the vicinity of the Agate Basin site, Moss Agate Arroyo is approximately .55 km (.34 mile) wide and 24 m (80 feet) deep (Figures 1.3, 1.4, 1.5, 5.1). Bedrock in the general study area is the Carlile shale of Upper Cretaceous age (Love *et al.*, 1955), which strikes north-west–southeast and dips 4° to the southwest. Exposures of Carlile shale are randomly distributed along the deflated crests of bedrock ridges. The 2–7° slopes that rim the valley are covered by colluvium, which varies in thickness from 15 to 90 cm (.5 to 3 feet). The composition of the colluvium varies from clay to clayey sand, percentages of which vary with proximity to local outcrop sources. Paired Holocene alluvial terraces, which are present along most of the drainage systems in northeastern Wyoming (L. B. Leopold and J. P. Miller 1954), are not present within this study area. Minor nonpaired alluvial terraces of small areal extent (Figure 5.2) are randomly distributed adjacent to modern stream channels. These features are uncommon and lie .5–1.5 m (1.5–5 feet) above the modern channel. Minor knickpoints, .3–1 m (1–3 feet) high, are present along the grass-covered bottom of the main fifth-order stream and its tributaries. The spacing between knickpoints (headcuts) along the fifth-order stream varies from 91 to 182 m (300 to 600 feet). Knickpoints are common features along drainages located in semiarid environments (Schumm and Hadley 1957).

The colluvial slopes present along the valley of Moss Agate Creek are characterized by an abundance of miniature "scarps." These steplike features are cut into colluvium and consist of a near-vertical wall .3–.6 m (1–2 feet) high. The base of the wall adjoins a broad depositional surface that is inclined 2–5° in a downslope direction. These geomorphic erosional features are 15–45 m (50–150 feet) long.

The drainage divide (labeled S_3, Figure 5.4) at the head of Moss Agate Arroyo (Figures 5.1 and 5.4) is capped by sediment composed of arkosic sands and gravel. Two geomorphic features that resemble terraces are present on the northeast side of the valley of Moss Agate Arroyo, downslope from the drainage divide (Figure 5.4). These features are labeled S_1 and S_2 in ascending order. They lie 15 m (50 feet) and 21 m (71 feet), respectively, above the channel of the stream. A sandy, arkosic gravel is exposed on the S_1 surface. The S_2 surface is underlain by a bed about 30 cm (1 foot) thick composed of intermixed arkosic sand, gravel, cobbles, and granite boulders, .3–.6 m (1–2 feet) long. Cobbles of sandstone, granite, lineated mafic rocks, chert, quartzite, chalcedony, white quartz, and fragments of silicified wood are scattered over the S_2 surface. The arkosic sediments that underlie the main drainage divide and the S_1 and S_2 features rest on Carlile shale and are probably of Pleistocene age. They are derived from a terrain underlain by granitic rocks of Precambrian age. The closest outcrops of granite lie 52 km (32 miles) northeast of the Agate Basin site within the Precambrian core of the Black Hills (Petsch 1953). The closest granite outcrops in Wyoming are located in the Hartville Uplift, at a point 60 km (37 miles) to the southwest (Love *et al.* 1955). The mode of origin of the S_1 and S_2 features is unknown. If they are interpreted as alluvial terraces, which they resemble, problems arise as to how they formed at the head of a small drainage basin. Geologic field mapping over a much larger area than that encompassed by this report is required before a plausible explanation can be formulated.

THE MOSS AGATE ARROYO DRAINAGE BASIN

The ephemeral stream that drains Moss Agate Arroyo and its tributaries occupies an elongate, fifth-order drainage basin 4.57 km (2.84 miles) by 2.74 km (1.9 miles), an area of 12.5 km² (5.4 square miles). The overall gradient of the fifth-order channel that traverses Moss Agate Arroyo is .02. Topographic relief within the fifth-order basin is 91 m (300 feet).

From an archaeological and geologic viewpoint, the most important tributary of Moss Agate Arroyo is Sheaman Draw. This third-order stream drains to the southeast and joins Moss Agate Arroyo at a point on the eastern edge of the study area (Figures 1.4 and 5.2). The Sheaman site, which contained Clovis artifacts, lies on the northeastern bank of Sheaman Draw at a point .67 km (.42 mile) northeast of the Agate Basin site (Figures 1.4 and 5.2). Within the mapped area of this report, Sheaman Draw is the only tributary to Moss Agate Arroyo that contains sediments of pre-Altithermal age.

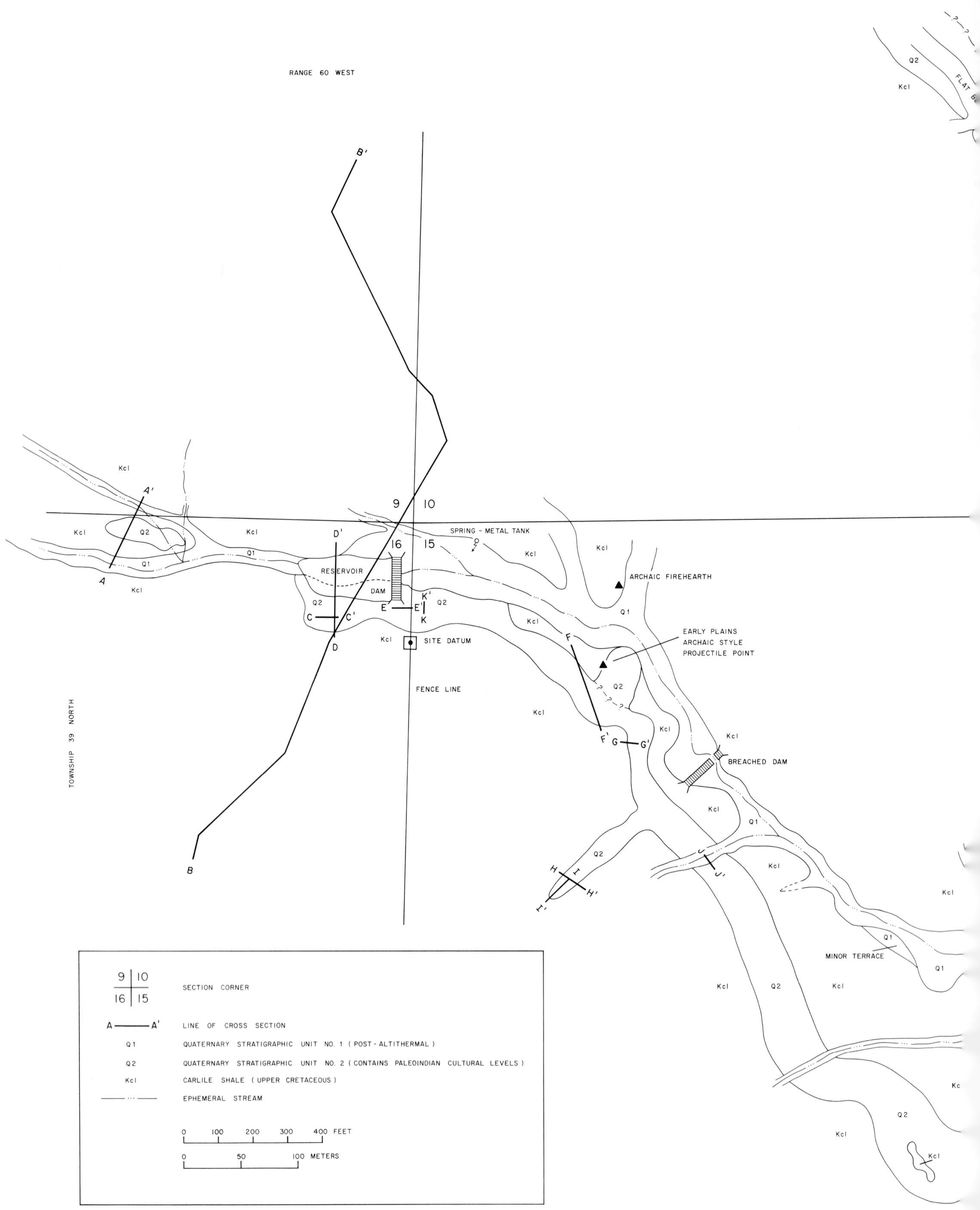

RANGE 60 WEST

Q2

Kcl

FLAT B

B'

Kcl

9 | 10

A'

Kcl   Q2   Kcl   SPRING – METAL TANK

Kcl   Q1   Kcl

Q1   16 | 15   Kcl

A   D'   ARCHAIC FIREHEARTH

Kcl   RESERVOIR   Q1

Q2   DAM   Kcl   EARLY PLAINS
C   C'   E   E' K' Q2   ARCHAIC STYLE
              E   K   Kcl   PROJECTILE POINT

D   Kcl ◆ SITE DATUM   F

D   Q2

FENCE LINE   Kcl

Kcl   F' G G'   Kcl

Kcl   BREACHED DAM

Kcl

Q2   Q1

H I H'   J J'

I' H'   Q2   Kcl   Kcl

TOWNSHIP 39 NORTH   MINOR TERRACE

Q1

Kcl   Q2   Kcl

Kc

Q2

Kcl   Kcl

9 | 10
16 | 15   SECTION CORNER

A ——— A'   LINE OF CROSS SECTION

Q1   QUATERNARY STRATIGRAPHIC UNIT NO. 1 (POST – ALTITHERMAL)

Q2   QUATERNARY STRATIGRAPHIC UNIT NO. 2 (CONTAINS PALEOINDIAN CULTURAL LEVELS)

Kcl   CARLILE SHALE (UPPER CRETACEOUS)

————   EPHEMERAL STREAM

0   100   200   300   400 FEET

0   50   100 METERS

FIGURE 5.2 **Plane table map of the Agate Basin site area, Niobrara County,
Wyoming.**

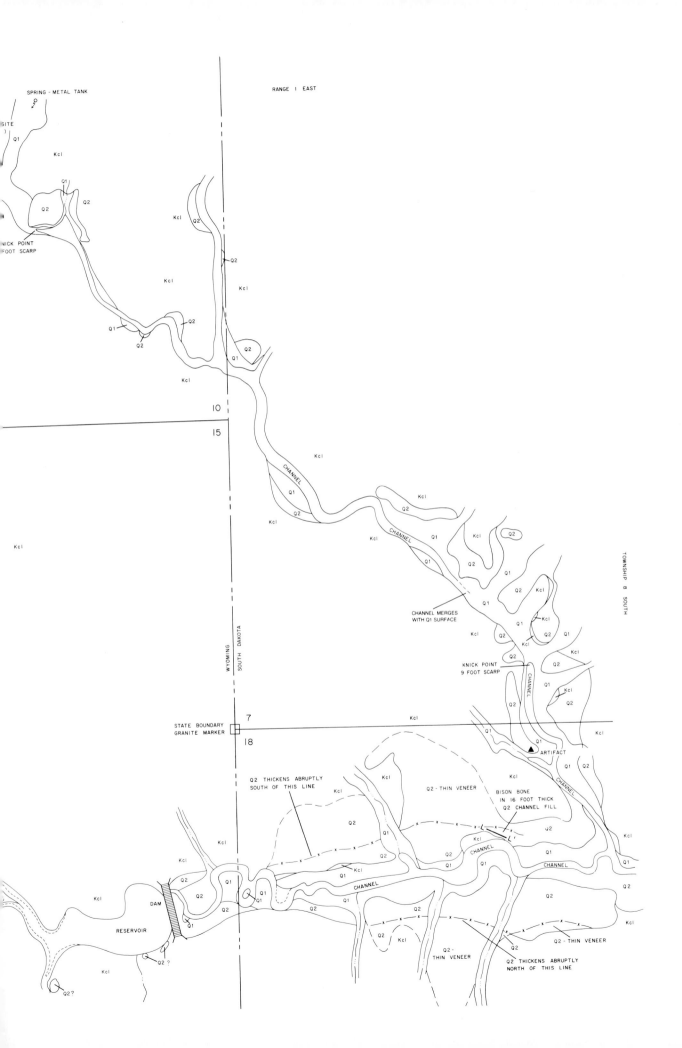

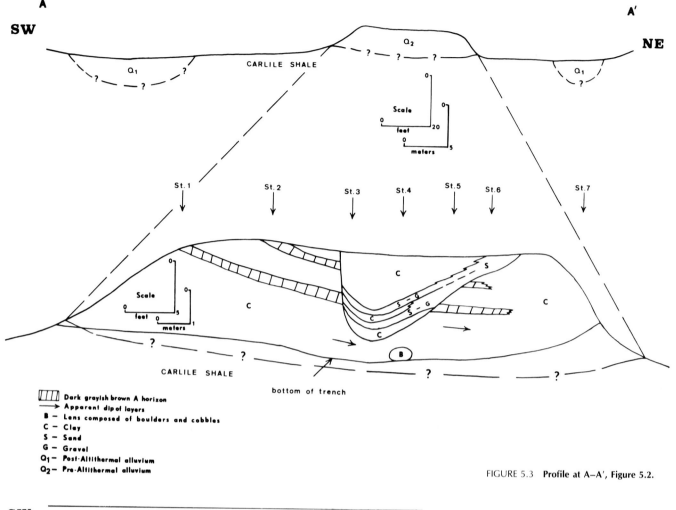

A   A'

SW

NE

Q₂

Q₁   CARLILE SHALE   ?   ?   ?   Q₁
?   ?   ?
?   ?   ?

Scale

0   0
feet   20
0
meters   5

St.1   St.2   St.3   St.4   St.5 St.6   St.7

Scale

0   0
feet   5
0
meters   1

C   S
S   C
S – G
S – G
C   C
C

C

?   B

CARLILE SHALE   ?   ?

bottom of trench

⊞ Dark grayish brown A horizon
→ Apparent dip of layers
B – Lens composed of boulders and cobbles
C – Clay
S – Sand
G – Gravel
Q₁ – Post-Altithermal alluvium
Q₂ – Pre-Altithermal alluvium

FIGURE 5.3   Profile at A–A', Figure 5.2.

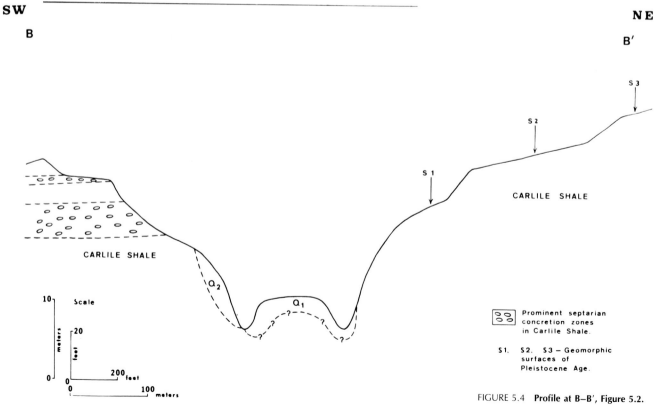

SW   NE

B   B'

S 3

S 2

S 1

CARLILE SHALE

CARLILE SHALE

Q₂

Q₁

?   ?   ?   ?

Scale

10

20
0
feet

200 feet
0
0   100 meters

⊙⊙ Prominent septarian
    concretion zones
    in Carlile Shale.

S1, S2, S3 – Geomorphic
    surfaces of
    Pleistocene Age.

FIGURE 5.4   Profile at B–B', Figure 5.2.

The fifth-order ephemeral stream that drains Moss Agate Arroyo empties into the north fork of Moss Agate Creek at a point 3.66 km (2.27 miles) southeast of the Agate Basin site. The north fork of Moss Agate Creek in turn empties into a drainage system that joins the Cheyenne River at a point in South Dakota 11.3 km (7 miles) northeast of the Agate Basin site. The Cheyenne River is the master stream within this portion of Wyoming and South Dakota. It drains to the southeast.

The Moss Agate Arroyo drainage system flows to the southeast, whereas the north fork of Moss Agate Creek drains to the northeast. Both of these drainage directions are at nearly right angles to the southwest dip of regional bedrock. The drainage courses of third- or higher-order stream channels are arranged in a rectangular pattern. The predominant orientation of these streams is N 38° W ± 14.5° (N = 35); the secondary direction is N 68° E ± 8.7° (N = 13). The rectangular stream pattern is evident along the fifth-order stream that drains Moss Agate Arroyo (Figures 1.4 and 5.1). Its channel drains S 50° E from the Agate Basin site for a distance of .91 km (.6 mile). At this point the stream channel abruptly changes direction to N 80° E, a direction it maintains until the junction with Sheaman Draw, a distance of .7 km (.45 mile). The rectangular stream pattern is herein attributed to structural control by a regional bedrock joint system. Additional evidence for joint control of stream courses is the direct alignment of the heads of third- or higher-order streams that are on the opposite sides of the same gravel-capped drainage divide. This widespread drainage pattern is very evident on U.S. Geological Survey 7.5 minute topographic maps of Twentyone Divide quadrangle and Mule Creek SE quadrangle, both of which straddle the Wyoming–South Dakota boundary. The Agate Basin site is located on the Mule Creek SE quadrangle map.

The Paleoindian cultural horizons at the Agate Basin and Brewster sites are encased in a perched, alluvial channel fill deposit (hereafter called the Q_2 unit) that parallels and lies southwest of Moss Agate Arroyo. The alluvium lies within an arroyo-like depression herein called the Q_2 paleochannel. The Q_2 paleochannel parallels Moss Agate Arroyo for a downstream distance from the Brewster site of 1 km (.6 mile), at which point it merges into the modern valley of Moss Agate Creek. A soil horizon associated with the Agate Basil cultural horizon is present within the sediments of the Q_2 unit. This soil horizon can be identified to the southeast of the Agate Basin site for a distance of 1 km (.6 mile). Over this distance, the gradient on top of the Agate Basin soil horizon is .0156. The sinuosity factor of the Q_2 paleochannel along the same horizontal interval is 1.51.

Strictly speaking, the gradient on top of the Agate Basin soil horizon is not a stream gradient but more closely corresponds to the gradient of the bank (valley slope) that bordered the stream. There can be a divergence between the valley slope and stream gradients, particularly if the sediment load contains a high silt–clay content (which is the situation in the Agate Basin area). In channels with a high silt–clay content the valley slope is three times that of the channel gradient (Schumm 1977:112). Thus the stream gradient adjacent to the surface on which the Agate Basin soil formed was probably less than .0156. The gradient along the parallel portion of the modern channel of Moss Agate Creek is .028, and the sinuosity factor is 1.15. The modern channel of Sheaman Draw

FIGURE 5.5   Locations of channel gradient measurements.

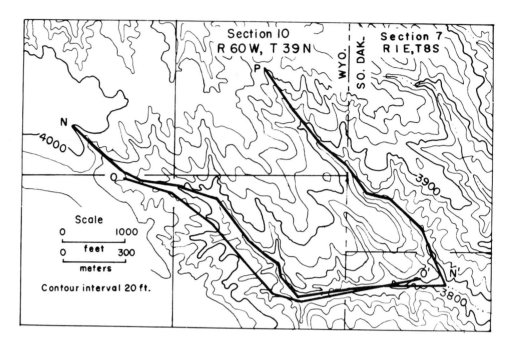

has a gradient of .04 and a sinuosity factor of 1.23 for a distance of 1 km (.6 mile) downstream from the Sheaman site. In all probability, the stream that drained the Q_2 paleochannel had a lower gradient and was more sinuous than the modern streams in the same area (see Figures 5.5 and 5.6).

In cross section, the Q_2 channel has the outline of an arroyo. In the thickest preserved portions of the channel, the observed angle of contact between the

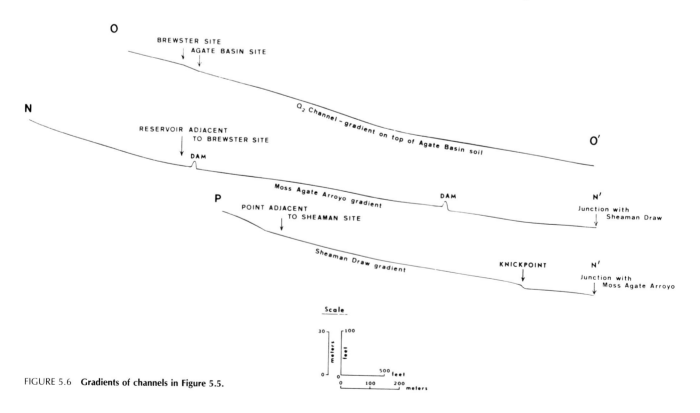

FIGURE 5.6   Gradients of channels in Figure 5.5.

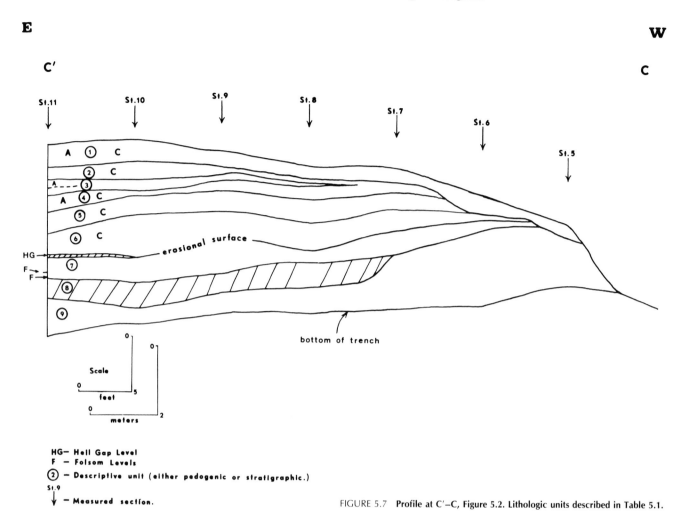

E   W

C′   C

FIGURE 5.7   Profile at C′–C, Figure 5.2. Lithologic units described in Table 5.1.

HG— Hell Gap Level
F — Folsom Levels
② — Descriptive unit (either pedogenic or stratigraphic.)
St.9
↓ — Measured section.

channel fill and the Carlile shale decreases from 60–70° in the highest reaches of the channel wall to 12° in the lowest observed portions of the channel wall. The maximum observed thickness of the Q_2 unit is 7.62 m (25 feet). This was observed in a trench excavated at the Brewster site (Figure 5.8). The bottom of the Q_2 unit was not exposed in the trench and it is estimated that a 1.5 m (5 foot) thickness of Quaternary sediment lies below the deepest portion of the trench. The preserved width of the Q_2 paleochannel varies from 37 m (120 feet) at the Agate Basin site to 70 m (230 feet) at the junction of Sheaman Draw and Moss Agate Creek. Between the Brewster site and a Q_2 channel remnant located 192 m (630 feet) to the northwest, at the position of cross section A–A′ (Figure 5.3), the gradient on top of the soil horizon that contained Folsom artifacts is .038. The gradient along the modern stream channel between the two aforementioned locales is .041. The preserved width of the Q_2 paleochannel at the position of cross section A–A′ is 17 m (55 feet). However, inspection of cross section A–A′ shows that only the southwest side of the original Q_2 paleochannel is still preserved. In all probability the original width of the Q_2 channel at the locale of cross section A–A′ was 30 m (100 feet). At the Agate Basin site, the Q_2 paleochannel, at the time of Folsom occupation, was probably 7.6 m (25 feet) deep

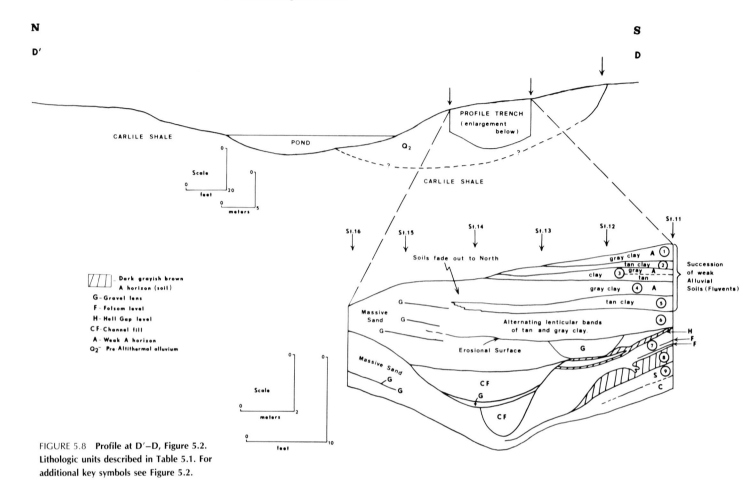

FIGURE 5.8 Profile at D'−D, Figure 5.2.
Lithologic units described in Table 5.1. For
additional key symbols see Figure 5.2.

and 37 m (120 feet) wide; its walls were steep and the arroyo floor was essentially flat. This situation contrasts with the modern setting at the Agate Basin-Brewster site area. Whereas the 7.6 m (25 foot) depth of the modern draw of Moss Agate Arroyo at the Agate Basin site is nearly the same as the thickness of the Q_2 unit, the width of the modern depression is nearly twice that of the ancient arroyo. This situation is evident on cross section D'−D (Figure 5.8).

Another possible difference between the modern and ancient drainage systems is the general lack of evidence of tributaries to the Q_2 paleochannel. The modern fifth-order stream has numerous tributaries, whereas only three were identified for the Q_2 paleochannel. Admittedly, this may reflect a lack of geologic preservation for some of the tributaries to the Q_2 channel. The sediment pattern in the upper portion of the Q_2 unit at the Agate Basin site suggests the possibility of a tributary stream emptying sandy sediment into the main channel, though no mappable evidence of a tributary presently exists (see Figure 5.8). The arkosic sands within the Q_2 channel also argue for the presence of some former tributaries, as these materials had to have been carried down from the higher elevations adjacent to the main drainage divide.

That portion of the Q_2 paleochannel that lies outside the modern fifth-order stream channel was probably abandoned as an active channel in late Altithermal time (4500–7000 years B.P.). This is suggested by the presence of Early Archaic style projectile points within sediments located at the top of the

Q_2 channel plus the development of the late Altithermal soil (see Reider, this chapter, Section 2) on the sediments filling the Q_2 paleochannel. The modern channel of Moss Agate Creek crosses the Q_2 paleochannel in the vicinity of the Brewster site (Figures 5.1 and 5.2). This situation suggests that the stream course that occupied the Q_2 channel was abandoned as a result of stream piracy. The modern fifth-order stream apparently eroded headward from a point just west of the Wyoming–South Dakota state line and eventually cut through the Q_2 paleochannel. This resulted in abandonment of the Q_2 paleochannel and the creation of a new hydraulic base level for the fifth-order drainage basin. The development and headward migration of the modern fifth-order stream probably resulted from a drop in the regional water table. Haynes (1968) has postulated a gradual regional lowering of the ground water table in the western United States during Holocene time and a resultant incision of stream channels. A change in soil types within the Q_2 channel also suggests a lowering of the water table in post-Pleistocene time (Reider, this chapter, Section 2). A modern example of a dramatic change in stream character is present within the study area. An earth-filled dam was constructed across Moss Agate Arroyo in 1963 (Tom Beebe, personal communication). This dam is just east of the Wyoming–South Dakota line (Figure 5.2). A marked contrast in sinuosity (Figure 5.2) and channel depth is seen on both sides of the dam. Immediately downstream from the dam, the modern stream channel has a sinuosity of 2.7 over a horizontal distance of 137 m (450 feet). Downstream from this point, the stream channel straightens and has a sinuosity figure of 1.25. This compares with a 1.15 sinuosity for that portion of the stream channel upstream from the dam. Downstream from the dam the modern stream channel is 3 m (9 feet) deep and is bounded by near-vertical walls. Upstream from the dam, in contrast, the channel is shallow (slopes of 4–8°) and grass covered, and marked by occasional minor knickpoints .3–1 m (1–3 feet) high. Deep channel incision has taken place along Sheaman Draw for a distance of 229 m (750 feet) upstream from its junction with the main fifth-order stream. This deep channel abruptly terminates at a knickpoint 3 m (9 feet) high. Upstream from this knickpoint, the channel is also shallow, grass covered, and marked by occasional minor knickpoints. The setting described appears to have developed after the earthen dam was built in 1963. The pond behind the dam retained normal floodwaters, which contain a high bed load of silt and sand. Those waters that did move over the dam's spillway would probably have carried a bed load lower than that of normal floodwaters and would consequently have been more erosive and able to cut a deep channel. A decrease in bed load will result in higher stream sinuosity (Schumm 1977:177). This type of reaction to lower bed load content might explain the marked increase in channel sinuosity immediately downstream from the dam. The impoundment of floodwaters behind the dam would also result in a decrease in moisture content of the channel sediment downstream from the dam. This "drying out" process would have contributed to the ability of the stream to incise a deep channel. This scenario is hypothetical, as hydrologic data are not available for Moss Agate Arroyo. The fluvial event or series of events that created the anomalous change in sinuosity and channel incision downstream from the dam must have occurred sometime between 1963, the time the dam was built, and July 1973. Aerial photographs taken in July 1973 display the same channel features, in the same locations and with the same dimensions, as were mapped by plane table in the fall of 1979 (Figure 5.2). There has been no observable lateral movement or headward erosion along the channel during the past 8 years. The development of the presently incised channel is an example of the exceeding of the extrinsic threshold as defined by Schumm (1977:7).

QUATERNARY SEDIMENTS   A brief discussion of the arkosic Pleistocene sediments and Holocene colluvium has already been presented and will not be repeated. The main item in this discussion will be the description of the sediments that occupy the modern alluvial channels and the Q_2 paleochannel.

A total of 12 cross sections (Figure 5.3, 5.4, 5.7–5.16) are reproduced here. The cross sections show the overall spatial relationship between various sedimentary and pedogenic units. The position of the cross sections are shown in Figure 5.2. A number of stratigraphic sections were measured in the field, along the line of each cross section. The location of each measured section is shown on its respective cross section.

The alluvial deposits are divided into two main units, Q_1 and Q_2. Unit Q_1 comprises the ephemeral stream deposits that occupy the modern stream channels. These sediments are of post-Altithermal age. Unit Q_2 was defined previously.

The sediments within the Q_1 and Q_2 units are all derived from older rocks located within the fifth-order drainage basin. Clay (which ranges in clastic content from silty to sandy clay) and sand are the predominant constituents of the Q_1 and Q_2 units. The clay mineralogy is described by Reider (this chapter, Section 2). Essentially all of the clay and silt and much of the sand were derived from the Carlile shale. The Carlile is a dark gray, marine shale with silty–sandy shale zones and lenticular interbeds of sandstone. Sandstone lenses 1.5–3.0 m (5–10 feet) thick are exposed at the crests of ridges located in the eastern portion of the study area. Septarian concretion zones are also a prominent feature within the Carlile shale. The concretions vary in length from 30 to 60 cm (1 to 2 feet) and are composed primarily of calcite and calcareous siltstone. Broken concretion fragments of siltstone are abundant within some channel fill deposits. Two prominent concretion zones are well exposed immediately south of the Agate Basin–Brewster site area. Granite cobbles and boulders as well as arkosic sands are also present in the Q_2 unit. These materials are derived from the previously described Pleistocene deposits which lie on the northwest side of the valley of Moss Agate Arroyo. (For a detailed description of the lithology of the Q_2 unit, see Table 5.1).

The sediments in both Q_1 and Q_2 units are poorly sorted. Evidence for this consists of the mechanical grain size analyses presented by Reider in this volume, plus field observations. Layers of clay with randomly distributed inclusions of coarse-grained clasts are a common occurrence, as are individual beds composed of mixed sand, silt, and clay. Graded stratification characterized by an upward decrease in grain size within a given bed, though common in most fluvial deposits, was observed only rarely within the exposures present in site excavations or backhoe trenches.

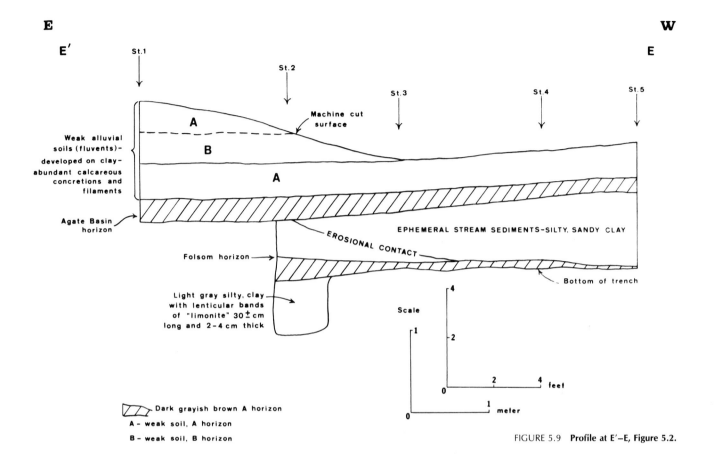

E   W

E'   E

St.1   St.2   St.3   St.4   St.5

A

Machine cut surface

Weak alluvial soils (fluvents)- developed on clay- abundant calcareous concretions and filaments

B

A

Agate Basin horizon

EPHEMERAL STREAM SEDIMENTS-SILTY, SANDY CLAY

EROSIONAL CONTACT

Folsom horizon

Bottom of trench

Light gray silty, clay with lenticular bands of "limonite" 30±cm long and 2-4 cm thick

Scale

4

1

2

2

0

2   4   feet

0

1   meter

Dark grayish brown A horizon
A – weak soil, A horizon
B – weak soil, B horizon

FIGURE 5.9   Profile at E'–E, Figure 5.2.

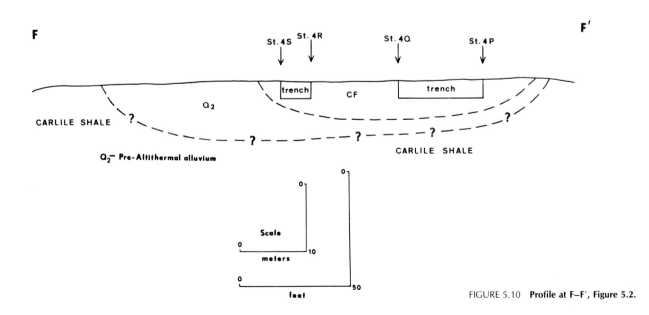

NW   SE

F   St.4S St.4R   St.4Q   St.4P   F'

trench   CF   trench

CARLILE SHALE   ?   Q₂

Q₂– Pre-Altithermal alluvium

?   ?   ?   ?   ?

CARLILE SHALE

Scale

0

0

0

0   10

meters

0   50

feet

FIGURE 5.10   Profile at F–F', Figure 5.2.

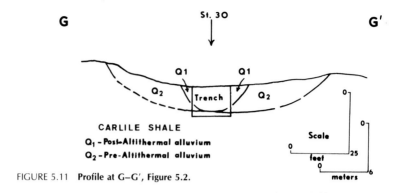

SW
NE

FIGURE 5.11   Profile at G–G', Figure 5.2.

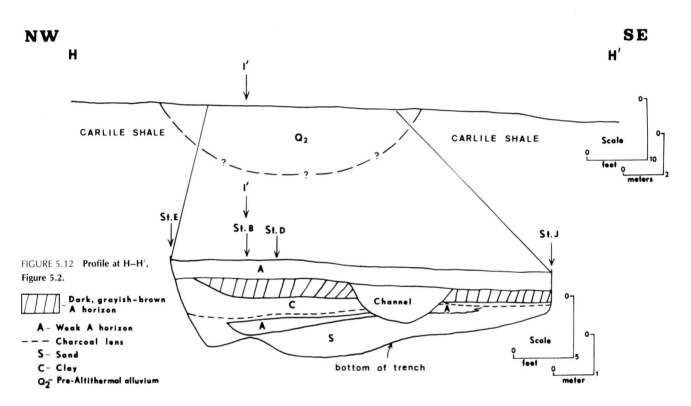

NW
SE

FIGURE 5.12   Profile at H–H', Figure 5.2.

[//]: # (legend)
▨ – Dark, grayish–brown
      A horizon

A – Weak A horizon

– – – Charcoal lens

S – Sand

C – Clay

Q₂ – Pre-Altithermal alluvium

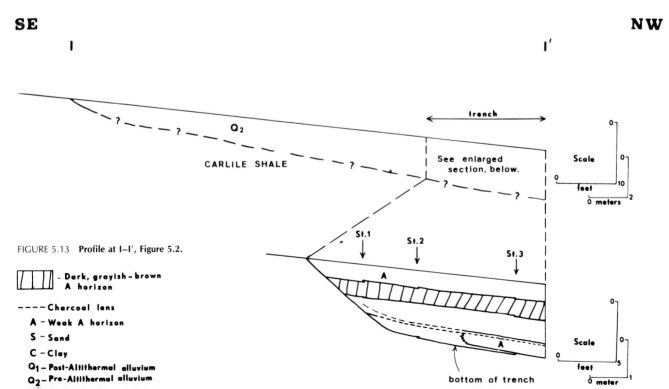

SE
NW

FIGURE 5.13   Profile at I–I', Figure 5.2.

▨ – Dark, grayish–brown
      A horizon

– – – – Charcoal lens

A – Weak A horizon

S – Sand

C – Clay

Q₁ – Post-Altithermal alluvium

Q₂ – Pre-Altithermal alluvium

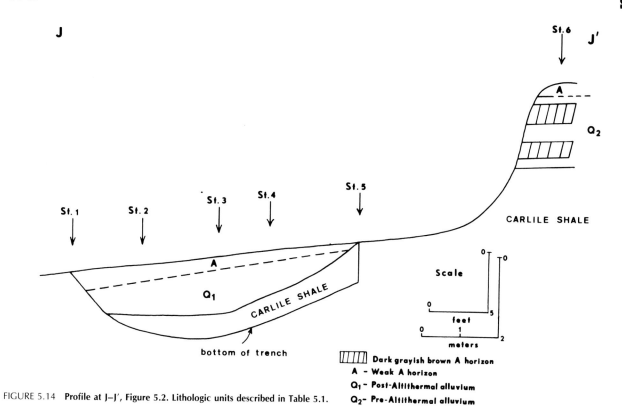

NW

J

SE

St. 6
J'

A

Q₂

CARLILE SHALE

St. 1   St. 2   St. 3   St. 4   St. 5

A

Q₁

CARLILE SHALE

bottom of trench

Scale

feet

meters

Dark grayish brown A horizon
A – Weak A horizon
Q₁– Post-Altithermal alluvium
Q₂– Pre-Altithermal alluvium

FIGURE 5.14   Profile at J–J′, Figure 5.2. Lithologic units described in Table 5.1.

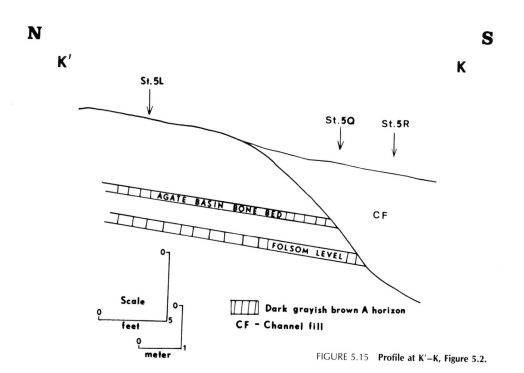

N

S

K'

K

St. 5L

St. 5Q   St. 5R

AGATE BASIN BONE BED

CF

FOLSOM LEVEL

Scale

feet

meter

Dark grayish brown A horizon
CF – Channel fill

FIGURE 5.15   Profile at K′–K, Figure 5.2.

[323]

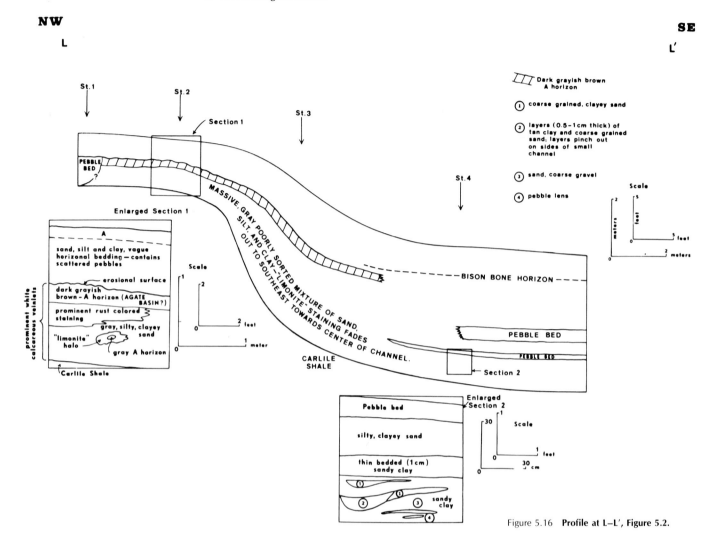

Figure 5.16   **Profile at L–L', Figure 5.2.**

The poor sorting present in most of the sediments within the study area probably results from the fact that all of the sediments are locally derived and have been transported very short distances. The upstream distance from the Agate Basin site to the head of the Q_2 paleochannel could not have exceeded 518 m (1700 feet), as this is the distance of the site from the present edge of the drainage divide that borders the fifth-order valley on the northeast (Figures 1.3 and 5.1).

The sand grains and coarse granitic clasts within the sediments of the Q_1 and Q_2 units are rounded to well rounded. This derives from the fact that most of the sand grains and coarser-grained fractions have been recycled from older sediments. The quartz sands are mainly derived from the mature sandstones of the Upper Cretaceous Carlile Shale; the pebbles, cobbles, and boulders composed of granite are derived from Pleistocene alluvial deposits. The only angular clasts of note are broken septarian concretion fragments composed of calcareous siltstone. These fragments tend to be very angular and are abundant in portions of the Q_2 unit. Weathered, septarian concretions readily break along natural lines of weakness and are subsequently transported downslope by erosional

TABLE 5.1

Field Descriptions of Selected Stratigraphic Sections in the General Agate Basin Site Area

Unit	Bed	Description	Thickness (cm)
		Measured section located at station 3, cross section J-J' (Figure 5.14).	
		Section starts at surface and is measured downward.	
Q₁	4	A horizon of modern azonal soil, light gray, sandy, calcareous.	30.4
	3	Alluvial channel deposit—entire bed is composed of lenticular, horizontal bands of sand. Bands are 6–8 cm thick and 90–155 cm long. Some bands contain "hint" of laminae 1–2 mm thick. Most sand within the bed is coarse to very coarse grained, though some very fine grained sand lenses are present. Most bands contain 5% gray tabular, fissile shale fragments derived from the Carlile shale. The broad surfaces of the shale flakes are parallel to bedding planes. Angular to subangular septarian concretion fragments (pebble size) are randomly distributed throughout the entire bed. There is no apparent increase of pebble concentration in the basal portion of the bed. Septarian concretion fragments constitute 6% of the bed. A few elongate, 2-cm-long, rounded white quartz pebbles are present. Three coarse-grained sand lenses do contain a concentration of pebbles.	134.1
	2	Clay, gray, sandy, massive.	30.0
	1	Carlile shale bedrock. Shale is altered, has "gummy" appearance.	30.0
		Measured section at Agate Basin site, in center of main excavation area. Plane table stadia station 5L. Measured at N 085, W 025 (Figures 1.12 and 5.15)ᵃ	
		Section starts at surface	
Q₂	7	Surface soil, a horizon, light gray, composed of clay; very calcareous, contains few scattered coarse quartz grains (.5–1 mm), also abundant root fibers and fiber-size root molds. (.1 mm wide). Bed is composed of colluvium, massive appearance.	33.5
		Beds 7 and 6 are separated by erosional surface.	
	6	Pebble zone; poorly sorted mixture of light gray, silty, calcareous clay and elongate, rounded pebbles, no apparent stratification. Coarse fraction composes about 25% of bed and consists of a mixture of light gray silty shale fragments; "clusters" (5–10 mm long) of fine-grained sand, rounded, well sorted; few red hematitic siltstone fragments (10 mm long), isolated quartz and red granite pebbles 3–4 mm long. Some pebbles are coated with white, amorphous-appearing CaCO₃ and CaSO₄ (?). Some 1–2 mm-long, noncalcareous crystalline clusters in clay fraction. Sample contains about 7% quartz sand grains, very fine to fine grained. The grains are randomly distributed as isolated grains or as clusters of contiguous sand grains. Bed has light yellow, "rusty" mottling.	3.0
	5	Clay, light gray, slightly silty, slightly calcareous, massive appearance; contains abundant plant fiber molds (.2–.5 mm wide); about 5% of bed consists of white gypsiferous (?) veinlets and round crystalline clusters (1–5 mm long). Some gypsum (?) veinlets form a network of 5–10 mm-long, "parallelograms," probably ped surfaces. Tabular pieces of charcoal (.10–.5 mm long) are scattered throughout the bed and constitute less than 1% of bed. Bed is a buried paleosol horizon.	36.0
	4	Horizontally banded bed composed of light gray, calcareous clay. Some clay is slightly sandy. Bands are 2.5–20 cm thick and undulate slightly. Bed contains abundant white, noncalcareous veinlets, .2–.4 mm wide and 2–5 mm long, abundant fiber root molds, (.2 mm wide-5 mm long). Some elongate white crystalline "concretions" (1–3 mm long) are scattered throughout the clay. A 1 cm-thick, slightly undulating to horizontal pebble layer lies 63.5 cm below top of bed.	97.5

(continued)

TABLE 5.1 (Continued)

Unit	Bed	Description	Thickness (cm)
		A 1 cm-thick horizontal layer that contains charcoal fragments, a few rounded, .5 mm-long granite pebbles, and chert debitage lies 18 cm above the base of the bed. The charcoal fragments range from .1 to 2 mm in length but some large 5–10 mm-long pieces of charcoal are also present.	

Descriptions of samples in Bed 4 examined under the binocular microscope follow:

Interval from top of Bed 4 (cm)

0–4		Clay, light gray, calcareous, slightly silty, abundant gypsum (?) veinlets (.2–.4 mm wide, 2–5 mm long); abundant plant fiber molds (.2 mm wide, 2–5 mm long); some crystalline sypsum (?) masses (1–3 mm long).	
23–30		Clay, light gray, slightly silty, trace of fine-size quartz sand grains. Approximately 1% of sample consists of scattered fine to medium, well-rounded quartz sand grains. Some irregularly shaped crystalline gypsum (?) "masses" (2 mm long). Few plant fiber molds (.1 mm wide); few medium-size, rounded grains of granite.	
47–58		Clay, medium tannish gray, abundant plant fiber molds (.2 mm wide, 1–2 mm long). Some white, gypsum (?) "inclusions" (2–3 mm long); trace of very fine sand grains.	
74–82		Clay, light gray, slightly silty, full of fiber root molds (.2 mm wide, 1–5 mm long). Isolated white crystalline gypsum (?) masses (1–5 mm long) comprise about 3% of sample. A few (rare), 1–2 mm-long fragments of charcoal were observed.	
93–97.5		Clay, medium gray, slightly silty; contains abundant charcoal grains (.1–2 mm long); some are irregular in shape and some are elongate; charcoal about 1% of sample and irregularly distributed. Elongate masses of crystalline gypsum (?) (.5–1 mm wide and 1–5 mm long) and white gypsum (?) veinlets are abundant; plant fiber molds (.1–.2 mm wide) are present.	

A near-horizontal, undulating erosional surface with 15–30 cm of relief (from "trough" to "crest") separates Beds 4 and 3.

| | 3 | This bed is the Agate Basin paleosol that contains the Agate Basin archaeological, cultural horizon. It has a massive appearance and is composed of brownish black clay, silty, slightly calcerous with prominent white, amorphous-appearing, noncalcareous "caliche" veinlets and irregularly shaped masses (1–2 mm long) of gypsum (?). The white "caliche" veinlets and gypsum (?) masses comprise about 10% of the bed. Scattered charcoal grains (.1–1 mm long) comprise less than 1% of bed. Trace of isolated fine-grained quartz grains. Root molds (.2–1 mm wide, 2–3 mm long) are abundant (about 5%). | 13–28 |

Descriptions of samples in Bed 3 examined under the binocular microscope follow:

TABLE 5.1 (Continued)

Unit	Bed	Description	Thickness (cm)
		Interval from top of Bed 3 (cm)	
		11–18 Clay, light grayish tan, 20–30% silt content, few scattered, isolated, subangular, coarse quartz grains. White, elongate, slightly calcareous, isolated "caliche" masses (1–5 mm long) comprise about 3% of sample. Root fiber molds (.2 mm wide) comprise about 2% of sample.	
		30–36 Clay, light tannish gray, silty; contains less than 1% isolated, white "caliche" masses (1–2 mm long); contains scattered fiber root molds; trace of .1 mm-long charcoal flecks; one piece of granite, rounded, elongate, 5 mm long.	
		The contact between Beds 3 and 2 is not sharp but gradational over about 3 cm. It is a pedogenic contact.	
	2	Clay, light tan, massive with caliche veinlets. Contains bone fragments and charcoal grains.	46
		Descriptions of samples in Bed 2 examined under the binocular microscope follow:	
		Interval from top of Bed 2 (cm)	
		11–17 Clay, light tan, silty (20–30%); contains few randomly scattered, coarse, angular quartz grains; contains about 2% root fiber molds (.2 mm wide). Isolated white elongate masses (1–5 mm long) of "caliche" comprise about 3% of sample.	
		30–35 Clay, light tannish gray, silty; about 1% white "caliche" masses (1–2 mm long); sample does not react to acid; contains scattered fiber root molds, trace of .1 mm-long charcoal granules; elongate granite pebble (5 mm long).	
		Beds 2 and 1 are separated by undulating contact surface with 8 cm of relief.	
	1	Folsom soil horizon; contains artifacts. Clay, dark brownish gray, slightly silty, massive; slight reaction to acid; trace of elongate to round charcoal grains (.2–1 mm long); contains less than 1% white claiche masses (1–2 mm long) on broken surface; some noncalcareous caliche masses have crystalline appearance; some masses contain vugs (.1 mm diameter) lined with microcrystals.	15–26
		Measured section in Brewster site area located at stadia station 11 on cross sections C–C′ and D′–D (Figure 5.8).	
		Section starts 2.77 m below ground surface. All descriptions are from field notes.	
Q₂	4	Top of bed coincides with Hell Gap cultural level. Bed is composed primarily of sand, light tan, fine-grained, silty, clayey (clay content increases from base of bed to top). Bed is composed of alternating horizontal lenses .6–8 cm wide and 60–91 cm long. Some bands are slightly undulating; contact between lenses is vague in places. Some bands are gray and others contain gray "streaks." An isolated bison bone occurs 7.5 cm from the base of the bed.	67
		Contact between Beds 4 and 3 is indistinct and changes laterally.	
	3	Top of bed coincides with the top of the Folsom soil. The Folsom cultural level lies at the top of Bed 3. The bed embraces the A	51

(continued)

TABLE 5.1 (Continued)

Unit	Bed	Description	Thickness (cm)
		horizon of the Folsom paleosol and is dark brownish gray to black. It is composed of silty to sandy clay that is horizontally banded. Individual clay bands are lenticular.	
		The succession of observed bands at the point of measured section follows:	

Band thickness from top of Bed 3 (cm)

.6	Clay, black
5	Clay, brownish gray
2.5	Clay, black
7.6	Clay, brownish gray
1.25	Clay, black
5	Sand, grayish tan, fine grained, clayey, massive; contains caliche nodules
30	Clay, silty, black, about 15% of layer randomly distributed "caliche" nodules (2–5 mm long)

Unit	Bed	Description	Thickness (cm)
		Base of Bed 3 coincides with base of A horizon of Folsom paleosol.	
	2	Sand, light tan, fine grained, clayey, massive light-rust-colored mottling.	46
		Vague contact between Beds 2 and 1.	
	1	Clay, light gray; bed composed of horizontal lenses 5–13 cm thick and 50–122 cm long; contact between some lenses is vague.	59
		Randomly distributed rust-colored (limonitic ?) streaks within some bands; altered, rust-colored concretion fragments are horizontally distributed; some are nearly altered to clay. "Caliche" nodules (2–3 mm long) are abundant and randomly distributed.	
		The bottom of the trench did not reach Carlile shale bedrock.	

[a]This section is indurated with white calcareous and noncalcareous salts. These minerals are the Cca horizon of the Altithermal soil.

processes. The concretion fragments observed in the Q_1 and Q_2 units display only minor signs of abrasion.

Q_1 Unit

The Q_1 unit is well exposed in the deep incised gully along the southern portion of Sheaman Draw. It was also exposed in two backhoe trenches, the positions of which are shown on cross sections G–G' (Figure 5.11), and J–J' (Figure 5.14). This unit was deposited under an ephemeral stream regime in post-Altithermal time. The lithology and stratification within this unit were not studied in detail but were observed. These features are similar to those observed in the upper portion of the Q_2 unit. The maximum observed thickness of the Q_1 unit is 3 m (9 feet), though thicker deposits undoubtedly exist. The areal distribution of the Q_1 unit is shown in Figure 5.2.

Q_2 Unit

The maximum observed thickness of the Q_2 unit is 7.6 m (25 feet). This areal distribution of the unit is shown in Figure 5.2. Inspection of the cross sections shows that the Q_2 unit can be divided into two main subunits. The older unit contains the Paleoindian cultural horizons. The stratification within the lower subunit is characterized by abundant examples of planar, horizontal bedding. The most prominent type is lenticular stratification (Picard and High 1973:150). At the Agate Basin site, individual beds range from 30 to 70 cm in thickness. These beds are commonly composed of horizontal to slightly undulating bands that are .5–1.5 cm thick and .5–3 m long. The bands are usually composed of silty to sandy clay. Bands composed of sand with the same dimensions are commonly interlayered between the clay bands. This type of stratification occurs in beds that are composed predominantly of coarse clastics. One such 55-cm thick bed is present 30 cm above the Agate Basin cultural horizon at the Agate Basin site. It consists primarily of lenses of angular septarian concretion fragments 1–3 cm long. Some coarse-grained quartz sand lenses are interlayered with the septarian lenses in the central portion of the unit. Horizontal beds (.3–1 m thick) with a massive, nonbanded appearance are nearly as abundant within the Q_2 unit as those that are banded. On close inspection some of the massive beds contain a vague horizontal banding. The massive beds are composed of silty clay or sand and in places mixtures of both.

Horizontal, discontinuous stratification (Picard and High 1973:147) is also present in the basal subunit of Q_2 but is much more limited in occurrence. Within beds of this type, individual strata vary from 2 to 3 mm in thickness and 5–25 cm in length. The horizontal, discontinuous stratification occurs primarily in sandy units but was observed in clay beds with a high silt–sand content. A few minor examples of micro cross-lamination were noted at the top of some horizontal, discontinuous stratification units.

An occurrence unusual for the study area was noted in the basal portion of the Q_2 unit in a backhoe trench depicted in cross section A′–A′ (Figure 5.3). A bar composed of mixed granite and sandstone cobbles (10–20 cm in length) is encased in a 1.5-m thick unit composed of sandy clay. The bar is convex upward, 36 cm high and 60 cm wide at the base. Partially composed of some nearly boulder-size clasts, the bar obviously formed in a high-velocity stream regime.

Lenticular stratification is developed in shifting and fluctuating sedimentary regimes. Horizontal, discontinuous stratification is indicative of deposition by high-velocity currents (Picard and High 1973). The basal subunit was deposited under an ephemeral stream regime of fluctuating hydraulic environments including episodes of high-velocity deposition. Periods of nondeposition are marked by the presence of well-developed paleosols.

Three prominent soils are associated with the Clovis, Folsom, and Agate Basin–Hell Gap cultural horizons. Reider (this chapter, Section 2), has described these soils and has interpreted the Clovis soil as a gley soil that formed in a water-saturated environment under cool climatic conditions. The Folsom and Agate Basin–Hell Gap soil horizons developed above the water table under increasingly drier and probably warmer conditions. The vertical interval between the Folsom and Agate Basin–Hell Gap soils in the Agate Basin–Brewster site area varies between .82 and 1.22 m (2.7 and 4 feet) and decreases in a downstream direction.

The Agate Basin and Folsom soils are widespread within the basal subunit of the Q_2 unit. They can be recognized in most of the cross sections where both are present. The Clovis soil is the most restricted and has been identified only at the Sheaman and Agate Basin site locales. In some cases only one of the late Pleistocene soils is present within a local area, and then identification becomes a problem.

The presence of the aforementioned soils indicates that periods of stability and nondeposition intervened between periods of sedimentation. The fact that the soils were not destroyed by fluvial channel scouring also suggests that a moderate hydraulic regime predominated throughout most of the sedimentation period of the basal subunit of the Q_2 unit even though episodes of deposition under a high velocity regime did take place (e.g. cobble bars).

The fluvial regime of the basal subunit was brought to an abrupt close sometime after the formation of the Agate Basin–Hell Gap soil approximately 10,000 years B.P. At this time a prolonged episode of stream cutting and filling was inaugurated. These cut-and-fill sequences are evident on most of the cross sections and constitute the upper subunit of the Q_2 unit. On cross section D′–D (Figure 5.8), at least four episodes of cut and fill can be recognized within the upper subunit. Channel fill sediments consist of alternating lenticular clay and sand lenses, which vary from .2 to 1.5 m in thickness. Thin gravel lenses about 5 cm thick and .3–2 m long are a common sedimentary feature within the thicker sandy clay or sand units. Most sediments within the upper subunit are poorly sorted. Channel beds generally have a massive appearance, though beds about 60 cm thick composed of interlayered lenses of sand and gravel 2–10 cm thick are not uncommon.

A succession of three weak alluvial soils can be recognized within the upper subunit at the Brewster site. Apparently periods of nondeposition were long enough for weak soils to develop. The major erosional episode that initiated the cut-and-fill sequence was probably caused by a climatic shift to semiarid conditions. A shift to more arid conditions is also indicated by the presence of the late Altithermal calcareous and alkaline soil (Reider, this volume), which permeates the Q_2 unit. This soil is wide-spread over the western United States (Haynes 1968). At the Hell Gap archaeological site, located in Wyoming 120 km (75 miles) southwest of the Agate Basin site, the late Altithermal soil is developed on sediment that is younger than 5740 years B.P. (Haynes 1968:608).

The sand–shale ratio within the entire Q_2 unit varies with locale rather than time. There is no pronounced gross lithologic change in a vertical direction. This situation is apparent on cross section D′–D (Figure 5.8), in which the sand content within the entire Q_2 unit increases from south to north rather than vertically. As previously mentioned, this lateral change in sand content may have resulted from prolonged contribution of sediment from a nearby tributary stream. Sediment derivation from a local source is evident at the Sheaman site, where the predominant lithology within the entire Q_2 unit is arkosic sand. This situation is not surprising, as Pleistocene sediments are located nearby in an upslope position.

In late Pleistocene time, during the Clovis occupation, it is possible that a small spring-fed stream did flow through the Q_2 channel. Minor springs currently exist along Moss Agate Arroyo, and one of them is just north of the Agate Basin site (Figure 5.2). The gleyed nature of the Clovis soil would indicate the presence of a water table at or near the surface, which in turn suggests the presence of a stream. A stream may have persisted until the time of the Agate Basin–Hell Gap occupation.

2. SOIL DEVELOPMENT AND PALEOENVIRONMENTS
richard g. reider

PURPOSE AND
METHODOLOGY

Soils of the Agate Basin site (Figures 1.3, 1.4, and 1.5) and vicinity were investigated in the field during the summers of 1978 through 1980. The emphasis of study was the morphologies and genesis of soils (Boyd 1980) formed in alluvial and/or colluvial sediments of a buried and abandoned paleoarroyo (Albanese 1977) of Moss Agate Creek. These soils are associated with Folsom, Agate Basin, and Hell Gap cultural levels at the site itself, as well as with a Clovis level at the Sheaman site nearby. Overlying soils were also studied.

The pedologic studies were undertaken so that the soils could be used as interpretive tools in paleoenvironmental reconstruction, to aid in understanding conditions prevalent during and following the Paleoindian occupation of the area. In addition, soil stratigraphy of the site itself was studied, as was the stratigraphy in upstream and downstream locations. Radiocarbon dates and artifactual materials associated with the soils have provided a time framework for reconstructing events in the late Pleistocene (the Pleistocene–Holocene boundary is considered here to be approximately 8000 B.P.).

Soil profiles were taken in three locations (Figure 2.13) and described following the methods of the Soil Conservation Service (Soil Survey Staff 1962). Samples of soil horizons were analyzed in the laboratory for the following characteristics: particle size by the hydrometer method (Bouyoucos 1927, 1962); pH using a 1:1 soil paste and an electronic pH meter; calcium carbonate equivalency (Piper 1950); percentage of organic matter (Walkley and Black 1934); and percentage of total carbon for selected horizons by combustion (total carbon analysis by Jane V. Thomas, chemist, Natural Resources Research Institute, University of Wyoming). Clay mineralogy was determined by x-ray diffraction for selected horizons.

PHYSICAL GEOGRAPHY OF
THE SITE

Moss Agate Creek and its tributaries (Figures 1.3, 1.4, and 1.5) have cut near the site into Carlile shale (Cretaceous), which in the area gently dips southwestward off the Black Hills into the Powder River Basin (Whitcomb 1965). On uplands in the local area are eolian cover sands of late Pleistocene age, which, in combination with Pleistocene or Tertiary alluvial units, have supplied sandy materials to soils and sediments formed in or deposited near the arroyo bottom at various times in the late Pleistocene and Holocene. The uplands are cuestas formed on resistant beds of the Carlile shale, and Moss Agate Creek and its tributaries have been guided along less resistant units forming numerous strike valleys.

Vegetation in the area is characterized by a sagebrush–shortgrass community represented by western wheatgrass (*Agropyron smithii*), blue grama grass (*Bouteloua gracilis*), needle-and-thread grass (*Stipa comata*), prairie sandreed grass (*Calamovilfa longifolea*), big sagebrush (*Artemisia tridentata*), and prickly pear cactus (*Opuntia sp.*) (Soil Conservation Service 1973).

The climate of the area is semiarid. Average annual precipitation is approximately 35 cm. Mean monthly temperatures range from about −7.2°C in January to 23.3°C in July (Becker and Alyea 1964a, 1964b).

THE SOIL OF CLOVIS AGE

The soil datable to Clovis time at the Agate Basin site (Figure 5.17) is a modified Wiesenboden or Low Humic or Humic Gley Soil (Baldwin *et al.* 1938; Bunting 1965; Ruhe 1970; Thorp and Smith 1949) or Haplaquoll (Soil Survey Staff 1975), which indicates impeded soil drainage along the bottom of the paleoarroyo in late Pleistocene time. This soil may exist as two or more thin soils having dark A horizons separated by weathered alluvium (B horizons), or as a thicker single soil near the site (Area 3). On a morphological and stratigraphic basis, it is traceable along arroyo cuts to a soil containing in situ Clovis materials at the Sheaman site approximately 1 km northeast of the Agate Basin site. Charcoal near the top of the A horizon of this soil at the Agate Basin site yields a date of 11,450 ± 110 years B.P. (SI-3734).

The field description for this soil as a twofold unit from the Agate Basin site is shown in Table 5.2. Laboratory data are listed in Table 5.3, and the soil's stratigraphic position is shown in Figure 5.18. As a whole, the soil contains two dark A horizons, each of which is underlain by thin grayish leached bands (A2 horizons). The black color of the A horizon suggests significant organic buildup at the soil surface during pedogenesis under impeded drainage, and the presence of grasses and sedges. However, organic matter percentages presently do not exceed 1.5% in these A horizons. This is not uncommon for buried A horizons,

FIGURE 5.17 A two-part soil of Clovis age (Area 1). The thick, dark A horizon at the top is underlain by a light-colored, leached A2 horizon, beneath which is a reddish mottled and gleyed B horizon. In turn, another dark A horizon underlies this sequence, below which is a thin, light-colored, leached A2 horizon and a strongly gleyed and mottled B horizon. Discontinuous dark and broken A horizons, which indicate periodic burial of such horizons on the arroyo bottom, occur at the base of the exposure in gleyed sediments. Rodent burrowing has subsequently mixed or altered the whole exposure. Trowel is approximately 25 cm long.

TABLE 5.2
Field Description of the Clovis-Age Soil

Location: See Figure 2.13.
Parent material: Alluvium
Elevation: 1173 m
Drainage: Well drained
Remarks: Colors and consistence under moist conditions.

A11cab   0–18 cm thickness. Dark reddish brown (5YR 2.5/2) clay loam; weak, coarse subangular blocky structure; friable consistence; common, medium, generally rounded or slightly oblong to irregularly shaped lime concretions in soft masses; violent effervescence; gradual smooth boundary.

A12cab   18–36 cm thickness. Black (5YR 2.5/1) clay loam; weak, medium to coarse subangular blocky structure; friable consistence; common, medium, generally rounded or slightly oblong to irregularly shaped lime concretions in soft masses; violent effervescence; abrupt wavy boundary.

A2cab   36–44 cm thickness. Not described.

B2ircabg   44–54 cm thickness. Brownish yellow (10YR 6/6) sandy clay loam; weak, coarse subangular blocky structure; friable consistence; few, fine, generally rounded or slightly oblong to irregularly shaped lime concretions in soft masses; common, medium, generally rounded or slightly oblong to irregularly shaped mottling in seams and soft masses; slight effervescence; abrupt wavy boundary.

A11cab   54–62 cm thickness. Very dark gray brown (2.5Y 3/2) clay loam; weak, coarse subangular blocky structure; friable consistence; common, fine, irregularly shaped lime concretions in soft masses; slight effervescence; abrupt wavy boundary.

A12cab   62–70 cm thickness. Very dark gray to black (5YR 2.5/1) clay loam; weak, coarse subangular blocky structure; very friable consistence; common, fine, irregularly shaped lime concretions in soft masses; strong effervescence; abrupt wavy boundary.

A2cab   70–73 cm thickness. Not described.

B2cabg   73–78 cm thickness. Gray brown (10YR 5/2) clay loam; weak, coarse subangular blocky structure; friable consistence; few, fine, generally rounded or slightly oblong to irregularly shaped lime concretions in soft masses; very strong effervescence; abrupt wavy boundary.

Ccabg   78–101+ cm thickness. Light gray brown to very dark gray brown (2.5Y 6/2 to 10YR 3/2) clay loam; weak, coarse subangular blocky structure; friable consistence; few, fine, generally rounded or slightly oblong to irregularly shaped lime concretions in soft masses; common, medium, irregularly shaped mottling in seams; slight effervescence on concretions to no effervescence on matrix.

TABLE 5.3
Laboratory Data for the Clovis-Age Soil

Horizon	Thickness (cm)	Percentage of sample >2 mm	Percentage of sand 2000–50 μm	Percentage of silt 50–2 μm	Percentage of clay <2 μm	pH 1:1	Percentage CaCO$_3$	Percentage of organic matter
A11cab	0–18	0	21.2	41.4	37.3	9.1	11.0	1.5
A12cab	18–36	.21	27.8	33.0	39.2	9.1	11.5	1.5
A2cab[a]	36–44	—	—	—	—	—	—	—
B2ircabg	44–54	3.08	53.4	24.3	22.3	8.8	3.0	.1
A11cab	54–62	0	34.9	35.7	29.4	8.5	3.0	.6
A12cab	62–70	0	21.7	46.6	31.7	8.5	4.5	1.1
A2cab[a]	70–73	—	—	—	—	—	—	—
B2cabg	73–78	.27	30.2	39.0	30.8	8.7	14.0	.5
Ccabg	78–101+	.12	36.6	32.7	30.7	8.3	2.0	.3

[a]Not sampled.

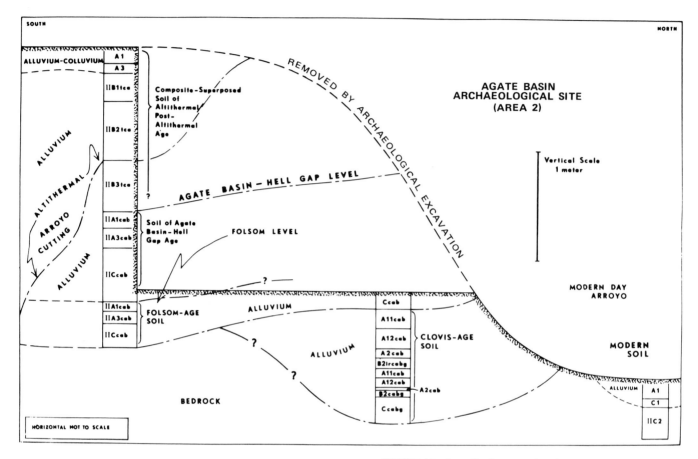

FIGURE 5.18 Generalized cross-section of soil stratigraphy at Area 2.

based on work at other archaeological sites in Wyoming by the author, and is easily explainable in view of the ephemeral character of organic matter in soils once burial occurs (Birkeland 1974).

The dark color of the A horizons at present is enhanced by carbonaceous coatings on sand grains. In an attempt to determine the fate of organic matter in the A horizons, samples were analyzed for total carbon by combustion, and this yielded organic carbon values no greater than 2.87%. The mean total carbon for A horizons of surface soils was 1.34%, and 1.94% for buried A horizons of the Clovis-age soil. It appears, then, that the A horizons of the Clovis-age soil were once rich in organic matter. Following burial the organic matter was nearly totally decomposed by microbial or other action, and it is now largely present in the form of organic coatings. The decomposition probably resulted in a loss of orrganic carbon through release of carbon dioxide.

The subsoils of the soil shown in Table 5.2 consist of mottled, ironstained, and gleyed B horizons formed in alluvium; the mottling and iron staining are stronger in the upper of the two B horizons. Below the lower B horizon, or included within it, are broken or discontinuous dark A horizons. This suggests that soil formation occurred under waterlogged conditions, and that the soil was periodically buried and formation was interrupted by sedimentation along the arroyo bottom.

TABLE 5.4
Field Description of the Folsom-Age Soil

Location:	See Figure 2.13.
Parent material:	Alluvium
Elevation:	1173 m
Drainage:	Well drained
Remarks:	Colors under moist conditions; consistence under dry conditions.

IIA1cab	0–8 cm thickness. Very dark gray brown (10YR 3/2) clay; moderate, fine to medium subangular blocky structure; friable consistence; common, fine, generally rounded or slightly oblong to irregularly shaped lime concretions in soft masses and filaments or threads; no clay films; slight effervescence; abrupt smooth boundary.
IIA3cab	8–18 cm thickness. Very dark gray brown (10YR 3/2) clay loam; moderate, fine to medium subangular blocky structure; friable consistence; common, fine, generally rounded or slightly oblong to irregularly shaped lime concretions in soft masses and filaments or threads; no clay films; slight effervescence; abrupt smooth boundary.
IICcab	18+ cm thickness. Gray brown to pinkish gray (2.5Y 5/2 to 7.5YR 6/2) silty clay; moderate, fine to medium subangular blocky structure; friable consistence; common, fine, generally rounded or slightly oblong to irregularly shaped lime concretions in soft masses and filaments or threads; no clay films; slight effervescence. Limonitic staining in coarse-textured pockets.

The soil overlying the Clovis level consists of A–C horizonation. Although it was difficult to study this soil in good exposures at the site because of disturbance from excavation, it appears to be an Alluvial Soil (Baldwin *et al.* 1938; Thorp and Smith 1949) or Fluvent (Soil Survey Staff 1975) grading toward a Humic Gley or Haplaquoll. Field and laboratory data for this soil are given in Tables 5.4 and 5.5 The soil stratigraphic position is shown in Figures 5.18 and 5.19.

The soil contains in situ Folsom materials near the top of the A horizon and thus dates to about 10,800 B.P. Being an Alluvial Soil or Fluvent, it contrasts sharply with the more strongly developed Humic Gley or Haplaquoll of Clovis age, and may signify improved drainage along the arroyo bottom during Folsom occupation. Nevertheless, localized strong mottling and weak iron staining occur in the C horizon of the soil, which may indicate some periodic, perhaps seasonal, saturation of the soil profile. Alternatively, the weaker iron oxidation and lack of gleying, as well as the absence of thick black A horizons, could be a result of a lesser time of soil formation as compared to the Clovis-age soil. In this

THE SOIL OF FOLSOM AGE

TABLE 5.5
Laboratory Data for the Folsom-Age Soil

Horizon	Thickness (cm)	Percentage of sample >2 mm	Percentage of sand 2000–50 μm	Percentage of silt 50–2 μm	Percentage of clay <2 μm	pH 1:1	Percentage CaCO$_3$	Percentage of organic matter
IIA1cab	0–8	a	20.1	34.8	45.1	7.4	1.5	.6
IIA3cab	8–18	a	22.1	47.1	30.7	7.6	1.0	.6
IICcab	18+	a	18.6	40.7	40.7	8.1	3.0	.5

*a*Not recorded.

FIGURE 5.19 **Soil exposures in Area 2. The Folsom-age soil occurs in alluvium in the bottom of the exposure at the level of the stake (obscured). Overlying this is the soil of Agate Basin–Hell Gap age, the A horizon of which is at the level of the shovel blade, which rests on an Agate Basin–Hell Gap level. Above the latter soil is a composite calcareous–saline soil of Altithermal/post-Altithermal age, which contains an argillic B horizon and an accumulation of salts and carbonates. These compounds have been superposed into underlying soils.**

case, drainage conditions along the bottom of the paleoarroyo could have been much the same as during Clovis time.

Folsom occupation of the Agate Basin site took place on the soil of Clovis age or its remnants, or on alluvial–colluvial surfaces that bury the Clovis-age soil by only a few centimeters in positions away from the arroyo bottom. In addition, Folsom occupation occurred near the top of the Alluvial Soil described here (Tables 5.4 and 5.5), which formed near the bottom of the arroyo.

The variety of surface conditions for this occupation appears to be a result of geomorphic instability between Clovis and Folsom occupations. The stratigraphic relationships and character of the soil of Folsom age suggest a drying of the climate following Clovis occupation of the area but preceding Folsom occupation. This may have been punctuated by a drop in the water table, thus resulting in improved soil drainage conditions along the arroyo bottom. A return of geomorphic stability appears to have caused shifting of the arroyo generally southward by a few meters at the site (Area 2), and the abandonment of the poorly drained arroyo of Clovis age on the north.

The soil of Agate Basin–Hell Gap age overlies the Folsom-age soil by as much as approximately 1 m and is composed of A–C horizonation. It is an Alluvial Soil or Fluvent that developed along the bottom and sides of the paleoarroyo. It contains in situ Agate Basin and Hell Gap materials in close association near the top of the IIA12cab horizon, indicating an age of about 10,000 to 10,400 B.P. for the soil. Field and laboratory data for this soil are given in Tables 5.6 and 5.7. The stratigraphic position of the soil is shown in Figures 5.18 and 5.19.

The soil of Agate Basin–Hell Gap age closely resembles the Folsom-age soil morphologically and genetically. It indicates that soil drainage near the arroyo bottom had improved compared to drainage during Clovis occupation.

The stratigraphy at the site suggests that there was marked arroyo cutting and filling following Folsom occupation but preceding Agate Basin–Hell Gap occupations. Although the stratigraphy is unclear on this point, erosion can be seen in the form of channel cuts that appear to truncate Folsom levels and in places cut deeply enough to incise the Clovis-age soil. This erosion may account for the occurrence of Folsom-age materials immediately above the in situ Folsom level at the site (Area 2).

If the stratigraphy has been correctly interpreted, the implications are that the water table dropped sufficiently between the Folsom and the Agate Basin-Hell Gap occupations to initiate a marked channel cutting and filling episode that formed in conjunction with headward erosion of the paleoarroyo. As a consequence, sediments filling this cut are composed predominantly of clayey materials derived from the Carlile shale and preexisting soils, but on occasion these sediments contain alluvial lenses of sands derived from the cover sands or other coarse units of the uplands. The assembled evidence suggests that the drying episode between the Folsom and Agate Basin–Hell Gap occupations was

THE SOIL OF AGATE BASIN–HELL GAP AGE

TABLE 5.6
Field Description of the Soil of Agate Basin–Hell Gap Age

Location: See Figure 2.13.
Parent material: Alluvium
Elevation: 1173 m
Drainage: Well drained
Remarks: Colors under moist conditions; consistence under dry conditions.

IIA1cab   0–15 cm thickness. Dark brown (10YR 3/3) clay; moderate, fine to medium subangular blocky structure; friable consistence; common, fine, generally rounded or slightly oblong or irregularly shaped lime concretions in soft masses and filaments or threads; few, thin clay films that line tubular or interstitial pores; slight effervescence; clear smooth boundary.

IIA3cab   15–33 cm thickness. Dark brown (10YR 4/3) clay; moderate, fine to medium subangular blocky structure; friable consistence; common, fine, generally rounded or slightly oblong to irregularly shaped lime concretions in soft masses and filaments or threads; no clay films; slight effervescence; clear smooth boundary.

IICcab   33–56 cm thickness. Olive brown (2.5Y 4/4) clay loam; moderate, fine to medium subangular blocky to prismatic structure; friable consistence; common, fine, generally rounded or slightly oblong to irregularly shaped lime concretions in soft masses and filaments or threads; no clay films; slight effervescence; clear smooth boundary.

TABLE 5.7
Laboratory Data for the Soil of Agate Basin–Hell Gap Age

Horizon	Thickness (cm)	Percentage of sample >2 mm	Percentage of sand 2000–50 μm	Percentage of silt 50–2 μm	Percentage of clay <2 μm	pH 1:1	Percentage CaCO₃	Percentage of organic matter
IIA1cab	0–15	*a*	12.1	32.7	55.2	7.5	1.5	.7
IIA3cab	15–33	*a*	20.5	34.6	44.8	7.6	2.0	1.0
IICcab	33–56	*a*	26.7	38.7	34.6	7.7	.5	.4

*a*Not recorded.

followed by geomorphic stability, perhaps associated with a more humid climate during Agate Basin–Hell Gap occupations. This return to geomorphic stability resulted in the formation of the Azonal Soil or Fluvent of Agate Basin–Hell Gap age.

SOILS ABOVE THE AGATE BASIN–HELL GAP LEVEL

The Agate Basin–Hell Gap level is immediately overlain by clayey alluvial sediments less than a meter to several meters in thickness at the site (Area 1 and Brewster area). Above these sediments is a major unconformity (Figure 5.18) caused by arroyo incision, which in places cuts deeply into the sediments and soils associated with Paleoindian groups. Only locally did this cutting avoid erosion of some of the late Pleistocene cultural levels, soils, and sediments. This cutting appears to be of Altithermal age and is thought to represent a significant drop in the water table brought about by the aridity of the Altithermal climate (Haynes 1968). The unconformity thus probably marks the Pleistocene–Holocene boundary.

Sediments and soils above the unconformity differ markedly from those beneath. Above, the sediments, which appear to be culturally sterile, are locally sandier and more calcareous. They contain considerable clay in some places, derived partly from the reworking of Carlile shale. Weak Alluvial Soils or Fluvents occur within the sediments, but the whole sequence is characterized by prominent accumulation of calcium carbonate and other salts. The sandier nature of these sediments was derived from incision of the paleoarroyo and its headward growth into areas containing eolian sands or other sandy units on the uplands. When the arroyo became filled with these sediments, soil formation occurred at the top of the sequence, and takes the form of a strongly developed composite soil at the modern surface near the site.

The soil composite, classed as a Ustollic Haplargid or Natrargid (Soil Survey Staff 1975) or Gray Desert Soil or Sierozem (Baldwin *et al.* 1938; Thorp and Smith 1949), is described in Tables 5.8 and 5.9. The stratigraphic position of the soil appears in Figures 5.18 and 5.19. The soil probably denotes pedogenesis that occurred once the paleoarroyo was filled with sediments, as well as pedogenesis that occurred since the time the arroyo was abandoned by renewed arroyo incision in post-Altithermal time. Thus, the soil signifies pedogenesis spanning Altithermal, Neoglacial, and modern episodes.

The strong carbonate accumulation in this soil is visually evident in the

TABLE 5.8

Field Description of Composite Soil above Agate Basin–Hell Gap Level
(Altithermal/Post-Altithermal)

Location: See Figure 2.13.
Parent material: Alluvium–colluvium 0–25 cm; alluvium 25–149 cm
Elevation: 1173 m
Drainage: Well drained
Remarks: Colors under moist conditions; consistence under dry conditions.

A1	0–15 cm thickness. Light olive brown (2.5Y 5/4) clay loam; moderate, very fine subangular blocky and single-grain structure; soft consistence; disseminated lime concretions; no clay films, strong effervescence; abrupt smooth boundary.
A3	15–25 cm thickness. Gray brown (2.5Y 5/2) clay; moderate, very fine to fine angular to subangular blocky structure; friable consistence; few, fine, irregularly shaped lime concretions in filaments or threads; no clay films; slight effervescence; clear smooth boundary.
IIB1tca	25–50 cm thickness. Dark gray brown (2.5Y 4/2) clay; moderate, fine to medium subangular blocky to prismatic structure; friable consistence; few, fine, irregularly shaped lime concretions in filaments or threads; few thin, clay films that line tubular or interstitial pores; slight effervescence; gradual smooth boundary.
IIB2tca	50–103 cm thickness. Dark gray brown (2.5Y 4/2) clay; moderate, fine to medium subangular blocky to prismatic structure; friable consistence; few, fine irregularly shaped lime concretions in filaments or threads; few thick, clay films that line tubular or interstitial pores; slight effervescence; gradual smooth boundary.
IIB3tca	103–149 cm thickness. Dark gray brown (2.5Y 4/2) clay; moderate, fine to medium subangular blocky to prismatic structure; friable to firm consistence; common, fine, generally rounded or slightly oblong to irregularly shaped lime concretions in soft masses and filaments or threads; many moderately thick clay films that line tubular or interstitial pores; slight effervescence; abrupt smooth boundary.

---

field, but the process may be characterized more by the accumulation of soluble salts other than calcium carbonate, rather than by calcium carbonate itself. Analysis was not done on the nature of these salts, but pH values in this soil of greater than 8, and greater than 9 in some profiles below this soil, suggest that sodium salts affect the present pH values in varying degree. In contrast, the percentages of calcium carbonate (Table 5.9) are not excessively large in the composite soil. However, this may be only a reflection of the fine-grained sediments of this profile and others in the vicinity. Fine-grained materials would have large pore space to accommodate the carbonates and salts, thus leading to small percentages.

The B horizon of the composite soil contains clay films. The presence of clays, carbonates, and other salts in the soil could be explained in at least two ways. First, the unit may have initially formed under a relatively humid climate during the early Altithermal, at which time clay illuviation took place; the climate may later have become drier, culminating in accumulation of carbonates and salts at the expense of clays. Generally speaking, the soil would then indicate that conditions during the late Altithermal and thereafter were dry enough to cause formation of carbonates and salts in the soil. The present dry climate of the area would be conducive to the accumulation of these compounds.

The second explanation, considered more probable, is that the marked accumulation of sodium salts along with some calcium carbonate could have resulted in deflocculation of clays (Birkeland 1974) and their migration and

TABLE 5.9
Laboratory Data for the Composite Soil above the Agate Basin–Hell Gap Level (Altithermal/Post-Altithermal)

Horizon	Thickness (cm)	Percentage of sample >2 mm	Percentage of sand 2000–50 μm	Percentage of silt 50–2 μm	Percentage of clay <2 μm	pH 1:1	Percentage CaCO₃	Percentage of organic matter
A1	0–15	a	43.9	22.9	33.3	8.1	5.0	1.2
A3	15–25	a	13.3	22.7	64.0	7.8	3.0	.6
IIB1tca	25–50	a	10.3	28.5	61.1	8.2	2.5	.6
IIB2tca	50–103	a	14.0	30.7	55.3	8.1	2.0	.6
IIB3tca	103–149	a	5.6	32.9	61.6	7.7	.5	.6

ᵃNot recorded.

accumulation in the subsoil approaching a natric B horizon (Soil Survey Staff 1975). In this case, clay translocation and accumulation of carbonates and salts would be virtually contemporaneous in Altithermal and post-Altithermal times. The source for the salts and some carbonates is probably the Carlile shale, but carbonates are thought to be largely of atmospheric origin (eolian, decomposition of organic matter, and/or carbon dioxide dissolved in meteoric waters) based on decreasing density of calcium carbonate and other salts downward through the stratigraphy.

Development of the paleosol of Altithermal age and younger soils above the Agate Basin–Hell Gap level, especially the composite soil discussed here, has resulted in superposition (Hunt 1972) of this collective pedogenesis onto underlying sediments and paleosols. Hence carbonates, and to some extent soluble salts, of the upper soils, which indicate a drying of climate, have been infused onto the lower units, which give indication of relatively humid conditions, thus imparting alkaline pH values on formerly acidic soils (Humic Gleys or Haplaquolls) or less basic soils (Alluvial Soils or Fluvents) of late Pleistocene age. In fact, carbonate or salt stringers and veinlets from this superposition permeate downward with decreasing density below the Clovis-age soil into bedrock.

This superposition process has also been noted at the Carter/Kerr-McGee Paleoindian site in the Powder River Basin near Gillette, Wyoming, where a calcareous soil of probable Altithermal age has been superposed onto Humic Gley soils (Haplaquolls and Argiaquolls) of Clovis, Folsom, Agate Basin, Hell Gap, and Cody ages (Reider 1980a). Therefore, as is the case at the Carter/Kerr-McGee site, the late Pleistocene soils of the Agate Basin site are modified paleosols affected by later environments.

Such superposition of calcareous or saline soils of Altithermal and younger ages onto late Pleistocene soils or sediments has been noted at other archaeological sites in Wyoming (Haynes and Grey 1965; Reider 1979, 1980b), and has been observed by the author at a number of other localities in Wyoming and Colorado. These calcareous soils, although varying to some extent in kind and degree of development, are analogous to the Altithermal paleosol or caliche recognized by L. B. Leopold and J. P. Miller (1954) in Wyoming's Powder River Basin.

An attempt was made to discern the clay mineralogy for soils of Altithermal/post-Altithermal and late Pleistocene ages in the area to see if the mineralogy might vary given the marked climatic, vegetative, and drainage differences under which the soils formed. However, the strong presence of clay minerals in the Carlile shale prevents differentiation of clay minerals inherited from parent material or shale and those of pedogenic origin. Montmorillonite, kaolinite-chlorite (undifferentiated), and illite are the dominant clay minerals in all horizons analyzed, and no significant variation in relative contents appears to exist between the samples.

CLAY MINERALOGY

The soil currently forming in alluvium at the bottom of the modern arroyo was studied for comparison with past pedogenic conditions in the area. Data for this soil are shown in Tables 5.10 and 5.11. The stratigraphic position is shown in Figure 5.18.

THE MODERN SOIL

The modern arroyo soil is a thin and weakly developed Alluvial Soil or Fluvent, which contrasts sharply with the Humic Gleys (Haplaquolls) of late Pleistocene age and the calcareous–saline soils (Alluvial Soils or Fluvents and Gray Desert, Sierozem, or Haplargid or Natrargid soils—see Baldwin *et al.* 1938; Soil Survey Staff 1975; Thorp and Smith 1949) of Altithermal and post-Altithermal ages. The modern soil appears to be no more than several hundred years old, based on its weak development and geomorphic–stratigraphic position along the drainageway. Generally, it indicates good soil drainage and moderate accumulation of organic matter at the soil surface. In addition to indicating a relatively young and brief period of soil formation, the soil denotes improved soil drainage as compared to late Pleistocene conditions and less impregnation

TABLE 5.10

Field Description of the Modern Soil on the Arroyo Bottom

Location: See Figure 2.13.
Parent material: Alluvium 0–24 cm; Carlile shale 24–81+ cm
Elevation: 1170 m
Drainage: Well drained
Remarks: Colors and consistence under moist conditions.

A1   0–18 cm thickness. Dark gray brown (2.5Y 4/2) clay loam; weak, very fine to fine sub-angular blocky structure; friable consistence; few, fine, generally rounded or slightly oblong mottling concentrated in segregated areas; slight effervescence; abrupt smooth boundary.

C1   18–24 cm thickness. Olive brown (2.5Y 4/4) clay loam; weak, fine to medium subangular blocky structure; friable consistence; few, fine, generally rounded or slightly oblong lime concretions in soft masses; few, fine, generally rounded or slightly oblong mottling concentrated in segregated areas; slight effervescence; abrupt wavy boundary.

IIC2   24–81+ cm thickness. Yellowish brown to dark gray brown (10YR 5/6 to 10YR 4/2) silty clay; weak, medium to coarse subangular blocky and platy structure; friable consistence; common, fine, generally rounded or slightly oblong lime concretions in filaments or threads; common, fine to medium, generally rounded or slightly oblong mottling concentrated in segregated areas; slight effervescence.

TABLE 5.11
Laboratory Data for the Modern Soil on the Arroyo Bottom

Horizon	Thickness (cm)	Percentage of sample >2 mm	Percentage of sand 2000–50 μm	Percentage of silt 50–2 μm	Percentage of clay <2 μm	pH 1:1	Percentage CaCO$_3$	Percentage of organic matter
A1	0–18	1.30	42.8	28.6	28.6	8.0	2.0	2.8
C1	18–24	3.47	30.8	34.6	34.6	8.0	3.0	1.6
IIC2	24–81+	0	3.7	45.1	51.2	8.0	4.0	.8

of materials with carbonates and salts as compared to soils dating as old as Altithermal time.

CONCLUSIONS   Major conclusions drawn from a study of soils and soil stratigraphy of the Agate Basin site may be summarized as follows:

1. The soil of Clovis age indicates poor drainage along the arroyo bottom under a high water table developed in response to relatively humid climatic conditions. The soil is classed as a modified Wiesenboden or variety of Humic Gley or Haplaquoll. The poor drainage is characterized by mottling and gleying of subsoils and by the accumulation of thick, dark organic A horizons under grasses, sedges, and perhaps some woodland. Weak, broken, or discontinuous leached A2 horizons frequently underlie the dark surface A horizons. These Humic Gley soils no longer form in the area, and are mapped in Wyoming as modern soils (Wiesenboden) in the extreme western part of the state (Ravenholt et al. 1976) at elevations of 1780–2100 m where frostfree seasons are only 30–50 days. They may exist in areas of the state not yet surveyed. Nonetheless, they are also known at the Garrett Allen site (48CR301) in Carbon County, Wyoming, at an elevation of approximately 2160 m in sediments containing Late Prehistoric and Woodland cultural levels, and possibly other cultural components as old as McKean (ca. 4500 B.P.).

2. The soil of Folsom age at the bottom of the paleoarroyo appears to be an Alluvial Soil or Fluvent grading toward a Humic Gley or Haplaquoll. It is thought that this soil indicates improved soil drainage along the arroyo bottom in post-Clovis to Folsom time, but its weaker development as compared to the Clovis-age soil may denote only a brief time of formation under high-water-table conditions similar to those of Clovis time. Nonetheless, between Clovis and Folsom occupations, there appears to have been some weak arroyo cutting and/or shifting, such that the axis of the poorly drained arroyo of Clovis age was locally abandoned. This cutting and shifting may have been in response to a drying of climate and lowering of the water table following Clovis occupation, causing downcutting of the stream system. These conditions could have resulted in the improved soil drainage that appears possible between Clovis and Folsom time and may have been the major factor involved in the formation of the Folsom-age Alluvial Soil or Fluvent.

3. The soil of Agate Basin–Hell Gap age is also an Alluvial Soil or Fluvent.

It demonstrates improved soil drainage along the arroyo bottom during Agate Basin and Hell Gap occupations as compared to Clovis time. It is less mottled than the Folsom-age soil and lacks gleying, which suggests further improvement of soil drainage. Like the Folsom-age soil, it indicates much less accumulation of organic matter in the A horizon and lacks signs of intense leaching (A2 horizons).

Like the conditions immediately preceding development of the Folsom-age soil, there appears to have been an episode of marked arroyo cutting preceding development of the soil of Agate Basin–Hell Gap age. Although stratigraphic relationships are unclear, this cutting could be responsible for Folsom materials in the sediments. The incision was deep enough to erode into and below soils of Folsom and Clovis ages and may have been a result of drying of climate preceding Agate Basin and Hell Gap occupations, as is suggested for events between Clovis and Folsom occupations. Thus, soil formation during Agate Basin and Hell Gap time could have been in response to more humid conditions following this drying. Perhaps occupations in the area during Folsom, Agate Basin, and Hell Gap times, and even in Clovis time, were influenced to a degree by larger game populations that coincided with more moist conditions and improved grass and herb cover. These conditions seem to correlate with a stabilization of geomorphic surfaces, which was concomitant with soil formations.

4. Following Agate Basin–Hell Gap occupation of the Agate Basin site, alluviation buried the soil of Agate Basin–Hell Gap age with as much as several meters of clayey sediments derived from the Carlile shale. Subsequently, the soils associated with the Paleoindian sequence at the site were cut by deep arroyo incision, producing a major unconformity that seems to coincide with marked climatic change to drier and warmer conditions at the Pleistocene–Holocene boundary (ca. 8000 B.P.). Soils above the unconformity are weak Alluvial Soils or Fluvents within alluvium, but the sequence is dominated by a composite soil at the surface of the abandoned paleoarroyo that classifies as a Haplargid, Natrargid, or Sierozem. This calcareous–saline soil is strongly developed and probably marks both semiarid and desert conditions in Altithermal time to the present. This soil has superposed itself deeply into preexisting soils and sediments dating to late Pleistocene time, thereby impregnating formerly acid soils with carbonates and salts.

In consequence, the Pleistocene–Holocene boundary seems to be evidenced in sediments of the paleoarroyo by a shift from soils indicating varying degrees of poor drainage to those demonstrating good soil drainage under more arid environments, which have basically continued to modern times. The most severely dry or long-term aspect of this trend appears to be the Altithermal interval during which time the Haplargid, Natrargid, or Sierozem probably reached its penultimate development.

5. The composite soil just described completed the sedimentation and sequence of soil development of the paleoarroyo of Moss Agate Creek. Following this, the arroyo system cut to its present position, generally shifting northward by several tens of meters near the site (Area 1), where it cut essentially headward along the alluvium–bedrock contact. There may have been several periods of soil formation within this new cut-and-fill sequence, for the modern soil at the bottom of the arroyo signifies only very recent soil formation, perhaps no more

than several hundred years old, in a thin veneer of alluvium over bedrock. Older soils of this time may have been removed just prior to the formation of this soil. Generally, it is thought that the present cutting-and-filling cycle of the arroyo is of Neoglacial age.

There is evidence for several periods of soil formation during this time. It consists of weak soils (Fluvents) with A–C horizonation, both at the surface and buried, formed in colluvium along slopes leading to the uplands. Frequently they bury the composite soil of Altithermal and post-Altithermal age in the paleoarroyo. The degree of development of these soils is equivalent to that of the modern soil on the arroyo bottom. These colluvial soils have formed intermittently along the slopes in conjunction with a series of cat steps or terracettes with back slopes of less than .5 m height, which are actively retreating upslope. It appears the retreat of these features results in a compage of soils of various young ages formed in colluvium or pedisediment across the slopes, and that this slope instability correlates with the active cutting of the modern arroyo as it is controlled by its present base level, prevailing climate, and grazing intensity.

6. In total, soils and soil stratigraphy of the Agate Basin site give good evidence of climatic shift from late Pleistocene through Altithermal and on to modern times. As stated by Reider (1980a) for soils of the Carter/Kerr-McGee site, the Wiesenboden or Humic Gleys (Haplaquolls) of the Agate Basin site lend credence to the idea that such soils may prove to be good indicators of stratigraphic age in the region and may be good markers within buried paleoarroyos for any future identification of Paleoindian cultural levels. Furthermore, this study helps to substantiate the existence and nature of the Altithermal paleosol or caliche identified by L. B. Leopold and J. P. Miller (1954) in the Powder River Basin.

3. VEGETATION ECOLOGY
clayton marlow

Vegetative communities reflect the influence of local climate, soils, and topography. Agate Basin, like much of the immediately adjacent Powder River Basin, is a mosaic of shortgrass prairie and Wyoming Basin shrub steppe. The Shortgrass Prairie province described by R. G. Bailey (1976) is characterized by hot summers and cold winters, with the majority of precipitation occurring during the summer. Hot summers and cold winters are also typical of the Wyoming Basin province (R. G. Bailey 1976) but here early spring is the period of peak precipitation. At Agate Basin two precipitation peaks occur, one in late May and early June and the second in September. This climatic pattern allows species from both the shortgrass prairie and the Wyoming Basin to intermingle forming a shortgrass–shrub steppe.

Big sagebrush (*Artemisia tridentata*), saltbush (*Atriplex* ssp.), rabbit brush

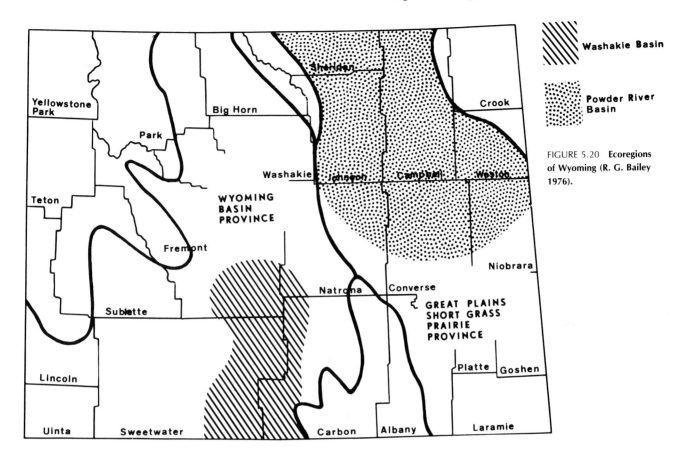

Washakie Basin

Powder River Basin

FIGURE 5.20 Ecoregions of Wyoming (R. G. Bailey 1976).

(*Chrysothamnus* ssp.), and black greasewood (*Sarcobatus vermiculatus*) dominate the vegetative associations of the Wyoming Basin province (Figure 5.20) but are either absent or form only minor components of ravine or riparian plant communities in the shortgrass prairie. Olson and Zimmerman (1979) did not report any of these general or species from their study area in south-central South Dakota. Studies conducted by Tolstead (1941) and Hanson and Whitman (1938) in western North Dakota list blue grama (*Bouteloua gracilis*), western wheatgrass (*Agropyron smithii*), sedges (*Carex* ssp.) needle-and-thread grass (*Stipa comata*), buffalo grass (*Buchloe dactyloides*), prairie sandreed (*Calamovilfa longifollia*), and little bluestem (*Andropogon scoparius*) as dominants of the shortgrass prairie. At Agate Basin, climate and soils filter out poorly adapted species from both provinces, creating a unique shrub–grass community.

Wyoming big sagebrush (*Artemisia tridentata wyomingensis*) forms an overstory above a shortgrass association dominated by western wheatgrass, blue grama, threadleaf sedge (*Carex filifolia*), needle-and-thread grass, and prairie junegrass (*Koeleria cristata*). This assemblage, or at least three of the six species, dominated 25 of the 37 communities surveyed in the northern Powder River Basin (Marlow 1978). Differences in species dominance result from changes in soils or topography. The arroyo present at the Agate Basin site creates its own microclimate, and a distinctive flora pattern has emerged.

The additional moisture and reduced evapotranspiration rate resulting from the deep arroyo form a mesic plant community. Western snowberry (*Sym*

TABLE 5.12
**Probable Agate Basin Vegetation Association
10,000–11,000 B.P.**

Arroyo	Uplands
Populus tremuloides	Artemisia tridentata
Deschampsis caespitosa	vaseyana[a]
Poa ampla	Artemisia tridentata
Poa pratensis[c]	wyomingensis[b]
Carex eleocharis[c]	Agropyron
Carex nebraskensis[c]	dasystachyum
Agropyron	Agropyron smithii[b]
trachycaulum	Agropyron spicatum[a]
Achillea millefolium[c]	Bouteloua gracilis[b]
Rosa woodsii[c]	Poa secunda[b]
Symphoricarpos	Poa canbyii[a,b]
occidentalis[c]	Koeleria cristata[b]
Lupinus caudatus[c]	Carex eleocharis[a]
Geranium richardsonii	Carex filifolia[b]
Artemisia tridentata	Stipa comata[b]
vaseyana	

[a]North- and east-facing slopes.
[b]South- and west-facing slopes and ridge tops.
[c]Present in current plant community.

phoricarpos occidentalis), woods rose (Rosa woodsii), Kentucky bluegrass (Poa pratensis), thick-spike wheatgrass (Agropyron dasystachyum), tail-cup lupine (Lupinus caudatus), western yarrow (Achillea millefolium), and prairie thermopsis (Thermopsis rhombifolia) cover the bottom and sides of the Agate Basin arroyo. Not only is the species composition different from the surrounding shrub steppe, but the above ground biomass produced by the arroyo community is more than twice that of the surrounding shrub–grass association.

Pollen analysis of sediments collected from sites in South Dakota, North Dakota, Manitoba, Saskatchewan, and Minnesota (H. E. Wright 1970) and northeastern Kansas (Wells 1965) indicate that spruce (Picea ssp.), fir (Abies ssp.), pine (Pinus ssp.), and other boreal tree species occupied the region between 15,000 and 12,500 years B.P. By 10,670 B.P. spruce had apparently retreated north as far as Pickerel Lake in northeastern South Dakota (H. E. Wright 1970). Subsequent layers of Pickerel Lake sediment reveal a change from riparian woodland consisting of birch (Betula ssp.), elm (Ulmus ssp.), and oak (Quercus ssp.) to prairie at 8000 to 9000 years B.P. P. S. Martin (1975) reports that a vast, treeless prairie stretching from Manitoba to the Gulf of Mexico cannot be traced back in the fossil record beyond 11,000 B.P. Micromammal fossils from the Agate Basin site appear to fit this pattern.

Faunal remains from the Folsom level (Walker, this volume, Chapter 4, Section 6) particularly the microtine rodents, indicate that the microclimate of the then-existing arroyo was cool and damp. Potential vegetation for this site 10,000–11,000 years B.P. is shown in Table 5.12. H. E. Wright (1970) shows that as spruce began to decrease about 10,000 B.P., birch, elm, and oak began to dominate the pollen rain. Quaking aspen (Populus tremuloides), a contemporary of the spruce–fir forest, could continue to exist during the rise of previously

TABLE 5.13
Probable Agate Basin Vegetation Association
9300–10,200 B.P.

Arroyo	Uplands
Populus tremuloides[a]	Artemisia tridentata
Artemisia tridentata	wyomingensis
vaseyana	Agropyron
Symphoricarpos	dasystachyum
occidentalis	Agropyron smithii
Rosa woodsii	Agropyron spicatum[a]
Agropyron	Bouteloua gracilis
dasystachyum	Poa canbyii
Agropyron smithii	Poa secunda
Agropyron	Koeleria cristata
trachycaulum[a]	Carex filifolia
Poa pratensis	Carex eleocharis[a]
Carex eleocharis	Stipa comata
Carex nebraskensis	
Achillea millefolium	
Lupinus caudatus	
Thermopsis rhombifolia	

[a]Infrequent occurrence within association.

mentioned deciduous species, and there are stands of aspen found in the southern Black Hills today. In fact, as was mentioned before, a relict stand of quaking aspen was recently found only 8 miles east of the Agate Basin site. However, 700–800 years later, 9300–10,200 B.P., the tree overstory was becoming so open that the drying trend within the arroyo was accelerated. This is based on disappearance of the red-backed vole (*Clethrionomys gapperi*). The continued dominance of both the meadow vole (*Microtus pennsylvanicus*) and the long-tailed vole (*Microtus longicaudus*) suggests that a fairly substantial shrub cover still existed at the site (Table 5.13).

As the drying and warming trend continued, aspen, slender wheatgrass (*Agropyron trachycaulum*), mountain big sagebrush (*Artemisia tridentata vaseyana*), and bluebunch wheatgrass (*Agropyron spicatum*) disappeared from the arroyo and upland plant associations. This change was probably complete by 8000 B.P., since H. E. Wright (1970) suggests this date as the approximate beginning of prairie dominance in the Central Plains. Shifts in plant community composition and species dominance during the postglacial period would have improved conditions for large grazers such as bison but probably had little effect on human plant-gathering strategies.

Prehistoric occupation sites appear to be more closely correlated to plant species diversity and seasonality than to the relative abundance of edible species (Marlow 1978 and 1979). Vegetative associations of the Powder River Basin generally have a low species diversity, and the current arroyo and upland associations at Agate Basin are no exception. Eight edible and one medicinal species occur in the present (8000 B.P. to present) plant community (Table 5.14). However, during the Agate Basin and Folsom occupations of the area, there was only one more edible plant in the species assemblage.

TABLE 5.14
Edible and Medicinal Plant Species at the Agate Basin Site[a]

Species	Use
Achillea millefolium[b,c]	Medicinal
Agropyron dasystachyum[b,c]	Seeds eaten
Agropyron smithii[b,c]	Seeds eaten
Agropyron trachycaulum[b]	Seeds eaten
Carex nebraskensis[b,c]	Seeds eaten
Koeleria cristata[b,c]	Seeds eaten
Rosa woodsii[b,c]	Fruit eaten
Symphoricarpos occidentalis[b,c]	Fruit eaten
Thermopsis rhombifolia[c]	Seeds eaten

[a]Based on Hellson and Gadd 1974; Gilmore 1977; and Jennings 1978.
[b]Folsom and Agate Basin–Hell Gap occupation period.
[c]8000 B.P. to present.

Prairie junegrass (*Koeleria cristata*) and prairie thermopsis (*Thermopsis rhombifolia*) produce edible seeds in late June; the other grass and shrub species do not produce seeds and fruit until late August or September. However, gatherers could not rely on harvesting material from all eight species, even following the seasonal development patterns. Western wheatgrass reproduces both vegetatively (rhizomes), and sexually (seeds). Generally, this cool-season grass* reproduces vegetatively, causing a limited or nonexistent seed crop. Adverse weather conditions may limit seed production by reliable species at other times. So by choosing areas of high vegetative diversity, gatherers could reduce the likelihood of "crop failure" and increase units of foodstuff collected per unit labor. The low diversity and widely separated seed maturity periods at Agate Basin probably caused it to be a less desirable gathering locality than the Black Hills 10–15 miles to the east and north. This situation could have existed since 10,000 years B.P. Although not well suited for human utilization, the vegetative associations at Agate Basin are well suited for bison.

Popp and Dahlgren (1979) reported that bison (*Bison bison*) in Wind Cave National Park, South Dakota, preferred cool-season grasses during spring and early summer, shifted to warm-season species during late summer, and then returned to cool-season grasses in the autumn. However, Peden *et al.* (1974) found that bison grazing on the shortgrass prairie of northeastern Colorado preferred warm-season grasses throughout the year, except during the spring when cool-season species were selected. Either grazing model will fit the vegetation pattern at Agate Basin. The lush Agate Basin arroyo association, dominated by cool-season grasses, would attract bison in the early spring and again in late summer or fall; summer and winter would have found the herds grazing in uplands dominated by the warm-season species blue grama (*Bouteloua gracilis*).

---

*Cool-season genera, such as *Agropyron*, *Poa*, *Stipa*, and *Carex*, initiate growth early in the spring, reach maximum development by late spring, and become semidormant during the summer; they then resume growth in the fall if adequate moisture is available. *Warm-season genera*, such as *Andropogon*, *Bouteloua*, and *Buchloe*, initiate growth in late spring and grow continuously through the summer, reaching maximum standing crop by fall. Regrowth does not occur until the following spring.

Herds at or below the range carrying capacity would not have had to leave the Powder River Basin (Figure 5.20) on seasonal migrations in search of more forage. Instead, seasonal dietary preference allowed bison to move from plant species to plant species and remain in the basin. The paucity of bison kill sites in the Washakie Basin (Figure 5.20) strengthens this hypothesis. Vegetative associations in the Washakie Basin are dominated by one or more shrub species and contain one warm-season grass, sand dropseed (*Sporobolus cryptandrus*). Sand dropseed is limited in its distribution and has low animal palatability; hence, grazing in the basin may have been limited to spring or early fall. By contrast, the widespread distribution of the highly palatable warm-season blue grama in association with cool-season wheatgrasses and bluegrasses at Agate Basin could have attracted bison to the site throughout the year, thus providing a reliable food base for human exploitation. The shortgrass–shrub steppe of Agate Basin and the rest of the Powder River Basin provided excellent bison range into the present time.

To sum up, changes in climate 12,000 to 15,000 years ago caused the retreat of the Wisconsin ice sheet. These same climatic changes caused the decline of the boreal forest stretching across North Dakota and South Dakota, Nebraska, and Kansas. For a short time afterward, an assemblage of deciduous tree species replaced the declining conifers. The arroyo existing at the Agate Basin site may have contained a relict quaking aspen community during 10,000 to 11,000 years B.P. Upland plant communities during the same period began to provide good bison range; human gatherers found a limited supply of edible plants with only one brief harvest period, late summer and early fall.

By the time the Agate Basin–Hell Gap cultures were using the arroyo site as a bison trap, the aspen and its several understory codominants were gone. The edible plant resource, however limited, had altered very little during this change and would remain relatively stable until present times. Potential carrying capacity for bison continued to increase until approximately 8000 years B.P. when the shortgrass prairie reached its present geographic distribution. The mixture of cool- and warm-season grasses in the Agate Basin locality and the rest of the Powder River Basin probably allowed bison to stay in the immediate area year-round. It would seem, then, that Agate Basin was prime hunting territory, and not a plant-processing site with opportunistic exploitation of big game.

4. POLLEN ANALYSIS
jane m. beiswenger

Pollen analysis of eastern Wyoming samples has been difficult because the sediments are usually oxidized. Preliminary samples (50 cm³) from Agate Basin did not yield any pollen. Thus, larger quantities (200 cm³) of sediment were used for this study in an attempt to concentrate sufficient amounts of pollen for analysis.

TABLE 5.15

Pollen Samples from Agate Basin

Level No.	Level	Location (provenience if known)	Collector
1	Pond surface	—	G. Frison
2	Agate Basin	South profile	G. Zeimens
3	Intermediate	Control block, center of site	G. Zeimens
4	Folsom	N 110'–110'10" E 5'–6'6"	B. Bradley
5	Sand below Folsom	N 112'–112'10" E 9'–10'4"	B. Bradley
6	Dark clay be-low Folsom	N 112'–112'10" E 9'–10'4"	B. Bradley
7	Dark organic base of Folsom	53 cm below surface	R. Lewis
8	Dark organic	87 cm below surface	R. Lewis
9	Sandy loam, organic	103 cm below surface	R. Lewis
10	Deepest black	N 78.5'–85' W 23.5'–25.5'	R. Lewis

METHOD   Nine samples were collected in June and July of 1979 from different levels of the Agate Basin site. A sample of surface mud was collected from a nearby pond for the purpose of comparison. Table 5.15 gives the location, level, and collector of each sample. A 200-cm³ sample (approximately 1 cup) of sediment from each level was prepared for pollen analysis by the following procedure.

Each sample was placed in a 1000-ml beaker with 200 ml distilled water. Small amounts of concentrated HCl were added and the sample was stirred after each addition. This was continued until there was no reaction with the addition of fresh HCl. The sample was stirred vigorously and allowed to stand for 45 seconds after the motion of the liquid ceased. The supernatant was poured through a No. 60 screen into a clean beaker, and the sediment was discarded after it had been checked for pollen. The sample was again stirred vigorously and allowed to settle at successively longer intervals, ending with 2½ minutes. The supernatant was transferred to a 50-ml plastic tube and centrifuged. The resulting sediment was treated with concentrated HC, HF and 10% KOH. The sediment was then mixed with ZnBr (specific gravity, 2.0) and centrifuged for 30 minutes in 12-ml glass test tubes. The ZnBr containing the suspended and floating material was diluted with acidified, distilled water and centrifuged. If sufficient pollen was present, the sample was acetolyzed for 1 minute in a boiling water bath with a mixture of nine parts acetic anhydride and one part H_2SO_4. The sample was washed with glacial acetic acid, then distilled water and mounted in glycerine jelly for microscopic examination.

TABLE 5.16
**Pollen Types Identified in Different Levels of
the Agate Basin Site**

Level 2 (Agate Basin)	Level 3 (Intermediate)	Level 4 (Folsom)
Picea	*Pinus*	*Pinus*
Pinus	Cf. *Populus*	*Carya*
Celtis type	*Artemisia*	*Pterocarya*
Onagraceae	Chenopodiaceae	*Tilia* type
Carya	Leguminosae	*Celtis* type
Pterocarya	Gramineae	*Ulmus* type
Tilia type		Cf. Aceraceae
Compositae		Cf. *Sarcobatus*
Artemisia		*Alnus*
Salix		*Salix*
Gramineae		Compositae
Leguminosae		*Artemisia*
Saxifragaceae		Gramineae
		Chenopodiaceae
		Caryophyllaceae

Level 5 (Sand below Folsom)	Level 6 (Dark clay below Folsom level)	Level 7 (Dark organic at base of Folsom)
Pinus	*Pinus*	*Pinus*
Carya	*Ephedra*	*Alnus*
Cf. *Thuja*	*Carya*	*Carya*
Ephedra	*Celtis* type	Cf. *Ulmus*
Celtis type	*Salix*	*Artemisia*
Juglandaceae type	*Artemisia*	Compositae
Cf. *Sarcobatus*	*Alnus*	*Salix*
Salix	Gramineae	Gramineae
Compositae	Compositae	Cyperaceae
Artemisia	Umbellifereae	
Gramineae	Leguminosae	
Chenopodiaceae	Ericaceae	
Saxifragaceae	Caryophyllaceae	
	Chenopodiaceae	

RESULTS

Six of the nine samples from the Agate Basin site contained a sufficient amount of pollen for analysis. Level 8 (87 cm below surface) and level 9 (103 cm below surface) yielded a small amount of pollen, and the deepest black level was barren. A few grains were well preserved; however, most of the pollen was severely oxidized, with 19–49% of the grains unidentifiable. Corrosion of the wall of the pollen grain, caused by the interaction of iron and oxygen in ground water (Tschudy 1969) is a frequent problem in iron rich sediments. Beiswenger (1978) reported increasingly higher percentage of poorly preserved pollen correlated with increasing depth in oxidized samples from western Colorado. Hall (1981) has described the same phenomenon in samples from Oklahoma. In addition to problems of oxidation, redeposition may occur. Grains of *Carya*, not in the modern flora of this area, were present in level 2 (Agate Basin), level 4 (Folsom), and three other levels. Grains of *Pterocarya* were identified in both the Agate Basin and Folsom levels. This genus has not been present in North America since the Pliocene (E. B. Leopold and H. D. MacGinitie 1972) and is evidence that some portion of each of these samples is redeposited Tertiary sediment.

Redeposition is a danger when concentrating pollen from large quantities of sediment in an area where strata of differing geological ages are exposed. And, it is likely to occur during violent rainstorms or during the periods of high winds which are so prevalent on the High Plains. Using a large amount of sediment was necessary to obtain enough pollen for observation; unfortunely it did not provide relaible results in this study. Had the redepositon indicator been absent, and the majority of the grains well preserved, one could have some confidence that the pollen spectrum reflected the climatic conditions during the deposition of the sediments of the site. This has been the case in some samples from western Colorado and northern Wyoming (Beiswenger, unpublished data).

Since redeposition is a factor in both occupation levels and is a probable factor in the other samples, I have not made percentage calculations. Pollen types are listed according to their occurrence in the various levels in Table 5.16, but these cannot be used for a climatic reconstruction of the Quaternary in the Agate Basin area. Modern pollen percentages from the mud sample are given in Table 5.17, since these could be useful to future studies in this part of Wyoming.

CONCLUSIONS   The Agate Basin samples were not found suitable for a pollen study. Small samples did not contain enough pollen for analysis. Pollen preparations from large quantities of material contained *Pterocarya* grains demonstrating the presence of redeposited Tertiary material in the Agate Basin sediments.

TABLE 5.17

Pollen Percentages for a Sample of Surface Mud from the Agate Basin Area

Pollen type	Percentage
Pinus	23.3
Abies	.5
Populus	.3
Picea	.8
Alnus	.3
Artemisia	40.3
Gramineae	.3
Cf. *Salix*	.8
Caryophyllaceae	.8
Cyperaceae	1.1
Cf. Citaceae (*Helianthemum* type)	.3
Leguminosae	.8
Ranunculaceae	1.9
Umbellifereae	.5
Eleagnus	.3
Compositae	11.4
Sarcobatus	1.6
Chenopodiaceae	9.3
Typha	.3
Cf. *Polygonum*	.3
Undifferentiated monocot	.5
Unknown	3.0
Unidentifiable	1.7

5. PHYTOLITH STUDIES

rhoda owen lewis

Opal phytoliths, minute silica bodies, are formed in plants during the maturation process. Soluble silica is absorbed with water by the roots and is deposited in and around cells of the plants. These distinct and identifiable plant remains are then deposited in the soil during the decaying process. Opal phytoliths are relatively resistant to many of the factors that can cause destruction of plant pollen. They can therefore be used as an aid in determining paleovegetation in sites with poor or no pollen preservation. Phytolith results can be used in conjunction with and to enhance the pollen analyses from a site because phytolith production is high in monocotyledons, whereas pollen production is high in dicotyledons.

FACTORS IN PHYTOLITH PRESERVATION

Phytolith counts from the Agate Basin site have been unsatisfactory and no real definitive information on the paleobotany from this site has resulted. The area is well watered naturally, and supports a relatively lush grass cover today. At the time of the Agate Basin bison kill, the area is believed to have been relatively wet, which suggests that the site area was also then covered by grass. The soil at Agate Basin is somewhat alkaline, ranging between pH values of 7.6 and 8.3 (Lewis 1979b:57). Of the samples tested, only the least alkaline con-

TABLE 5.18

1978–1979 Phytolith Results, Agate Basin Site

		Count[a]				
Provenience	Level	Festucoid	Chloridoid	Panicoid	Elongate	pH
N 95–100 E 5–10	Bone level				P	
W 20 N 92	Deepest level below bone		1		P	
N 95–100 E 5–10	Bone level	1			P	
N 90–92 W 20.5–22	10.7–10.85′ BD[b] hearth, dark brown sandy clay	1			P	
N 90–95 W 10–15	9.5′ BD, first carbon layer below sand				P	
N 92 W 20	Between deepest level and bone level	2			P	
Plane table station 22	Unit 1, 4″ thick, bone bed scattered bone				P	7.7
Plane table station 22	Unit 2, 5″ thick, dark gray sandy clay—massive bone at base	1			P	7.9
Plane table station 22	Unit 4, 22″ thick	1	3	1	P	7.6
Plane table station 22	Unit 5, light gray clay				P	8.0
Plane table station 22	Unit 6, 12″ thick				A	8.3
N 88.8 W 10–22.5	Sample 12, between Folsom level and bedrock; 13′9″–14′2″ BD				P	

(continued)

TABLE 5.18 (*Continued*)

Provenience	Level	Festucoid	Chloridoid	Panicoid	Elongate	pH
				Count[a]		
N 88.8 W 10–22.5	Sample 10, intermediate level between Agate Basin main level and Folsom level; 12′11″–13′4″ BD				A	
N 88.8 W 10–22.5	Sample 1, 5′8″–6′3″ BD				A	
N 88.8 W 10–22.5	Sample 2, 6′8″–7′3″ BD				A	
N 88.8 W 10–22.5	Sample 3, 7′1″–8′5″ BD				A	
N 88.8 W 10–22.5	Sample 4, 9′7″–9′11″ BD				A	
N 88.8 W 10–22.5	Sample 5, 10′10″–11′2″ BD				A	
N 88.8–91.2 W 10.0–22.5	Main bone level				P	
	Soil sample from around bones in main Agate Basin level				P	
	1979 Samples					
	Level I, 41″ BS[c] light brown sandy loam, some organic stringers				A	
	Level II, 35″ BS, dark organic level				P	
	Level III, 31″ BS, sandy, gravelly clay, oxidized				A	
	Level IV, 21″ BS, dark organic level, base of Folsom level				A	
	Level V, 9″ BS Folsom level				A	
N 91–93 E 24.5–22	Hearth area, Folsom level				P	
N 91–93 E 24.5–22	Area around hearth, Folsom level				A	
E 0–5 N 80–85	14′5″ BD, upper calcite level, upper Folsom level				P	
E 0–5 N 80–85	15′6″ BD, lower Folsom level, brown sand calcite deposits				A	
E 0–5 N 80–85	15′6″ BD, lower Folsom level, brown sand calcite deposits				A	
E 0–5 N 80–85	16′8″ BD, charcoal flecks thru level, calcite, dark clayey sand, below Folsom				P	
E 0–5 N 80–85	18′6″ BD, lower level, tan orangey sand				P	

[a]1 represents less than 5; 2, 6–15; 3, 16–25; 4, 26 or more. A indicates absence, P, presence.
[b]BD is depth below site datum.
[c]BS is depth below ground surface at collection point.

tained identifiable phytoliths in significant quantities. Phytolith preservation can be severely affected by heavily alkaline soils (Rovner 1975:130), but the alkalinity at Agate Basin is not as high as at both the Horner (Wyoming) site and Hudson–Meng (Nebraska) site (Lewis 1979b:57). It is suggested that fluctuations of the water table, which may have occurred at Agate Basin, in conjunction with an alkaline soil caused raising and lowering of the alkalinity, and that the pH factor measured today may not in fact reflect the conditions over the past 10,000 years. A high prehistoric pH factor combined with a leaching process could have been the cause of phytolith destruction at Agate Basin.

The only sample that contains significant amounts of phytoliths is from Albanese's plane table station 22 and is from the Agate Basin cultural level (Albanese, personal communication). The difference in phytolith counts between this sample and the others examined suggests the possibility of contamination and I would hesitate to predict the paleovegetation from the results of this one sample.

METHODOLOGY

The soil samples from Agate Basin were prepared in two different ways for phytolith examination. The first 11 samples discussed in Table 5.18 were subjected to the methodology discussed in Lewis (1979b:16–17) and they were mounted permanently on slides, which are stored at the Anthropology Department of the University of Wyoming. The last 21 samples were examined in a Sedgwick–Rafter counting chamber using the method described by Lewis (1979a). Phytoliths observed in both the slides and the chamber were classified according to Twiss *et al.* (1969:111–112).

Table 5.18 summarizes the phytolith information presently available from this series of soil samples from Agate Basin. Value labels have been assigned to phytolith counts in the festucoid, chloridoid, and panicoid classes: less than 5 (1), 6–15 (2), 16–25 (3), and 26 or more (4). The elongate class will be designated only by presence (P) or absence (A).

During the spring of 1980, eight additional phytolith samples from Agate Basin and four phytolith samples from the Sheaman site were examined using the Sedgwick–Rafter counting chamber. On the basis of phytolith evidence observed during this initial examination, samples 1K022 and 1K017 from Agate Basin and sampels 2, 3, and 4 from the Sheaman site were made into permanent slides. The results from both examinations are included in Tables 5.19 and 5.20.

CONCLUSIONS

The results of the phytolith studies at Agate Basin have been consistent but disappointing. Although phytoliths have aided in paleobotanical reconstructions at other sites in this geographic region, other studies at Agate Basin (e.g., faunal taphonomy) have contributed much more paleoecological information than can be obtained from the phytolith studies.

TABLE 5.19
1980 Phytolith Results, Agate Basin Site

Provenience	Level	Count[a]			
		Festucoid	Chloridoid	Panicoid	Elongate
N 88.8 W 10–22.5	1K015 Sample 6 11′4″–11′8″ BD				A
N 88.8 W 10–22.5	1K016 Sample 7 11′8″–12′ BD				P
N 88.8 W 10–22.5	1K017 Sample 8 12′–12′4″ BD			1	P
N 88.8 W 10–22.5	1K018 Sample 9 12′5″–12′11″ BD				P
N 88.8 W 10–22.5	1K020 Sample 11 13′4″–13′8″ BD				P
N 100 W 00–10	1K022 Agate Basin bone bed 11′9″–12′2″ BD	1			P
N 105 W 00–10	1K023 Upper Folsom level 12′–12′4.5″ BD				P
N 100 W 00–10	1K024 Folsom bone bed 13′2″–13′8″ BD				P

[a]1 represents less than 5. A indicates absence; P, presence.

TABLE 5.20
1980 Phytolith Results, Sheaman Site

Provenience	Level	Count[a]			
		Festucoid	Chloridoid	Panicoid	Elongate
Unknown	Sample 1 5 pen lengths BS				P
Unknown	Sample 2 50 cm BS				P
Unknown	Sample 3 90 cm BS				P
Unknown	Sample 4 12 cm BS	2	1		P

[a]1 represents less than 5; 2, 6–15. P indicates presence.

6. FOSSIL NONMARINE GASTROPODS
emmett evanoff

Fossil nonmarine gastropods at the Agate Basin site indicate that moist, vegetation-rich conditions existed during the Clovis and Folsom occupations. Comparable composition and relative abundances of gastropod taxa in two assemblages from the Clovis and Folsom levels (Figure 5.21) indicate similar original environments for these levels. The mollusk assemblages from this site are composed of abundant terrestrial snails and uncommon freshwater snails (Table 5.21).

The terrestrial snails include both widespread, drought-resistant gastropods (xeric taxa), and gastropods restricted to more moisture-rich habitats (mesic taxa). The most abundant terrestrial snails are *Discus cronkhitei, Vallonia gracilicosta,* and *Zonitoides arboreus* (Figure 5.21). *Discus cronkhitei* and *Zonitoides arboreus* presently inhabit damp humus in wooded areas (Taylor 1960), but can also occur in thick grass litter adjacent to semipermanent water bodies (personal observation along the Niobrara River, Sioux County, Nebraska). *Vallonia gracilicosta* is abundant and widespread throughout the Great Plains (La Rocque 1970) in riparian habitats and moist microhabitats under shrubs in drier areas. The less abundant snails *Catinella* spp., *Cionella lubrica, Euconulus fulvus,* and *Succinea* spp. typically occur in moist, vegetation-rich habitats. *Oxyloma* spp. typically lives on mud and vegetation usually within 15 cm of

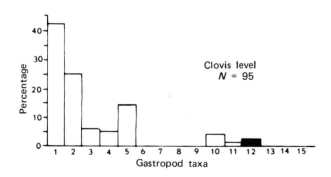

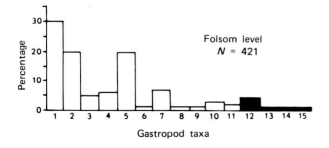

FIGURE 5.21 **Percentages of gastropod taxa from the Agate Basin site. White bars represent terrestrial snails, and shaded bars represent freshwater snails. Numbers refer to species listed in Table 5.21.**

TABLE 5.21
Fossil nonmarine Gastropods from the Clovis and Folsom Levels at the Agate Basin Site[a]

Numbers (Figure 5.21)	Taxa	Relative abundance[b] Clovis	Folsom
	Terrestrial gastropods		
	Family Endodontidae		
1	*Discus cronkhitei* (Newcomb) 1865	A	A
	Family Valloniidae		
2	*Vallonia gracilicosta* Reinhardt 1883	A	A
3	*Vallonia cyclophorella* Sterki 1893	C	C
4	*Vallonia* sp.	C	C
	Family Zonitidae		
5	*Zonitoides arboreus* (Say) 1916	C	A
6	*Euconulus fulvus* (Muller) 1774		R
	Family Succineidae		
7	*Succinea* spp.		C
8	*Catinella* spp.		R
9	*Oxyloma* spp.		R
10	Succineidae: genera? and spp.? indet.	R	R
	Family Cionellidae		
11	*Cionella lubrica* (Muller) 1774	R	R
	Freshwater gastropods		
	Family Lymnaeidae		
12	*Stagnicola palustris* (Muller) 1774	R	C
13	*Fossaria parva* (Lea) 1841		R
14	Lymnaeidae: genera? and spp.? indet.		R
	Family Physidae		
15	*Aplexa hypnorum* (Linnaeus) 1758		R

[a]All gastropod specimens are stored at the Department of Anthropology, University of Wyoming, Laramie.
[b]A = abundant ($N > 20\%$); C = common ($20\% \geq N > 5\%$); R = rare ($5\% \geq N$).

water (Taylor 1960), and therefore indicates the proximity of an ancient water body to the Agate Basin site. *Vallonia cyclophorella* occurs in habitats similar to those of *Vallonia gracilicosta*, but is restricted in its distribution to the Rocky Mountains and the western Great Plains (Bequaert and Miller 1973).

Freshwater snails are uncommon in these fossil gastropod assemblages, but their presence, like that of *Oxyloma*, indicates the existence of an ancient body of water. *Stagnicola palustris* is extremely abundant and widespread in modern intermittent and perennial water bodies in the High Plains (Taylor 1960). *Fossaria parva* is a semiaquatic snail, which often occurs with *Oxyloma* spp. *Aplexa hypnorum* typically inhabits intermittent water bodies (Taylor 1960). These freshwater snails collectively suggest that the aquatic habitats proximal to the Agate Basin site were intermittent. Geologic evidence indicates that springs existed near the site during the Clovis and Folsom occupations (Frison, personal communication, 1981), which would have provided suitable habitats for these freshwater gastropods.

The association of abundant, principally mesic terrestrial snails with uncommon freshwater snails indicates that the Agate Basin site was moist, heavily vegetated, and near a body of water during the Clovis and Folsom occupations. Springs near the site probably provided ample moisture for the dense riparian habitat required by the terrestrial snails.

Chapter six
SUMMARY AND CONCLUSIONS

george c. frison
dennis stanford

When the Agate Basin site was first investigated, in the early 1940s, Early Man in the New World was an accepted fact. The relative chronology and absolute dates of the cultural complexes, however, were uncertain. The taxonomy of the late Pleistocene bison was less well known and understood, and archaeologists were not yet deeply concerned with the details of bison procurement and many other aspects of faunal analysis. Roberts (1943) was well aware that the Agate Basin site was a manifestation of Early Man, but he probably was unaware that anything approaching an overall understanding of the site would require a long period of investigation utilizing many experts in many disciplines along with extensive analysis. Had World War II not intervened, the Agate Basin site would undoubtedly have been properly investigated in the 1940s, and a serious loss of irreplaceable data might have been avoided.

However, it was unlikely that a highly visible bone bed containing such sought after artifacts as Agate Basin projectile points would remain undisturbed for very long. The site suffered significant damage up until the Brewster site excavations in 1959 and the Bass and Roberts site work in 1961. These investigations were not large enough, nor did they involve the breadth of disciplinary studies necessary for recovering sufficient data to lead to a satisfactory explanation of past site activities. These 1959 and 1961 excavations also triggered a fresh round of site depredations that continued for over a decade. It was fortunate that much of the site was too deeply buried to be within the reach of hand tools.

Systematic survey and testing of the Agate Basin site locality from 1971 to 1974 indicated that large parts were still intact. A field season in 1975 and analysis of the results provided significant amounts of cultural materials but relatively little in terms of explanation of past site activities. Five more years of

[361]

investigations provided a data base sufficient to allow some positive statements—and much speculation—on the nature of the Paleoindian use of the Agate Basin site locality. Many specialties, including geology, paleontology, paleobotany, taphonomy, palynology, biology, soil science, animal behavior, phytolith analysis, and lithic analysis, added increments of knowledge to form the present picture.

The evidence of Paleoindian cultural activities found to date in the Agate Basin site locality occurred in arroyo bottoms. Some of the cultural materials recovered were redeposited, and some were in situ. We must assume that as much and probably more cultural activity occurred outside of the arroyo, but these higher occupational surfaces no longer exist. The character of the land surface has changed also. The present arroyo with gently sloping banks and a number of small tributaries contrasts sharply with the wide-bottomed, steep-sided arroyo we are certain was present during Paleoindian times.

In general, the paleoarroyo was aggrading during Paleoindian times although minor periods of downcutting are also suggested. To date there are no known in situ Clovis cultural deposits in the main paleoarroyo in the vicinity of Areas 1, 2, and 3, but redeposited cultural materials there are of Clovis age, although no diagnostic items have yet been recovered. However, in situ Clovis-age deposits may yet be discovered, since a large part of the deposits filling the paleoarroyo are still intact.

However, the Clovis deposits in a tributary arroyo (the Sheaman site) are in situ. The Sheaman site was probably a relatively large site originally, as is suggested by remnants of thick, redeposited levels downstream from the site location that contain redeposited charcoal, bone fragments, and an occasional stone flake. The Sheaman site also is in the bottom of a paleoarroyo, but it is close to an interstream divide where it resembled a swale more than a true arroyo. Probably here also occupation was not limited to the swale but degradation subsequent to the Clovis occupation has removed this evidence. A swale would not appear to be the ideal camping spot during wet weather and alternative locations must have been allowed for.

Chert objects of cultural origin were distributed throughout the Clovis level and were altered to varying degrees depending upon their proximity to intense heat. No evidence indicates the heat was culturally related and it may have occurred as long as 1000 years after the Clovis occupation. The exact nature of the burn is highly conjectural. Bison commonly bed in similar locations and a concentration of tall grass and bison dung might have produced sufficient heat. Equally likely is burning of a heavy brush cover.

Two bison calf mandibles at the Sheaman site stronlgy suggest a springtime or immediate postcalving time of occupation but the sample is too small for a close time-of-year determination. The true meaning of the heavy concentration of red ocher throughout much of the Clovis occupation level is a subject of speculation, but ocher can be obtained locally with relative ease. Red ocher is present in somewhat lower concentrations in the Folsom levels in Areas 2 and 3, but is absent in the Agate Basin and Hell Gap levels.

The focus of activity for the Folsom, Agate Basin, and Hell Gap cultural groups was apparently bison procurement. Insufficient evidence of a Clovis cultural group was recovered to do much more than establish its former presence and the fact that certain aspects of lithic reduction were performed. However, the time of year of bison procurement during Folsom, Agate Basin, and Hell Gap times was during the cold months. Some sort of communal efforts are strongly suggested that resulted in more economic goods (meat) being taken than could be used from day to day. Consequently, some form of storage was necessary and it is argued that the frozen meat cache was the strategy adopted. The animals were skinned, cut into sections, and piled. Protection from carnivores and scavengers was necessary but this could have been solved in various ways. A hide covering, reinforced by small timbers, covered with snow, and glazed with ice would have been effective and would have allowed access by the human group as needed. The lack of features commonly associated with the preparation of dried meat and its products as was common in Late Prehistoric communal bison kills further supports the concept of the frozen meat cache in Paleoindian times.

The exact reasons for choosing this locality for winter bison procurement are unclear but many possibilities exist. The area is today, and undoubtedly was in Paleoindian times, prime bison winter range. There is a strong suggestion, however, that another deciding factor of the use of Agate Basin site locality for bison procurement was topographic. The combination of landforms present appears to have operated in favor of the hunters and required a minimum of effort to provide successful entrapment. The configuration of the paleoarroyo at any given time undoubtedly figured very strongly in the actual location of any given bison procurement event. Regardless of the hunters' experience, many subtle things affect bison behavior and the location of a trap or corral must first be tested to confirm its value.

It is generally accepted that geologic processes of the past are ongoing. A manifestion of what might be an analog of the Agate Basin site topography in Paleoindian times was made some distance away and consists of a deep, wide, steep-sided, intermittent arroyo with a channel that meanders from one side to the other (Figure 6.1). The width of the arroyo varies and the channel bottom occasionally displays sharp drops that interrupt an otherwise even gradient. The banks are high enough and steep enough to contain bison and an impediment of logs and brush across a constricted location would now provide an effective trap. A number of animals killed in the cold months could be butchered and the meat piled on the floodplain but out of the main channel and allowed to freeze. Subsequent aggrading in the arroyo would preserve some evidence of the activity unless later periods of arroyo cutting removed the aggraded deposits. Erosion of the present surface of the arroyo would remove the evidence of human activity performed there. This is, of course, a hypothetical reconstruction, but one that is believed reasonable based on the present body of evidence from the Agate Basin site.

The Folsom levels in Areas 2 and 3 are in situ although some disturbance is indicated by a small amount of cultural materials in the sediments above the occupation level in Area 2. These materials apparently either were scoured from the surface of the occupation floor or resulted from cutting into the occupational floor upstream from Area 2, since the Folsom level was essentially intact in the excavated areas in Area 2.

The claim of the presence of structures in the Folsom level in Area 2 is,

FIGURE 6.1   A location near Agate Basin that is thought to resemble the paleolandf⋯m at Agate Basin.

admittedly, based on weak evidence. Even if structures were pres⋯nt, it is difficult to regard them as family living structures, since they are s⋯uated on the
arroyo floodplain where unseasonal thawing could have produ⋯ed flooding.
They may have served other purposes related to bison procurement or carcass
utilization. They might have been shaman structures involved with bison procurement or more simple features placed and used to house the equipment
needed to process frozen bison carcasses. Certainly projectile poin⋯ manufacture
occurred in the vicinity of the proposed structure along with the r anufacture of
bone and antler items. A strong argument for the presence of a st⋯ucture can be
made also by the bison ribs driven into the ground, which were v⋯ry likely pegs
to hold down a lodge or other covering.

The Folsom occupation area was quite extensive, considering that parts of
individual artifacts were recovered nearly 100 m apart with no reason to suspect
that the intervening area is not a continuous site. There were almost certainly
many more bison killed than were represented in the Folsom occupation levels
excavated. The report of a pile of skulls in the Folsom level during the Brewster
site excavations along with the bison bone recovered during the later University
of Wyoming–Smithsonian excavations leaves the strong impression that a rela-

tively large bone bed was present at one time in Area 3. If the presently recovered evidence is a true indicator, however, the Folsom bison kills were relatively small in comparison to known Paleoindian bison kills of the Hell Gap, Alberta, and Cody time periods.

There is a remarkable similarity between the manufactured bone items at the Lindenmeier site and those found in the Folsom level at Agate Basin, even though both assemblages are small. The bone and antler projectile points at Agate Basin along with the other items and manufacture discards of the same material suggest that Folsom cultural groups possessed an extensive and sophisticated bone and antler manufacture technology. The stone tool assemblage supports this also. The wide range of manufactured stone, bone, and antler tool and weaponry types argues for a sophisticated tradition of fine workmanship in other areas such as wood- and hide-working. Any talented and perceptive user of tools soon realizes that Folsom tool assemblages were the products of true artisans.

The recovery at the Hanson site (Frison and Bradley 1980) and the Agate Basin site of several Folsom projectile points and bifaces that were broken at various stages of manufacture has revealed the entire manufacture sequence of both the bifaces and projectile points. Fluting of Folsom points seems reasonably well explained even though there probably were alternative means of accomplishing the fluting process. However, the reasons for fluting projectile points are still unclear. It was a wasteful process and did not measurably increase the utility of the point as a lethal device. Fluting appears to have taken on attributes of a ritual procedure or perhaps even an art form.

The Agate Basin component in Area 2 represented a relatively large bison-procurement effort that could have easily involved a hundred or more animals. However, the dentition studies suggest more than a single event. Area 2 is not believed to have been an actual kill location, but was probably close to one. Area 1 was very likely a kill area but the evidence to document this more clearly was lost.

Two concentrations of bones within the bone bed in Area 2 are postulated to have been piles of butchered and frozen sections of bison carcasses. The distribution of bones and tools outward from these piles is further postulated as the result of processing frozen meat in preparation for human consumption, which probably took place elsewhere, possibly on land surfaces that no longer exist. The tool assemblage was a simple but effective one and similar to many others found in butchering and processing sites throughout the entire period of prehistoric communal bison procurement on the Plains.

Agate Basin projectile points are a distinctive and lethal form of Paleoindian weaponry. The technology and the final product as seen and described in the Agate Basin projectile point assemblage should provide archaeologists with an adequate means to separate Agate Basin assemblages from other Paleoindian assemblages, at least in most cases, provided adequate site samples are present for comparisons. The Frazier site (Wormington, personal communication) materials are unquestionably Agate Basin as are the Agate Basin component materials from the Hell Gap site (Irwin-Williams et al. 1973), although the complete report on Hell Gap is lacking and badly needed for comparative purposes in High Plains Paleoindian studies.

Farther afield, a close similarity to Agate Basin materials is claimed for several site assemblages in the Keewatin District, Northwest Territory (J. V. Wright 1976). The Keewatin materials appear to fit within the range of variation of the Agate Basin site materials, but a comparison between kill site and camp site is difficult if not of questionable veracity, as Wright admits; it involves comparing what may be a projectile point assemblage representing different manufacture stages with a kill site assemblage representing completed projectile points and broken specimens that were subsequently reworked to a functional condition. Husted (1969) has used the term *Agate Basin-like* in describing projectile points from the Bighorn Canyon area of Wyoming. Again there are similarities between the assemblages, at least in outline form, but the production technology of the Bighorn Canyon materials has not yet been adequately studied.

Dating of the Keewatin and the Agate Basin-like materials from Bighorn Canyon is also a problem. A date of around 8000 years B.P. or slightly more is suggested for the Keewatin materials (J. V. Wright 1976:89) and dates from around 8000 to nearly 9000 B.P. are given for the Bighorn Canyon cave site occupation levels that produced Agate Basin-like projectile points (Husted 1969:11, 31, 32, 52, 82). The Agate Basin levels at the Agate Basin site and the Hell Gap site are dated at over 10,000 B.P. At the Agate Basin site there seems little doubt that the Hell Gap projectile point came directly out of the Agate Basin type. In fact, there is a strong suggestion of some mixing of the two types in the Agate Basin level at the Agate Basin site. It is an uncomfortable feeling to attempt to hypothesize direct relationships between cultural groups separated by several hundred years on the basis of projectile point morphology alone, and also without intermediate evidence to support the relationship. However, a very small number of Agate Basin points recovered in good context do demonstrate a slight shoulder that is reminiscent of the Hell Gap point type and this could be used to argue for a direct lineal relationship between Agate Basin and Hell Gap.

The relationship between Agate Basin and Folsom is certainly open to question. There does not appear to be any known lanceolate unfluted projectile point type on the High Plains that might be considered ancestral to the Agate Basin type unless it is the Goshen type suggested from the Hell Gap excavations and dated at around 10,800 to 11,000 B.P. (Irwin-Williams *et al.* 1973:52). In fact, the next oldest cultural complex material and that closely related stratigraphically and by absolute dates in at least two High Plains sites besides Agate Basin—Hell Gap (Irwin-Williams *et al.* 1973) and Carter/Kerr-McGee (Frison 1977)—is Folsom.

Approaching the problem in the sense of moving from early to late on the time scale, the question that arises is what happened to Folsom. Using projectile point typology, the present evidence suggests that Folsom disappeared quite abruptly in a way almost analogous to the disappearance of many species of animals at about the same time—unless, of course, Midland is a cultural complex that immediately followed Folsom, as is suggested from the Hell Gap site investigations (Irwin-Williams *et al.* 1973:82). In this case Agate Basin could have been part of a continuum from Folsom to Midland to Agate Basin. However, on the High Plains, whether or not Midland is a separate cultural complex or part of Folsom is still an open question; unfluted Folsom points do appear in

Folsom components, and sites that can provide adequate samples and stratigraphy with which to study the Folsom–Midland problem fully (see Judge 1970) are not yet known.

The weight of evidence at this time on the High Plains argues for cultural continuity from Folsom to Agate Basin, even though there is a radical change in the two projectile point types. Wormington (personal communication) feels strongly that intentional fluting is present on one of the Frazier site Agate Basin projectile points and Agogino (1970) argues for the same kind of intentional fluting. If the fluting claimed for Agate Basin projectile points does indicate continuity of a human population from Folsom to Agate Basin, it is evident from this that many aspects of Paleoindian cultural systematics are not yet clear. On the other hand, abrupt changes in material cultural items are not uncommon.

The Hell Gap cultural complex is now better understood with the investigation of the Casper site in Wyoming (Frison 1974), the Jones–Miller site in eastern Colorado (Stanford 1978), and the Carter/Kerr-McGee site in Wyoming (Frison 1977), in addition to the earlier type site investigations (Irwin-Williams *et al.* 1973, Agogino and Galloway 1965). Hell Gap seems to have derived directly out of Agate Basin and there may even be some overlap in time. Hell Gap was the last known Paleoindian group to use the Agate Basin site as a bison-procurement location. Aggradation of the arroyo may have been a determining factor, since the general area did still witness continued bison killing during the later Paleoindian periods. Hudson–Meng (Agenbroad 1978) was an Alberta kill a short distance south of Agate Basin and Carter/Kerr-McGee to the northwest contained a Cody complex kill. The Hawken site directly to the north demonstrated communal bison killing carried over into Early Plains Archaic times.

The post-Paleoindian geologic history of the Agate Basin site is not yet well understood. Deep trenching of the alluvial deposits in the old arroyo is evident and could possibly represent Altithermal conditions. Subsequently, however, the aggrading continued until the filling of the post-Paleoindian arroyo cut, and sometime later the geologic processes began that resulted in the present topography. Archaic fire pits along Moss Agate Arroyo indicate that the present character of the landscape had been largely achieved more than 2000 years ago.

Neither the full range of sources nor the methods of distribution of raw flaking materials during Paleoindian times are yet understood. Knife River flint played an important role in the tools and weaponry of the Folsom and Agate Basin cultural groups, and its source was nearly 800 km to the north; the source of the distinctive Flat-Top chert is about half that distance in the opposite direction. The cultural systematics of the Paleoindian cannot be fully understood until the mechanisms of distributions of raw materials are resolved.

Paleoecological reconstruction based on geology, soils, small mammals, snails, vegetation, pollen, and phytoliths need to be continued and further refined. The results of *Bison* population studies do not seem to fit the appropriate biological models possibly for cultural reasons. It is not unlikely that animals of different age, size, and sex were butchered and processed in different ways. Taphonomic studies offer perhaps the greatest potential for resolving many paleoecological, biological, and cultural problems encountered in Paleoindian studies. Archaeologists must have more and better information concerning the events between the biocoenose and the thanatocoenose in animal kill, butchering, and processing sites before accurate reconstructions of Paleoindian economics can be realized.

The full potential of taphonomic studies in producing paleoecological and paleocultural data is far from being realized. One relatively narrow-focused area of inquiry that might be profitably explored lies in further studies of bison dentition in situations where large samples of animals were obtained in communal kills, as demonstrated in the main Agate Basin component in Area 2 and also in Area 1 before it was needlessly destroyed. The Agate Basin component data indicate what must be considered as extremely large annual increments of tooth wear (see Table 4.8). At the beginning of the second year in late Pleistocene bison, M_1 was fully erupted and the average height of the tooth that had to last the animal for the rest of its life was about 55 mm. This meant that 9 years later, M_1 was worn away and the animal's remaining life span was severely limited, since the loss of M_1 impaired the animals's food intake and increased the wear on M_2 and M_3. The inevitable result, particularly where forage was limited, was death.

From this, it would appear that tooth wear on bison might be an indicator of the kind and amount of forage available to the animals, although other factors, such as competition for forage, must also be considered. For example, at one extreme, bison forced to graze very short grass in sandy or gravelly soil have been observed to pick up enough rock that tooth enamel was actually chipped away, resulting in extremely fast wear extending even beyond the occlusal surfaces. At the other extreme, bison that live in areas of tall, lush forage demonstrate relatively small amounts of tooth wear. Studies by G. Haynes (personal communication, 1981) on bison molars from Wood Buffalo National Park, Alberta and Northwest Territories, Canada, indicate yearly increments of tooth wear of as low as around 1mm. The Wood Buffalo National Park herd feeds on relatively lush grass and has very little competition from other grazers.

The tooth wear observed on the Agate Basin bison indicates some kind of severe stress, although its exact nature is not yet decipherable from the data base. A working hypothesis is that significant climatic change after Clovis times negatively affected the animal carrying capacity of the High Plains, and the bison were experiencing considerable difficulty in adjusting to these changes. Even so, a shortened life span as a result of increased tooth wear was not enough to endanger the species. Unfortunately, there are, as yet, no adequate samples with which to gain some knowledge of tooth wear on Clovis-period bison. Such data would probably reveal something of the lifeways of the earlier bison and provide a basis for determining whether the amount and kind of stresses the species was subjected to at that time were similar to those of Agate Basin times.

If large annual increments of tooth wear as it is recorded in kill sites is an indication of a bison population under stress, this may also figure strongly in the procurement process. Weather, time of day, time of year, feed conditions, vegetative cover, terrain, and animal condition are all interacting forces that affect both the short and long term aspects of animal behavior. It may have been that the bison population under stress was more susceptible to a procurement pattern of communal hunting. Many subtle changes in behavior are perceptible only by the experienced hunter but these alter procurement procedures.

Geologic studies are indispensable to Paleoindian studies. The two are inseparable, but, unfortunately, investigators in each discipline lack the necessary familiarity with the principles of the other. Stratigraphy, identification of paleolandforms, and the problems of stream transport figure strongly in the interpretation of the Agate Basin site since the aspects of Paleoindian life carried out within the confines of an arroyo's walls are all that remained. The proper assessment of bison procurement depends on accurate identification of the landforms that were involved. To maximize cultural interpretations from geologic deposits, the expertise of a person knowledgeable in the processes and interpretation of late Pleistocene and Recent period geology is mandatory.

The same can be argued for soil studies. Correlations between soils of the same age from area to area can be a strong adjunct to the archaeologist in circumstances where cultural diagnostics are lacking. Soils are also strong and reliable indicators of past climatic conditions. Paleoindian studies would lose a large share of their potential for paleoecological and cultural interpretations without the contributions of soils and geologic specialists.

It is unfortunate that the pollen and phytolith studies were inconclusive at the Agate Basin site. It may be a result of our own deficiencies in present recovery methods or it may be attributable to problems of site preservation. It does not indicate that we should abandon these studies; instead, continued effort should be made to develop new and more reliable recovery methods, and to find out why the present problems exist.

Nonmarine mollusks were preserved in large numbers in Clovis and Folsom levels at the Agate Basin site, and they could be important paleoecological indicators. Their presence in Folsom and Clovis levels and their absence in the Agate Basin and Hell Gap levels may be significant in terms of climatic change. More collections of snails in reliable stratigraphic contexts of Paleoindian age are needed for a better understanding of the taphonomics of snail remains before too much optimism is expressed. However, the validity of both geological and mollusk studies are strengthened by the fact that the results from both indicate the presence of running water in the paleoarroyo during Clovis and Folsom times.

The taphonomics of small mammal remains allow a broader basis for paleoecological interpretations during Folsom and Hell Gap times. By looking at the areas of sympatry of the different species of small mammals involved, it is possible to actually view modern analogs of past plant and small mammal communities. The results of research from several disciplines including geology, soils, and taphonomics of invertebrates and small mammals now point to similar paleoecological conditions at the Agate Basin site. This is encouraging for future research.

The period of time from Clovis to late Plano or from about 12000 to 10,000 years ago witnessed the changes that took place in climate from the late Pleistocene to the present (see, e.g., Bryson 1974). During this same period the last of the major Pleistocene faunal extinctions occurred, including the mammoth, the camel, and the horse. The bison survived, but selective factors were at work to bring about gradual changes in size and skull morphology throughout the ensuing Holocene period. Shifts of small-mammal populations that were more sensitive to ecological changes than the large ones also document these changes. Major vegetation changes occurred at this time, along with the general character of the landscape. The agate Basin site provides a record of this, albeit one that is incomplete.

In conclusion, the collection, analysis, and interpretation of archaeological data are constrained by the metholology of the discipline as a science, but also by the uniqueness of each investigator's approach. Interpretation is based on concepts that range from known and accepted fact to pure conjecture. The greater the number of facts, the stronger the conclusions will be. However, no two investigators are in total agreement on where the line between fact and conjecture should be drawn. Consequently, the present results for the Agate Basin site must be considered statements of progress, rather than conclusions.

A large, undisturbed data base remains at the Agate Basin site. It must and can be adequately protected. It is a source of great value for future Paleoindian studies, and should be exploited judiciously. Paleoindian studies are experiencing a period of development and testing of new methods of inquiry involving other disciplines. Until the full potential of these other disciplinary studies are realized, final interpretations of Paleoindian sites in particular and archaeological sites in general will be subject to constant revision. This is not an undisirable situation; on the contrary, it is an indication of a healthy discipline that is continually trying to improve its methodology. The greatest danger lies in the failure or inability to test these new methodologies properly and accept or discard them on the basis of rigid scientific proof.

APPENDIX

Agate Basin Site Artifact Data[a]

Figure number	Ownership	Catalog number	Material	Maximum thickness (mm)
2.19a	U.W.	OA012	K	7.4
2.19b	U.W.	OA123	C	5.9
2.19c	U.W.	OA045	C	9.4
2.19d	U.W.	OA061	C	8.1
2.19e	U.W.	11308	C	6.9
2.19f	U.W.	OA006	C	5.4
2.19g	U.W.	96565	C	10.4
2.19h	U.W.	OA276	C	8.5
2.19i	U.W.	96597	C	4.4
2.19j	U.W.	OA131	C	12.1
2.19k	U.W.	96596	K	7.6
2.19l	U.W.	96426	C	5.6
2.19m	U.W.	96586	C	4.5
2.19n	U.W.	OA286	C	6.2
2.19o	U.W.	96591	C	9.2
2.19p	U.W.	96589	C	5.0
2.19q	U.W.	OA193, OA024	C	3.2
2.19r	U.W.	OA017	C	3.8
2.19s	U.W.	OA066	C	5.2
2.19t	U.W.	OA296	C	2.4
2.20a	U.W.	OA476, OA018, OA223	C	5.3
2.20b	U.W.	OA439	C	8.6

[a]The Steege and Duguid collections have been presented to the Smithsonian Institution.

Abbreviations. *Ownership:* S.I., Smithsonian Institution; U.W., University of Wyoming; ST, Louis Steege; DU, James Duguid; JS, Josephine Spencer. *Material Type:* K, Knife River flint; C, chert; Q, quartzite; P, porcelainite; L, calcite; S, sandstone; G, granite; B, bone; A, antler, I, ivory.

(continued)

Figure number	Ownership	Catalog number	Material	Maximum thickness (mm)
2.21a	U.W.	96570	C	11.5
2.21b	U.W.	OA316	C	7.5
2.21c	U.W.	96594	C	6.7
2.21d	U.W.	OA293	C	4.9
2.21e	U.W.	OA047	C	2.5
2.21f	U.W.	OA099	C	3.0
2.21g	U.W.	OA026	C	3.9
2.21h	U.W.	OA132	C	3.1
2.21i	U.W.	OA303	C	4.5
2.21j	U.W.	96557	C	3.9
2.21k	U.W.	OA101	C	10.5
2.21l	U.W.	OA178	C	9.0
2.21m	U.W.	96558	C	3.5
2.21n	U.W.	OA338	C	2.5
2.21o	U.W.	OA096	C	1.9
2.21p	U.W.	OA098	C	2.6
2.21q	U.W.	OA309, OA053	C	5.0
2.21r	U.W.	OA030	C	2.1
2.21s	U.W.	OA400	C	3.9
2.21t	U.W.	OA107	C	2.4
2.21u	U.W.	OA109	C	2.8
2.21v	U.W.	OA172	C	5.0
2.21w	U.W.	OA100	C	5.5
2.21x	U.W.	OA191	C	5.2
2.21y	U.W.	96515	C	2.1
2.21z	U.W.	96542	C	2.0
2.21aa	U.W.	96541	C	1.9
2.22a	U.W.	OA305, 96575	Q	10.2
2.22b	U.W., S.I.	OA119, 508,114	Q	5.1
2.22c	U.M.	96571	C	7.2
2.22d	U.W.	96569	C	6.7
2.22e	U.W.	OA355	C	7.0
2.22f	U.W.	96599	C	5.6
2.22g	U.W.	OA046	C	4.4
2.22h	U.W.	OA173	C	10.0
2.22i	U.W.	OA247	C	6.4
2.22j	U.W.	96574	C	4.3
2.22k	U.W.	96573	C	5.3
2.22l	U.W.	OA067	C	5.7
2.22m	U.W.	OA299	C	6.7
2.22n	U.W.	OA055	C	5.0
2.23a	U.W.	OA038	C	7.9
2.23b	U.W., S.I.	OA189, 508,113	C	7.3
2.23c	U.W.	OA089	Q	6.5
2.23d	U.W.	96598	C	6.3
2.23e	U.W.	OA295	C	10.2
2.23f	U.W.	OA062	C	11.4
2.23g	U.W.	OA121	C	7.2
2.23h	U.W.	OA277	C	6.0
2.23i	U.W.	OA086	C	6.3
2.23j	U.W.	96592	Q	11.4
2.23k	U.W.	OA320	C	15.4
2.24	U.W.	OA173	C	10.0
2.25a	U.W.	OA039, 96566	Q	5.5
2.25b	U.W.	OA032	K	9.2
2.25c	U.W.	96587	K	9.4
2.25d	U.W.	96567	K	8.1
2.25e	U.W.	96564	C	10.5

Figure number	Ownership	Catalog number	Material	Maximum thickness (mm)
2.25f	U.W.	96563	Q	13.2
2.25g	U.W.	OA294	C	16.9
2.25h	U.W.	OA391, 96599	C	10.1
2.26a	U.W.	96600, 96548	C	4.5
2.26b	U.W., S.I.	96550, 96503, 508,112	Q	4.6
2.26c	U.W.	OA059	C	5.4
2.26d	U.W.	96502	Q	7.1
2.26e	U.W.	96501	Q	3.7
2.26f	U.W.	OA020	C	4.5
2.26g	U.W.	OA112	C	3.9
2.26h	U.W.	96533	C	5.1
2.26i	U.W.	OA078	C	6.1
2.26j	U.W.	96544, OA106	C	5.4, 2.9
2.26k	U.W.	OA288	C	6.9
2.26l	U.W.	96504	Q	6.1
2.26m	U.W.	OA085	C	4.5
2.26n	U.W.	96545	C	5.4
2.26o	U.W.	96526	C	5.7
2.26p	U.W.	96506, 96508, 96509	C	4.1
2.26q	U.W.	96505	C	1.8
2.26r	U.W.	96530	C	1.9
2.26s	U.W.	OA093	C	7.4
2.26t	U.W.	OA082	C	3.2
2.26u	U.W.	OA174	C	2.5
2.26v	U.W.	96532	C	7.5
2.26w	U.W.	OA110	C	5.0
2.26x	U.W.	96507	C	4.7
2.27	U.W.	96554	C	29.6
2.28a	U.W.	OA160	G	57.0
2.28b	U.W.	C3477	Q	33.9
2.29	U.W.	OA267	G	44.3
2.30	U.W.	OA460	Q	39.2
2.31	U.W.	OA461	Q	50.2
2.32	U.W.	OA462	Q	94.5
2.33	U.W.	96562, OA169	S	37.0, 10.8
2.34	U.W.	OA009	S	55.0
2.35	U.W.	OA463	S	33.1
2.36	U.W.	OA323	L	22.1
2.37	U.W.	OA124	L	20.0
2.38	U.W.	OA115	G	35.2
2.41a	DU	JD111	P	—
2.41b	DU	JD113	C	—
2.41c	DU	JD90	C	—
2.41d	U.W.	OA175	K	4.6
2.41e	U.W.	OA438	C	2.1
2.41f	U.W.	OA431	C	6.1
2.41g	U.W.	OA430	C	6.0
2.41h	U.W.	OA423	C	1.6
2.41i	U.W.	OA176	C	3.6
2.41j	U.W.	OA429	C	7.7
2.41k	U.W.	OA425	C	3.6
2.41l	U.W.	OA414	C	7.5
2.41m	U.W.	OA415	Q	6.1
2.41n	U.W.	OA413	C	3.9
2.41o	U.W.	OA410	C	4.1
2.41p	U.W.	OA412	C	5.6
2.41q	U.W.	OA417	C	5.5

(continued)

Figure number	Ownership	Catalog number	Material	Maximum thickness (mm)
2.41r	U.W.	OA419	C	5.0
2.41s	U.W.	OA411	Q	9.5
2.41t	U.W.	OA404	C	2.3
2.41u	U.W.	OA421	C	8.0
2.41v	U.W.	OA402	Q	6.8
2.41w	U.W.	OA409	Q	10.0
2.41x	U.W.	OA416	C	6.5
2.48a	S.I.	508,014	K	6.2
2.48b	S.I.	508,015	K	6.0
2.48c	S.I.	508,016	K	6.8
2.48d	S.I.	508,017	K	7.9
2.48e	S.I.	508,018	K	8.7
2.48f	S.I.	508,019	K	7.0
2.48g	S.I.	508,020	K	6.0
2.48h	S.I.	508,021	K	6.2
2.48i	S.I.	508,022	K	7.0
2.48j	S.I.	508,023	K	5.9
2.48k	S.I.	508,024	K	6.9
2.48l	S.I.	508,025	K	6.1
2.48m	S.I.	508,026	K	7.4
2.48n	S.I.	508,027	K	5.5
2.49a	S.I.	508,028	K	6.8
2.49b	S.I.	508,029	K	5.9
2.49c	S.I.	508,030	K	9.1
2.49d	S.I.	508,031	K	8.7
2.49e	S.I.	508,032	K	6.2
2.49f	S.I.	508,033	K	6.1
2.49g	S.I.	508,034	K	7.4
2.49h	S.I.	508,035	K	6.4
2.49i	S.I.	508,036	C	7.8
2.49j	S.I.	508,037	C	8.4
2.49k	S.I.	508,038	C	7.1
2.49l	S.I.	508,039	C	6.6
2.49m	S.I.	508,040	C	8.9
2.49n	S.I.	508,041	C	5.8
2.49o	S.I.	508,042	C	7.1
2.50a	S.I.	508,043	C	8.2
2.50b	S.I.	508,044	C	6.6
2.50c	S.I.	508,045	C	6.3
2.50d	S.I.	508,046	C	5.9
2.50e	S.I.	508,047	C	6.4
2.50f	S.I.	508,048	C	7.5
2.50g	S.I.	508,049	C	6.9
2.50h	S.I.	508,050	C	7.1
2.50i	S.I.	508,051	Q	8.1
2.50j	S.I.	508,052	Q	6.5
2.50k	S.I.	508,053	Q	6.8
2.50l	S.I.	508,054	Q	5.0
2.50m	S.I.	508,055	Q	7.6
2.50n	S.I., U.W.	508,056, 11220	C	6.9
2.50o	S.I.	508,057	Q	6.5
2.50p	S.I.	508,058	Q	5.9
2.50q	S.I.	508,059	K	6.8
2.50r	S.I.	508,060	Q	7.2
2.50s	S.I.	508,061	Q	7.9
2.50t	S.I.	508,062	Q	7.8
2.51a	U.W.	35002a	K	7.6
2.51b	U.W.	35006a	K	6.1

Figure number	Ownership	Catalog number	Material	Maximum thickness (mm)
2.51c	U.W.	35005a	K	7.9
2.51d	U.W.	35007a	K	7.3
2.51e	U.W.	35003a	Q	7.4
2.51f	U.W.	03431	K	7.2
2.51g	U.W.	11317	K	7.0
2.51h	U.W.	35004a	C	7.3
2.51i	U.W.	35010a	P	7.3
2.51j	U.W.	35011a	C	6.7
2.51k	U.W.	35009a	Q	6.2
2.51l	U.W.	OA387	C	5.4
2.51m	U.W.	35008a	Q	9.0
2.52a	U.W.	96602, 11294, 11291	K	5.5
2.52b	U.W.	96601, 96237	K	8.0
2.52c	U.W.	96118a	K	7.2
2.52d	U.W.	96107a	K	7.8
2.52e	U.W.	11318	Q	7.0
2.52f	U.W.	96228	K	6.9
2.52g	U.W.	96205	K	6.3
2.52h	U.W.	OA051	K	6.1
2.52i	U.W.	11307	K	6.1
2.52j	U.W.	96058	K	8.3
2.52k	U.W.	98605	K	7.5
2.53a	U.W.	96071	K	7.1
2.53b	U.W.	11323	K	7.3
2.53c	U.W.	OA379	K	5.5
2.53d	U.W.	96097	K	7.8
2.53e	U.W.	OA273	K	8.0
2.53f	U.W.	OA268	Ḱ	8.4
2.53g	U.W.	11328	K	6.4
2.53h	U.W.	C3430	K	5.9
2.53i	U.W.	96057	K	6.3
2.53j	U.W.	11298	K	6.2
2.53k	U.W.	96078	K	5.9
2.53l	U.W.	00196	K	5.7
2.53m	U.W.	96221	C	6.5
2.53n	U.W.	96085	C	7.8
2.53o	U.W.	96060	C	8.8
2.53p	U.W.	96042	C	6.8
2.53q	U.W.	OA060	C	6.9
2.54a	U.W.	96603	C	7.0
2.54b	U.W.	96000	C	7.7
2.54c	U.W.	96604	C	7.5
2.54d	U.W.	11330	C	8.2
2.54e	U.W.	OA090	C	8.0
2.54f	U.W.	96213	C	5.1
2.54g	U.W.	96124a	C	4.9
2.54h	U.W.	96038	C	6.5
2.54i	U.W.	C3432	C	7.4
2.54j	U.W.	96068	C	8.0
2.54k	U.W.	96074	C	4.9
2.54l	U.W.	11310	C	6.1
2.54m	U.W.	96081	C	4.2
2.54n	U.W.	OA382	C	6.0
2.54o	U.W.	96076	Q	6.0
2.54p	U.W.	96087	Q	8.1
2.54q	U.W.	96092	Q	6.3
2.54r	U.W.	96112a	Q	7.8

(continued)

Figure number	Ownership	Catalog number	Material	Maximum thickness (mm)
2.54s	U.W.	11329	Q	7.9
2.54t	U.W.	11331	Q	7.1
2.54u	U.W.	96202	Q	6.4
2.54v	U.W.	96054	Q	5.7
2.54w	U.W.	96061	Q	6.4
2.54x	U.W.	96059	Q	5.0
2.54y	U.W.	96212	Q	7.7
2.54z	U.W.	11272	Q	6.2
2.55a	U.W.	11319	K	7.0
2.55b	U.W.	11332	K	4.9
2.55c	U.W.	11333	K	7.9
2.55d	U.W.	11326	K	6.4
2.55e	U.W.	11329	K	8.8
2.55f	U.W.	11315	C	6.2
2.55g	U.W.	11300	Q	8.6
2.55h	U.W.	11312	Q	7.0
2.55i	U.W.	11297	Q	3.6
2.55j	ST	1	K	8.6
2.55k	ST	2	Q	8.9
2.55l	ST	3	Q	6.1
2.55m	ST	4	C	7.3
2.55n	ST	5	K	6.5
2.55o	U.W.	11316, 96044	C	6.0
2.56a	S.I.	508,073	K	7.5
2.56b	S.I.	508,074	C	7.7
2.56c	S.I.	508,075	K	—
2.56d	S.I.	508,076	C	9.2
2.56e	S.I.	508,077	C	7.2
2.56f	S.I.	508,078	C	6.3
2.56g	S.I.	508,079	C	6.9
2.56h	S.I.	508,080	C	7.0
2.56i	S.I.	508,081	Q	6.7
2.56j	S.I.	508,082	C	6.9
2.56k	S.I.	508,083	K	7.1
2.56l	S.I.	508,084	C	7.4
2.56m	S.I.	508,085	Q	8.1
2.56n	S.I.	508,086	Q	5.7
2.56o	S.I.	508,087	Q	6.9
2.56p	S.I.	508,088	K	5.5
2.56q	S.I.	508,089	C	7.5
2.56r	S.I.	508,090	K	8.5
2.56s	S.I.	508,091	Q	—
2.56t	S.I., U.W.	508,092, 96211	Q	6.7
2.57a	DU	JD96	K	7.1
2.57b	DU	JD100	K	7.5
2.57c	DU	JD114	K	5.6
2.57d	DU	JD102	K	9.2
2.57e	DU	JD101	K	8.2
2.57f	DU	JD91	C	8.9
2.57f	U.W.	OA274	C	8.9
2.57g	DU	JD93	C	7.9
2.57h	DU	JD95	K	6.9
2.57i	DU	JD92	K	6.5
2.57j	DU	JD99	K	7.3
2.57k	DU	JD112	K	7.2
2.57l	DU	JD87	Q	5.4
2.57m	DU	JD104	Q	7.3

Figure number	Ownership	Catalog number	Material	Maximum thickness (mm)
2.57n	DU	JD94	Q	6.9
2.57o	DU	JD110	Q	7.3
2.57p	DU	JD109	C	8.5
2.58a	J.S.	1	C	—
2.58b	J.S.	2	C	—
2.58c	J.S.	3	C	—
2.58d	J.S.	4	C	—
2.58e	J.S.	5	C	—
2.58f	J.S.	6	C	—
2.58g	J.S.	7	Q	—
2.58h	J.S.	8	C	—
2.58i	J.S.	9	C	—
2.58j	J.S.	10	C	—
2.58k	J.S.	11	C	—
2.58l	J.S.	12	C	—
2.59a	U.W.	35001a	C	7.7
2.59c	U.W.	OA176, 96094, 96094a, OA458	K	8.1
2.61a	U.W.	11285	C	10.5
2.61b	U.W.	96216	C	9.5
2.61c	U.W.	96226	C	6.0
2.61d	U.W.	96224	C	11.7
2.61e	U.W.	96096	Q	8.7
2.61f	U.W.	OA271	Q	11.6
2.61g	U.W.	96593	Q	7.6
2.61h	DU	JD88	C	—
2.61i	U.W.	96209	Q	9.3
2.61j	U.W.	11286	Q	18.8
2.61k	U.W.	11287	Q	19.3
2.62a	U.W.	OA475	C	15.5
2.62b	U.W.	96585	C	9.0
2.62c	U.W.	96234	C	8.5
2.62d	U.W.	OA042	C	10.5
2.62e	U.W.	OA050	C	13.8
2.62f	U.W.	OA001	C	10.5
2.62g	U.W.	11283	C	13.0
2.62h	U.W.	96049	C	10.4
2.62i	S.I.	508,093	C	—
2.63a	DU	JD97	K	—
2.63b	U.W.	96097	K	8.0
2.63c	U.W.	OA270	K	11.9
2.63d	U.W.	96222	K	9.2
2.63e	U.W.	11334	K	7.8
2.63f	U.W.	11309	C	18.3
2.63g	U.W.	OA002	C	10.0
2.63h	U.W.	96588	C	13.1
2.63i	U.W.	OA133, 96206	K	8.8
2.63j	U.W.	96204	C	12.4
2.64a	S.I.	508,063	Q	—
2.64b	S.I.	508,064	Q	—
2.64c	S.I.	508,065	C	—
2.64d	S.I.	508,066	P	—
2.64e	S.I.	508,098	Q	—
2.64f	S.I.	508,099	Q	—
2.64g	U.W.	OA450	C	9.9
2.64h	S.I.	508,067	C	—
2.64i	S.I.	508,068	C	—

(*continued*)

Figure number	Ownership	Catalog number	Material	Maximum thickness (mm)
2.64j	U.W.	96062	Q	5.9
2.64k	S.I.	508,100	C	—
2.64l	U.W.	OA272	Q	13.3
2.64m	U.W.	OA326, OA275	P	12.4
2.64n	U.W.	OA449	C	7.4
2.65a	DU	JD105	K	—
2.65b	U.W.	OA269	Q	11.1
2.65c	DU	JD98	Q	11.3
2.66a	U.W.	96225	C	5.9
2.66b	S.I.	508,094	C	—
2.66c	S.I.	508,095	C	—
2.66d	DU	JD85	Q	—
2.66e	DU	JD89	C	—
2.66f	U.W.	96076	C	2.2
2.66g	S.I.	508,096	C	—
2.66h	DU	JD86	K	4.5
2.66i	U.W.	OA325, 96114	K	8.7
2.66j	U.W.	96219	C	5.6
2.66k	U.W.	11278	C	7.5
2.66l	U.W.	11295	Q	9.9
2.66m	U.W.	96084	C	4.8
2.66n	U.W.	96065	C	5.4
2.66o	U.W.	96045	C	8.1
2.66p	U.W.	96283	C	4.9
2.66q	S.I.	508,097	Q	9.1
2.66r	U.W.	96090, OA364	C	8.9
2.66s	U.W.	96098	C	9.9
2.66t	U.W.	11273	C	7.8
2.67a	U.W.	96065	C	5.4
2.67b	U.W.	96076	C	2.2
2.67c	U.W.	11273	C	7.8
2.68	U.W.	11302	C	8.5
2.69a	U.W.	11335	SD	27.4
2.69b	U.W.	OA306	Q	33.6
2.69c	S.I.	508,117	Q	—
2.69d	U.W.	OA451, OA452	C	20.4
2.69e	U.W.	OA453, OA454	C	19.4
2.69f	U.W.	OA455	C	12.8
2.69g	S.I., U.W.	508,111, OA456	C	5.7
2.69h	U.W.	OA457	C	4.0
2.69i	S.I.	508,110	C	—
2.70a	U.W.	11281	C	14.1
2.70b	U.W.	11281	C	14.1
2.70c	U.W.	11281	C	23.5
2.70d	U.W.	OA377	C	32.5
2.70e	U.W.	11274	C	22.7
2.70f	U.W.	C3469	C	23.4
2.70g	U.W.	OA467	C	22.7
2.70h	U.W.	11288	C	26.9
2.70i	U.W.	OA468	C	26.7
2.71a	U.W.	96051	C	9.4
2.71b	U.W.	96048	C	8.6
2.71c	U.W.	96095	C	5.6
2.71d	U.W.	96214	C	6.5
2.71e	U.W.	OA173	C	7.8
2.71f	S.I.	508,101	C	—
2.71g	S.I.	508,102	C	—
2.71h	U.W.	96038	C	6.6

Figure number	Ownership	Catalog number	Material	Maximum thickness (mm)
2.71i	U.W.	OA477	C	6.5
2.71j	U.W.	96077	C	10.6
2.71k	U.W.	11305	C	6.8
2.71l	U.W.	96108	C	8.2
2.71m	U.W.	11304	C	7.7
2.71n	S.I.	508,103	C	—
2.71o	U.W.	11271	C	8.2
2.71p	U.W.	11303	C	10.1
2.71q	S.I.	508,104	C	—
2.71r	U.W.	96220	C	6.7
2.71s	U.W.	11296	C	4.5
2.71t	U.W.	11289	C	6.5
2.72a	U.W.	96056	Q	12.4
2.72b	U.W.	OA266, C3419	C	13.0
2.72c	U.W.	11313	C	8.5
2.72d	U.W.	11290	C	7.0
2.72e	U.W.	96217	C	13.5
2.72f	DU	JD108	Q	6.0
2.72g	S.I.	508,105	Q	—
2.73a	U.W.	11277, 11282	Q	11.4
2.73b	U.W.	11284	C	13.8
2.73c	U.W.	96105	Q	10.2
2.73d	U.W.	96104	C	11.7
2.73e	S.I.	508,106	C	—
2.73f	S.I.	508,069	Q	21.0
2.73g	S.I.	508,107	Q	—
2.73h	S.I.	508,108	Q	—
2.73i	S.I.	508,070	Q	—
2.73j	S.I.	508,071	Q	—
2.73k	S.I.	508,072	P	—
2.73l	S.I.	508,109	Q	—
2.74a	U.W.	OA378	Q	39.2
2.74b	U.W.	C3489	Q	42.0
2.75	S.I.	508,116	Q	44.3
2.76	U.W.	OA459	Q	64.8
2.79a	U.W.	96577	C	7.2
2.79b	U.W.	96578	Q	6.7
2.79c	U.W.	96581	C	7.9
2.79d	U.W.	96580	C	7.0
2.79e	U.W.	96582	C	7.5
2.79f	U.W.	96579	C	15.4
2.79g	U.W.	OA300	C	4.4
2.79h	U.W.	96584	C	8.5
2.79i	U.W.	96583	C	4.0
2.79j	U.W.	OA400	C	8.3
2.79k	U.W.	OA192	C	8.2
2.79l	U.W.	OA063	C	6.8
2.79m	U.W.	30737	C	8.1
2.79n	S.I.	508,115	C	—
2.82	U.W.	OA403	S	13.3
2.83a	U.W.	OA151	Q	7.4
2.83b	U.W.	96231	Q	6.5
2.83c	U.W.	OA140	Q	7.9
2.83d	U.W.	OA150	C	8.2
2.83e	U.W.	OA152	C	7.0
2.83f	U.W.	96230	Q	7.0
2.83g	U.W.	OA146	Q	7.6

(continued)

Figure number	Ownership	Catalog number	Material	Maximum thickness (mm)
2.83h	U.W.	OA147	Q	6.5
2.83i	U.W.	OA148	Q	10.0
2.83j	U.W.	OA161	Q	7.0
2.83k	U.W.	OA159	Q	7.4
2.83l	U.W.	OA149	Q	7.0
2.83m	U.W.	OA324	C	6.2
2.83n	U.W.	OA155	C	7.2
2.83o	U.W.	96210	P	4.7
2.85a	U.W.	OA416	C	6.5
2.85b	U.W.	OA421	C	8.0
2.89a	U.W.	E1031	B	—
2.89b	U.W.	E1038	B	—
2.91a	DU	JD103	C	—
2.91b	DU	JD84	Q	—
2.91c	U.W.	E1067	C	7.7
2.91d	U.W.	E1065	Q	8.5
2.91e	U.W.	OA442	C	—
2.91f	U.W.	E1064	C	10.7
2.92a	U.W.	E1000	C	8.1
2.92b	U.W.	E1013	C	8.0
2.92c	U.W.	E1062	C	8.6
2.92d	U.W.	E1008	Q	12.7
2.92e	U.W.	E1002	C	9.7
2.92f	U.W.	E1027	C	13.0
2.93a	U.W.	E1028	C	12.1
2.93b	U.W.	E1066	C	11.3
2.93c	U.W.	E1071	C	10.9
2.93d	U.W.	E1063	C	9.9
2.93e	U.W.	30757	C	11.3
2.93f	U.W.	E1060	C	5.6
2.93g	U.W.	E1065	C	4.4
2.93h	U.W.	E1061	C	10.2
2.94	U.W.	OA469	C	7.7
2.95	U.W.	OA467	Q	3.4
2.96	U.W.	OA447: 1–14	C	22.0
2.97	U.W.	E1015	C	42.5
2.98	U.W.	OA470	Q	39.7
2.99	U.W.	E1052	I	14.2
2.100	U.W.	OA464	B	—
2.101	U.W.	OA465	B	—
2.102	U.W.	OA466	B	—
2.103a	U.W.	F1443	B	—
2.103b	U.W.	F1822	B	—
2.104	U.W.	F1365	B	—
2.106	U.W.	OA010	A	—
2.107	U.W.	OA471, OA472	B	15.1
2.109a	U.W.	OA420	A	21.5
2.109b	U.W.	OA154	A	13.6
2.109c	U.W.	OA156	B	5.2
2.109d	U.W.	OA122, OA027	B	8.4
2.109e	U.W.	F1037	B	—
2.109f	U.W.	F1687	B	—
2.109g	U.W.	F1024	B	2.0
2.109h	U.W.	OA142	B	3.3
2.109i	U.W.	E1026	B	25.5
2.109j	U.W.	OA448	B	10.3
2.109k	U.W.	OA005	B	3.8
2.109l	U.W.	OA282	B	—

Figure number	Ownership	Catalog number	Material	Maximum thickness (mm)
2.109m	U.W.	F1719	B	—
2.110	U.W.	OA474	A	5.8
2.111a	U.W.	OA004	B	1.7
2.111b	U.W.	C3478	B	1.3
2.112a	U.W.	F1568	B	—
2.112b	U.W.	F1715	B	—
2.112c	U.W.	OA097	B	—
2.113a	U.W.	OA109	B	9.6
2.113b	U.W.	OA111	B	10.2
2.114a	U.W.	OA435	B	2.4
2.114c	U.W.	OA464	B	2.0
2.114d	U.W.	OA466	B	1.8
2.114e	U.W.	OA465	B	2.2
2.115	U.W.	OA441	A	3.1
2.116	DU	JD107	B	—
2.117	U.W.	OA321	B	10.8
2.118a	U.W.	11327	B	3.6
2.118b	U.W.	OA117	B	8.8
3.1a	U.W.	11281: 1–10	C	35.5
3.1b	U.W.	11281: 11–15	C	10.0
3.2a	U.W.	OA063	C	6.8
3.2b	U.W.	OA110	C	5.0
3.3	U.W.	OA288, 96505, 96506, 96508, 96509, 96530	C	6.9
3.4	U.W.	96527	C	3.2
3.5	U.W.	96507	C	4.7
3.8	U.W.	96548, 96600	C	4.5
3.11a, b	U.W.	OA447: 1–3	C	5.3
3.11c, d	U.W.	OA447: 4–14	C	13.5
3.13a, b	U.W.	OA448: 1–5	C	7.5
3.13c, d	U.W.	OA442: 1–3	C	6.8
3.14a, b	U.W.	OA445: 1–2	C	4.1
3.14c, d	U.W.	OA444: 1–2	C	4.0
3.16	U.W.	OA483	C	2.3
3.17	U.W.	OA484	Q	5.0
4.1	U.W.	F1396		
4.2a	U.W.	16578		
4.2b	U.W.	F1392		
4.3a	U.W.	F1324		
4.3b	U.W.	16378		
4.4	U.W.	F1524		
4.5a	U.W.	F1330		
4.5b	U.W.	F1356		
4.6	U.W.	F1394		
4.7	U.W.	F1479		
4.8	U.W.	F1479		
4.15	U.W.	F1883		
4.16	U.W.	F1876		
4.17	S.I.	F1877, B571		
4.18	U.W.	F1880		
4.19	U.W.	F1871		
4.20a	U.W.	F1878		
4.20b	U.W.	F1882		
4.21a	U.W.	F1870		
4.21b	U.W.	F1879		
4.22	U.W.	F1872		
4.23	U.W.	F1868		

(continued)

Appendix

Figure number	Ownership	Catalog number	Material	Maximum thickness (mm)
4.24	U.W.	F1873		
4.25	U.W.	F1874		
4.26a	U.W.	F1881		
4.26b	U.W.	F1875		
4.30	U.W.	F1869		
4.33a	U.W.	F1001		
4.33b	U.W.	F2113		
4.33c	U.W.	F1016		
4.33d	U.W.	F1175		
4.33e	U.W.	F2121		
4.33f	U.W.	F1012		
4.33g	U.W.	F1680		
4.33h	U.W.	F2028		
4.33i	U.W.	F1682		
4.34a	U.W.	F1022		
4.34b	U.W.	F1507		
4.34c	U.W.	F1013		
4.34d	U.W.	F1002		
4.34e	U.W.	B0095		
4.34f	U.W.	F1014		
4.34g	U.W.	F1015		
4.34h	U.W.	F1255		
4.36A	U.W.	F1157		
4.36B	U.W.	F1237		
4.36C	U.W.	F1155		
4.36D	U.W.	F1069		
4.36E	U.W.	F1154		
4.36F	U.W.	F1139		
4.36G	U.W.	F1149		
4.36H	U.W.	F1129		
4.36I	U.W.	F1150		
4.36J	U.W.	F1152		
4.36K	U.W.	F1146		
4.36L	U.W.	F1145		
4.36M	U.W.	F1102		
4.36N	U.W.	F1103		
4.36O	U.W.	F1084		
4.36P	U.W.	F1125		
4.36Q	U.W.	F1125		
4.36R	U.W.	F1101		
4.36S	U.W.	F1153		
4.36T	U.W.	F1100		
4.36U	U.W.	F1092		
4.36V	U.W.	F1130		
4.37b	U.W.	E1075		
4.38	U.W.	F2138		
4.39a	U.W.	F1478		
4.39b	U.W.	F1518		
4.40a	U.W.	B1574		
4.40b	U.W.	F0006		
4.41a	U.W.	F2332		
4.41b	U.W.	0109F		
4.41c	U.W.	0209F		

REFERENCES

Adams, D.
    1979   The cheetah: Native american. *Science 205*:1155–1158.

Agenbroad, L. D.
    1978   *The Hudson–Meng site: An Alberta bison kill site in the Nebraska High Plains.* Washington, D.C.: University Press of America.

Agogino, G. A.
    1970   Occasional, purposeful fluting of Agate Basin points. *Occasional Papers of New Mexico Academy of Science 1970*:13–15.

Agogino, G. A., and W. D. Frankforter
    1960   The Brewster site: An Agate Basin–Folsom multiple component site in eastern Wyoming. *The Masterkey 34* (3):102–107.

Agogino, G. A., and E. Galloway
    1965   The Sister's Hill site. A Hell Gap site in north-central Wyoming. *Plains Anthropologist 10*:190–195.

Albanese, J.
    1974   Geology of the Casper archeological site. In *The Casper site: A Hell Gap bison kill on the High Plains,* edited by G. C. Frison. New York: Academic Press. Pp. 173–192.
    1977   Paleotopography and Paleoindian sites in Wyoming and Colorado. In *Paleoindian lifeways,* edited by E. Johnson. *The Museum Journal 17*:28–47. Lubbock: West Texas Museum Association, Texas Tech University.

Alexander, H. L., Jr.
    1963   The Levi site: A Paleo-Indian campsite in central Texas. *American Antiquity 28*:510–528.

Anderson, E.
    1974   A survey of the late Pleistocene and Holocene mammal faunas of Wyoming. *Geological Survey of Wyoming, Report of Investigations 10*:79–87.

Armstrong, D. D.
    1972   Distribution of mammals in Colorado. *Museum of Natural History, University of Kansas, Monograph* No. 3.

Bailey, R. G
    1976   *Ecoregions of the United States.* (Map). Washington, D.C.: U.S. Forest Service.

Bailey, V.
    1900   Revision of American voles of the genus *Microtus.* U.S. Department of Agriculture, North American Fauna 17.

References

1915   Revision of the pocket gophers of the genus *Thomomys*. *U.S. Department of Agriculture, North American Fauna 39*.

Baldwin, M., C. E. Kellogg, and J. Thorp
1938   Soil classification. In *Soils and men, yearbook of agriculture, 1938*. Washington, D.C.: U.S. Government Printing Office. Pp. 979–1001.

Banfield, A. W. F.
1974   *The mammals of Canada*. Toronto: University of Toronto Press.

Bass, W. M.
1970   Excavations of a Paleo-Indian site at Agate Basin, Wyoming. *National Geographic Society Research Reports, 1961–1962 Projects*:21–25.

Bass, W. M., and F. Roberts
1961   Field notes on file, Smithsonian Institution, Washington, D.C.

Becker, C. F., and J. D. Alyea
1964a   *Precipitation probabilities in Wyoming*. Agricultural Experiment Station Bulletin 416. Laramie: University of Wyoming.

1964b   *Temperature probabilities in Wyoming*. Agricultural Experiment Station Bulletin 415. Laramie: University of Wyoming.

Becker, C. F., L. O. Pochop, and J. D. Alyea
1977   *Probabilities of freeze in Wyoming*. Agricultural Experiment Station Bulletin 381R. Laramie: University of Wyoming.

Bedord, J. N.
1974   Morphological variation in bison metacarpals and metatarsals. In *The Casper site: A Hell Gap bison kill on the High Plains*, edited by G. C. Frison. New York: Academic Press. Pp. 199–240.

Beiswenger, J. M.
1978   Pollen analysis of samples from Threemile Gulch Site, Colorado. In, K. T. Jones, Archaeological investigations of Threemile Gulch Site, Rio Blanco County, CO, *Reports of the Laboratory of Public Archaeology*, Ft. Collins, Colorado, No. 20, pp. 73–77.

Bekoff, M.
1978   *Coyotes—biology, behavior and management*. New York: Academic Press.

Bequaert, J., and W. Miller
1973   *The mollusks of the arid Southwest, with an Arizona checklist*. Tucson: University of Arizona Press.

Bernard, S. R., and K. F. Brown
1978   Distribution of mammals, reptiles and amphibians by BLM physiographic regions and A. W. Kuchler's association for the eleven western states. *U.S. Department of Interior Bureau of Land Management Technical Note* No. 301.

Binford, R.
1978   *Nunamiut Ethnoarchaeology*. New York: Academic Press.
1981   *Bones: Ancient Men and Modern Myths*. New York: Academic Press.

Birkeland, P. W.
1974   *Pedology, weathering, and geomorphological research*. New York: Oxford University Press.

Bonnichsen, R.
1973   Some operational aspects of human and animal bone alteration. In *Mammalian osteo-archeology: North America*, edited by B. Miles Gilbert. Columbia: Missouri Archeological Society. Pp. 9–25.
1979   Pleistocene bone technology in the Beringian refugium. *National Museum of Man, Mercury Series*, Paper No. 89. Ottawa: National Museum of Canada.

Bordes, F.
1961   Typologie du Paleolithique Ancien et Moyen. *Publications de l'Institue de l'Universite de Bordeaux*, Memorie No. 1.
1972   *A tale of two caves*. New York: Harper & Row.

Bouyoucos, G. J.
1927   The hydrometer as a new and rapid method for determining the colloidal content of soils, and the hydrometer as a new method for the mechanical analysis of soils. *Soil Science 23*:319–332, 343–354.
1962   Hydrometer method improved for making particle size analysis of soils. *Agronomy Journal 54*:464–465.

Bowles, J. B.
1975   Distribution and biogeography of mammals of Iowa. *The Museum, Texas Tech University Special Publication* No. 9.

Boyd, T. L.
1980   Paleopedology of the Agate Basin archeological site, eastern Wyoming. Master's thesis, Department of Geography, University of Wyoming, Laramie.

Bradley, B.
    1974   Comments on the lithic technology of the Casper site materials. In *The Casper site: A Hell Gap bison kill on the High Plains,* edited by G. C. Frison. New York: Academic Press. Pp. 191–197.

Brodkorb, P.
    1964   Catalogue of fossil birds: Part 2 (Anseriformes through Galliformes). *Bulletin Florida State Museum, Biological Series* 8(3):195–335.

Brumley, J. H.
    1973   Quantitative methods in the analysis of butchered faunal remains: A suggested approach. *Archaeology in Montana* 14(1):1–40.
    1975   The Cactus Flower site in southeastern Alberta: 1972–1974 excavations. *National Museum of Man, Mercury Series,* Paper No. 46. Ottawa: National Museum of Canada.

Bryson, R. A.
    1970   Character of climatic change, and the end of the Pleistocene [abstract] *AMQUA, Abstracts First Biennial Meeting,* Pp. 20–22.
    1974   A perspective on climatic change. *Science* 184:753–760.

Bunting, B. T.
    1965   *The geography of soil.* Chicago: Aldine.

Butler, B.
    1963   An Early Man site at Big Camas Prairie, south-central Idaho. *Tebiwa* 6:22–33.

Chittenden, H. M., and A. T. Richardson
    1905   *Life, letters and travels of Father Pierre Jean DeSmet, S.J., 1801–1873,* Vol. 3. New York: P. Harper.

Chomko, S. A.
    1978   Paleoenvironmental studies at Prospects Shelter, Wyoming [abstract]. *AMQUA, Abstracts Fifth Biennial Meeting,* p. 193.
    1979   Late Pleistocene environments and man in the western Big Horn Mountains, Wyoming. Paper presented at the Forty-fourth Annual Meeting, Society for American Archaeology, Vancouver, British Columbia, April 23–25, 1979.

Clark, G. R., and M. Wilson
    1981   The Ayers–Frazier Bison Trap (24PE30): A Late Middle period bison kill on the lower Yellowstone River. *Archeology in Montana* 22(1):23–77.

Clayton, L., W. Bickley, and W. Stone
    1970   Knife River flint. *Plains Anthropologist* 15:282–289.

Cleveland, C. G.
    1976   Experimental replication of butchered artiodactyl bone, with special reference to archeological features at 45FR5. *Washington Archaeological Research Center, Project Report* No. 46. Pp. 30–48.

CLIMAP Project Members
    1976   The surface of the Ice Age earth. *Science* 191:1131–1137.

Corner, R. G.
    1977   A late Pleistocene–Holocene vertebrate fauna from Red Willow County, Nebraska. *Transactions, Nebraska Academy of Science* 4:77–93.

Crabtree, D.
    1966   A stoneworker's approach to analyzing and replicating the Lindenmeier Folsom. *Tebiwa* 9:3–39.

Crompton, A. W., and K. Hiiemae
    1969   How mammalian molar teeth work. *Discovery* 5:23–24.

Davis, L. B.
    1976   *Missouri River Breaks area: Archaeological and historical value.* Billings, Montana: Bureau of Land Management.

Davis, L. B., and J. W. Fisher, Jr.
    n.d.   Prehistoric utilization of pronghorn antelope in the Northwestern Plains. Manuscript on file, Department of Sociology, Montana State University, Bozeman.

Deaver, K., and G. S. Greene
    1978   Faunal utilization at 45AD2: A prehistoric archaeological site in the channeled scablands of eastern Washington. *Tebiwa* 14:1–21.

Dillon, L. S.
    1956   Wisconsin climate and life zones in North America. *Science* 123:167–176.

Dottrens, E.
    1946   1. Etude Preliminaire: Les Phalanges Osseuses de Bos Domesticus. *Revue Suisse de Zoologie* 53:739–774.

Duffield, L. F.
    1970   Some Panhandle aspect sites in Texas, their vertebrates and paleoecology. Doctoral dissertation, University of Wisconsin, Madison.

References

1973   Aging and sexing the post cranial skeleton of bison. *Plains Anthropologist* 18:132–139.

Eakin, D.

1979   The vertebrate fauna from the Garrett Allen site 48CR301, Wyoming. Paper presented at the Thirty-seventh Annual Meeting, Plains Anthropological Conference, Kansas City, Missouri.

Egan, H.

1917   *Pioneering the West 1846–1878*, edited by W. M. Egan. Richmond, Utah: Howard R. Egan estate.

Empel, W., and T. Roskosz

1963   Das Skellett der Gliedmassen des Wisents, *Bison bonasus* (Linnaeus, 1758). *Acta Theriologica* 37:259–297.

Eshelman, R. E., E. B. Evenson, and C. W. Hibbard

1972   The peccary, *Platygonus compressus* Le Conte, from beneath Late Wisconsinan till, Washtenau County, Michigan. *Michigan Academician* 5(2):243–256.

Figgins, J.

1933   A further contribution to the antiquity of man in America. *Proceedings of the Colorado Museum of Natural History* 12:4–8.

Finch, W. I., F. C. Whitmore, Jr., and J. D. Sims

1972   Stratigraphy, morphology, and paleoecology of a fossil peccary herd from western Kentucky. *U.S. Geological Survey, Professional Paper* No. 790.

Findley, J.

1951   Habitat preferences of four species of *Microtus* in Jackson Hole, Wyoming. *Journal of Mammalogy* 32(1):118–120.

Fletcher, A., and F. La Flesche

1906   The Omaha tribe. *Bureau of American Ethnology Annual Report* No. 27.

Frison, G. C.

1970   The Glenrock Buffalo Jump, 48CO304: Late Prehistoric period buffalo procurement and butchering. *Plains Anthropologist Memoir* No. 7.

1971   Shoshonean antelope procurement in the upper Green River Basin, Wyoming. *Plains Anthropologist* 16(54), Part 1:258–284.

1973   The Wardell Buffalo Trap 48SU301: Communal procurement in the Upper Green River Basin, Wyoming. *Anthropological Papers of the Museum of Anthropology, University of Michigan* 48:1–111.

1974   *The Casper site: A Hell Gap bison kill on the High Plains.* New York: Academic Press.

1976   Cultural activity associated with prehistoric mammoth butchering and processing. *Science* 194:728–730.

1977   The Paleo-Indian in the Powder River Basin. Paper presented at the Thirty-fifth Plains Anthropological Conference, Lincoln, November 17–19, 1977.

1978a   Animal population studies and cultural inference. In Bison procurement and utilization: A symposium, edited by L. Davis and M. Wilson. *Plains Anthropologist Memoir* No. 14. Pp. 44–52.

1978b   *Prehistoric hunters of the High Plains.* New York: Academic Press.

Frison, G. C., and B. Bradley

1980   *Folsom tools and technology of the Hanson site, Wyoming.* Albuquerque: University of New Mexico Press.

Frison, G. C., and C. Reher

1970   Age determination of buffalo by teeth eruption and wear. *Plains Anthropologist Memoir* No. 7. Pp. 46–47.

Frison, G. C., and D. N. Walker

1978   The archeology of Little Canyon Creek Cave and its associated late Pleistocene fauna [abstract]. *AMQUA Abstracts, Fifth Biennial Meeting,* p. 200.

Frison, G. C., D. N. Walker, S. D. Webb, and G. M. Zeimens

1978   Paleo-Indian procurement of *Camelops* on the Northwestern Plains. *Quaternary Research* 10(3):385–400.

Frison, G. C., M. Wilson, and D. N. Walker

1978   The Big Goose Creek site: Bison procurement and faunal analysis. *Occasional Papers on Wyoming Archeology* No. 1.

Frison, G. C., M. Wilson, and D. J. Wilson

1976   Fossil bison and artifacts from an early Altithermal period arroyo trap in Wyoming. *American Antiquity* 41:28–57.

Frison, G., and G. Zeimens

1980   Bone projectile points: An addition to the Folsom cultural complex. *American Antiquity* 45:231–237.

Galloway, E., and G. Agogino

1961   The Johnson site: A Folsom campsite. *Plains Anthropologist* 6:205–208.

Gilbert, B. M., L. D. Martin, and S. A. Chomko
    1978   Paleontology and paleoecology of Natural Trap Cave, Wyoming: 20,000–10,000 B.P. [abstract]. *AMQUA Abstracts, Fifth Biennial Meeting,* p. 203.

Gilmore, M. R.
    1924   Old Assiniboine Buffalo Drive in North Dakota. *Indian Notes* 1:204–211.
    1977   *Uses of plants by the Indians of the Missouri River region.* Lincoln: University of Nebraska Press.

Graham, R. W.
    1979   Paleoclimates and late Pleistocene faunal provinces in North America. In *Pre-Llano cultures of the Americas: Paradoxes and possibilities,* edited by R. L. Humphrey and D. S. Stanford. Washington, D.C.: Anthropological Society of Washington: Pp. 49–69.

Grant, P. R.
    1970   Experimental studies of competitive interaction in a two-species system: II. The behavior of *Microtus, Peromyscus,* and *Clethrionomys* species. *Animal Behavior* 18:411–426.
    1971   Experimental studies of competitive interaction in a two-species system: III. *Microtus* and *Peromyscus* species in enclosures. *Journal of Animal Ecology* 40:323–350.
    1972   Interspecific competition among rodents. *Annual Review of Ecology and Systematics* 3:79–106.

Grayson, D. K.
    1981   A critical view of the use of archaeological vertebrates in paleoenvironmental reconstruction. *Journal of Ethnobiology* 1(1):28–38.

Grinnell, G.
    1961   *Pawnee, Blackfoot and Cheyenne.* New York: Charles Scribner's Sons.

Guilday, J. E., and P. Parmalee
    1972   Quaternary periglacial records of voles of the genus *Phenacomys* Merrian (Cricetidae: Rodentia). *Quaternary Research* 2:170–175.

Guilday, J. E., H. W. Hamilton, and A. D. McGrady
    1971   The Welsh Cave peccaries (*Platygonus*) and associated fauna, Kentucky Pleistocene. *Annals of the Carnegie Museum* 43(9):249–320.

Guthrie, R. D.
    1968a   Paleoecology of the large mammal community in interior Alaska during the late Pleistocene. *American Midland Naturalist* 79(2):346–363.
    1968b   Paleoecology of a late Pleistocene small mammal community from interior Alaska. *Arctic* 21(4):223–244.

Hager, M. W.
    1972   A Late Wisconsin–Recent vertebrate fauna from the Chimney Rock Animal Trap, Larimer County, Colorado. *University of Wyoming, Contributions to Geology* 11(2):63–71.

Hall, E. R.
    1951   A synopsis of the North American lagomorpha. *University of Kansas, Museum of Natural History Publications* 5(10):119–202.

Hall, E. R., and E. L. Cockrum
    1953   A synopsis of the North American microtine rodents. *University of Kansas, Museum of Natural History Publications* 5(27):373–498.

Hall, E. R., and K. R. Kelson
    1959   *The mammals of North America.* New York: Ronald Press. (2 vols.)

Hall, S. A.
    1981   Deteriorated pollen grains and the interpretation of Quaternary pollen diagrams. *Review of Palaeobotany and Palynology* 32:193–206.

Hanson, H. C., and W. Whitman
    1938   Characteristics of major grassland types in western North Dakota. *Ecological Monograph* 8:57–114.

Hargrave, L. L.
    1972   Comparative osteology of the chicken and American grouse. *Prescott College Studies in Biology* No. 1.

Haury, E.
    1953   Artifacts with mammoth remains, Naco, Arizona. 1. Discovery of the Naco mammoth and the associated projectile points. *American Antiquity* 19:1–14.

Hay, O. P.
    1923   The Pleistocene of North America and its vertebrated animals from the states east of the Mississippi River and from the Canadian provinces east of longitude 95°. *Carnegie Institute of Washington Publication* No. 322.

Haynes, C. V., Jr.
    1968   Geochronology of late Quaternary alluvium. In *Means of correlation of Quaternary successions, Proceedings VII INQUA Congress,* Volume 8, edited by R. B. Morrison and H. E. Wright, Jr., Salt Lake City: University of Utah Press. Pp. 591–631.

References

Haynes, C. V., Jr., and D. C. Grey
    1965   The Sister's Hill site and its bearing on Wyoming postglacial alluvial chronology. *Plains Anthropologist* 10:196–217.

Haynes, G.
    1980   Evidence of carnivore gnawing on Pleistocene and recent mammalian bones. *Paleobiology* 6(3):341–351.

Hellson, J. C., and M. Gadd
    1974   Ethnobotany of the Blackfoot Indians. *Canadian Ethnological Series Paper* No. 19.

Hester, J. J.
    1972   Blackwater locality No. 1: A stratified Early Man site in eastern New Mexico. *Fort Burgwin Research Center Publication* No. 8.

Hibbard, C. W.
    1949   Techniques of collecting microvertebrate fossils. *Contributions of the Museum of Paleontology, University of Michigan* 8(2):7–19.
    1956   *Microtus pennsylvanicus* (Ord) from the Hay Springs local fauna of Nebraska. *Journal of Paleontology* 30(5):1263–1266.
    1958   Summary of North American Pleistocene mammalian local faunas. *Papers of the Michigan Academy of Science, Arts and Letters* 43:3–32.
    1968   Paleontology. In Biology of *Peromyscus*, edited by J. A. King. *American Society of Mammalogists, Special Publication* No. 2. Pp. 6–26.
    1970   Pleistocene mammalian local faunas from the Great Plains and Central Lowland provinces of the United States. In *Pleistocene and Recent environments of the central Great Plains*, edited by W. Dort, Jr., and J. K. Jones, Jr. Lawrence: University of Kansas Press. Pp. 395–433.

Hoffman, R. S., and J. K. Jones, Jr.
    1970   Influence of late-glacial and post-glacial events on the distributions of recent mammals on the northern Great Plains. In *Pleistocene and Recent environments of the central Great Plains*, edited by W. Dort, Jr., and J. K. Jones, Jr. Lawrence: University of Kansas Press. Pp. 355–394.

Hoffmann, R. S., and D. L. Pattie
    1968   *A guide to Montana mammals.* Missoula: University of Montana Press.

Hole, F., and R. Heizer
    1973   *An introduction to prehistoric archeology (3rd ed.).* New York: Holt, Rinehart and Winston.

Holmes, W.
    1919   Handbook of aboriginal American antiquities. *Bureau of American Ethnology Bulletin* No. 60.

Hunt, C. B.
    1972   *Geology of soils.* San Francisco: W. H. Freeman.

Husted, W. M.
    1969   Bighorn Canyon archeology. *Smithsonian Institution, River Basin Surveys Publications in Salvage Archeology* No. 12.

Irwin-Williams, C., H. Irwin, G. Agogino, and C. V. Haynes, Jr.
    1973   Hell Gap: Paleo-Indian occupation on the High Plains. *Plains Anthropologist* 18:40–53.

Jennings, J. D.
    1978   Prehistory of Utah and the eastern Great Basin. *University of Utah Anthropological Papers* No. 98.

Jepsen, Glenn L.
    1953   Ancient buffalo hunters of northwestern Wyoming. *Southwestern Lore* 19:19–25.

Johnson, M. L., C. W. Clanton, and J. Girard
    1948   The sagebrush vole in Washington State. *The Murrelet* 39(3):44–47.

Jones, J. K., Jr.
    1953   Geographic distribution of the pocket mouse, *Perognathus fasciatus. University of Kansas, Museum of Natural History Publications* 5:515–526.

Judge, W.
    1970   Systems analysis and the Folsom–Midland question. *Southwestern Journal of Anthropology* 26:40–51.
    1973   *Paleoindian occupation of the central Rio Grande Valley in New Mexico.* Albuquerque: University of New Mexico Press.

Koch, W.
    1935   The age order of epiphyseal union in the skeleton of the European bison. *Anatomical Record* 61:371–376.

Kurtén, B.
    1953   On the variation and population dynamics of fossil and recent mammal populations. *Acta Zoologica Fennica* 76:1–122.
    1964   Population structure in paleoecology. In *Approaches to paleoecology,* edited by J. Imbrie and N. Newell. New York: Wiley. Pp. 91–106.

Lahren, L. A., and R. Bonnichsen
    1974   Bone foreshafts from a Clovis burial in southwestern Montana. *Science 186:*147–150.
La Rocque, A.
    1970   Pleistocene Mollusca of Ohio: Terrestrial Gastropoda. *State of Ohio, Division of Geological Survey, Bulletin 62(3):*555–800.
Leopold, E. B., and H. D. MacGinitie
    1972   Development and affinities of Tertiary floras in the Rocky Mountains. In *Floristics and paleofloristics of Asia and eastern North America,* edited by A. Graham. Amsterdam: Elsevier. Pp. 147–200.
Leopold, L. B., and J. P. Miller
    1954   A post-glacial chronology for some alluvial valleys in Wyoming. *U.S. Geological Survey Water Supply Paper* No. 1261.
Lewis, G. E.
    1970   New discoveries of Pleistocene bisons and peccaries in Colorado. *U.S. Geological Survey Professional Paper* No. 700B. Pp. B137–B140.
Lewis, R.
    1979a   Continued investigations of opal phytoliths from Wyoming archeological sites. Paper presented at the Thirty-seventh Plains Anthropological Conference, Kansas City, Missouri.
    1979b   Use of opal phytoliths in paleo-environmental reconstruction. Unpublished master's thesis, Department of Anthropology, University of Wyoming, Laramie.
Long, C. A.
    1965   The mammals of Wyoming. *University of Kansas, Museum of Natural History Publications 14(18):*493–758.
Lorrain, D.
    1968   Analysis of the bison bones from Bonfire Shelter. In D. S. Dibble and D. Lorrain, Bonfire Shelter: A stratified bison kill site, Val Verde County, Texas. *Texas Memorial Museum, Miscellaneous Papers* No. 1. Pp. 77–132.
Love, J. D., J. L. Weitz, and R. K. Hose
    1955   Geologic map of Wyoming. Washington, D.C.: U.S. Geological Survey.
Lundelius, E. L., Jr.
    1967   Late-Pleistocene and Holocene faunal history of central Texas. In *Pleistocene extinctions,* edited by P. S. Martin and H. E. Wright, Jr. New Haven: Yale University Press. Pp. 287–319.
Lyman, R. L.
    1978   Prehistoric butchering techniques in the Lower Granite Reservoir, southwestern Washington. *Tebiwa 13:*1–25.
Madden, C. T.
    1978   Mammoths (*Mammuthus*) from the Colby site. In G. C. Frison, *Prehistoric hunters of the High Plains.* New York: Academic Press. Pp. 391–401.
Maglio, V. J.
    1973   Origin and evolution of the Elephantidae. *American Philosophical Society, Transactions 63(3):* 1–149.
Mandelbaum, D.
    1940   The Plains Cree. *Anthropological Papers of the American Museum of Natural History 37:*155–316.
Marlow, C. B.
    1978   *Plant resources of the Powder River Basin. Archeological Survey of the Western Powder River Basin* (Vol. 3). Cheyenne: Wyoming Recreation Commission. Pp. 68–101.
    1979   Cultural plant resources of Wyoming's eastern Red Desert. Manuscript on file at Wyoming Recreation Commission, Cheyenne.
Martin, L. D., and B. M. Gilbert
    1978   Excavations at Natural Trap Cave. *Nebraska Academy of Sciences, Transactions 6:*107–116.
Martin, L. D., B. M. Gilbert, and D. B. Adams
    1977   A cheetah-like cat in North American Pleistocene. *Science 195:*981–982.
Martin, L. D., B. M. Gilbert, and S. A. Chomko
    1979   *Dicrostonyx* (Rodentia) from the late Pleistocene of Northern Wyoming. *Journal of Mammalogy 60(1):*193–195.
Martin, P. S.
    1967   Pleistocene overkill. *Natural History 76:*32–38.
    1975   Vanishings and future of the prairie. In B. F. Perkins, *Geoscience and man: Grasslands ecology* (Vol. 10). Baton Rouge: Louisiana State University School of Geoscience. Pp. 39–51.
Martin, P. S., and H. E. Wright, Jr.
    1967   *Pleistocene extinctions: The search for a cause.* New Haven: Yale University Press.

References

Matthews, J. V., Jr.
    1976   Arctic–steppe—An extinct biome. *AMQUA Abstracts, Fourth Biennial Meeting.* Pp. 72–77.

Maxwell, M. H., and L. N. Brown
    1968   Ecological distribution of rodents on the High Plains of eastern Wyoming. *Southwestern Naturalist* *13*(2):143–158.

Myers, T. P., M. R. Voorhies, and G. Corner
    1980   Spiral fractures and bone pseudotools at paleontological sites. *American Antiquity 45:*483–490.

Nelson, E. W.
    1909   The rabbits of North America. *United States Department of Agriculture, North American Fauna* No. 20.

Nowak, R. M.
    1979   North American Quaternary *Canis. University of Kansas, Museum of Natural History Monograph* No. 6.

Olson, G. D., and L. J. Zimmerman
    1979   A cultural resources reconnaisance of the federal lands on the east bank of Lake Francis Case, South Dakota. Report on file, U.S. Army Corps of Engineers, Omaha, Nebraska

Osgood, W. H.
    1900   Revision of the pocket mice of the genus *Perognathus. U.S. Department of Agriculture, North American Fauna* No. 18.
    1909   Revision of the mice of the American genus *Peromyscus. U.S. Department of Agriculture, North American Fauna* No. 28.

Peden, G. G., G. M. Van Dyne, R. W. Rice, and R. M. Hansen
    1974   The trophic ecology of *Bison bison* L. on shortgrass plains. *Journal of Applied Ecology 11:* 489–498.

Peterson, R.
    1978   Projectile point re-utilization patterns at the Agate Basin site. *Wyoming Contributions to Anthropology 1:*139–147.

Petsch, B. C.
    1953   Geologic map of South Dakota. Vermillion: South Dakota State Geological Survey.

Picard, M. D., and L. R. High, Jr.
    1973   *Sedimentary structures of ephemeral streams.* New York: Elsevier.

Piper, C. S.
    1950   *Soil and plant analysis.* New York: Interscience.

Popp, J. K., and R. B. Dahlgren
    1979   Seasonal range use patterns and food habits by bison at Wind Cave National Park. Paper presented at the South Dakota Section Meeting of the Society for Range Management, Rapid City, 1979.

Ravenholt, H. B., W. R. Glen, and K. N. Larson
    1976   *Soil survey of the Star Valley area, Wyoming–Idaho.* Washington, D.C.: U.S. Soil Conservation Service, Government Printing Office.

Rawn, V.
    n.d.   Small mammal remains from the Jones–Miller site, Colorado. *Smithsonian Contributions to Anthropology* (in press).

Ray, C. E., C. S. Denny, and M. Rubin
    1970   A peccary, *Platygonus compressus* Le Conte, from drift of Wisconsinan age in northern Pennsylvania. *American Journal of Science 268:*78–94.

Ray, V. F.
    1932   The Sanpoil and Nespelemi Salishan peoples of northeastern Washington. *University of Washington Publications in Anthropology 5:*1–237.

Regan, A. B.
    1934   Some notes on the history of the Uintah Basin in northeastern Utah to 1850. *Proceedings, Utah Academy of Science, Arts and Letters 11:*55–64.

Reher, C. A.
    1970   Population dynamics of the Glenrock *Bison bison* population. In G. C. Frison, The Glenrock Buffalo Jump, 48CO304. *Plains Anthropologist Memoir* No. 7. Appendix II.
    1973   The Wardell *Bison bison* sample: Population dynamics and archaeological interpretation. In G. C. Frison, The Wardell Buffalo Trap 48SU301: Communal procurement in the upper Green River Basin, Wyoming. *University of Michigan, Anthropological Papers* No. 48. Appendix II.
    1974   Population study of the Casper site Bison. In *The Casper site: A Hell Gap bison kill on the High Plains,* edited by G. C. Frison. New York: Academic Press.

Reher, C., and G. Frison
    1980   The Vore site, 48CK302, a stratified buffalo jump in the Wyoming Black Hills. *Plains Anthropologist Memoir* No. 16.

Reider, R. G.
    1979   Preliminary report on the soils and soil stratigraphy of the Grayrocks Dam site, Platte County, Wyoming. Report to the Missouri Basin Power Project. Manuscript on file with the Office of the Wyoming State Archeologist, University of Wyoming, Laramie.
    1980a Late Pleistocene and Holocene soils of the Carter/Kerr-McGee archeological site, Powder River Basin, Wyoming. *Catena* 7:301–315.
    1980b Paleopedology of the Guffy Peak 11 archeological site, Fremont County, Wyoming. Report to Powers Elevation Company, Archeological Division, for Rocky Mountain Energy, Denver.

Repenning, C. A.
    1980   Faunal exchanges between Siberia and North America - Evidence from quaternary land mammals remains in Siberia, Alaska, and the Yukon Territory. *Canadian Journal of Anthropology* 1(1):45–50.

Robbins, C. S., B. Brunn and H. S. Zim
    1966   *Birds of North America.* Golden Press, New York.

Roberts, F. H. H.
    1935   A Folsom complex: A preliminary report on investigations at the Lindenmeier site in northern Colorado. *Smithsonian Miscellaneous Collections* 94:1–35.
    1942   Archeological and geological investigations in the San Jon District, eastern New Mexico. *Smithsonian Miscellaneous Collections* 103(4):1–30.
    1943   A new site. *American Antiquity* 8:100.
    1951   The early Americans. *Scientific American* 184(2):15–19.
    1961a The Agate Basin complex. In *Homenaje a Pablo Martinez del Rio.* Mexico City: Instituto Nacional de Anthropologia y Historia. Pp. 125–132.
    1961b 1961 Excavations at Agate Basin, Wyoming. *Plains Anthropologist* 7:89–91.

Romer, A. S.
    1966   *Vertebrate paleontology* (3rd ed.). Chicago: University of Chicago Press.

Rovner, I.
    1975   Plant opal phytolith analysis in Midwestern archaeology. *Michigan Academician* 8:129–137.

Ruhe, R. V.
    1970   Soils, paleosols, and environment. In *Pleistocene and Recent environments of the central Great Plains,* edited by W. Dort, Jr., and J. K. Jones, Jr. Lawrence: University of Kansas Press. Pp. 37–52.

Schumm, S. A.
    1977   *The fluvial system.* New York: Wiley.

Schumm, S. A., and R. F. Hadley
    1957   Arroyos and the semiarid cycle of erosion. *American Journal of Science* 255:161–174.

Scott, G. R., and R. M. Lindvall
    1970   Geology of new occurrences of Pleistocene bisons and peccaries in Colorado. *U.S. Geological Survey Professional Paper* No. 700B. Pp. B141–B149.

Sellards, E. H.
    1952   *Early Man in America: A study in prehistory.* New York: Greenwood Press.

Semken, H. A., Jr.
    1980   Holocene climatic reconstructions derived from the three micromammal-bearing cultural horizons at the Cherokee Sewer site, northwestern Iowa. In *The Cherokee excavations: Holocene ecology and human adaptations in northwestern Iowa,* edited by D. C. Anderson and H. A. Semken. New York: Academic Press. Pp. 67–99.

Shaw, L., and G. C. Frison
    1979   Evidence for pre-Clovis in the Big Horn Basin. Paper presented at the Forty-fourth Annual Meeting of the Society for American Archaeology, Vancouver, British Columbia, April 23–25, 1979.

Skinner, M. F., and O. C. Kaisen
    1947   The fossil *Bison* of Alaska and preliminary revision of the genus. *American Museum of Natural History Bulletin* 89:123–256.

Soil Conservation Service
    1973   Natural vegetation, Wyoming. U.S. Department of Agriculture, Soil Conservation Service Map M7-E-22902-N. Washington, D.C.: U.S. Government Printing Office.

Soil Survey Staff
    1962   *Soil survey manual.* Agricultural Handbook 18. Washington, D. C.: U.S. Government Printing Office.
    1975   *Soil taxonomy.* Agricultural Handbook 436. Washington, D.C.: U.S. Government Printing Office.

Sollberger, J. B.
    1977   On fluting Folsom: Notes on recent experiments. Bulletin Texas Archeological Society 48:47–52.

Stanford, D.
    1974   Preliminary report of the excavation of the Jones–Miller Hell Gap site, Yuma County, Colorado. *Southwestern Lore* 40:30–36.

References

1978   The Jones–Miller site: An example of Hell Gap bison procurement strategy. In Bison procurement and utilization: A symposium. *Plains Anthropologist Memor* No. 14. Pp. 90–97.

1979   The Selby and Dutton sites: Evidence for a possible pre-Clovis occupation of the High Plains. In *Pre-Llano cultures of the Americas: Paradoxes and possibilities*, edited by R. L. Humphrey and D. S. Stanford. Washington, D.C.: Anthropological Society of Washington. Pp. 101–123.

Stebbins, R. C.
    1966   *A field guide to western reptiles and amphibians*. Boston: Houghton Mifflin.

Steward, J. H.
    1938   Basin–plateau aboriginal sociopolitical groups. *Bureau of American Ethnology Bulletin* No. 120.

Stuckenrath, R., and J. E. Mielke
    1972   Smithsonian Institution radiocarbon measurements VII. *Radiocarbon 14*(2):401–412.

Sundstrom, C., W. G. Hepworth, and K. L. Diem
    1973   Abundance, distribution and food habits of the pronghorn. *Wyoming Game and Fish Commission Bulletin* No. 12.

Taylor, D.
    1960   Late Cenozoic molluscan faunas from the High Plains. *U.S. Geological Survey Professional Paper* No. 337.

Thorp, J., and G. D. Smith
    1949   Higher categories of soil classification. *Soil Science* 67:117–126.

Tikhomirov, B. A.
    1958   Natural conditions and vegetation in the mammoth epoch in northern Siberia. *Problems of the North* 1:168–188.

Tolstead, W. L.
    1941   Plant communities and secondary succession in southcentral South Dakota. *Ecology* 22(3): 322–328.

Tschudy, R. H.
    1969   Relation of palynomorphs to sedimentation. In R. H. Tschudy and R. A. Scott (eds.), *Aspects of Palynology*, Wiley-Interscience, New York, pp. 79–96.

Turner, R. W.
    1974   Mammals of the Black Hills of South Dakota and Wyoming. *University of Kansas, Museum of Natural History, Miscellaneous Publications* No. 60.

Twiss, P. C., E. Suess, and R. M. Smith
    1969   Morphological classification of grass phytoliths. *Proceedings of the Soil Science Society of America* 33:109–114.

U.S. Weather Bureau
    1964   Climatic summary of the United States—supplement for 1951 through 1960: Colorado. Washington, D.C.: U.S. Government Printing Office. 86 pp.

    1965   Climatic summary of the United States—supplement for 1951 through 1960: Utah. Washington, D.C.: U.S. Government Printing Office. 67 pp.

von den Driesch, A.
    1976   A guide to the measurements of animal bones from archeological sites. *Harvard University Peabody Museum Bulletin* 1:1–136.

Walker, D. N.
    1974   A Pleistocene gyrfalcon. *The Auk* 91:820–821.

    1975   A cultural and ecological analysis of the vertebrate fauna from the Medicine Lodge Creek site (48BH499). Unpublished master's thesis, Department of Anthropology, University of Wyoming, Laramie.

    1977   An occurrence of muskoxen in a Wyoming archeological site. Paper presented at the Thirty-fifth Plains Anthropological Conference, Lincoln, Nebraska, November 17–19, 1977.

    1980   The Garnsey site canid. In Late prehistoric bison procurement in southeastern New Mexico: The 1978 season at the Garnsey site (LA18399), edited by J. D. Speth and W. S. Parry. *Technical Reports, Museum of Anthropology, University of Michigan* No. 12. Pp. 344–365.

    1982   A late Pleistocene *Ovibos* from southeastern Wyoming. *Journal of Paleontology* 56(2):486–491.

Walker, D. N., and G. C. Frison
    1979   The continual domestication of wolf/dog hybrids on the Northwestern Plains. Paper presented at the Forty-fourth Annual Meeting of the Society for American Archaeology, Vancouver, British Columbia, April 23–25, 1979.

    1980   The late Pleistocene mammalian fauna from the Colby mammoth kill site, Wyoming. *University of Wyoming, Contributions to Geology* 19(1):69–79.

    1982   Studies on Amerindian dogs 3: Prehistoric wolf/dog hybrids from the Northwestern Plains. Journal of Archaeological Science 9:125–172.

Walkley, A., and I. A. Black
    1934   An examination of the Degtjareff method for determining soil organic matter and a proposed modification of the chromic acid titration method. *Soil Science 37*:29–38.
Weaver, J.
    1978   The wolves of Yellowstone. *U.S. Department of Interior, National Park Service, Natural Resources Report* No. 14.
Weaver, J. E.
    1968   *Prairie plants and their environment, a fifty-year study in the Midwest.* Lincoln: University of Nebraska Press.
Webb, S. D.
    1965   The osteology of *Camelops. Bulletin of the Los Angeles County Museum, Science 1*:1–54.
Wells, P. V.
    1965   Scarp woodlands, transported grassland soils, and concept of grassland climate in the Great Plains region. *Science 148*:246–249.
    1970   Vegetational history of the Great Plains: A post-glacial record of coniferous woodland in southeastern Wyoming. In *Pleistocene and Recent environments of the central Great Plains,* edited by W. Dort, Jr., and J. K. Jones, Jr. Lawrence: University of Kansas Press. Pp. 185–202.
Wendland, W.
    1978   Holocene Man in North America: The ecological setting and climatic background. *Plains Anthropologist 23*(82):273–287.
Wheat, J. B.
    1972   The Olsen–Chubbuck site: A Paleo-Indian bison kill. *Society for American Archaeology, Memoir* No. 26.
Wheeler, R. P.
    1954   Selected projectile point types of the United States: 2. *Bulletin of the Oklahoma Anthropological Society 2*:1–5.
Whitaker, J. O., Jr.
    1967   Habitat relationships of four species of mice in Vigo County, Indiana. *Ecology 48*:867–872.
Whitcomb, H. A.
    1965   Groundwater resources and geology of Niobrara County, Wyoming. *U.S. Geological Survey Water Supply Paper* No. 1788.
White, T. E.
    1952   Observations on the butchering technique of some aboriginal peoples: I. *American Antiquity 17*(4):337–338.
Williams, D. F., and H. H. Genoways
    1979   A systematic review of the olive-backed pocket mouse, *Perognathus fasciatus* (Rodentia, Heteromyidae). *Annals of the Carnegie Museum 48*(5):73–102.
Wilmsen, E. N., and F. H. H. Roberts, Jr.
    1978   Lindenmeier, 1934–1974: Concluding report on investigations. *Smithsonian Contributions to Anthropology* No. 24.
Wilson, M.
    1974   The Casper site local fauna and its fossil *Bison.* In *The Casper site, a Hell Gap bison kill on the High Plains,* edited by G. C. Frison. New York: Academic Press. Pp. 125–171.
    1975   Holocene fossil *Bison* from Wyoming and adjacent areas. Unpublished master's thesis, Department of Anthropology, University of Wyoming, Laramie.
    1978   Archaeological kill site populations and the Holocene evolution of the genus *Bison.* In Bison procurement and utilization, edited by L. Davis and M. Wilson. *Plains Anthropologist Memoir* No. 14. Pp. 9–23.
Witkind, M.
    1971   An archaeological interpretation of the Roberts Buffalo Jump site, Larimer County, Colorado. Unpublished master's thesis, Department of Anthropology, Colorado State University, Fort Collins.
Wood, A. E.
    1935   Evolution and relationships of the Heteromyid rodents. *Annals of the Carnegie Museum 24*:73–262.
Wood, W. R., and D. L. Johnson
    1978   A survey of disturbance processes in archaeolgoical site formation. In *Advances in archaeological method and theory* (Vol. 1), edited by M. Schiffer. New York: Academic Press. Pp. 315–381.
Wormington, H. M.
    1957   Ancient man in North America. *Denver Museum of Natural History, Popular Series* No. 4.
Wright, H. E., Jr.
    1970   Vegetational history of the Central Plains. In *Pleistocene and Recent environments of the central*

References

Great Plains, edited by W. Dort, Jr., and J. K. Jones, Jr. Lawrence: University of Kansas Press. Pp. 157–172.

Wright, J. V.
    1976   The Grant Lake site, Keewatin District, N.W.T. *National Museum of Man, Mercury Series,* Paper No. 47. Ottawa: National Museum of Canada.

Zeimens, G. M., and D. N. Walker
    1974   Bell Cave, Wyoming: Preliminary archaeological and paleontological investigations. *Geological Survey of Wyoming, Report of Investigations* 10:88–90.

Zeimens, G. M., and S. Zeimens
    1974   Volumes of bison astragali. In *The Casper site: A Hell Gap bison kill on the High Plains,* edited by G. C. Frison. New York: Academic Press. Pp. 245–246.

NAME INDEX

SUBJECT INDEX

STUDIES IN ARCHAEOLOGY

Consulting Editor: Stuart Struever

Department of Anthropology
Northwestern University
Evanston, Illinois

Charles R. McGimsey III. **Public Archeology**

Lewis R. Binford. **An Archaeological Perspective**

Muriel Porter Weaver. **The Aztecs, Maya, and Their Predecessors: Archaeology of Mesoamerica**

Joseph W. Michels. **Dating Methods in Archaeology**

C. Garth Sampson. **The Stone Age Archaeology of Southern Africa**

Fred T. Plog. **The Study of Prehistoric Change**

Patty Jo Watson (Ed.). **Archeology of the Mammoth Cave Area**

George C. Frison (Ed.). **The Casper Site: A Hell Gap Bison Kill on the High Plains**

W. Raymond Wood and R. Bruce McMillan (Eds.). **Prehistoric Man and His Environments: A Case Study in the Ozark Highland**

Kent V. Flannery (Ed.). **The Early Mesoamerican Village**

Charles E. Cleland (Ed.). **Cultural Change and Continuity: Essays in Honor of James Bennett Griffin**

Michael B. Schiffer. **Behavioral Archeology**

Fred Wendorf and Romuald Schild. **Prehistory of the Nile Valley**

Michael A. Jochim. **Hunter-Gatherer Subsistence and Settlement: A Predictive Model**

Stanley South. **Method and Theory in Historical Archeology**

Timothy K. Earle and Jonathon E. Ericson (Eds.). **Exchange Systems in Prehistory**

Stanley South (Ed.). **Research Strategies in Historical Archeology**

John E. Yellen. **Archaeological Approaches to the Present: Models for Reconstructing the Past**

Lewis R. Binford (Ed.). **For Theory Building in Archaeology: Essays on Faunal Remains, Aquatic Resources, Spatial Analysis, and Systemic Modeling**

James N. Hill and Joel Gunn (Eds.). **The Individual in Prehistory: Studies of Variability in Style in Prehistoric Technologies**

Michael B. Schiffer and George J. Gumerman (Eds.). **Conservation Archaeology: A Guide for Cultural Resource Management Studies**

Thomas F. King, Patricia Parker Hickman, and Gary Berg. **Anthropology in Historic Preservation: Caring for Culture's Clutter**

Richard E. Blanton. **Monte Albán: Settlement Patterns at the Ancient Zapotec Capital**

R. E. Taylor and Clement W. Meighan. **Chronologies in New World Archaeology**

Bruce D. Smith. **Prehistoric Patterns of Human Behavior: A Case Study in the Mississippi Valley**

Barbara L. Stark and Barbara Voorhies (Eds.). **Prehistoric Coastal Adaptations: The Economy and Ecology of Maritime Middle America**

Charles L. Redman, Mary Jane Berman, Edward V. Curtin, William T. Langhorne, Nina M. Versaggi, and Jeffery C. Wanser (Eds.). **Social Archeology: Beyond Subsistence and Dating**

Bruce D. Smith (Ed.). **Mississippian Settlement Patterns**

Lewis R. Binford. **Nunamiut Ethnoarchaeology**

J. Barto Arnold III and Robert Weddle. **The Nautical Archeology of Padre Island: The Spanish Shipwrecks of 1554**

Sarunas Milisauskas. **European Prehistory**

Brian Hayden (Ed.). **Lithic Use-Wear Analysis**

William T. Sanders, Jeffrey R. Parsons, and Robert S. Santley. **The Basin of Mexico: Ecological Processes in the Evolution of a Civilization**

David L. Clarke. **Analytical Archaeologist: Collected Papers of David L. Clarke. Edited and Introduced by His Colleagues**

Arthur E. Spiess. **Reindeer and Caribou Hunters: An Archaeological Study**

Elizabeth S. Wing and Antoinette B. Brown. **Paleonutrition: Method and Theory in Prehistoric Foodways.**

John W. Rick. **Prehistoric Hunters of the High Andes**

Timothy K. Earle and Andrew L. Christenson (Eds.). **Modeling Change in Prehistoric Economics**

Thomas F. Lynch (Ed.). **Guitarrero Cave: Early Man in the Andes**

Fred Wendorf and Romuald Schild. **Prehistory of the Eastern Sahara**

Henri Laville, Jean-Philippe Rigaud, and James Sackett. **Rock Shelters of the Perigord: Stratigraphy and Archaeological Succession**

Duane C. Anderson and Holmes A. Semken, Jr. (Eds.). **The Cherokee Excavations: Holocene Ecology and Human Adaptations in Northwestern Iowa**

Anna Curtenius Roosevelt. **Parmana: Prehistoric Maize and Manioc Subsistence along the Amazon and Orinoco**

Fekri A. Hassan. **Demographic Archaeology**

G. Barker. **Landscape and Society: Prehistoric Central Italy**

Lewis R. Binford. **Bones: Ancient Men and Modern Myths**

Richard A. Gould and Michael B. Schiffer (Eds.). **Modern Material Culture: The Archaeology of Us**

Muriel Porter Weaver. **The Aztecs, Maya, and Their Predecessors: Archaeology of Mesoamerica, 2nd edition**

Arthur S. Keene. **Prehistoric Foraging in a Temperate Forest: A Linear Programming Model**

Ross H. Cordy. **A Study of Prehistoric Social Change: The Development of Complex Societies in the Hawaiian Islands**

C. Melvin Aikens and Takayasu Higuchi. **Prehistory of Japan**

Kent V. Flannery (Ed.). **Maya Subsistence: Studies in Memory of Dennis E. Puleston**

Dean R. Snow (Ed.). **Foundations of Northeast Archaeology**

Charles S. Spencer. **The Cuicatlán Cañada and Monte Albán: A Study of Primary State Formation**

Steadman Upham. **Polities and Power: An Economic and Political History of the Western Pueblo**

Carol Kramer. **Village Ethnoarchaeology: Rural Iran in Archaeological Perspective**

Michael J. O'Brien, Robert E. Warren, and Dennis E. Lewarch (Eds.). **The Cannon Reservoir Human Ecology Project: An Archaeological Study of Cultural Adaptations in the Southern Prairie Peninsula**

Jonathon E. Ericson and Timothy K. Earle (Eds.). **Contexts for Prehistoric Exchange**

Merrilee H. Salmon. **Philosophy and Archaeology**

Vincas P. Steponaitis. **Ceramics, Chronology, and Community Patterns: An Archaeological Study at Moundville**

George C. Frison and Dennis J. Stanford. **The Agate Basin Site: A Record of the Paleoindian Occupation of the Northwestern High Plains**

in preparation

William J. Folan, Ellen R. Kintz, and Laraine A. Fletcher. **Coba: A Classic Maya Metropolis**

James A. Moore and Arthur S. Keene (Eds.). **Archaeological Hammers and Theories**

Lewis R. Binford. **Working At Archaeology**